Observing God's World

Third Edition

Gregory Rickard
Gregory Parker

 A Beka Book Pensacola, FL 32523-9100
an affiliate ministry of PENSACOLA CHRISTIAN COLLEGE

A Beka Book® Science and Health Series

Science	Health
K5 God's World	
1 Discovering God's World	• Health, Safety, and Manners 1
2 Enjoying God's World	• Health, Safety, and Manners 2
3 Exploring God's World	• Health, Safety, and Manners 3
4 Understanding God's World	• Developing Good Health
5 Investigating God's World	• Enjoying Good Health
6 **Observing God's World**	• Choosing Good Health
7 Science: Order and Reality	• A Healthier You
8 Matter and Motion in God's Universe	• Let's Be Healthy
9 Science of the Physical Creation	• Health in Christian Perspective
10 Biology: God's Living Creation	• Life Management under God
11 Chemistry: Precision and Design	• Sex, Love, and Romance
12 Physics: The Foundational Science	*(Sex Education from the Bible)*

Observing God's World

Third Edition

Staff Credits

Editors: Naomi Sleeth, Gregory Parker, Marion Hedquist, Delores Shimmin
Consultants: Rebecca Ross; Shane Smith, Ph.D.; Stephen McAlister; Ed Rickard, Ph.D.
Designer: John Halbach
Production Artists: Tim Keenan, Jeremy Knepshield, Andrew Macarthur, Rohn Gibson
Illustrators: Bill Bailey, Steven Hileman, Brian Jekel, Tim Keenan, Jeremy Knepshield,
    David Russell, Aaron Birchler, Terry Breen, Dave Bowers, Steve Gammel

A Beka Book, a Christian textbook ministry affiliated with Pensacola Christian College, is designed to meet the need for Christian textbooks and teaching aids. The purpose of this publishing ministry is to help Christian schools reach children and young people for the Lord and train them in the Christian way of life.

Cataloging Data
Rickard, Gregory.
        Observing God's world / Gregory Rickard,
    Gregory Parker. — 3rd ed.
    —p. : col. ill.; 26 cm. (A Beka Book Science Series)
    Includes index.
    For grade 6.
    1. Science — Study and teaching (Elementary)
II. Parker, Gregory. III. A Beka Book, Inc.
Library of Congress: Q161.2 .R52 027 2001
Dewey System: 570

Credits are listed on page 425 which is an extension of this copyright page.

Contents

Plentiful Plants .... page 2

Chapter 1

Observing Invertebrates .... page 92

Chapter 2

Our Fascinating Earth .... page 166

Chapter 3

God's Great Universe .... page 234

Chapter **4**

Exploring Space .... page 298

Chapter **5**

Matter and Chemistry .... page 358

Chapter **6**

Special Features

Plentiful Plants

Have you ever considered how much of our lives is affected by plants? In the summer, we mow the grass; and in the fall, we spend days raking up huge piles of leaves. On cold winter evenings, we enjoy the warmth of a crackling wood fire; in the spring, we are thrilled with the beauty of the flowers blooming all around us.

God created plants in a wealth of shapes and sizes. Some are very beautiful; others have particularly fascinating designs or manners of growth. But above all else, God made plants to be useful. Many of the clothes we wear are made from cotton, a material made from plants. Wood is used in a variety of ways in the houses we build. The books we read are printed on paper, another plant product. And, of course, much of the food we eat comes from the roots, stems, leaves, or fruits of plants.

Warmth, clothing, building materials, transportation, and food are some of the most important uses for plants; but plants have many other uses that you may not be aware of. As a result of study throughout history, people have learned much about the possible uses of plants. You will learn more about how plants help us as you read this chapter.

1.1 Leaves: The Food Factories

When we look at a plant, we often notice its leaves first. Some plants have very large leaves that look like the ears of an elephant; others have bunches of tiny, needlelike leaves that shimmer in the sunlight. Because leaves have interesting smooth or jagged shapes, attractive colors, and a variety of arrangements on the stem, they give beauty to plants.

Working all the day long

Essential leaves. Is adding variety and beauty to our world the only purpose for leaves? You might think so if you were to watch a leaf for several hours, or even days. It never does anything but hang from its plant. It never even moves, unless stirred by the wind. But that leaf is not as lazy as it seems.

Every leaf is a complex mechanism working to produce food for the plant by means of a chemical process called

photosynthesis [fō′tō·sĭn′thĭ·sĭs]. Without the food produced by photosynthesis in the leaves, plants could not grow. And without plants, there would be no food for animals and people. *All life depends on plants because plants are the only living things that can make their own food.* The next time you look at the unusual or beautiful leaves on a plant, remember that the job of photosynthesis, occurring unseen within the leaves day by day, is an essential part of God's plan for life on earth.

Leaves in action. Photosynthesis is carried out by tiny cells in the leaf, too small to be seen by the human eye. Let's look at an enlarged view of the inside of a typical leaf to help us understand how this important process works.

A leaf needs three ingredients in order to do its work: *water, air,* and *light*. The plant gets *water* from the ground and transports it to the leaf through the roots and stem. *Air* enters the leaf through holes or pores called **stomata** [stō′mə·tə: "little mouths"], located on the underside of the leaf. Each **stoma** (singular of *stomata*) is so extremely small that there may be tens of thousands of them in a leaf section the size of a quarter. The third ingredient, *light,* comes from the sun. Because sunlight is necessary for photosynthesis, the leaf can do its work only during the daytime.

Photosynthesis. In order to manufacture food from these three ingredients, the leaf uses a special tool known as **chlorophyll** [klôr′ə·fĭl], the *pigment,* or coloring, that makes plants green. As sunlight enters the leaf, some of its energy is absorbed by tiny packages of chlorophyll called **chloroplasts** [klôr′ə·plăsts], contained in the cells of the leaf. The energy of the sun splits the water, provided by the roots and stems, into simpler chemicals called *hydrogen* and *oxygen*. The oxygen (a gas) is released through the stomata into the air, where it is available to be

plant cells

vein

stoma

Cutaway of leaf

breathed by people and animals. The hydrogen is combined with carbon dioxide (a gas taken from the air) to form a type of sugar called **glucose**—*the food plants need to live.* The glucose is shipped away for storage or used in other parts of the plant.

Besides photosynthesis, another important job of leaves is to construct chemicals, such as **proteins** and **vitamins,** that the plant needs for nourishment. Whenever we eat vegetables, our bodies make use of these proteins and vitamins for our own nourishment.

Photosynthesis

chlorophyll absorbs sunlight; water splits into hydrogen and oxygen

carbon dioxide enters through the stomata

hydrogen

water moves up the stem to the leaves

glucose

oxygen exits through the stomata

🍁 A look at leaf anatomy

Take a close look at a leaf growing on a tree or a bush. Notice its color. How does the color of the top surface compare with that of the bottom? Is the leaf all one color? Is it green, or yellow, or red? Observe its shape. Is it rounded or pointed at the tip? Is the edge jagged or smooth? Feel the texture of its surface. Is it smooth, or furry, or rough? Does the bottom feel different from the top? Look around your yard for leaves with other shapes, colors, and textures.

A strong skeleton. Carefully examine the structure of one of the leaves you found. The leaf is joined to its plant by a **stem.** The stem is strong yet flexible, so that even in violent storms the leaf is not torn away. The stem also contains many conducting channels or tubes. Some of these tubes bring water and minerals to the leaf, and others take food from the leaf to the rest of the plant.

Spreading outward from the stem and across the leaf is a network of large and small **veins.** These veins are like strong pipes serving both to transport liquids and to reinforce the structure of the thin, fragile leaf. Examine the pattern of the veins on your leaf. Do they run side by side lengthwise along the leaf, or do they branch out from both sides of a central vein? On many leaves, all the smaller veins are joined to one especially large vein, called the **midrib,** that runs straight up the middle of the leaf.

top side underside

A green complexion. You should also notice that the top of the leaf looks different from the underside. The leaf is designed so that most of its food-making cells are arranged close to its top surface, the side that is turned toward the sunlight. Since most of the chlorophyll is near the top, the top of the leaf is usually greener than the bottom.

A smooth skin. Most leaves feel very smooth. The waxy covering that coats the skin of a leaf and prevents water from escaping is called the **cuticle.** Because the cuticle faithfully performs its job, materials can enter and exit the leaf only through the stomata or the stem.

Leaf anatomy

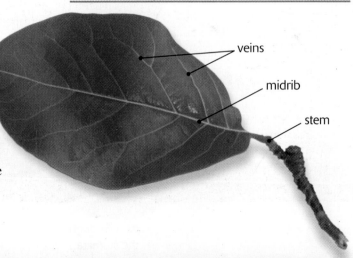

veins
midrib
stem

🍁 Special leaves

God has given some leaves special jobs to do. These unusual leaves have structures so unique that you might not recognize them as leaves at all. A **special leaf,** sometimes called a *modified leaf, is one that has a special design for a special task.* Some of these leaves include tendrils, spines, fleshy storage leaves, and the trapping leaves of insect-eating plants.

Twining climbers. Vines are plants that climb upward as they grow by clinging to tall objects such as walls or trees. Special leaves called **tendrils** are the "hands" with which a vine grasps a support structure. A tendril is designed to coil around any object it happens to touch. When the tendril touches something, the cells on the side opposite the point of contact begin to grow very rapidly, causing the tendril to bend and wrap around the object.

tendrils of cucumber vine

spines of prickly pear cactus

Prickly protection. The **spines** of cactuses are special leaves that contain no chlorophyll. Their function is to protect the water-storing stem of the cactus plant. This plant grows in hot, dry regions, where animals would destroy the cactus to get at its water if God had not given the plant special sharp spines for protection. These spines discourage animals from eating the cactus.

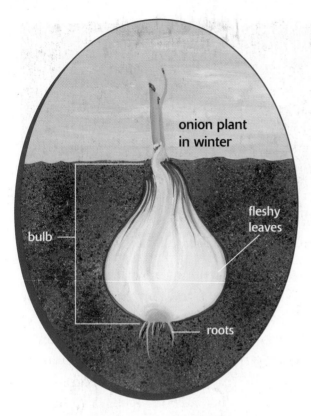

onion plant in winter

bulb

fleshy leaves

roots

Tasty storage space. The leaves of some plants, such as the onion, grow partially below the ground. In the winter, the upper tubular leaves of the onion die, but the fleshy bases of the leaves remain in the earth, wrapped around the tiny plant to insulate it from the cold ground and to nourish the plant when it begins to grow again in the spring. The many layers of lower leaves that remain below the ground form a **bulb.** This bulb is the onion that we eat.

Insect eaters. Plants such as the Venus flytrap, bladderwort, pitcher plant, and sundew have unusual leaves that can trap and digest small insects. Because of their unusual diet, these plants are called **insectivorous** [ĭn'sĕk·tĭv'ər·əs: insect-eating] **plants.** Insectivorous plants contain chlorophyll for manufacturing their own food, but they also obtain some food from the bodies of their victims.

The leaves of the **Venus flytrap** are hinged so that they can close like the jaws of a steel trap. An insect that crawls into the flytrap's leaf touches tiny trigger hairs that cause the two halves of the leaf to slam together. In order to prevent the leaf from closing at a false alarm, God has designed the trigger hairs in such a way that the leaf closes only if a hair is touched two times in a row, or if two hairs are touched at least one time each. When the trapped insect has been digested, the leaf opens and waits for its next meal to happen along.

Venus flytrap

bladderwort

bladder catching mosquito larva

Another insect-eating plant with trigger hairs is the **bladderwort.** This underwater plant has hollow, bladderlike leaves filled with water. When an unsuspecting insect or small crustacean bumps into one of the hairs positioned at the bladder's opening, the leaf suddenly expands. The creature finds itself caught in an inescapable current as water is sucked into the expanding leaf. After digesting its victim, the leaf shrinks down to set the trap again.

The **pitcher plant** attracts insects with its bright colors and the aroma of its honeylike nectar. When an insect lands on the rim of the slippery pitcher leaf, it slides helplessly down past many tiny hairs. These hairs point downward, allowing the insect to "drop in" but not to crawl out. After the insect dies, it is slowly digested in a liquid at the bottom of the pitcher.

Insects are attracted to the **sundew** by the plant's glistening bait—its sticky "dewdrops." When an insect crawls over the sundew plant, it steps into the dewdrops and gets stuck. The leaf's long hairs or tentacles then close over the insect to prevent its escape, and juices in the tentacles digest the insect.

pitcher plant

sundew

the Green machine

Did you ever notice the wide variety of leaves that God has on display in your own back yard? Narrow grass leaves, hand-shaped maple leaves, and needlelike pine leaves are only a few of the many different kinds you might find. Try to collect a sample of each type of leaf that grows in your yard. You will be surprised at how many different shapes you discover. Leaf shapes can be divided into four main groups: needlelike leaves; scaly leaves; long, thin leaves; and broad, flat leaves.

You can find **needlelike leaves** on trees and bushes throughout the year because these leaves are always green, even after the leaves of other trees have fallen from their branches. Needlelike leaves are what you will most likely find on your Christmas tree. Some needlelike leaves are long and spindly, and others are short and stubby. They may be soft and flexible, or firm and prickly like straight pins. Can you find a tree with needlelike leaves in your yard?

Scaly leaves are very small. If you look closely at one of the tiny *branchlets* (small branches) on a plant with scaly leaves, you will see that the branchlet is covered by a flat layer of tiny green scales that look like scales on a fish. Each scale is an individual leaf. Scaly leaves, like needles, are green year round. Look for scaly leaves on orna-mental shrubs planted around your house.

Leaves of the third group—**long, thin leaves**—can usually be found growing on the ground beneath your feet. This group includes the blades of grass that must

be cut often to keep your yard looking trim and neat. As you are looking for long, thin leaves to collect, you may be surprised at how many different kinds of grass leaves are in your lawn. Be sure to get whole leaves and not ones shortened by a lawn mower.

needlelike leaves

scaly leaves

long, thin leaves

The fourth group has **broad, flat leaves.** You will find them on a wide variety of trees, bushes, and plants throughout your yard. In a temperate climate, most of these leaves change colors and later fall to the ground during the autumn months. When you look closely at leaves of this fourth group, you will notice that they come in many different shapes and sizes and that no two leaves are identical. However, leaves from the same plant are very similar. Some leaves are heart-shaped, while others are oval or oblong. Can you find a leaf that looks like an arrowhead? How about a teardrop? You might even find a leaf with "fingers."

Broad leaves differ not only in shape, but also in what kind of edges they have. Some leaves have **smooth** edges with no bumps or bulges. Others have **toothed** edges like the row of sharp teeth on a saw blade. **Wavy** edges have many bumps or curves. Many types of leaves have **lobed** edges. Lobes stick out like fingers or thumbs from the main part of the leaf. Be sure to look for smooth, toothed, wavy, and lobed leaves in your yard.

As you collect samples of leaves found in your yard, keep them moist by placing them between some damp paper towels in a plastic bag or paper sack. Divide your leaf collection into the four leaf groups so that you can easily examine your findings. Choose some of the more interesting leaf shapes to start a back yard leaf collection.

In order to make your collection last for a long time, you will need to press your leaves. The quickest way to press them is to use an iron, some waxed paper,

Broad, flat leaves

smooth edges

toothed edges

lobed edges

a piece of cardboard, and some scrap cloth. Ask an adult to help you. Use the piece of cardboard as an ironing board. Preheat the iron to a medium setting and then place a sheet of waxed paper on the cardboard. Carefully place a leaf or two on the waxed paper, making sure that each leaf lies flat. When the leaves are in position, place a second sheet of waxed paper over the leaves. Cover the waxed paper with the piece of scrap cloth. By this time, the iron should be hot enough to be used. Place the hot iron on the cloth and slide it around as if you were ironing a shirt. Make sure that each part of the leaf gets ironed for at least twenty seconds. The heat from the iron not only flattens and dries out the leaf but also melts the wax on

the paper to provide a protective coating for the leaf. Remove the cloth and the waxed paper from the cardboard. Carefully peel the waxed paper from the leaf. You should notice that the leaf is shinier than it was before. What do you think makes it shinier?

Now you can make an exhibit with your newly pressed leaves by gluing them to construction paper. Label each leaf, telling where you found it and to which of the four basic leaf groups it belongs. If your leaf belongs to the broad, flat leaf group, also tell what kind of edge it has. Do any of your classmates have similar leaves? Do any of them have leaves completely different from yours?

Comprehension Check 1.1

1. What is the chemical process whereby plants produce food inside their leaves?

2. What is the pigment or coloring that gives plants their green color?

3. What is the food plants need to live?

4. What are the three main structural parts of a leaf?

5. What kind of leaf has a special design for a special function?

6. Name four insectivorous plants.

1.2 Roots and Stems

There is more to a plant than meets the eye. When you look at a plant, you are really looking at the plant's **shoot system,** every part of the plant visible above the ground. Leaves, stems, twigs, trunks, flowers, and fruit all make up the shoot system. The other part of the plant, located below the ground, is called the **root system.**

Many plants have as much or more growth underground as they do above ground. Although a tree appears to end abruptly at ground level, its thick trunk is actually connected to a vast system of roots that spread outward below the surface much like the tree's branches do up above. If you have ever seen a large tree that has been blown over in a violent storm, you may have noticed some of the root system still connected to the trunk.

In this section, you will learn about roots and their aboveground counterparts, stems. Trunks, branches, and twigs are all considered stems because, although larger and woodier, they serve the same purposes as do the thin green stems of flowers.

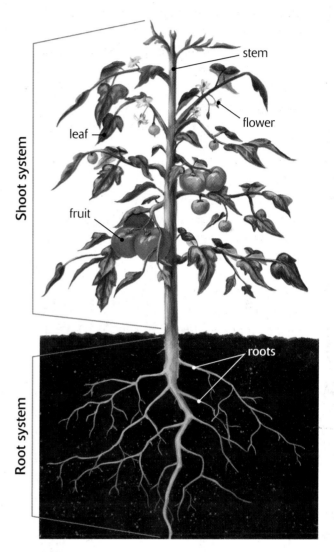

Parts of a tomato plant

Getting to the root of the matter

Roots do all of their work in the dark. They are hidden, but they are essential to plant growth. Have you ever stopped to consider what would happen if all the roots in the world started to grow upward instead of downward? How strange all the plants would look! But roots never do that. God designed roots so that they always grow downward into the soil, no matter how the original seed was laid in the ground. Roots are not beautiful, but without them there would be no showy flowers, no towering trees, no fields of waving grass.

Soil explorers. Roots serve many important purposes. They anchor the plant in the soil and keep soil from being washed away by water or blown away by the wind. But the main job of a root is to absorb water and minerals for the plant's use.

Water is the life of a plant. Without water, the plant cannot make its food, glucose, through photosynthesis. Even after the glucose is produced, it must remain dissolved in water in order for nourishment to travel to all parts of the plant. If the plant's cells are not kept filled with water, the plant will wilt. Water carries dissolved minerals up to the leaves to be used in manufacturing proteins, vitamins, and other important chemicals.

Plants that find moisture near the surface of the ground send out a broad, shallow network of roots. Grasses have this sort of root system. If you were to dig up a small square of grass out of your lawn using a trowel, you would see that the roots of grasses resemble a mass of stringy fibers. Other plants must send their roots down deep into the ground to find water. A plant that sends one main root particularly deep is said to have a **taproot.** Have you ever pulled dandelions out of a lawn or flower bed? If so, you have had firsthand experience trying to dig out their taproots. One taproot we often eat is the carrot.

Root systems

grass   dandelion   carrot

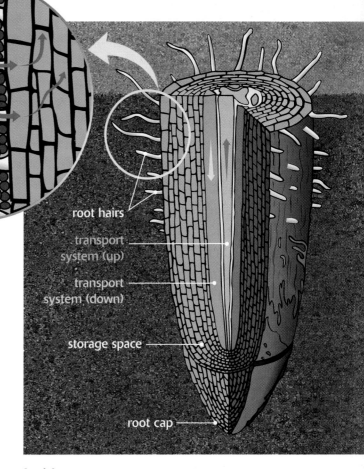

water enters root hairs

root hairs

transport system (up)

transport system (down)

storage space

root cap

Inside a root

In its search for water, a root digs through the soil by growing longer. A root grows only at its tip, which is covered by a layer of tough protective cells called a **root cap.** The root cap enables the delicate root tip to push its way through the hard ground without being damaged. **Root hairs,** tiny projections near the end of the root, worm their way between individual particles of soil to find water and dissolved minerals. These materials are absorbed through the cell membranes of the root hairs and then transported to the rest of the plant in tiny liquid-carrying tubes.

Roots are very efficient at absorbing water. In fact, they absorb much more than the plant actually needs. Most of the water taken in through the roots is released by evaporation through the stomata of the leaves. Each stoma is opened and closed by two **guard cells** that together surround the tiny opening. When water is plentiful, the stomata open wide to allow much water to leave the leaf. But when water is scarce, the stomata close to keep water in. By giving plants the ability to control the rate of evaporation, God has made it possible for them to survive in periods of dry weather, when the roots are unable to take in enough water to meet the plant's needs.

The plant warehouse. Roots are the shipping and receiving warehouse for the plant. They ship water and dissolved minerals up to the leaves for use in photosynthesis and other chemical processes. They also store extra glucose, the food made by the leaves.

Plants break down, or "burn," glucose in order to release the chemical energy stored in the sugar molecules. This chemical energy supplies the energy needed by the plant for growth. But leaves are so efficient that they make more food than the plant can use all at once. Extra glucose is sent down to the roots to be kept until needed.

carrot   beet   turnip

The roots store this extra sugar by converting it into substances called **starches.** Vegetables such as carrots, beets, and turnips are food-storing roots made mostly of starches. One thing you notice when eating any of these vegetables is that starchy vegetables do not taste very sweet. Other roots such as sweet potatoes and sugar beets are much sweeter, because they have not converted all of their sugar into starch.

When a plant needs its food reserve, the roots change starch back into sugar, and the sugar moves throughout the plant. Most plants make use of their stored food in the spring, when they need energy to grow new leaves. Until these new leaves can begin manufacturing food, the plant must rely on its stored sugar for nourishment.

Special roots. Many plants have roots that carry out special jobs for the plant. The roots of climbing plants such as *ivy* help the plant

to cling to its support. Certain desert plants have roots that produce harmful chemicals to keep other plants from growing close by and using up the plant's water supply.

Some unusual plants called **epiphytes** [ĕp′ə·fīts′] never touch the ground. They grow in the tops of trees. The *vanilla plant* (from which we get vanilla flavoring) has green open-air roots that carry out photosynthesis. *Spanish moss,* an epiphyte that covers many old trees in the South, has no roots at all. Its water is provided by rain and its nutrients by dead cells from the tree it lives on.

ivy on wall

roots

vanilla plant

Spanish moss

Stems: the plant superhighway

A two-way street. Much of a plant's work is done underground. Like tiny miners, roots take in water and minerals from the soil. These important resources are next carried to the leaves, the plant factory, by pipeline tissues in the stem. The pipelines, formed from special tube-like cells joined end to end, allow liquids to move up and down the stem much as blood flows through the veins and arteries of your body.

A stem contains two sets of pipelines. One set conducts water and minerals upward, from the roots to the leaves. The other set carries dissolved food in the other direction, from the leaves to the stem itself and to the roots.

Isn't it amazing that a tall tree can pull water all the way up its stem to the very topmost leaves? Scientists have discovered that water is drawn up the stem as a result of evaporation through the stomata of the leaves. Leaf cells that release water into the air become rather *dehydrated*, or dried out. These drier cells refill themselves by taking water from other nearby cells, which in turn draw water from the leaf's veins. Like tiny water pipes, the leaf veins draw water from other tiny "pipes" in the branch, which in turn connect to water vessels

in the stem. These vessels stretch downward through the trunk and roots, where the water is replenished by root hairs that absorb moisture from the soil.

water and minerals UP

dissolved food DOWN

glucose is made in the leaves

excess water leaves plant

glucose is stored in roots and stem

water and dissolved minerals enter at root hairs

Plant transport system

the Green machine

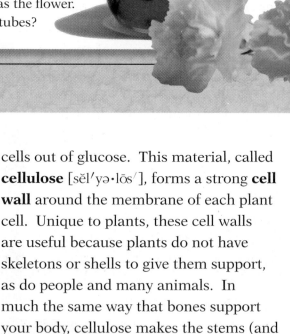

An easy way to demonstrate that water travels upward through the stem of a plant is to place the stem of a white flower in colored water. You will need a *glass or pint-sized jar, water, food coloring, scissors, a magnifying glass,* and *two or three white carnations.*

Fill the glass one-third full of water, and then add ten or fifteen drops of food coloring. With the scissors, trim the end of the stems before placing the flowers into the colored water. Leave the flowers in the water overnight.

Look at the flowers the next day. Have they changed in any way? What caused the change? With the scissors, cut one of the flower stems above the water line. Study the cut through the magnifying glass. You should be able to see some strawlike tubes the same color as the flower. What are these tubes?

A platform for leaves. The upper part of the stem, or **stem tip,** produces the plant's growth. First, cells at the stem tip divide, making twice as many cells. As the new cells are added, the plant grows taller. Next, the new cells begin to lengthen. They do not grow fatter, however. God has designed the stem so that its cells grow in only one direction, thus giving the plant height. When the long cells in the stem fill with water, they become firm, enabling the plant to stand upright and spread its leaves to the sunlight.

The stem is strengthened by a tough, fibrous material manufactured by plant cells out of glucose. This material, called **cellulose** [sĕl′yə·lōs′], forms a strong **cell wall** around the membrane of each plant cell. Unique to plants, these cell walls are useful because plants do not have skeletons or shells to give them support, as do people and many animals. In much the same way that bones support your body, cellulose makes the stems (and other parts) of plants stiff and firm, without taking away all their flexibility.

Special stems. In addition to carrying materials, most stems also store food or water. Some plants have stems that are especially suited to this job. The white potato, for example, is actually a food-storing stem, while the thick, spongy stem of the cactus stores water. The stem of the cactus is also designed to carry out the plant's photosynthesis, since the spines contain no chlorophyll. Because it lacks large, broad leaves with their many stomata, the cactus plant is better able to keep its water from evaporating in hot weather.

Some stems have other unique jobs. A **stolon** [stō′lŏn], also called a **runner,** is a stem that grows along the surface of the ground. Every so often along its length the stolon sends down roots that begin another plant. Many grass plants have stolons. **Rhizomes** [rī′zōmz′] are thick storage stems that produce new plants but differ from stolons in that they grow just below the ground instead of on the surface. Some vines have stems that function as

tendrils (you will remember that some other vines have tendrils that are leaves and not stems).

Thorns are protective stems much like leaf spines.

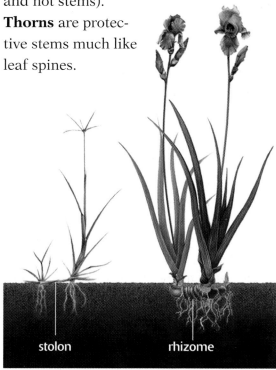
stolon   rhizome

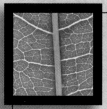

the
Green
machine

Tropism triumphs

What do you do when something is blocking your path? You go around it. What do you do when you need something that is just out of reach? You stretch for it. What do you do when you fall? You pick yourself up. These actions are natural responses to situations that come your way.

Plants cannot walk or run or move like people, but they still have a God-given ability to respond suitably to the situation. If a seedling's upward growth is blocked by a stone or a fallen log, the growing tip changes its path until the way is clear for it to push upward again. If a bush is planted near a river, it stretches its roots toward the water until they reach the riverbank. If a flowerpot topples over, the plant's roots continue to grow downward and its stem upward, even though the plant is lying on its side. Such growth adaptations in plants are known as **tropisms** [trō′pĭz′əmz]. *A tropism is the growth of a plant in response to a condition in its environment.*

With the right materials, you can produce tropisms in plants yourself. The following experiments demonstrate four different kinds of tropisms:

To get started, you will need *two glasses or jars, a wire screen, water, several beans, cotton balls,* and *some paper towels.* (If you soak the beans the night before, they will sprout faster). Pack one of the jars with moistened paper towels and place six to eight beans between the jar and the paper towels. Make sure the beans are equally spaced around the inside wall of the jar. Fill the second jar with moistened cotton balls, and then cover the jar opening with the wire screen. Lay six to eight beans on the wire screen.

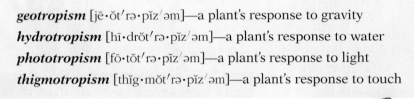

geotropism [jē·ŏt′rə·pĭz′əm]—a plant's response to gravity

hydrotropism [hī·drŏt′rə·pĭz′əm]—a plant's response to water

phototropism [fō·tŏt′rə·pĭz′əm]—a plant's response to light

thigmotropism [thĭg·mŏt′rə·pĭz′əm]—a plant's response to touch

Tropisms

geotropism

hydrotropism

phototropism

thigmotropism

Cover the beans with more moistened cotton. Keep the cotton and the paper towels moist throughout the experiment. The beans will sprout and will continue to grow if they remain moist.

After a few days, the young bean plants should be big enough for you to continue the experiment. Notice in which direction the roots are growing. Are the bean roots in the first jar growing in the same direction as the bean roots on the wire screen? Cover the first jar with a piece of cardboard and carefully turn it over so that the roots point upward. Lift the screen off the second jar and remove the cotton from within the jar. Return the screen to the jar, making sure that the cotton on the screen is moist. Watch the roots in both jars for several days. Do they continue growing in the same direction? Is the group of bean plants on the screen an example of geotropism or hydrotropism? Which of these two tropisms do you think is stronger? Why?

The best way to see phototropism taking place is to set a potted plant in a sunny spot in your room. What direction are the leaves facing after two days? Turn the plant around. Watch what the leaves do in the next several days.

You can see thigmotropism in action by placing a nail next to a tendril of a vine growing on a fence or tree near your home. Place the nail next to the tendril in such a way that you can leave the nail in position overnight; you may want to position the nail so that the tendril is lightly touching it. Check the tendril the following morning. How has the tendril changed? Why would God give a tendril the ability to curl itself around an object? Some tendrils curl to the right, while others curl to the left. Which way does your tendril curl?

Comprehension Check 1.2

1. What are the two systems of a plant?

2. What is the one main root that a plant sends particularly deep?

3. What is the layer of tough protective cells that protects the delicate root tip as the root pushes its way through the hard ground?

4. What are the tiny projections near the end of a root that help the root absorb water and minerals?

5. What are plants that never touch the ground called? Give two examples.

6. What tough, fibrous material forms a strong cell wall around each plant cell?

1.3 Flower, Fruit, and Seed

We all enjoy flowers for their beauty and fragrance, but were you aware that they also serve an important purpose? Without the seeds that are formed in flowers, more than half of all the kinds of plants in the world would not be able to reproduce.

🍁 Design for beauty

The most noticeable parts of a flower are its brightly colored **petals.** Besides decorating the landscape with their color, petals also help to attract bees or other creatures to the flower. **Sepals** [sē′pəlz] usually look like smaller, green versions of the petals and are located beneath them, although some flowers have sepals the same size and color as the petals themselves. Sepals enclose and protect a developing flower, or **bud,** until it opens up as a fully formed blossom.

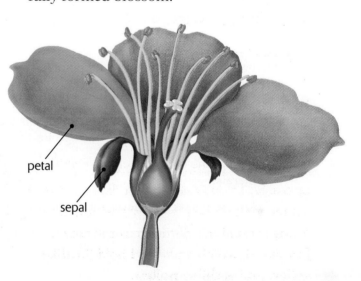

petal

sepal

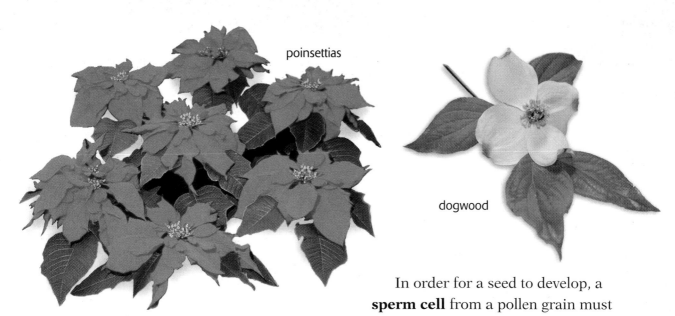

poinsettias

dogwood

Some flowers are bordered by colorful leaves called **bracts.** Bracts serve the same function as do petals—to attract insects to the flower—but have a much different structure. In some cases, the bracts take the place of the petals completely. The poinsettia, which we often see at Christmastime, has no true petals. Its yellow flower is surrounded by very large, bright red (or white) bracts. Although the flower of the dogwood tree has very tiny petals, the white bracts are what gives the tree its spectacular appearance when it is in bloom.

Design for reproduction

In the middle of the flower, surrounded by the petals, is a long tube called the **pistil.** The fat base of the pistil, the **ovary** [ō′və·rē], holds one or more undeveloped seeds, or **ovules** [ō′vyo͞olz]. Also in the center of the flower, usually positioned in a ring around the pistil, are the **stamens** [stā′mənz], which make and hold dustlike yellow grains called **pollen.**

In order for a seed to develop, a **sperm cell** from a pollen grain must unite with an **egg cell** stored inside an ovule—a process known as **fertilization.** A flower may be fertilized by its own pollen or by pollen from another flower. The pollen is first deposited on the pistil, which has a flat tip—the **stigma**—specially designed to receive the pollen. This transfer of pollen from the stamen to the pistil is called **pollination.** Bees and other insects such as flies, wasps, and butterflies are the most frequent **pollinators,** but birds, bats, and the wind also pollinate flowers.

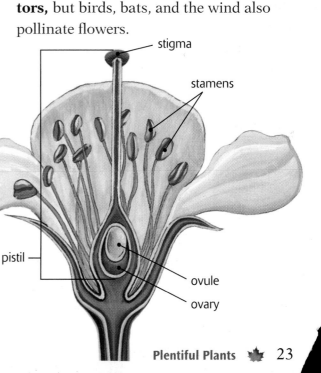

stigma

stamens

pistil

ovule

ovary

honeybee coated with pollen leaving flower

As the bee feeds on the nectar, which it will use to make honey, it brushes against the pollen-coated stamens. Some of the pollen grains stick to the fine hairs on the bee's body. The bee carries this pollen with it when it flies on to the next flower. As the bee crawls over the flower, pollen is brushed onto the stigma.

God has designed flowers so that the process of pollination is beneficial both to the flowers and to the creatures that pollinate them. A bee is drawn to a flower by its fragrance and bright color. (Most flowers smell sweet, although a few, designed to be pollinated by flies, smell like rotten meat.) The bee is lured deep into the flower in its search for **nectar,** a sweet liquid stored in the bottom of the bloom.

Once deposited on the stigma, a pollen grain goes into action. The hard outer casing on the pollen grain cracks open, and a special cell inside begins to lengthen, burrowing its way downward through the pistil and into an ovule. This cell forms a **pollen tube** down which two sperm cells travel from the pollen grain to the egg cell inside the ovule. When a sperm cell unites with the egg cell, the ovule begins to develop into a seed.

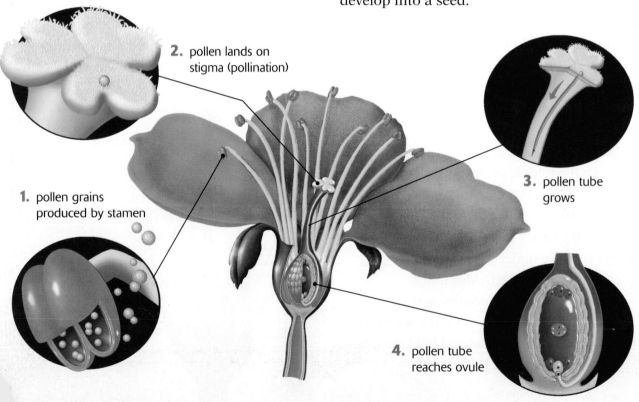

2. pollen lands on stigma (pollination)

1. pollen grains produced by stamen

3. pollen tube grows

4. pollen tube reaches ovule

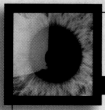

EYEwitness reporter

By dissecting [dĭ·sĕkt′ĭng] a flower (taking a flower apart for study), you can see how God uses a colorful blossom and a hungry insect to help a plant reproduce. You will need *a pin or paper clip, a flower, a magnifying glass,* and *a white piece of paper.* A big flower such as a lily or a daffodil is a good one to dissect because each part can be seen without a magnifying glass. You will, however, need a magnifying glass to view how pollen sticks to the stamens and how the ovules are arranged within the pistil.

Before you cut into the flower, make a sketch of what you already see (box 1). Try to show in your drawing the number of petals and the number of sepals the flower has. Remember that the sepals are not always green; they may be the same color as the petals they surround. You may also be able to include the parts sticking out from the center of the flower. Can you tell which is the pistil and which are the stamens? How does the pistil differ from the stamens? With colored pencils or crayons, color your drawing to match your flower. Label each part that you have drawn.

#1

#2

#3

You are now ready to cut the flower open. Place the flower on a white piece of paper, laying it flat so you can see the outside of the petals and the sepals. Poke the pin a short distance into the base of the flower, where the flower connects to the stem. Carefully slide the pin up the center of the flower all the way to the tip of the pistil so that the flower is split in half. Now gently pull the flower apart. Can you see several beadlike parts within the base of the pistil? These are the ovules. Study the ovules through the magnifying glass and make a sketch of what you see (box 2).

In order for the ovules to turn into seeds, they must unite with sperm cells stored inside pollen grains. With the help of the magnifying glass, you can see grains of pollen on the very tips of the stamens. Make a sketch of the pollen you see on the stamens (box 3). Discover how easy it is to brush off the dry, powdery pollen by pulling a stamen from the flower and brushing its tip across the white paper. Can you see the thin coat of colored powder on the paper? It is no wonder that an insect gets pollen on its legs when it touches a stamen.

Next, study the stigma, the very tip of the pistil, through the magnifying glass. You will notice that it appears to be very sticky.

start cutting here

Brush the stigma across the pollen on the paper. When you look at the pistil through the magnifying glass again, you should be able to see small particles of pollen sticking to the stigma. What do you think happens when an insect brushes against the stigma?

Once a pollen grain has reached the pistil, it grows a pollen tube down into the ovary. If your flower has already been pollinated, you may be able to see a pollen tube running through the middle of the pistil. Check to see if your pistil has a pollen tube.

Now report your findings by writing a short paragraph explaining how a flower reproduces.

Design for distribution

After fertilization has taken place, the flower fades and drops its petals. Its job is finished. But the ovary, where the seeds lie hidden, begins to experience an interesting transformation. Little by little, the plant gathers a supply of food around the seeds, and the ovary swells larger and larger. Eventually, ***the ovary becomes a fruit.*** A fruit may be many times larger than the original flower. A twenty-pound watermelon, for example, develops from an ovary less than a half inch across. Other fruits are very small. Each tiny grain on a head of wheat is an individual fruit.

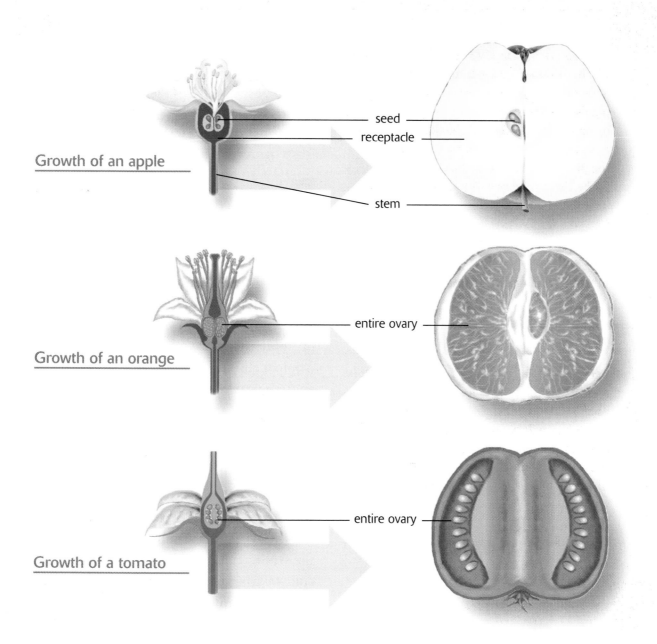

Growth of an apple

seed
receptacle
stem

Growth of an orange

entire ovary

Growth of a tomato

entire ovary

A fruit may be sweet and fleshy like an apple, or it may be dry like a nut or like the pod of a green bean. In everyday speech, we usually use the term *fruit* to refer only to those fruits that have a sweet taste. But scientifically speaking, a **fruit** is anything that forms from the ovary of a flower. Nuts, beans, peas, olives, and grains, as well as some common "vegeta-bles" such as tomatoes and cucumbers, are all actually *fruits*.

The most important function of fruits for the plants is to help scatter the seeds. A fleshy fruit may be eaten by an animal. The seeds within the fruit pass through the animal's digestive tract and are deposited in another location. Dry fruits help to scatter seeds in a variety of ways.

dandelion seeds

Some are equipped with tiny hooks that catch onto the fur of animals or the clothing of people. Others have wings or parachutelike structures that enable them to float on the wind. Some fruits with dry pods explode violently, shooting seeds away from the parent plant. If seeds were not scattered, very few would grow. After sprouting, the young seedlings would die from overcrowding.

burs caught in wild mustang's mane

Design for growth

Seeds do not necessarily begin to grow as soon as they fall into the ground. God has programmed into seeds the ability to remain **dormant,** or inactive, for long periods of time. Before a seed can sprout and begin growing, two things must be present: **moisture** and **warmth.** In tropical climates, temperatures are warm enough year round for seeds to begin growing, but seeds often remain dormant until after the rainy season has brought sufficient moisture to the soil. In temperate climates, however, the soil usually contains plenty of moisture for seeds to grow. But if seeds began to grow as soon as they matured, in the late summer or early fall, the young plants would soon die as the cold weather arrived. God has therefore built into many seeds a delay mechanism to keep them from sprouting right away. Some seeds have an especially hard coat that must decay before the seedling inside can get enough moisture to start growing. Others contain chemicals that keep them from sprouting until they have been exposed to a long period of cold temperatures. Most seeds lie dormant over the winter and then begin to grow in the spring, when the ground becomes warm once again.

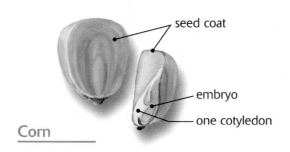

Corn

seed coat
embryo
one cotyledon

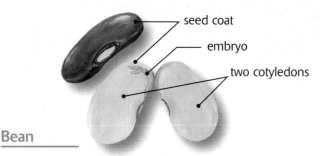

Bean

seed coat
embryo
two cotyledons

Each seed is a powerful growth package with three parts. (1) Within the seed is a living **embryo** [ĕm′brē·ō], or miniature undeveloped plant, made up of a tiny shoot that will become the stem and leaves, and a small root that will develop into the root system. (2) Each seed has one or two **cotyledons** [kŏt′əl·ēd′ənz] that contain stored food for the growing plant. Corn is an example of a plant with one cotyledon; peanuts and beans have two. (3) A **seed coat** covers and protects the embryo.

🍁 Design for variety

When God created the world, He gave man dominion over it. God wants us to study His creation and learn how to use it. Scientists who study plants are called **botanists.** Botanists learn as much as they can about all the varieties of plants in the world. From their study has come much knowledge about how to control plant diseases and stimulate plant growth.

By cross-fertilizing related plants with different characteristics, botanists can sometimes produce a new variety of plant called a **hybrid** [hī′brĭd]. Of course, scientists cannot change one *kind* to another *kind.* An apple will never be a cucumber, for example. *Like animals, plants always reproduce after their own kind.* This principle is one of the great laws that God established at the time of creation.

A successful hybrid has the desirable characteristics of each parent. Many of our food crops and ornamental flowers are hybrids. They are often larger, healthier, or more beautiful than related varieties that grow in the wild. Long-stemmed roses, large ears of corn, luscious apples, and disease-resistant wheat are examples of beneficial hybrids. Botanists have learned a great deal about plants, but there is still much more to learn.

hybrid apple

crab apples

Science Speaks

When Carl Linnaeus [lĭ·nē′əs: 1701–1778] was just a little boy in Sweden, he loved to study plants so much that people started calling him "the little botanist." It was not unusual for the Swedish townsfolk to see the young Linnaeus with his hands filled with different kinds of flowers and leaves he had found along the country road. While other boys his age were chasing snakes and catching frogs and spiders, Carl was collecting plants. As he studied the many different kinds of plants he found, he often wondered what their names were and how they were related to one another. Little was known in the early 1700s about the different kinds of plants, but Carl was determined to find out everything he could.

Carl Linnaeus, who later became known as *Carolus Linnaeus,* grew to become one of the greatest botanists in history. He wrote several books describing the many different kinds of plants he found and gave countless lectures proclaiming the wonders of God's creation displayed in a common flower. He invented the system of classifying plants and animals that is still in use today. He started a worldwide search for unusual and exotic plants, encouraging many of his colleagues and students to travel as far away as India, South America, and the South Pacific.

Linnaeus was convinced that all the related groups of plants and animals on the earth today have existed since Creation. (The Bible calls these related groups *kinds.*) He believed that although many variations have occurred within each kind as a result of generations of reproduction, each variation has the same basic characteristics that were given to the parent plant or animal in the beginning. No new kinds have appeared since Creation.

This belief led Linnaeus to the conclusion that plants sharing the same basic structures should also share the same group name. For instance, a sweetbrier rose, a China rose, and a French rose may look very different, but they all still share some common characteristics, such as the structure of their flowers. Therefore, according to Linnaeus's system of classification, each of these plants shares the same genus name, *Rosa.* Linnaeus also made sure each plant had a second name that would describe its specific structure. This species separates each plant from the others in its group. Because of his work in classifying plants and animals, Carolus Linnaeus is known today as the "Father of Taxonomy." (Taxonomy [tăk·sŏn′ə·mē] is the science of classification.)

1. What process involves a sperm cell from a pollen grain uniting with an egg cell stored inside an ovule?

2. What do we call the process of transferring pollen from the stamen to the pistil? Name three insects that commonly aid in this process.

3. What is a *fruit*?

4. Name the three parts of a seed.

5. What is a scientist who studies plants called?

6. Give the name of each flower part indicated in the diagram.

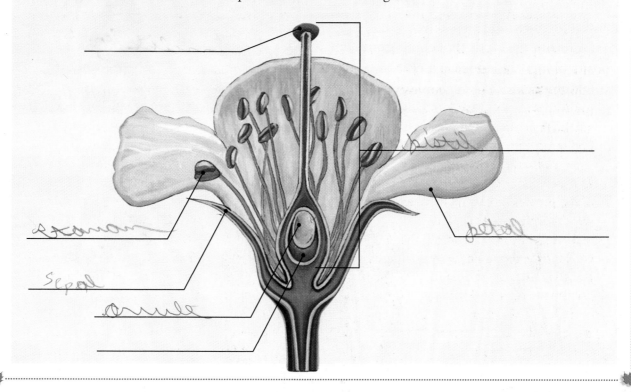

(handwritten labels: pistil, petal, stamen, sepal, ovule)

1.4 Plant Families You Should Know

Botanists have divided flowering plants into families according to the structure of their flowers and fruits. Some plant families include common plants that grow near your home. Others you may never see unless you visit a botanical garden or a tropical rain forest. A few plant families you should know are the **composite family,** the **pea family,** the **rose family,** the **lily family,** and the **grass family.**

🍁 Composites: Flowers of many parts

You are probably familiar with the composite family because it includes many of the different wildflowers that bloom in fields and along country roads. It is the largest family of flowering plants. Daisies, goldenrods, thistles, and dandelions are all considered composites because each flower you see is actually a combination of many flowers. The daisy has several petallike **ray flowers** and hundreds of tiny **disk flowers.** Some composites have only ray flowers, and some have only disk flowers.

A few of the foods that come from composite plants are lettuce, artichokes, and sunflower seeds. Some people even eat dandelions!

sunflowers

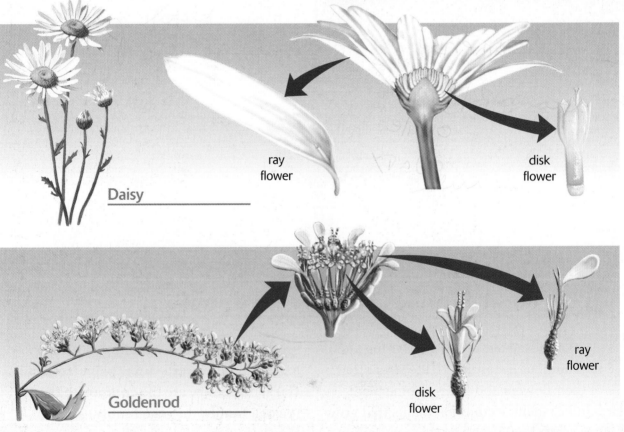

ray flower

disk flower

Daisy

Goldenrod

disk flower

ray flower

JUST for FUN

 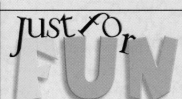

Can you figure out which of these flowers are composites? Do you know their names? Turn the book upside down to find the answers to these questions and to find the names of the other flowers on display.

Answers: The following numbers are composites: 1, 2, 3, 5, 7, 10, 11, 12. All of the flowers pictured are as follows: 1. Daisy 2. Aster 3. Black-eyed Susan 4. Butter-and-eggs (Toadflax) 5. Ironweed 6. Cardinal flower (Scarlet lobelia) 7. Goldenrod 8. Jewelweed (Touch-me-not) 9. Queen Anne's lace 10. Chicory 11. Tansy 12. Dandelion

🍁 Peas: The high-protein plants

If you have ever picked green beans or garden peas, you are familiar with members of the pea family. You may not realize, however, that other members of this large plant group include the clover and alfalfa [ăl·făl′fə] fed to cows, the ornamental sweet peas, wisterias, and redbuds grown for their showy flowers, and the bothersome kudzu [kŏod′zoo], a rapidly growing vine imported from China and Japan that can quickly take over an entire roadside or field. The pea family is the second largest family of flowering plants.

Packed in a pod. Members of the pea family are called **legumes** [lĕg′yoomz] because their fruits grow in the shape of a pod, or legume. Some legumes have smooth pods; others have prickly or bumpy pods. Clover has very tiny pods and the yard-long bean has pods that are three feet in length. When a legume is mature, the pod will dry out and split down the sides to release the seeds.

Protective petals. You can recognize most legumes not only by their pods but also by their flowers. The pea flower has one large petal that spreads out like a fan at the top of the blossom. Two smaller side petals, called wings, almost seem to flutter around two bottom petals that join together to form a pouch. The pouch surrounds and almost encloses the stamens and the pistil. In order to reach the nectar at the base of the flower, an insect must crawl through the small space within the pouch.

top petal

2 wings

pouch
(2 petals)

pea flower

wisteria

sweet pea

Necessary nitrogen. Plants need nutrients found in the soil in order to grow. Over time, some plants use so many nutrients that the soil no longer has enough nutrients for other plants to use. Legumes, however, give the soil more nutrients than they use. These extra nutrients are produced by bacteria, living on the roots of legumes, that take nitrogen from the air and change it into nutrients that plants can use.

Years ago, farmers discovered that after planting crops that use lots of nutrients from the soil, they could plant legumes and replenish the nutrients in the soil again. Today, most farmers also use fertilizer to build up the nutrients in the soil.

Essential and edible. Foods in the pea family that we commonly eat are peas, green beans, soybeans, alfalfa sprouts, peanuts, and candy made from licorice. You might also eat a little bit of protein produced in clover, alfalfa, and vetch; but by the time you eat it, the protein will be in the form of roast beef or a piece of steak.

One legume that has many uses is the peanut. George Washington Carver, a great Christian botanist, discovered over 300 products that could be made from peanuts—including ink, soap, shampoo, shaving cream, a milk substitute, and, of course, peanut butter.

Roses: Blessed with beauty and flavor

The beautiful flowers sent to sweethearts on Valentine's Day are not the only members of the rose family. Many other flowering plants belong to this colorful and fruitful plant group. All plants in the rose family have blossoms with five petals or with multiples of five. The wild rose has five petals that spread out like a star. *Blackberries, raspberries,* and *strawberries* also have blossoms with five petals. Other members of the rose family include *apples, peaches, pears, plums,* and *cherries.*

wild rose

strawberry

raspberry

hybrid roses

10, 15, 20, or more petals. Because God has allowed man to learn how to produce new plant varieties, apples are juicier, cherries are bigger, and blackberries are sweeter and less thorny than they ever were in the wild.

Lilies: Storehouse queens

Instead of having five petals or petals in multiples of five like the rose, flowers of the lily family have petals in multiples of three. The *day lily* is known for its long, narrow leaves and its tawny-orange, trumpetlike flower that lasts no longer than a day. You can find this bright flower blooming along roadsides and in meadows during the summer or in carefully cultivated gardens in the spring. Some interesting members of the lily family that bloom early in the spring are *tulips*, *hyacinths* [hī'ə·sĭnths], and *trilliums* [trĭl'ē·əmz]. Other lilies include the *tiger lily*, the *Easter lily*, and the *lily of the valley*.

Helpful hybrids.

Many plants in the rose family are hybrids. Different strains of the garden rose have been cross fertilized for many generations so that now they look quite different from the wild rose. Instead of having five petals, these roses now have

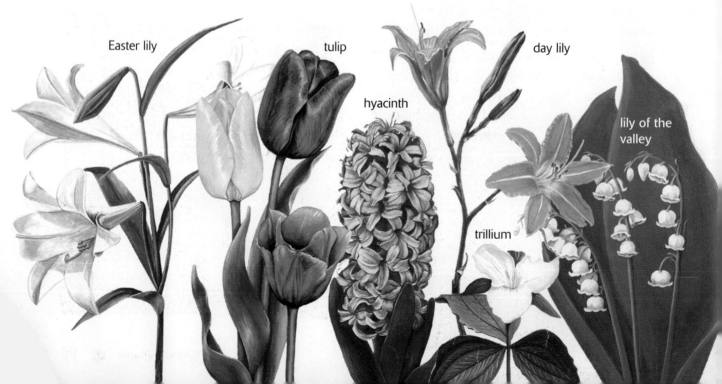
Easter lily
tulip
day lily
hyacinth
lily of the valley
trillium

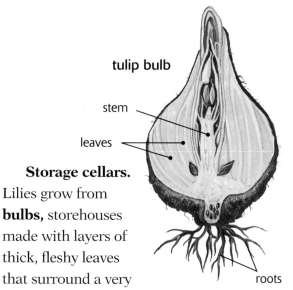

tulip bulb

stem

leaves

roots

Storage cellars.
Lilies grow from
bulbs, storehouses
made with layers of
thick, fleshy leaves
that surround a very
short stem. Bulbs are designed to store
food during the growing season so that the
plant can continue to live even after its leaves,
stem, and flowers have died away. At the
beginning of the next growing season, the
bulb sends out a new shoot, which becomes
the stem, leaves, and flowers of the new plant.

Some members of the lily family do not
have bulbs, but they still have thick leaves
that are used as food storehouses. Among
these plants are the cactuslike *aloes* [ăl′ōz]
and *yuccas* [yŭk′əz] found in desert climates.
The aloe vera plant is perhaps the most useful
of all lilies because the food stored in its
leaves can be used in soothing ointments and
lotions for the treatment of burns and other
skin disorders. One of the largest members
of the lily family is the *Joshua tree,* a form

Joshua tree

of yucca that grows in Arizona and Utah.
Its thick branches, which give it the appearance of a tree, support clusters of knifelike
leaves that point up to the hot desert sun.
Another large, treelike lily is the *kokerboom*
[kō′kər·bōōm′], which lives only in South
Africa and may grow to a height of 30 feet.
Baboons often climb to the top of the kokerboom to drink the sweet nectar from its
flowers.

kokerboom

aloe plant

Science Speaks

During the 1500s and 1600s, the Protestant Reformation came to England, and the English people became a people of one Book, the Bible. Their new love for God and understanding of His act of Creation led many Englishmen to a desire to study the things God has made. One of the greatest of the early English scientists was a Puritan botanist and naturalist, John Ray, who helped devise the system of classification of plants and animals that we use today.

John Ray, who lived in the 1600s, traveled all over the British Isles and the European Continent collecting specimens, making observations, and taking notes for a book on natural history that would include all of the known plants and animals. His work on classifying plants and animals was expanded by the great Swedish botanist Carolus Linnaeus in the 1700s. Near the end of his productive life, John Ray published his most popular and influential work, *The Wisdom of God Manifested in the Works of Creation*. In this book, the great scientist described many wonders of nature: the sun, moon, stars, rocks, trees, flowers, insects, birds, fish, and four-footed animals. He marveled at the variety of living things. "If the number of creatures be so exceeding great," he wrote, "how great . . . must needs be the Power and Wisdom of Him Who formed them all!" John Ray encouraged people to study science in order to better the lot of mankind and in order to appreciate more fully the greatness of God. "Let us then consider the Works of God," he said, "and observe the operations of His hands: let us take notice of, and admire His infinite wisdom and goodness in the formation of them."

🍁 *Grasses: Bountiful and beneficial*

Wheat, barley, rye, oats, rice, and *corn* are all members of the grass family, ***the most important family of food-producing plants.*** One third of the earth's land area is covered by grasses. Many of these grasses are cultivated and harvested to provide food. Others are cultivated to cover, beautify, and protect the land.

Although grasses have long, thin leaves (blades) like lilies, they do not have big flowers. Grasses have very small flowers, often the same color as the plant itself. These flowers do not need bright colors because they rely on the wind to pollinate them, instead of depending on insects.

God gave grasses two methods of reproduction so that they could provide more food for people and animals. The grass flowers, although small, produce seeds that are scattered by the wind. New plants can grow from these scattered seeds. But grass plants can also grow outward by sending out a creeping underground stem. These stems take root a short distance from the plant and begin to put out leaves. The new grass plants produced by the underground stems can start growing close to the parent plant even before the grass flower produces its seeds.

God also gave grasses the ability to withstand elements that would destroy most other plants. After being chopped, mowed, or eaten down to the roots, grasses can quickly grow back even when other plants would die. One reason grasses can spring back from such abuse is that most of the grass plant is actually underground, in its fibrous roots. When all of the leaves are destroyed, the grass plant can easily grow new leaves because of the great amount of nourishment in its roots.

Another reason grasses recover so quickly after being cut is that instead of growing at the stem tip as most other plants do, grasses grow at the base of every leaf. A grass leaf consists of two parts: the **blade** and the **sheath.** The

Typical grass plant

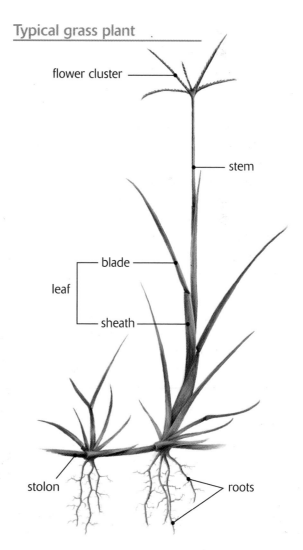

flower cluster

stem

leaf — blade

sheath

stolon

roots

blade is the long, narrow part that sticks out from the stem. The sheath is the part that is closely wrapped around the stem. When a blade of grass is chopped off by a cow or a lawn mower, the leaf continues to grow because the growing part—the sheath—is still intact. As the sheath grows, a new blade emerges from the stem.

Different kinds of grass

Cereal grasses. Did you know you eat grass every day? If you eat toast or cereal for breakfast, a sandwich for lunch, and spaghetti for dinner, you have eaten grass at all three meals!

Certain grasses, called **cereal grasses,** are harvested for the nutrients in their seeds. These seeds we call **grains.** Three of the most widely used grains are wheat, rice, and corn. *Wheat* is ground into flour, the main ingredient of breads, baked goods, breakfast cereals, and noodles such as spaghetti and macaroni. *Rice* is the chief food of over half the people in the world because it will grow in areas that are too hot or too wet for other grains. *Corn* is primarily fed to cattle and other livestock that furnish us with meat. Corn is also processed to make corn syrup, corn sugar, and corn oil, all of which are used for cooking. Of the three grains, many people enjoy corn the most, especially when it is in the form of popcorn or corn on the cob. Other grains that are widely used because of their nutritional value are oats, barley, and rye.

wheat

rice

corn

Turf grasses. The many grasses used to cover lawns, athletic fields, golf courses, and playgrounds are all considered **turf grasses.** These grasses beautify the land and protect it from erosion. Some common turf grasses are *Kentucky bluegrass, bentgrass, Bahia* [bä·ē′ə] *grass, Bermuda grass,* and *centipede grass.* Because some grasses grow best in drier climates, while others need more water, different turf grasses are often combined to keep lawns green throughout the year. Two unpopular wild grasses are *crab grass* and *quack grass.* Once established in a lawn, these tend to overrun the more beautiful turf grasses planted by man.

Woody grasses. *Bamboo* is a huge grass that grows primarily in Southeast Asia. Its stem can reach over 100 feet in height and can be as wide as one foot at its base. It certainly doesn't look like the grass that grows on our lawns! The giant panda, a rare animal that lives in Chinese bamboo forests, finds the leaves and the tender shoots of bamboo to be very tasty. The hollow, woody stems of bamboo are also used for building houses, bridges, furniture, fishing poles, and many other products.

Sugar cane, a much smaller woody grass, reaches a height of only 10 to 20 feet. It is filled with a sweet-tasting pulp that is very juicy when it is crushed. Once processed, the pulp becomes the sugar you may sprinkle on your cereal in the morning. Sugar cane is grown commercially in many tropical and subtropical countries.

sugar cane

bamboo

CONCEPTS
IN SCIENCE

Dicot?—or Monocot?

Biologists divide flowering plants into two basic groups: monocots and dicots. The seeds of **monocots** contain only *one cotyledon,* or food storage area. Their leaves usually have *parallel veins,* and their flower petals come in *multiples of three.* **Dicots,** on the other hand, have seeds with *two cotyledons.* Their *leaves are usually broad and flat,* with *veins that branch* out from the central midrib. Their flower petals come in *multiples of four or five.* Dicots and monocots also have different root systems: while monocots have *fibrous roots,* dicots usually have *taproots.* Can you tell which of the five plant families we have studied are dicots and which are monocots?

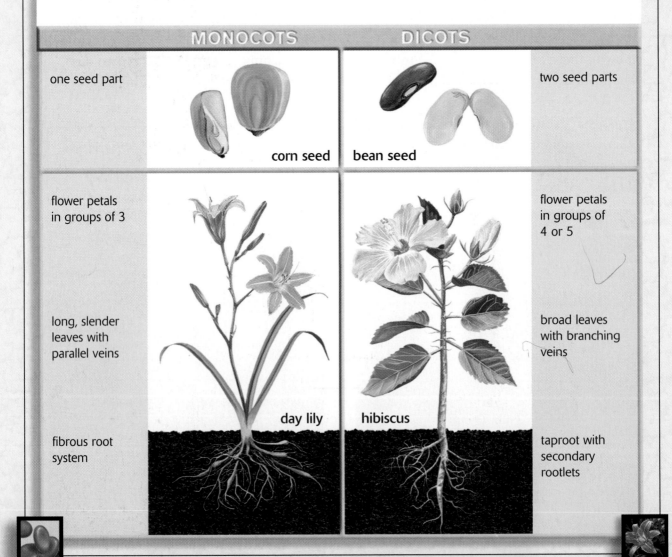

MONOCOTS

DICOTS

one seed part

corn seed

bean seed

two seed parts

flower petals in groups of 3

flower petals in groups of 4 or 5

long, slender leaves with parallel veins

broad leaves with branching veins

day lily

hibiscus

fibrous root system

taproot with secondary rootlets

1. What are the two types of flowers that make up a daisy? To what plant family do daisies belong?

2. Members of the pea family are called ____?____ .

3. To what family do blackberries, raspberries, and strawberries belong?

4. Lilies grow from a "storehouse" made with layers of thick, fleshy leaves that surround a very short stem. What is this storehouse called?

5. What is the most important family of the food-producing plants?

6. Examine the flowers and their characteristics and write the name of the correct family in the blank.

- largest flowering family
- two types of flowers make up the "one" flower

_____ family

- has 5 petals (1 large and 4 small)
- fruits grow in the shape of pods

_____ family

- small flowers
- two-part leaf (blade and sheath)
- can reproduce without flowers

_____ family

- petals grow in multiples of 5
- includes apples and cherries

_____ family

- petals grow in multiples of 3
- grows from bulbs

_____ family

Sketch it
TO SEE IT

Study the plants pictured on this page and draw them in the correct places in the vases. Think of the characteristics of each one as you draw it.

composite   pea   rose   lily   grass

Study other plants that belong to the five families you studied. Make a sketchbook with a drawing of at least one member of each family. Can you find plants that belong to other families?

Make a sketch of them and include them in your plant-family portrait book. With colored pencils or crayons, color the drawings you make. Display the best portraits for all to see.

1.5 The World of Trees

Trees are the giants of the plant kingdom. They tower high above all other growing things, as living monuments to God's power and glory. They are strong, massive, quiet, and beautiful, but also very useful.

Trees provide perches for birds and homes for many animals. Both people and animals are nourished by apples, cherries, oranges, peaches, dates, figs, coconuts, olives, pecans, and many other delicious and nutritious foods that grow on trees. Some food products such as chocolate, coffee, and maple syrup also come from trees. We can appreciate the warmth of a roaring wood fire on a winter night, and welcome the cool shade of a tree on a blazing hot day. Houses, tables, cabinets, and even parts of the desk you sit in can be made from the wood of trees.

sequoia trees

California
redwood

giant
sequoia

white oak

blue whale

🍁 Amazing trees

How would you describe a tree? You might begin by saying that a tree is a tall plant. You might add that a tree is made out of wood and has leaves and branches. A botanist would say that a **tree** is *a tall plant with a single woody stem*. Because it does not die after one season of growth, but lives for many years, it is called a **perennial** [pə·rĕn′ē·əl]. (Other plants, called **annuals** [ăn·yōō′əlz], grow only one year. **Biennials** [bī·ĕn′ē·əlz] are plants that live for two years.)

World record holders. Trees are the largest of all living things. Some are over 300 feet tall—taller than a thirty-story building! The largest mammal is the blue whale, sometimes measuring more than 100 feet in length. The tallest land animal, the giraffe, reaches a height of 18 feet. But the whale and the giraffe seem small when compared to a 360-foot **California redwood.** These redwoods are *the tallest living trees in the world*. Could you imagine building a tree house 300 feet in the air?

bristlecone pine

olive tree in Israel

Not only are trees the tallest living things, but they also are the oldest. **Dendrologists** [dĕn·drŏl′ə·jĭsts: scientists who study trees] have determined that the **bristlecone pines** of California are perhaps *the oldest living things on earth.* They date back four to five thousand years. Some of these trees sprouted soon after the Flood of Noah's day and were growing when Abraham walked the earth. The oldest sequoias are about 3500 years old. Some olive trees that are

still standing in Israel were alive during the time of Christ, about 2000 years ago, or began to grow shortly afterward.

Unusual trees. Many of the trees God created have interesting and unusual characteristics. The remarkable **banyan** [băn′yən] **tree** spreads outward by sending thick roots down from its branches to the ground. One banyan in India, with over 1700 of these root columns covering an area of three acres, forms a small forest all by itself. The state tree of

banyan tree

candlenuts

Hawaii, the **candlenut tree** or the kukui, has unusual nuts containing an oil that burns very well. Before electricity came to the islands, Hawaiians strung dried candlenuts together on the rib of a coconut leaf. Then the children set them on fire one at a time, each nut burning for two or three minutes, to provide light in the evening. The **baobab** [bā′ō·băb] **tree** of the African grasslands seems almost as wide as it is tall. It has a huge trunk that stores water to last throughout the dry season. An old baobab tree in Australia had a hollowed-out trunk so large that for a while it served as the town jail.

From seed to giant

The next time you are out for a walk in the woods or in a park, look for a tiny sapling growing in the shade of its parent tree. (The sapling will have the same sort of leaves that the adult tree has.) Compare the young plant with the older one. It is hard to imagine that once, many years ago, that huge tree was a small sapling, barely a foot tall. How do trees get to be so big?

The massive trunk of a tree is simply a very large stem. The stem grows lengthwise only at its tip, where a small knobby structure called a **bud** produces new growth. As the stem grows longer, small buds

baobab tree

bud

side bud

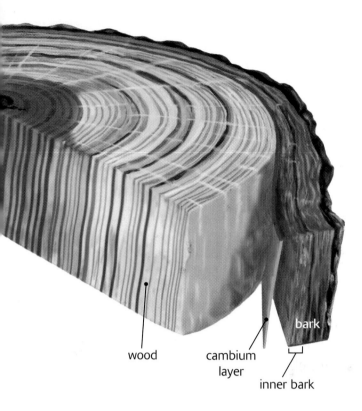

wood | cambium layer | inner bark | bark

The outward growth of a tree trunk takes place in a region just under the bark. If you were to pull away some of the bark, you would see a sticky, slimy film. It is here that cells divide to form new bark and new wood. This part of the tree where growth takes place is called the **cambium layer.**

🍁 Tree armor

The bark of a tree keeps the wood from drying out, protects the tree from the attacks of parasitic animals or plants, and protects from the invasion of disease. Some trees, such as the sequoia, have bark that protects them from fire. The inner layers of a tree's bark contain the pipelines that carry food from the leaves to the roots. If a ring of bark is removed from the trunk, a procedure known as **girdling** the tree, the tree eventually dies because nourishment is not able to reach the roots. *Since a tree needs its bark in order to survive, you should never pull any bark off a tree or carve into its trunk.*

appear on the sides of the stem. These buds grow outward from the stem and form branches. Each branch is tipped by a bud and is able to produce new side buds as well. The tree continues to grow throughout its life, enlarging its old branches and forming new ones. Take a look at the end of a twig on a low-hanging branch of a tree. Do you see the bud on the tip of the twig? Can you find any buds or new branches growing out of the side of the twig?

As a tree grows taller and more and more branches spread outward, the trunk of the tree must thicken in order to support the increasing weight of the branches and leaves. Trees enlarge their trunks (and branches) by adding one layer of new wood each year. As a result, the thickness of a trunk can help reveal the tree's age.

The outermost layers of bark on a tree are made up of dead cells, as are the surface layers of your own skin. When new wood and bark are formed on the inside, the old outer bark cannot stretch to make room. It cracks and spreads apart, giving the tree's trunk a rough texture. The older the tree gets, the more rough and cracked its bark becomes. The bark of each kind of tree has a unique texture and pattern of cracking. Very few trees grow so slowly that their bark does not crack. Trees such as the beech have smooth bark, and shed it only a little bit at a time.

You have already learned about many of the most important benefits of trees and other plants, such as producing oxygen for us to breathe, providing us with material for clothing and construction, and furnishing us with food. But there are countless other ways in which man has learned to make use of plants. Thousands of uses could be listed for trees alone. Here are a few examples:

- Certain **spices** and **flavorings** are made from the bark, leaves, roots, or fruits of trees. **Cinnamon,** for example, is the tasty bark of a tree. Nutmeg is a spice made by grating the seeds of the *nutmeg tree.* The flavoring for cola soft drinks comes from the nuts of the African *kola tree.*

- The fluffy **fiber** from the seed of the *kapok* [kā′pŏk] *tree* has been used to stuff pillows, mattresses, furniture cushions, and life preservers.

- Some rubbing ointments and throat lozenges, such as you might use when you have a cold, contain fragrant **oil** from the leaves of the *eucalyptus* [yōō′kə·lĭp′təs] *tree.*

- The **paper** this textbook is printed on is made from wood pulp.

- Painters use **turpentine** as a solvent to thin or mix paint, and **rosin** [rŏz′ĭn: dried turpentine] is used by musicians on the bows of their stringed instruments to create better contact with the strings. Both turpentine and rosin come from the *pine tree.*

- **Leather** is made from an animal hide that is treated with chemical preservatives. Until the 20th century, most leather was preserved using chemicals called **tannins** [tăn′ĭnz], which come from the bark and wood of trees such as *oaks* and *hemlocks.* Some leather is still preserved this way.

- A medicine known as **quinine** [kwĭ′nīn′] is taken from the bark of the South American *cinchona* [sĭng·kō′nə] *tree.* Quinine is used to treat people with malaria, a tropical disease carried by mosquitoes.

nutmeg

kapok

cinnamon

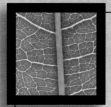

the Green machine

Each kind of tree has its own distinct bark, whether it be knobby or platelike, shaggy or fibrous, deeply cracked or smooth as paper. Hunting for different sorts of bark textures can be fun. You might enjoy starting a collection of bark rubbings from the various kinds of trees in your neighborhood.

All that is needed for taking a tree's bark print is a sheet of plain white paper and a dark-colored crayon. Hold the paper up against the tree, and then rub the side of the crayon lightly back and forth on the paper until you can see the pattern of the bark underneath. Try not to press down too hard, or the paper may tear. When you have finished, write the name of the tree, if you know it, beside the rubbing. Look for a variety of bark textures. Can you find a tree with smooth bark?

Life history of a tree

When a tree is cut down, a pattern of light and dark rings can be seen in the trunk. In the spring, when the tree begins to grow rapidly after the winter, the tree forms large cells to carry great quantities of water and

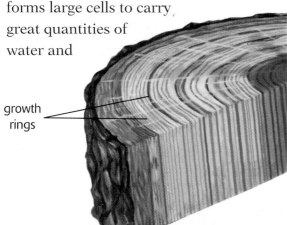

growth rings

food through the stem. This area of rapid growth appears as a light-colored band of wood. Then, in the summer, the tree grows more slowly forming smaller cells. The area of slower growth appears as a dark-colored band of wood. These light and dark bands make up the annual growth rings of the tree. *Each* **annual growth ring** *is made of an inner band of light spring wood and an outer band of dark summer wood. Together the two bands are one year's growth.* If you closely examine a piece of wood, you can often distinguish the annual rings that make up the "grain" of the wood. The exact age of the tree can be determined by counting the number of annual growth rings in the trunk.

The growth rings reveal many things about the history of the tree besides the tree's age. Studying the rings of a tree is like reading the tree's biography. Narrow rings are often the result of a drought that slowed the growth of the tree. If they occur near the center of the trunk, narrow rings tell us that larger trees may have prevented sunlight from reaching the tree when it was young. The younger tree would have grown more rapidly if it had not been shaded. A "v" marking in a ring tells us that a branch once grew at that point on the tree, and a scar may indicate damage done by fire.

Science & GREAT CHRISTIANS

David Livingstone
(1813–1873)

David Livingstone, the missionary-explorer who spent thirty years opening the interior of Africa to Christianity, commerce, and civilization, was born in a village in Scotland. His parents were devout Christians, and they brought up young David "in the nurture and admonition of the Lord." Because his family was extremely poor, David had to go to work in a local cotton mill at the age of ten to help support his family. Like many other poor factory children of his time, David worked from six o'clock in the morning until eight o'clock in the evening, every day of the week but Sunday, with time off only for breakfast and dinner. On an occasional half day's vacation, David would wander over the Scottish countryside, gathering specimens of plants and herbs and developing an interest in medicine.

David had an unquenchable thirst for learning. Once, he used a portion of his wages to buy a Latin grammar book. He propped the book up on his machine in the cotton mill so that he could study as he worked. He learned how to "tune out" the noise and distractions around him so that he could concentrate on his studies. To his great delight, the factory had an evening school for the workers. David attended school each evening from eight o'clock to ten o'clock. Learning was such a joy to him that he often sat up in his room until midnight reading books on travel and science (his favorite topics) and studying his lessons. But David's mother would finally enter the tiny chamber and make him blow out the candle, say his prayers, and climb into bed.

When he was sixteen, David Livingstone accepted Christ as his Savior, but he did not have full assurance of salvation until he was twenty. Because he believed that God was calling him to China as a medical missionary, he went to college to study medicine. After several years, he passed his medical examinations and was accepted as a candidate by the London Missionary Society. But war broke out, and the door to China closed.

One evening, David attended a lecture by Robert Moffat, the great pioneer missionary to Africa. When Moffat said that he had seen the smoke of a thousand villages that had never heard the gospel, David's interest in Africa was awakened.

Before Livingstone arrived in Africa in 1841, the interior of the "Dark Continent" was a blank spot on the map. While Livingstone was sailing to Africa, the kindly ship's captain, a Scotsman like Livingstone, taught him how to navigate (find directions) by studying the night sky. He showed him how to use a quadrant (a type of navigational instrument) to steer his course by the stars. On many a night at sea, Livingstone and the captain would be up until past midnight going over the principles of navigation. These lessons proved invaluable to Livingstone during his four expeditions across Africa to make future European settlement and missions possible. He discovered Lake Ngami [əng·gä′mē], traveled along the Zambezi [zăm·bē′zē] River, made maps of all the areas he explored, and became the first European to see "the smoke that thunders," Victoria Falls, which he named after his queen.

Wherever he went, David Livingstone carried his Bible, his medical bag, and his notebook. With the spirit of a true scientist, he kept accurate records of everything he saw and heard. Native peoples, exotic birds and plants, strange animals, rare diseases, and new places all found a place in his notebook.

The practice of medicine in Livingstone's time was still rather primitive, and he was one of the first to use such modern instruments as the stethoscope and the clinical thermometer. Malaria was then the great scourge of African exploration. Four previous European expeditions into the interior had failed because the malarial fever killed the Europeans so quickly, but Livingstone's use of the newly discovered quinine (from the bark of the cinchona tree) was able to reduce the mortality rate from 62 percent to 8 percent among the Europeans. Livingstone was also one of the first to connect mosquitoes with malaria, and he noted the outbreak of disease with the onset of the rains each year.

In all, Livingstone spent nearly thirty-two years in Africa attempting to win the souls and heal the bodies of the tribesmen he came to love.

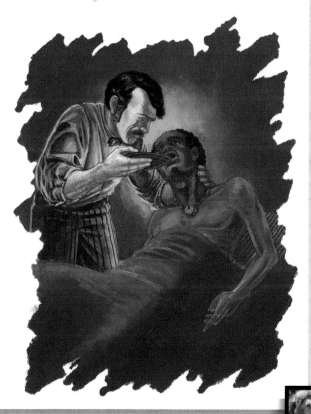

Comprehension Check 1.5

1. What is a tree?

2. What term describes a plant that lives for only one year? Two years? Many years?

3. What are the tallest living trees in the world? The oldest trees?

4. What do we call scientists who study trees?

5. What is the name of the structure at the tip of a stem that produces new growth?

6. What is the layer of the tree's trunk where new growth of bark and wood takes place?

7. What is made of an inner band of light wood and an outer band of dark wood? What do these bands tell us about a tree?

8. Why is girdling harmful to a tree?

1.6 Broadleaf Trees

If you were to go around your neighborhood looking at trees, you would probably find many with broad, flat leaves. Trees with this sort of leaf are called **broadleaf trees.** *Most broadleaf trees are flower-bearing, seed-producing plants.* Some trees have very noticeable flowers in the spring. These big, showy flowers are designed to be pollinated by animals and insects, which are attracted by bright colors. Other trees, like the plants in the grass family, have very small, plain-looking flowers that you would probably never notice unless you were looking for them. Such flowers are designed to be pollinated by the wind. Wind carries pollen from one blossom to another.

Broadleaf trees are sometimes referred to as **hardwood trees** because many of them have very hard and durable wood, excellent for the most demanding uses, such as in fine furniture. Not all broadleaf trees have hard wood, however. The balsa tree, for example, is a broadleaf tree, but its wood is extremely lightweight and soft. You may have had a toy glider or boat made of balsa wood.

Time for a vacation

Most broadleaf trees that grow in temperate climates are also **deciduous** [dĭ·sĭj′o͞o·əs] **trees.** The word *deciduous* refers to a tree that loses its leaves in the fall. There are several reasons why God has designed many trees to let go of

their leaves once a year. First, the tree is unable to manufacture food when the temperature drops below freezing, because frozen water cannot rise through the stem. Also, winter ice and snow accumulating on the broad surfaces of the leaves would cause branches to become so heavy that they would be torn from the tree. Since broadleaf trees do not need their leaves in the wintertime, they release them and remain dormant until the spring.

The autumn season would be a dismal time of year if God had not painted the dying leaves in bright shades of yellow, orange, and red. These brilliant fall colors are the result of blocked pipelines in the stems of the leaves. To prepare for winter, trees grow a wall of cork cells between the twig and the base of each leaf stem. This layer blocks the flow of water and minerals into the leaf. Cut off from nutrients,

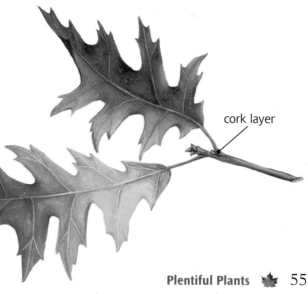

cork layer

the leaf stops manufacturing new chlorophyll. As the old chlorophyll gradually deteriorates, bright yellow and orange pigments in the leaf begin to show through. Although these other pigments are present year-round in the leaf, their colors are normally masked by the stronger green color of chlorophyll.

Besides stopping the flow of water into the leaf, the cork layer in the stem also keeps sugar from leaving the leaf. Although most of the vitamins and other important materials in the leaf are moved out for storage in the tree itself before the cork layer finishes growing, the last little bit of sugar is not able to get out in time. But even though this trapped sugar cannot be used by the tree, it is not wasted. Sunlight striking the leaf causes the leftover sugar to be made into bright red pigments. The fall leaves of many trees are given their red color as a result of this chemical reaction. (The same process turns a ripening apple from green to red.) Because the pigments are manufactured by sunlight, the amount of red in a tree's leaves is determined by the amount of sunshine the tree receives. Sunny autumns produce the most spectacular leaf colors.

Not all fall leaves are red, however. The leaves of many trees are colored primarily by orange or yellow pigments. Different blends of pigments in leaves give the fall landscape its full range of vivid colors— fiery reds, flaming oranges, deep golds, and brilliant yellows. Since green chlorophyll is needed to manufacture sugar, the appearance of other colors in fall leaves indicates that the job of making food for that year has been completed. Eventually, the layer of cork cells that has grown between the twig and the base of each leaf stem decays, and the leaf falls off the tree.

birch trees in autumn

![maple leaf icon] *Maples*

The maple tree's toothed leaves with three to five lobes make this common North American tree easy to recognize. Their V-shaped fruits, with tiny wings to catch the wind, can sail for miles on the breeze.

Maple trees are known for the especially bright colors of their fall leaves, and they are popular shade trees in residential neighborhoods. The **sugar maple,** found primarily in Canada and the northern forests of the United States, is the source of maple syrup, although some other maples are occasionally tapped for their sweet sap. The valuable white heartwood of the sugar maple is used to make bowling lanes and pins.

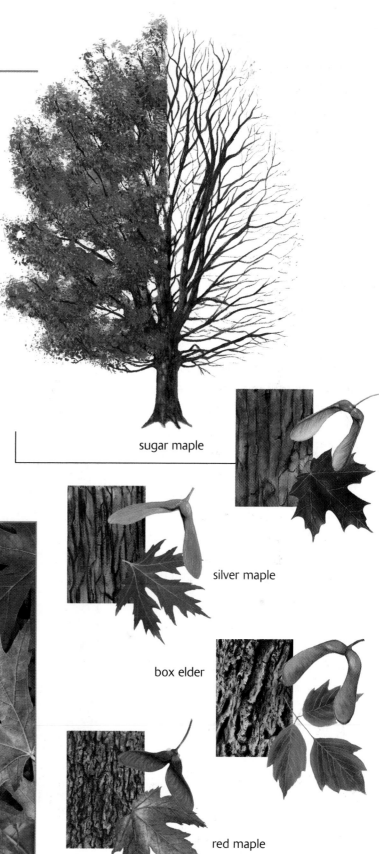

sugar maple

silver maple

box elder

red maple

silver maple leaves

Science and you

Most people like to put maple syrup on their pancakes, waffles, and French toast. You may have never tasted *real* maple syrup though, because most syrup sold in grocery stores today is artificially flavored. None of the imitations, however, taste quite like the genuine item.

Sugaring—the process of producing maple syrup and sugar—is a large industry in Canada and New England, where the sugar maple, the source of maple syrup, is a very important tree. Each year, the sugar maple brings millions of dollars to Vermont, Maine, and other northern states.

The sugar maple is named for its sweet sap. After glucose is produced in the leaves during photosynthesis, much of this sugar is stored over the winter as starch in the tree's trunk and roots. In the spring, the tree needs the stored food in order to begin growing and producing new leaves. The starch is changed back again, not into glucose, but into another kind of sugar known as **sucrose** [sōō′krōs]. Early spring weather, with its warm days and cold nights, causes the watery **sap** containing this sucrose to rise through the trunk up toward the tips of the branches.

Each spring, sugaring begins with a process called "tapping out." Farmers drill holes 1 1/2 to 2 inches deep into the larger trees and then hammer in small plastic or metal spouts. Large trees may have 3 or 4 holes drilled while very small

tapping the tree

trees will not have any. The spouts direct the syrup into plastic tubing that runs from tree to tree and then into a collecting tank, or into buckets hung directly below each spout and later emptied by hand.

The sap that comes out of the tree is mostly water, with only a little bit of sugar in it. Much of this water must be boiled away to make a thick, sweet syrup. Each bucketful of sap is taken to a sugarhouse, where the sap is boiled in a large heated tank called an *evaporator*. As the water evaporates, the sap becomes thick and turns into syrup.

boiling the sap

Workers must monitor the syrup carefully to make sure that it is boiled to precisely the right thickness. A product called *maple sugar* can also be made by boiling away all of the water, leaving only sugar crystals behind. It takes about 40 gallons of sap to make either 1 gallon of syrup or 4 1/2 pounds of sugar.

Once the syrup has been boiled to the right thickness, it passes out of the evaporator and through strainers that filter out gritty particles of sugar and other debris. From here, it is packaged in sterilized containers, where it waits to be bought and poured over someone's pancakes.

Elms

There are more than 15 varieties of elm, the most popular of which is the **American elm.** The American elm is a tall tree with a graceful, vaselike appearance. It may reach 130 feet in height. The way its branches curve away from the trunk and droop toward the ground reminds one of water spreading outward from a fountain.

The American elm, once widely planted as a shade tree, lined many city streets and shaded the lawns of many public buildings until, beginning in 1930, many elms were stricken by a fatal infection called **Dutch elm disease.** This disease, caused by a fungus, is most often spread by beetles that live within the tree's bark.

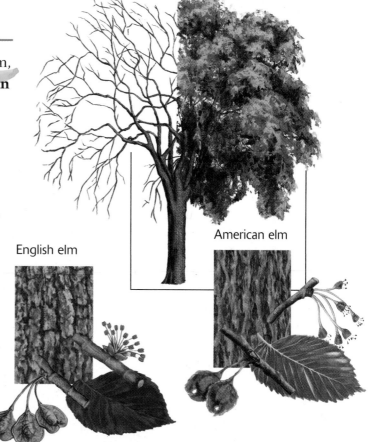

American elm

English elm

🍂 Oaks

A full-grown oak tree is a majestic sight. Its massive trunk is set into the ground like a pillar of granite, and its strong roots delve deep into the earth. Although oaks are not especially tall, their extremely thick and wide-spreading branches give them an impressive profile.

The fruit of the oak tree is the **acorn.** Although an oak tree's flowers easily go unnoticed, the bushels of acorns scattered under the tree in the fall are hard to miss. Acorns are rich energy sources for many animals, including squirrels, quail, deer, and mice. The edible acorns of the **white oak** were used as food by American Indians and pioneers.

The **live oak,** which grows in the warm South, is not a deciduous tree. It keeps its leaves until they are pushed off by new ones. It has been named the *live oak* because

white oak

red oak

live oak

large live oak in Louisiana

its leaves always look fresh and alive. This oak seldom grows over 50 feet tall, but its massive limbs, as thick as many tree trunks, grow outward horizontally much farther than the tree is high. Live oaks also have enormous root systems, which enable them to outlast the winds and surging waters of a hurricane. Many people have kept from drowning in floods by holding on to the branches of a live oak tree.

Oak wood has a very beautiful *grain* (the pattern of the growth rings in the wood), making it desirable for building furniture. Because of its strength, oak wood is preferred for railroad ties, floors, and other things that must be tough and durable. In the days of wooden ships, oak was considered the best ship timber.

paper birch

Birches

The **paper birch**, also known as the *canoe birch*, is the most common birch in North America. It can be found from coast to coast in Canada and in the northern United States. It is easily recognized by its smooth white bark, which is thin and papery. The bark peels off in layers on its own but should never be forcefully stripped from the tree, because to do so could kill the tree or at least result in the permanent loss of bark from the exposed part of the trunk.

Pioneers used birch bark as roofing and also as a writing surface. Indians spread the water-resistant bark over wooden frames to build wigwams and canoes.

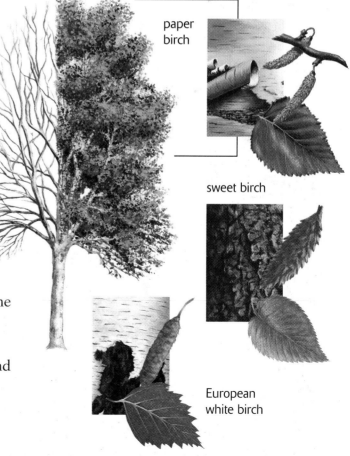

paper birch

sweet birch

European white birch

Willows

The willow family includes not just the willow trees themselves, but also the poplars. If you were to compare a willow leaf with a poplar leaf, you might find it difficult to believe that they came from trees that are closely related. The leaves of a willow are long and thin, but those of a poplar are nearly as broad as they are long.

Willows grow best along streams or near water. The drooping leaves and branches of many willows, especially the **weeping willow,** give them a graceful, almost mournful appearance. Some willow trees, such as the **pussy willow,** grow no larger than shrub size. Your mother may have used some of the soft, furry flowers of the pussy willow, which resemble cat's fur, to decorate your house.

Poplars, like willows, are found most often along streams and in other areas where water is available. The name *cottonwood,* used for many species of poplar, comes from the cottony tufts attached to the seeds. Cottonwoods were very useful to the settlers of the American plains. Because they grow extremely fast—up to 12 feet a year—these trees were frequently planted in rows to form a hedge (windbreak) that would break the force of the wind before it reached the house or barn. The trees also protected homesteads from dust storms, provided the necessary wood for building stockades, and fed livestock. Many of today's

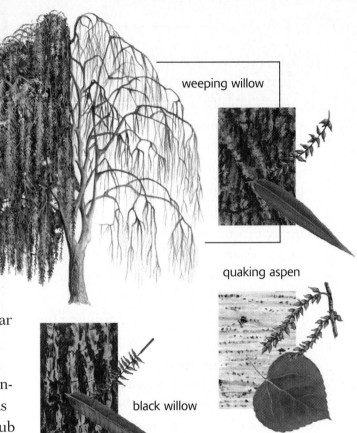

weeping willow

quaking aspen

black willow

ranchers profit from the blessings of the cottonwood just as early settlers did. But cottonwoods and other poplar trees also have their drawbacks: they are short-lived, and their wood is soft and not very durable.

Some species of poplars are called *aspens.* The **quaking aspen** gets its name from the tendency of its leaves to tremble in the slightest breeze.

weeping willow

EYEwitness reporter

Adopt a tree

Your assignment as a roving reporter is to choose your favorite tree and learn as much about it as you can by collecting samples and other sorts of information. Then, after becoming an expert on your tree, you will present a report of your discoveries to the class.

Perhaps you like a certain maple tree best because it has such colorful leaves in the autumn. You would want to press some autumn leaves so you can display them in your report. (Of course, you should obtain a leaf sample no matter what tree you choose.) If your tree is an oak, include an acorn or two if some are available. Or maybe your favorite tree is a type of conifer (see section 1.7). Be sure to get a couple of seed cones, and some pollen cones, too, if possible.

Whatever your choice, you may want to display a flower from the tree as well as a fruit, a few seeds, a bud, and maybe even a twig. By looking on the ground near the base of the tree, you might discover a seedling that is just beginning to sprout. This tiny descendant of your tree could be included in your report.

You might also find scattered around the tree some pieces of bark that have flaked off the trunk. You may collect a sample of loose bark, but do not pull bark off the tree! Instead, make a bark rubbing of your adopted tree. Do you see any similarities with other bark rubbings in your collection? How would you describe the texture of your tree's bark?

You can record the circumference of the tree trunk at eye level and compare it to the circumference of the tree at the level of your knees. To find the circumference, wrap a piece of string around the tree trunk at the height you want to measure and cut the string where it meets the other end. Then straighten the string and determine its length

with a measuring tape. How does the circumference of the tree trunk compare to the circumference of one of its lowest branches?

Are there any vertebrates that live in or around your tree? If so, what are they? How does your tree benefit the animals?

Find the common and scientific names of your adopted tree. You should be able to identify your tree by matching your observations with the descriptions in a field guide. The field guide will also tell you the family your tree belongs to as well as its natural habitat, its average height, and many other interesting details.

If possible, take a snapshot of your tree and include the picture in your report. Try to get the entire tree in the photo. You can estimate the height of the tree by taking the picture when someone is standing beside it and then comparing the heights of the tree and of the person in the developed photo. If your favorite tree is in your yard, you may be able to find some old family snapshots that have the tree in the background. Has it changed since those pictures were taken?

Once you have gathered all the samples and information for your report, you will want to make a display. A poster board or a large piece of construction paper would be ideal. Write a paragraph or two about your tree and include your written work somewhere on your display. Be sure to mount all the specimens and other items you collected so that everyone can get to know your favorite tree.

Comprehension Check 1.6

1. What tree group has flower-bearing and seed-producing plants, for the most part?

2. What do we call broadleaf trees that grow in temperate climates and lose their leaves in the fall?

3. What is the process of producing maple syrup and sugar?

4. Examine the trees and their characteristics and write the name of the correct family in the blank.

• good shade trees with especially colorful fall leaves
• a source of sugar and syrup

_____

- especially thick, wide-spreading branches
- produce acorns

_____

- grow best near water
- long, thin leaves and drooping branches
- graceful, almost mournful appearance
- poplars belong to this family

_____

- smooth, white, papery bark peels off in thin layers
- Indians covered wigwams and canoes with this bark

_____

- tall, graceful, vaselike appearance
- branches curve away from the trunk and droop toward the ground

_____

1.7 Conifers

 ### *The cone-bearers*

All trees produce seeds, but not all trees make their seeds by the same method. As you have already learned, most plants, including broadleaf trees, begin the reproductive process by forming flowers. After the flowers are pollinated by animals or wind, seeds form in the flower's ovary. Then the ovary itself turns into a fruit. Some trees, however, do not bear flowers; neither are their seeds encased in fruits. These trees are the *cone-bearing trees,* or **conifers.**

Jeffrey pine

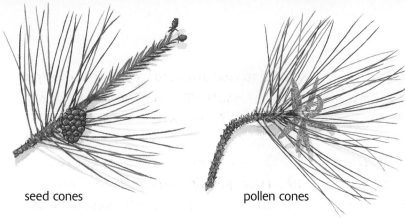

seed cones   pollen cones

Instead of bearing flowers, conifers produce two different kinds of cones. The **pollen cones** contain the pollen, and the **seed cones** contain the ovules to be pollinated. Because the tree relies on the wind to carry pollen from cone to cone, the pollen cones contain tremendous amounts of pollen to ensure that some of it will reach its destination. Even though the pollen of many types of conifers may be in the air at the same time, the seed cone can be pollinated only by pollen from its own kind of tree. God's plan for conifers, as for all other living things, is that each tree should reproduce only after its own kind.

A seed cone is pollinated and fertilized by a very complex and interesting process. First, the scales on the cone spread apart slightly to create openings to the interior of the cone, where two ovules are located on the top surface of each scale. The openings allow the wind to blow pollen grains into the cone. The ovules are pollinated when floating pollen grains land on them. But pollen grains cannot land just anywhere on the surface of an ovule. They must pass through a tiny opening in the wall of the ovule in order to reach the correct landing spot. To help the pollen grains find their way, the cone releases a small drop of sticky resin at the entrance to the wall of the ovule. After capturing an airborne grain of pollen, the drop of resin dries up, pulling the pollen grain through the opening. Once stuck to the surface of the ovule, the pollen grain cracks open, and the tube cell inside begins to lengthen, burrowing its way through the wall of the ovule and into the egg cell inside. After the tip of the pollen tube penetrates the egg cell, it bursts open and releases a sperm cell. When the sperm cell unites with the egg cell, the ovule begins to develop into a seed.

Once the seed cone has been pollinated, seeds begin to form inside the scales of the cone. The cone itself gradually becomes woody. It takes months or even years for the cone and its seeds to develop fully. In comparison with fully grown seed cones, pollen cones are rather small and insignificant, staying on the tree only long enough to complete their job of releasing pollen into the air.

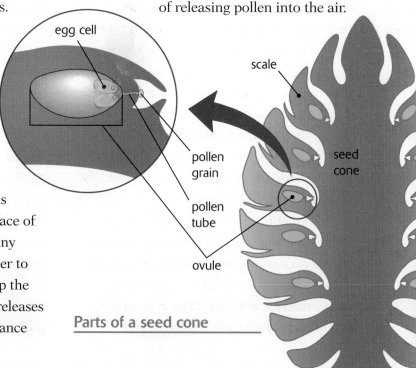

Parts of a seed cone

When the seeds are fully developed, the scales on the protective cone open up and the seeds fall out. The seeds of most conifers have tiny wings that carry the seeds quite a distance from the tree. Some conifers eventually release their cones, which fall to the ground carrying any remaining seeds with them, while other trees hang on to their cones as the scales fall off one at a time until the cones disintegrate completely.

Conifer characteristics

Huge trees with tiny leaves. Conifers and broadleaf trees differ in many ways besides in their method of forming seeds. They differ, for example, in their manner of growth. Most broadleaf trees have a full, rounded top, or *crown*. Because broadleaf trees put more energy into growing new side branches than they do into lengthening the main stem (the trunk), many of these trees grow outward as much as, or even more than, they grow upward. Although most broadleaf trees are not exceptionally tall, they are quite bushy and able to shade a large area below.

A typical conifer, on the other hand, has a very active bud at the tip of the main stem. Its trunk grows straight upward, sending out relatively short branches at right angles to the trunk. If you were to view a forest of tall conifers from a great distance away, perhaps from an airplane, the trees would resemble toothpicks with bunches of green bristles on their tips. Because of their tendency to grow primarily upward, conifers often grow to be much taller than broadleaf trees (although many types of conifers are bushy shrubs or short, stubby trees). The Douglas fir of the American Northwest, for instance, grows to a height of nearly 300 feet. The world's tallest trees, the redwoods and sequoias, are also conifers.

The huge stature of many conifers contrasts strongly with the size of their leaves, which are much smaller than those of broadleaf trees. Some conifers have *needles,* and others have *scales*—tiny leaves that overlap each other and tightly hug the branchlets of the tree.

Winter workers. There is another important difference between conifers and broadleaf trees. Most conifers are not deciduous, but are called **evergreens** because they keep their leaves year round, even in the winter.

The design of evergreen trees makes them well-suited to a winter lifestyle. Their thin needles or tiny scale-clad branchlets do not collect ice and snow as easily as broad, flat leaves would. Also, the shorter, more flexible branches of conifers droop readily to shake off ice and snow that would cause the massive branches of broadleaf trees to crack.

Even in the winter, an evergreen tree continues its food-making activities. To keep water in the plant at times when the ground is frozen and the plant is unable to draw more water up its stem, the needles or scales are coated with a very thick cuticle (waxy coating). The leaves also have many fewer stomata than large, broad leaves have. The tree carries out its photosynthesis very slowly, using the water contained in the tree itself. Even the shape of many conifers is an aid to winter food-making. Their pointed tops and steep sides help keep off a lot of snow that otherwise would block the leaves' access to sunlight.

The pine family

Most conifers belong to one of three different families: the pine family, the cypress [sī′prĭs] family, or the redwood family.

Pine trees are not the only members of the pine family. Spruces, firs, Douglas firs (which are not really firs at all!), hemlocks, and larches also belong to this group of trees.

Pines. Pine trees themselves can be easily identified because they are the only trees that have bundled needles: groups of needles wrapped firmly together at one end. Although the number of needles per bundle varies from one type of pine to another, most pine bundles contain between two and five needles.

One of the most important pine trees in the history of America is the **eastern white pine,** which once grew in extensive forests that blanketed many portions of the eastern United States. This pine was heavily lumbered because its wood is superior to that of other pines for use in construction. The tallest trees, which grew to over 200 feet, were made into masts for sailing ships. You can tell whether a pine is a white pine just by counting the needles in one bundle. A white pine is the only eastern variety with its needles in bundles of five.

In the American West, the **ponderosa** [pŏn′də·rō′sə] **pine** is one of the largest varieties, growing sometimes to about 250 feet. Another interesting pine is the **pinyon** [pĭn′yən] **pine,** which grows in the hot, dry climate of the southwestern states. This unusual conifer produces tasty edible nuts. Also, the needles of some pinyons are unique because they grow singly rather than in bundles.

eastern white pine

ponderosa pine

pinyon pine

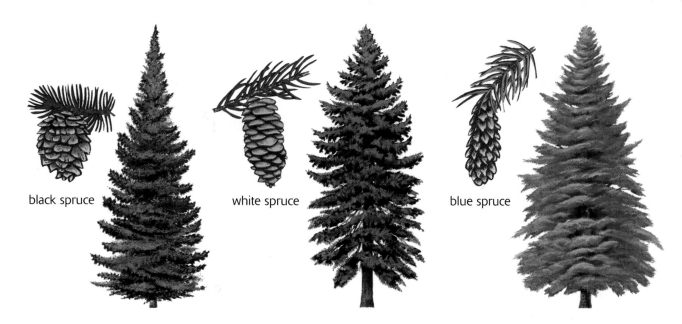

black spruce   white spruce   blue spruce

Spruces. Although members of the same family, pines and spruces differ in several respects. Unlike the bundled needles of pine trees, the needles of a spruce are joined individually to the branch. While spruce needles are short and stiff, pine needles tend to be longer and more flexible. Also, pines have rounded or flattened crowns, but spruces are sharply pointed at the top.

People living in warm southern regions will seldom see a spruce tree, except perhaps in a Christmas tree lot. Most spruce varieties are rugged trees that flourish in the cold North, or at high altitudes on mountain slopes. With their short limbs and pointed shape, spruces are perfectly suited to deal with large amounts of snow in the winter.

The two most common varieties of spruce in North America, the **black spruce** and the **white spruce,** grow widely across Canada and the northern United States.

balsam fir

A white spruce can be identified by the skunk-like odor its needles give off when crushed or broken. Another variety, the **blue spruce,** is an especially attractive tree with frosty blue needles. Blue spruces are often planted in yards as ornamentals.

Firs. Fir trees look much like spruces, but you can tell them apart if you know what to look for. Spruce cones hang from the underside of the branch, but fir cones stick straight up into the air. If you find whole cones underneath the tree, you have found a spruce, because fir cones do not fall off the tree in one piece but fall apart a little at a time while still on the branch. Also, spruce needles are stiff and sometimes prickly, whereas fir needles are usually blunt and soft.

One of the best-known fir trees is the **balsam** [bôl′səm] **fir,** which produces a fragrant liquid known as *Canada balsam.* Balsam firs are commonly used for lumber and papermaking; they are also popular as Christmas trees because of their fragrant smell.

Douglas firs. Douglas firs are not really firs at all. Rather, they make up another grouping within the pine family. Although sometimes called *false hemlocks,* they most closely resemble spruces. They can be distinguished by the long growths that hang out from between the scales of their seed cones.

Douglas firs become huge trees, reaching a height anywhere between 200 and 300 feet. Towering Douglas firs form vast forests along the Pacific coast of North America, particularly in Oregon and Washington, but also in Canada and California. The tree's large size and plentiful numbers, along with the usefulness of its strong, stiff wood, make the Douglas fir the chief lumber tree in the western United States.

Hemlocks. Hemlock trees can be distinguished from firs and spruces by looking at their cones. The cones of hemlocks hang down from the very tips of the branches. Spruce cones, however, hang farther up on the branch. The bark of the hemlock is one of the chief American sources of tannin, one substance used to tan leather.

Larches. Although most conifers are evergreens and most broadleaf trees are deciduous, there are exceptions. The live oak is an evergreen broadleaf tree. The **larches,** the most common of which in North America are the **tamaracks** [tăm′ə·răks′], however, are *deciduous conifers.* These trees are most impressive in the fall, when their needles turn to a deep gold color before falling to the ground.

hemlock

tamarack

Douglas fir

Science and you

Have you ever gone along with your family to the Christmas tree lot to pick out a live Christmas tree? If you have, you know that not all the trees are the same. Some are too tall to fit in your house. Some have large, bare patches. Not all Christmas trees are the same type of tree, either.

In America, the most popular Christmas trees are the balsam fir, the Douglas fir, the black spruce, and the Scotch pine.

The balsam fir can be recognized by the two silvery lines on the underside of each needle. The needles themselves are soft and flat, and the tree's balsam makes it particularly fragrant. Black spruce needles are stiffer than those of firs, but they are not prickly. The Scotch pine has needles in bundles of two. With your knowledge of conifers, you should be able to identify several the next time you are out hunting for a Christmas tree.

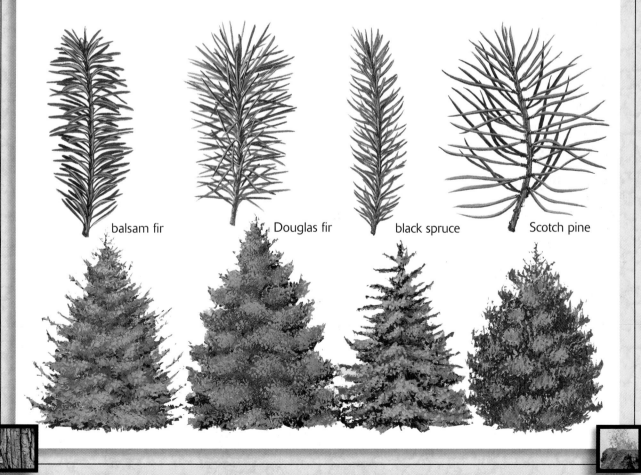

balsam fir   Douglas fir   black spruce   Scotch pine

The redwood family

The **redwood trees** of California are the tallest trees in the world. Many of these stately giants are more than 300 feet tall. (The tallest one still standing measures 367 feet!) It takes hundreds and hundreds of years for these trees to reach such heights. In fact, some redwoods have lived to be more than 2000 years old. One reason the redwood is able to survive for such a long time is that its bark, which can be as much as a foot thick, efficiently protects the tree from disease, fire, and insects. Because redwoods live for such a long time, some Indians of long ago thought the trees were immortal.

Although the *California redwood is the tallest of all trees,* one of its close relatives—the **giant sequoia**—wins a different award. *The sequoia is the largest of all trees.* The few sequoias left in the world grow in only one place—the western slopes of the Sierra Nevada [sĭ·ĕr′ə nə·văd′ə] range in California. The **General Sherman Tree,** the biggest sequoia, is more than impressive. This monstrous tree, estimated to be about 3500 years old, is 272 feet tall and 36 feet across at its base. It contains over 50,000 cubic feet of wood, weighing about 1000 tons. If the tree were cut down, thirty railroad cars would be needed just to haul its trunk away to the sawmill.

giant sequoia

California redwood

In our study of trees, it is interesting to note that God often produces huge results from tiny beginnings. The massive oak, for example, grows from a small acorn. But the much larger sequoia comes from a seed that is even smaller than a tomato seed.

General Sherman Tree (sequoia)

Another member of the redwood family is the **bald cypress.** It is a water-loving tree that can be found growing in the swamps, shallow lakes, and lagoons of the South. Often the bases of the trees are completely submerged in water with portions of the roots projecting out of the water in humps. Scientists are not sure of the function of these humps, called **knees,** although they probably supply oxygen to the waterlogged roots. The durable wood supplies valuable lumber. The bald cypress is an unusual tree because it is a deciduous conifer; like the larches and tamaracks, the bald cypress loses its needles in the fall.

bald cypress

🍁 *The cypress family*

Nearly all of the plants in the cypress family have scaly leaves. In fact, chances are that any scaly leafed tree or shrub growing in your yard is a member of the cypress family. Besides the cypresses themselves, this family of plants also includes the **cedars** and **junipers.** (The well-known bald cypress, however, belongs to a different family.) Junipers can be identified by looking at their seed cones, which have unusual fleshy coats that make the cones resemble berries.

Many cypress and juniper varieties grow only to the size of shrubs or small trees. Most cedars, on the other hand, become quite large. The **western red cedar** of the American Northwest, for example, may reach 200 feet in height.

The most interesting characteristic of the cedars is their aromatic wood. This attractive, reddish wood contains an oil that produces a pleasant fragrance. Because the oil in the wood repels moths, cedar wood is often used to build clothes closets and chests. Your mom may have a cedar chest she keeps garments or quilts in. Do you like the unusual smell that comes out of the chest when she opens it up? The oil from cedar wood is also used in perfumes. Because of its durability and resistance to decay, cedar wood has many other important uses; some houses are covered with cedar shingles or siding. The pencil you use may also be made out of cedar wood.

Unlike North American cedars, the famous **cedar of Lebanon,** the kind of tree Solomon used to build the Temple, is a member of the pine family rather than the cypress family. The needles of this tall, attractive tree form tufts on the branches. The wood is fragrant, much like that of North American cedars. Although it was once feared that most of the great cedars of Lebanon had been destroyed for their valuable wood, many of these trees are being grown and protected in the Middle East today.

western red cedar

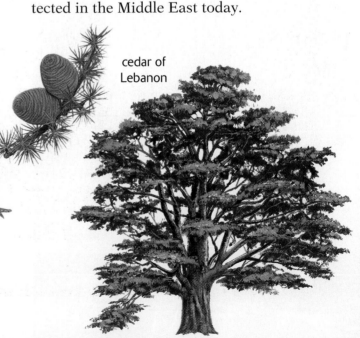

cedar of Lebanon

The flourishing palms

The palm tree is an evergreen, but not a conifer. It belongs in a completely different category. Whereas all of the trees we have studied so far are dicots [dī′kŏts], the palm tree—like grasses and lilies—is a monocot [mŏn′ə·kŏt′].

Palm trees like warmth. Whether a palm tree lives in a dusty desert or on a steamy tropical island, the tree is perfectly suited to its environment. The palm's leaves, called **fronds,** are some of the easiest leaves to recognize. Their large leaves are divided into many thin segments, a design that allows the trees to survive the fierce winds of hurricanes by making it difficult for the wind to "grab hold" of the leaves. The extensive fibrous root system also aids in protecting the palm from harsh weather. It would indeed be unusual to see a healthy palm tree uprooted after a violent hurricane. The palm's thick roots are also needed to gather and store water in desert conditions. A mature date palm in the middle of a desert may need up to 200 gallons of water a day in order to stay healthy and yield fruit.

A tasty nut. One of the most amazing fruits produced by a tree is the **coconut,** which grows on the coconut palm. The liquid inside the ripe fruit provides a refreshing drink known as *coconut milk.* The creamy, white interior, called *coconut meat,* is an important ingredient in many candy bars and cookies, as well as in coconut pie. The *coconut oil* extracted from the white meat is used in margarine, soaps, detergents, and cooking oil. The coconut is such a useful fruit that man has thought up more than one thousand uses for it.

palm tree

A world traveler. Many seeds are designed to travel long distances from their parent plant. Dandelion seeds, for instance, get from one place to another by flying through the air. Other seeds, like the coconut, float on the water. Air spaces inside the coconut make it light enough to stay afloat, bobbing on the surface like a little boat. Coconuts have been carried thousands of miles by ocean currents. As it is traveling, the seed inside the shell may become soaked with seawater and die. But if the shell is fairly watertight and is able to land on a warm beach before the seed dies, then the coconut may sprout. Though cast ashore on dry sand, it can draw nourishment from its own milk. The traveling coconut has spread the coconut palm to most of the islands and shores in the tropics.

coconut sprouting

Comprehension Check 1.7

1. Which tree family is cone-bearing?

2. What is the term for a tree that keeps its leaves all year round?

3. What is the name of the largest living sequoia?

4. Examine the trees and their characteristics and write the correct name in the blank.

• the largest of all trees
• General Sherman Tree is one

_____

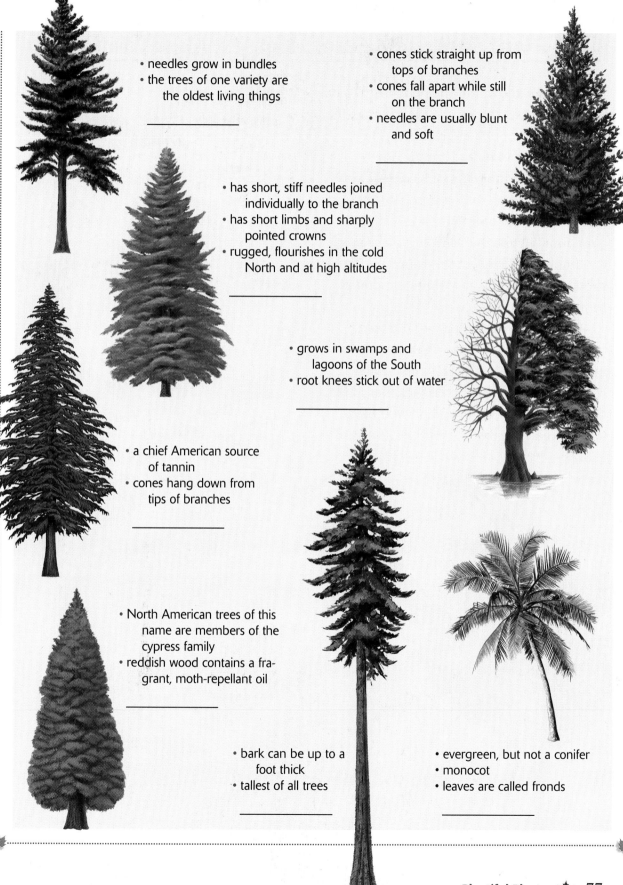

- needles grow in bundles
- the trees of one variety are the oldest living things

_____

- cones stick straight up from tops of branches
- cones fall apart while still on the branch
- needles are usually blunt and soft

_____

- has short, stiff needles joined individually to the branch
- has short limbs and sharply pointed crowns
- rugged, flourishes in the cold North and at high altitudes

_____

- grows in swamps and lagoons of the South
- root knees stick out of water

_____

- a chief American source of tannin
- cones hang down from tips of branches

_____

- North American trees of this name are members of the cypress family
- reddish wood contains a fragrant, moth-repellant oil

_____

- bark can be up to a foot thick
- tallest of all trees

_____

- evergreen, but not a conifer
- monocot
- leaves are called fronds

_____

1.8 Plant Surprises: Ferns, Mosses, Algae, and Fungi

You may know that the platypus [plăt′ĭ·pəs] does something that mammals just do not do—it lays eggs. The anaconda [ăn′ə·kŏn′də], on the other hand, a reptile that ought to lay eggs, does not—it gives birth to live young instead. The bat flies like a bird, even though it is a mammal, while the ostrich runs because it cannot fly. These surprises in creation show us that God is not limited to doing things in one specific way.

Some surprising plants that God created are *ferns, mosses, algae* [ăl′jē], and *fungi* [fŭn′gī]. These plants have some interesting characteristics that make them different from the plants you have already learned about.

Mammals don't lay eggs. But I do!

Mama!

Reptiles do lay eggs, but I don't!

Birds do fly. But I don't!

Mammals don't fly. But I do!

Read on to find what's surprising about us!

🍁 *Ferns: Frond flaunters*

You learned that most plants must bear seeds in order to reproduce. Each seed is a complex structure made of thousands of cells. *Ferns, however, do not bear seeds.* Instead, God has given these plants microscopic **spores,** each made of only one cell. These spores develop inside tiny structures called **spore cases.** If you look at a fern leaf, you may see some dark-colored spots arranged in an attractive pattern on the bottom of the leaf. Each spot contains millions of spores housed in a cluster of spore cases. When the spores are fully developed, the spore cases open, almost like little mouths, and release the spores into the air.

Another difference between a fern and most other plants is that *a fern grows sideways,* its stem creeping along the ground or just below the surface of the ground. The fern's roots, called **rhizoids** [rī′zoidz], grow downward from the underside of the stem, while the leaves, called **fronds,** grow upward from the upper side of the stem. The fronds are usually all you see of the plant.

spore cases

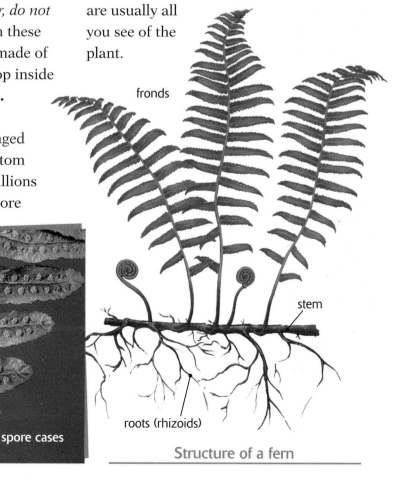

fronds

stem

roots (rhizoids)

Structure of a fern

Fern fronds, when they first appear, do not look like fully developed leaves. They are coiled tightly like the head of a fiddle, or a ball, on the end of the stem. As each frond grows, the "fiddlehead" slowly uncurls itself to reveal a large, beautiful leaf. The frond may be divided into many small leaflets, giving it a lacy appearance.

You should be able to find a few ferns when you hike in the woods near your home. Ferns usually grow in moist, shady areas near trees, rocks, or cliffs. They may also grow on the sides of buildings. Their fronds can be as short as one to two inches, or as long as one to two feet. A few ferns grow in cold climates; some can even be found on mountains north of the Arctic Circle. Most, however, live in warmer regions, especially in the tropics.

One type of fern, the **tree fern,** looks more like a palm tree than a fern. Instead of growing along the ground, its stem grows upward like the trunk of a tree. Found primarily in damp, mountainous regions of the tropics, this giant fern may reach a height of over fifty feet. Its fronds, which grow in one large cluster, are twelve to fourteen feet long.

uncurling fiddlehead

Mosses: Creeping carpets

If you have ever hiked through a forest, you have probably seen a patch of ground covered with a soft, spongy, green carpet. Although this carpet may seem too flat to be made of plants, it is actually a giant network of tiny plants called **mosses.**

Mosses are similar to ferns in several ways. Like ferns, mosses produce spores instead of seeds, and they grow sideways instead of upward; they may, as a result, spread over a rock, root, or tree trunk. They also prefer damp locations, often growing among the moist leaves and undergrowth of the forest floor. Mosses, like ferns, can grow on rocks, even on trees and the sides of buildings. They can be found in the tropics as well as in the Arctic.

green moss growing on rocks

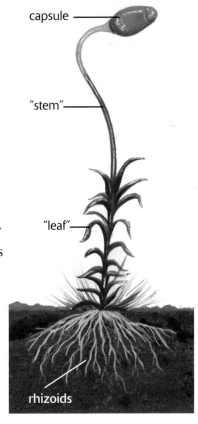

capsule

"stem"

"leaf"

rhizoids

Structure of a moss plant

Mosses do not have a network of tubes for moving nutrients and water back and forth, and they do not have true leaves, stems, or roots as ferns and most other plants do. A moss plant begins as a slender thread of connected cells that grows along the surface of the ground. This thread is so thin that in many places it may be only a single cell across. When threads of moss twist and weave together, they form the thick, green carpet that we see. Certain cells branch off from a thread to start new strings of cells. These new strings of cells become what look and act like roots, stems, and leaves. The "roots" are actually rhizoids like those in ferns and are necessary for obtain-ing nutrients from the soil and for anchoring the plant. The "leaves" use chlorophyll to make food for the plant, but because the "stems" do not have trans-port tubes, every cell must par-ticipate in moving food from the "leaves" to the rest of the plant. *By transferring food from cell to cell, the moss plant can grow in the same way as do other plants.*

Mosses are important plants because they hold soil so that it does not wash away. They also help other plants by keep-ing the soil moist. When they die, mosses enrich the soil. To keep household and garden plants from drying out, garden-ers often mix soil with a special type of moss called **peat moss.**

Algae: International inhabitants

Algae (singular: alga [ăl′gə]) can be found all over the world. They live in soil, on trees, and sometimes on the bodies of turtles and frogs. Certain algae that live in a coral polyp's tissues help it to secrete its skeleton. Algae form the green scum that blankets the surface of a pond. They make up a large part of the ocean plank-ton, an essential source of food for marine animals. A few kinds of algae live even in the Arctic snow. The slippery seaweeds you feel under your feet when you wade at the beach are a kind of algae.

algae on surface of pond

seaweed

Like mosses, algae do not need a system of tubes to transport food, because every cell either makes its own food or receives it from a nearby food-manufacturing cell. Many algae contain other pigments or colorings, in addition to chlorophyll, that determine whether the plants are classified as green, yellow, brown, or red algae.

Solitary algae. *Some algae are the smallest of all green plants.* Many are made of only one cell. Among the one-celled algae are the **diatoms** [dī′·ə·tŏmz′]— beautiful little plants that live in damp soil as well as in ponds, lakes, and oceans. Diatoms can be circular, oblong, triangular, square, or star shaped. Their glasslike coverings, which often exhibit intricate and lacy patterns, consist of two sections that fit together like a tiny jewel case. When diatoms die, their glassy cases collect in the soil or fall to the ocean floor, forming a substance called **diatomite.** Diatomite is used in many scouring powders, toothpastes, and filters.

Dinoflagellates [dī′·nō·flăj′·ə·lĭts], another kind of one-celled alga, resemble both animals and plants. Like animals, dinoflagellates move about from place to place. They swim in the ocean by means of two "hairs" or **flagella** [flə·jĕl′·ə] that whip around and propel them through the water. Unlike animals, however, dinoflagellates have chlorophyll and carry on photosynthesis. When water conditions are just right, one kind of dinoflagellate "blooms," or multiplies rapidly, giving off substances that color the water red. This "red tide" poisons sea creatures living near the surface of the water. People who eat animals that have absorbed some of red tide's toxic substances are in danger of being poisoned to death.

diatoms
(color added)

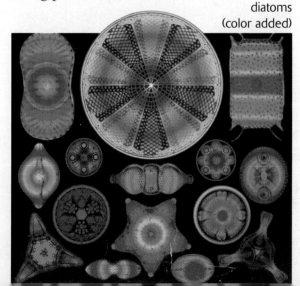

Sociable algae. Many algae join together in groups of cells. Some algae form **filaments,** long strings of cells laid end to end. If the hairs on your head were green, they would look a little like filaments. Filaments often attach themselves to rocks, making the rocks feel slimy. *Volvox,* a kind of green alga, forms a pale green, ball-shaped colony.

All large algae such as seaweed live in water. They are made of many cells, each having its own function. They have leaflike parts called **blades** and small berrylike **air sacs** that help the frond to float. **Holdfasts** take the place of roots and anchor the plants to the ocean floor. The largest alga, a kind of brown alga called **kelp,** often grows to be 200 feet long. Kelp grow upward until they reach the surface, where much of their great length floats on top of the water.

Serviceable algae. Algae are important to people in a variety of ways. In some parts of the world, people and farm animals eat seaweeds, because seaweeds are a good source of important minerals such as iodine. Algae are also used in the manufacturing of numerous products such as cosmetics, paints, films, plastics, medicines, and foods. **Algin** [ăl′jĭn] and **carrageenan** [kăr′ə•gē′nən], substances obtained from seaweed, are particularly useful in forming gels to thicken mayonnaise, pudding, ice cream, marshmallows, cheese, and other foods. Through the process of photosynthesis, algae also play an important role in providing the oxygen that people and animals need to breathe. Though often small and unnoticed, algae are important to life on earth.

bladder

blades

holdfast

Structure of kelp

giant kelp

🍁 Fungi: Friendly freeloaders

mold growing on bread

Can a plant live without chlorophyll? You have learned that chlorophyll is important because it enables a plant to produce food for itself. Therefore, it would only seem natural that a plant without chlorophyll could not survive. But God created many plants, called **fungi** (singular: fungus [fŭng′gəs]), that survive quite well without chlorophyll.

Mold, mildew, and *mushrooms* are three kinds of fungi you are probably familiar with. Mold usually shows itself on old bread or forgotten food and is often blue or black in color. Mildew is the slimy black or pink substance your mother asks you to wipe off the shower curtain or the lawn chairs every once in a while. Mushrooms are those strange-looking white or gray plants that grow in grass, on rocks, or on trees. Other kinds of fungi include *yeasts, rusts, smuts,* and *slime molds.*

Most fungi feed on dead matter such as fallen leaves or rotting logs. These plants are important because they help break down, or decompose, what they are feeding upon. They are much like garbage collectors who have the responsibility of removing wastes. Fungi that feed on dead matter are often called **saprophytes** [săp′rə·fīts′].

Other fungi, which prefer to feed on living matter, are called **parasites.** A parasite is *an organism (plant or animal) that gets its nourishment by attaching itself to another organism and continuously taking in that organism's body fluids.* One example of a parasite is the fungus that causes *athlete's foot,* a disease that eats away at the skin on your feet.

A third kind of fungus feeds on another living plant, but without harming it as a parasite would do. The fungus coexists with the other plant by providing nutrients that the plant needs in exchange for the food the fungus needs to stay alive. For instance, the *Japanese orchid* does not bloom until it becomes attached to the *honey fungus,* a kind of mushroom.

Many fungi are not easy to spot because they live beneath the surface of the ground, under the bark of a tree, or even in the skin of an animal or human being. A fungus consists of a network of cells strung together to form what is called the **mycelium** [mī·sē′lē·əm]. The mycelium, which looks somewhat like a flattened ball of threads, is the main part of the fungus. The rest of the fungus appears only when it is time to reproduce. Then, the mycelium sends a threadlike shoot up past the surface to the open air. This shoot contains spores within a kind of spore case. When the spore case opens, the spores are released to be spread by the wind. The shoot and the spore case are usually all that can be seen of the fungus plant.

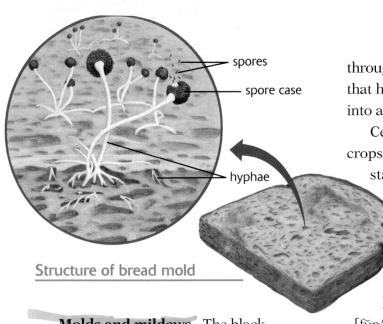

spores

spore case

hyphae

Structure of bread mold

Molds and mildews. The black bread mold you may have observed on an old piece of bread is so common that its spores can be found almost everywhere. Some have been discovered in the air over the North Pole, while others have been found hundreds of miles out to sea. The mold appears first as tiny, white, hairlike structures called **hyphae** [hī′fē]. Then tiny spore cases filled with hundreds of dark-colored spores form on some of the hyphae. When the spore cases burst, spores spread

throughout the air. If a spore lands on food that has been left out, the spore may grow into a new plant and spoil the food.

Certain kinds of mold can destroy crops of corn, wheat, potatoes, or other staple food products. One kind destroyed Ireland's potato crop in 1845. As a result, an estimated one million people died of starvation. Today, farmers can guard their crops from such harmful molds by spraying fungicide [fŭn′gĭ·sīd′] on plants.

Not all molds are harmful, however. If you have ever had an infection caused by bacteria, such as strep throat, your doctor may have given you **penicillin,** a drug made from one kind of mold. Other molds are used to make milk solids (curd) into cheese. The molds used to make Roquefort cheese and blue cheese give them their unique flavors. Another mold is used to make citric acid, an ingredient of foods, inks, and medicines.

Mildews are very similar to molds, except they sometimes grow on wet clothes and shower stalls instead of foods. Some mildews prefer to live on plants. These are usually white and powdery. Most mildews you may see are black, gray, or pink. Mildews are destructive but can be avoided by washing and drying wet clothing as soon as possible and by keeping shower stalls clean and dry. By carefully adding bleach to the water you use to wash clothes or scrub the bathroom, you can kill any mildew that has begun to establish itself.

mildew on lilac leaves

mushrooms

yeast causing bread
dough to rise

Mushrooms. The **mushroom** is somewhat different from other fungi because of its large spore-forming structure called the **fruiting body.** The fruiting body is much larger than the mushroom plant itself and is often in the shape of an umbrella or a cup. It consists of a central stalk, a cap, and several gills. The gills, which are usually located on the underside of the cap, hide the spores until they are ready to drop out. One mushroom, the *puffball*, has a fruiting body that can reach the size of a cantaloupe before it releases its spores. Other mushrooms display fruiting bodies with such a wide range of colors, shapes, and sizes that it is hard to believe that beneath the surface, each mushroom looks much the same.

Yeasts. If you have ever watched your mother or grandmother bake bread, you may have been surprised to see the dough expanding before your eyes. A special fungus called **yeast** causes bread to do this. Yeast is a single-celled fungus that converts sugar into alcohol and carbon dioxide. When the bread is baked, carbon dioxide and evaporated alcohol produce bubbles in the dough. These bubbles force the dough

to rise. The tiny air spaces left behind in the dough after the bubbles have escaped give the bread its light, fluffy texture.

Yeast spores do not grow if they are dry and have no sugar to feed upon. For this reason, a packet of yeast at the grocery store does not do anything until it is mixed with warm water and a little sugar.

Slime molds. One unusual kind of mold reveals itself in a slippery, slimy way as it grows on tree trunks and decaying logs. As with other kinds of fungi, **slime mold** is

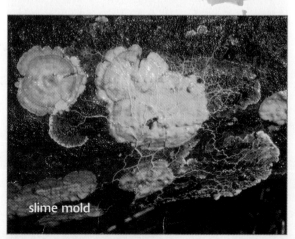

slime mold

normally hidden beneath the surface of the wood. However, when it is ready to reproduce, slime mold sends out sticky threads that have the consistency of glue. Eventually, the threads change into hard, spore-producing structures and do not return to their slippery forms. As the slime mold slides slowly along the surface of a log, it acts almost like a slug or other invertebrate, but its spore-producing structures show that it is indeed a plant.

Lichens. Some fungi and algae combine to form a different type of plant called a **lichen** [lī′kən]. The mycelium of the fungus surrounds the alga and provides the water and the nutrients the alga needs for photosynthesis. The alga, in turn, uses its chlorophyll to produce food for itself and for the fungus. Although the two plants are distinct, the fungus and the alga work together as one plant.

Lichens can be found throughout the world, often in places where other plants would not flourish. Sandy beaches and Arctic regions are two harsh places where lichens live. You can easily recognize many common lichens by their silvery green color. Some lichens are flat like pieces of bark, while others look like miniature bushes. Lichens break down dead plants and rocks into soil and enrich the soil wherever they grow.

Comprehension Check 1.8

1. What kind of plant does not bear seeds, but does have roots and leaves? Give the name for its roots.

2. Which type of plant does not have roots or true leaves, but grows from a slender thread of connected cells?

3. The world's smallest green plants belong to what group of plants?

4. Plants of which family do not contain chlorophyll? List five varieties of fungi we have studied.

5. What do we call an organism that attaches itself to another organism for nourishment?

6. Give the name for the large spore-forming structure of a mushroom.

7. What type of plant is actually a combination of fungi and algae?

the Nongreen machine

Working with yeasts

To watch yeast activate and grow you will need *a packet of yeast, five teaspoons of molasses, a plastic peanut butter jar with a lid,* and *some tap water.* Fill the jar two-thirds full with cool water and the five teaspoons of molasses. Dissolve the molasses in the water before pouring one-fourth packet of yeast into the mixture. Set the lid loosely on top of the jar to keep dust out, but do not screw it on tight. Let the yeast sit for two complete days.

When you remove the lid, what do you notice has happened to the yeast? Does the yeast smell? Has it changed in any way? If you look at a drop of yeast-molasses mixture through a *microscope* you will proba-

bly notice that each yeast cell has produced small buds. These buds will later break off and become new yeast cells.

Hunting mushrooms

How many different types of mushrooms grow in your neighborhood? If you live in the city, you may be able to find a few mushrooms in a nearby park or abandoned lot. Fallen logs and tree trunks would be the best places to look. If you live in the country, you should be able to find several different kinds of mushrooms growing in nearby woods, fields, or pastures.

When you go hunting for mushrooms, you should take along *a shovel or a hand trowel, garden gloves or plastic gloves, newspaper, masking tape,* and *a field guide to mushrooms.* The field guide will help you identify almost any mushroom you find. It is possible, however, that you might find a mushroom that is *extremely* poisonous, even though you think the field guide says it is edible. Very different kinds of mushrooms may be so similar in appearance that it is almost impossible to tell them apart. Therefore, it is important that you wear gloves in order to protect yourself from danger.

Collect at least one mushroom to take home for study. Use the shovel to loosen the soil around the fruiting body of the mushroom. Then brush away the soil to discover the mycelium. Try to pick up the entire mushroom. Wrap the mushroom in newspaper and seal it with a piece of masking tape.

causing bacteria. His discovery led to antibiotics that can help treat pneumonia, tuberculosis, strep throat, and many other diseases.

By studying bread molds, perhaps you too can make an important discovery. You will need *a half slice of bread, a pint jar with a cover, tap water,* and *dust from a window sill.* Soak the bread with tap water and place it in the jar. Sprinkle the window sill dust over the wet piece of bread and then close the jar. Set the jar in a warm place for several days.

When the mold appears, you will notice the white bread is covered with gray fuzz and black spots. The black spots are mold spore cases. If possible, study these spore cases through a *microscope.* The gray fuzz is a collection of hyphae growing on the bread.

Mold spores travel through the air and settle on any exposed food. If the food is moist and warm, the spores will grow into mold plants and eventually destroy the food. With this in mind, what can you do to prevent mold spores from destroying food in your kitchen?

When you are home, you can learn where the mushroom spores are stored within the mushroom cap. You will need *a knife* (not a kitchen knife!) and *a white index card or piece of white poster board that is slightly larger than the mushroom.* Ask for permission to use the knife in order to cut the cap away from the rest of the mushroom. Place the cap on the index card or piece of white poster board so that its gills are against the paper. Allow the mushroom to sit overnight, and then gently remove the cap. What do you see? The design on the paper shows where the spores were located within the cap. You can preserve this design by spraying it with hair spray and mounting it on a colorful piece of construction paper.

Do not eat any mushroom you collect in the wild. If you are hungry for mushrooms, ask your mom to buy some from the produce department at the grocery store.

Producing bread mold spores

Sir Alexander Fleming, a Scottish scientist, discovered a "wonder drug" called penicillin by studying bread molds. He learned that one type of bread mold produces a substance that destroys disease-

Chapter Checkup

Part A

I. Define these terms.

photosynthesis
tropism
pollination
fertilization
chlorophyll
bracts
stomata
glucose
cuticle
guard cells
cellulose
chloroplasts
embryo
botanist
shoot system
root system
root cap
taproot
root hairs
pistil

II. Describe the main function of the following parts.

petals
leaves
flowers
roots
stem
ovary
stamens
veins

III. Give the distinctions of the following plants or families.

pitcher plant
day lily
Venus flytrap
sundew
bladderwort
grasses
pea family
lily family
rose family
composite family

IV. Be able to recognize these families.

grasses
pea
lily
rose
composite

V. Tell why these people are important.

George Washington Carver
Carolus Linnaeus

Part B

I. Define these terms.

tree
perennial
annuals
biennials
dendrologists
cambium layers
annual growth ring
broadleaf trees
deciduous trees
sugaring
conifers
spores
fronds
rhizoid
kelp
mycelium
hyphae

II. Describe these plants.

ferns
mosses
algae
fungi
mildew
molds
mushroom
saprophytes
yeast
lichen

III. Describe these trees.

eastern white pine
ponderosa pine
pinyon pine
blue spruce
tamarack
giant sequoia
bald cypress

IV. Be able to recognize the following trees and their characteristics.

redwoods
sequoias
pines
oaks
willows
birches
maples
spruces
firs
cedars
palms
hemlocks

Observing Invertebrates

One interesting way to observe God's world is to study the multitude of animals that squirm, hop, wriggle, and prowl in every area of the earth. The members of this group range in size from tiny creatures that can be observed only through a microscope, to the giant blue whale, measuring up to 100 feet in length. Animals vary so much in shape, color, size, and habitat that there is no easy way you could study them all at one time.

For instance, it would be quite confusing to learn about the ostrich and the octopus together. God created both of these animals with so many different characteristics that they have little in common except the *o* that begins their names.

However, if you learned about several birds at the same time—like the penguin, the parrot, and the ostrich—you would be able to understand each animal better than if you studied them alone. And if you studied the clam and the snail along with the squid and the octopus, you would learn many ways in which these four creatures are similar.

You may already know that this *process of arranging animals or other things into groups according to their similarities* is called **classification.** Through classification, you can carefully observe one group of animals at a time.

2.1 Classification

Since the time when Adam named all the animals, people have enjoyed observing the design and variety in God's living creations all around the world. Some observers even took the time to write down things that make each plant or animal different and special. The more people looked and studied, the more kinds of plants and animals they found. Scientists soon realized that they needed some kind of "filing system" in order to keep track of them all. So many new kinds of creatures were being discovered each year that it became especially important to find a way to assign each one a name that all scientists would recognize.

 Let's get organized!

Many people worked on discovering and organizing new plants and animals; but in the 1700s, *Carolus Linnaeus* [lĭ·nē′əs] finally came up with a simple, practical method of classifying the plants and animals into groups according to their similarities. This basic system is still used today, although additional categories have been added since Linnaeus's time.

In this system, all living things may be organized into large groups called **kingdoms.** For centuries after Linnaeus, two main kingdoms were recognized: the plant *kingdom* and the animal *kingdom.* Each *kingdom* is divided into a few

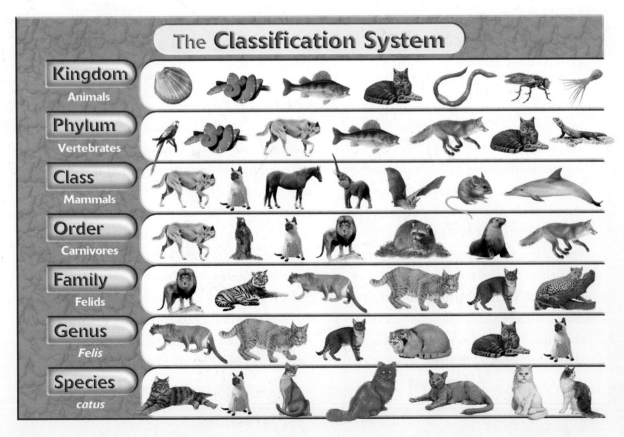

The Classification System

Kingdom Animals	
Phylum Vertebrates	
Class Mammals	
Order Carnivores	
Family Felids	
Genus Felis	
Species catus	

smaller groups called **phyla** [fī′lə: the singular is *phylum*]. Each *phylum* is divided into even smaller groups called **classes;** the *classes* are divided into smaller groups called **orders;** and the *orders* are divided into even smaller groups called **families.** As scientists put plants and animals into the groups, they look for ways that they are the same. If the plants and animals are very different, they are put into different groups. As the groups get smaller, the plants or animals in each group are more and more alike. Finally, the *families* are organized into **genera** [jĕn′ər·ə], and lastly the *genera* are divided into the smallest group, the **species** [spē′shēz].

The classification system moves from general to specific. The *kingdoms* are very large, general groups that include all plants and animals; but the *species* are much smaller groups of plants or animals that are very similar to each other. Linnaeus used the last two divisions

of the classification system—the genus and species names—to give each plant or animal its **scientific name.** The invention of the classification system allowed scientists to easily name each new plant and animal that was discovered.

At the time when Linnaeus was developing his system, all educated people in the Western world were familiar with the Latin and Greek languages. So scientists decided to use Latin and Greek terms for each scientific name. That way a French-speaking scientist could write about a specific creature and a Russian or English scientist could understand which animal was being discussed since they all knew Latin and Greek.

Animal Kingdom

Vertebrates

Invertebrates

Vertebrates and invertebrates

Members of the animal *kingdom* are either **vertebrates**—*animals with backbones*, or **invertebrates**—*animals without backbones*. You are already familiar with the five different types of vertebrates: *birds, mammals, fish, amphibians,* and *reptiles*. But vertebrates make up only about three percent of animal species. The vast majority of animals are invertebrates.

Invertebrates vary so much in size, shape, and body structure that many of them have little or nothing in common with each other except the fact that they have no bones. You may have seen a slimy snail, encased in a spiral shell, crawl across your windowsill. The snail does not look like a spider or a mosquito in any way, and yet it is an invertebrate just as they are. A tick on your dog looks nothing like the earthworm you may see in the garden, but they are both invertebrates. Butterflies and crabs, centipedes and sponges, sow bugs and sand dollars are all very different from each other. But they are all invertebrates: animals without backbones. As you learn about the invertebrates, you will also be learning more about classification.

Comprehension Check 2.1

Let's review classification.

1. What is classification?

2. Name the two kingdom divisions we have used in the classification of living things.

3. Which two divisions of the classification system are used to form the scientific name of a plant or animal?

4. What do we call animals that have backbones? What do we call animals without backbones?

Just for FUN

JOIN THE GROUP

(1) Decide whether the animals in each group below are vertebrates or invertebrates, and write **V** or **I** to the left of the number.

(2) If you wrote **V,** then to the right of the number write the first letter of the group the vertebrate belongs to: **B**irds, **M**ammals, **A**mphibians, **R**eptiles, **F**ish.

(3) Add a member to each vertebrate group. The name of the animal you add should begin with the same letter as the rest of the group members.

_____ 1. _____ donkey, dolphin, deer _____

_____ 2. _____ spider, sand dollar, sponge _____

_____ 3. _____ crocodile, copperhead (snake), chameleon _____

_____ 4. _____ butterfly, beetle, bug _____

_____ 5. _____ pelican, parrot, partridge _____

_____ 6. _____ salmon, seahorse, shark _____

2.2 Insects: The Most Numerous Arthropods

Arthropods: Invertebrates with External Skeletons

In order to study invertebrates more easily, scientists have divided them into several different *phyla* (section 2.1). Over 900,000 species of invertebrates belong to the phylum of creatures called **arthropods** [är′thrə·pŏdz′]—*invertebrates that have external skeletons, jointed appendages* (legs, antennae, etc.), *and segmented bodies*.

An arthropod's strong, lightweight **external skeleton (exoskeleton)** is made primarily of protein and a tough material called **chitin** [kīt′′n]. The external skeleton provides the arthropod with protection, strength, and support. All arthropods also have **jointed legs** and **segmented bodies** that provide great flexibility and allow the animals to crawl, walk, and even jump.

Arthropods range in size from the giant spider crab with a leg span of ten feet to the tiny mite that can be seen only with a microscope. You are already familiar with the largest group of arthropods—the insects. Other arthropods include crabs, spiders, and centipedes.

Six-legged superstars

About 90% of all arthropods belong to the *class* called **insects.** You are probably very familiar with insects, not only because you have studied them in past years, but also because they buzz through your house, ruin your picnics, and sting or bite you on hot summer days. Let's review what we already know about insects so that we can compare them to other arthropods.

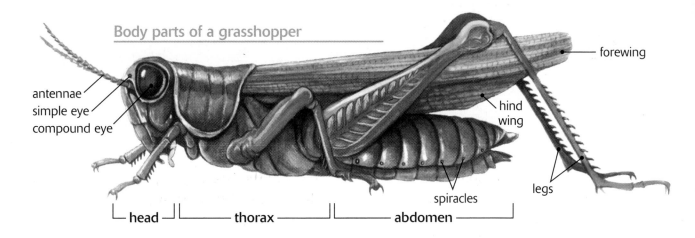

Body parts of a grasshopper

antennae
simple eye
compound eye

forewing

hind wing

spiracles

legs

head — thorax — abdomen

An insect has **three distinct body regions:** the *head,* the *thorax,* and the *abdomen.* All insects have one pair of **antennae** [ăn·těn′ē] that help them feel, hear, and taste. As adults, most insects have tiny **simple eyes** that help them see light and shadow as well as a pair of larger **compound eyes** that enable them to see in many directions at once. Air enters an insect's body through tiny openings in the abdomen called **spiracles** [spĭr′ə·kəlz] and travels through breathing tubes called **tracheae** [trā′kē·ē′] to **air sacs,** which are similar to lungs. All insects have **three pairs of jointed legs,** and most have **one or more pairs of wings;** insects are the only arthropods with wings.

 Metamorphosis

Most insects go through a startling transformation in appearance during their life.

This change in form, called **metamorphosis,** can be incomplete or complete.

Complete metamorphosis. The spectacular results of complete metamorphosis can be seen best in a butterfly or moth. After leaving the **egg,** the insect spends a good part of its life as a **larva,** a wormlike *eating and growing stage.* Insect larvae have hardy appetites, devouring almost any plant foliage in sight and often causing extensive damage to trees and crops. The larva of a butterfly or moth is a caterpillar. Next, the insect enters the *resting stage* of its life as a **pupa.** Butterflies rest in a chrysalis while moths rest in a cocoon. Finally, after these amazing changes have taken place, the insect begins the final stage of its life as an **adult** butterfly or moth.

Complete metamorphosis (ladybug)

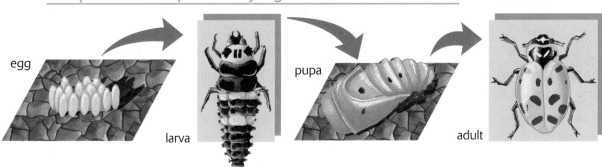

egg

larva

pupa

adult

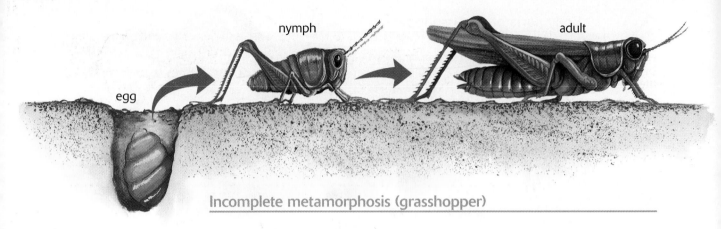

nymph

adult

egg

Incomplete metamorphosis (grasshopper)

Incomplete metamorphosis. An insect that goes through incomplete metamorphosis, such as a grasshopper, begins life as an **egg** and then becomes a **nymph** [nǐmf], or miniature, wingless adult. The nymph **molts** (sheds its external skeleton) several times, forming a new external skeleton each time it outgrows an old one. The nymph's major activity is the same as that of a larva experiencing complete metamorphosis—*eating.* After molting several times, the nymph eventually grows to be an **adult.**

Classifying insects

If one of every kind of insect living on earth were to pass before you in a huge group, it would be very difficult for you to find one particular insect in the crowd. However, the system of classification we studied in section 2.1 makes learning about insects much easier. For an example, let's look at the classification of a monarch butterfly.

A monarch butterfly belongs to the animal **kingdom** instead of the plant kingdom because it has the characteristics of an animal and not the characteristics of a plant.

Because the butterfly is an animal without a backbone but with an external skeleton and jointed feet, it is an invertebrate in the **phylum** of arthropods.

Since the butterfly has six legs, it belongs to the **class** called insects.

The class of insects is organized into about 25 or 30 different **orders.** Butterflies and moths belong to the order named *Lepidoptera* [lĕp/ĭ·dŏp/tər·ə], meaning "scale wings," because they have thousands of microscopic scales on their wings.

Although an order is a smaller group than a class, there are still hundreds of different kinds of butterflies and moths. Therefore, scientists divide orders into **families**—the monarch butterfly belongs to the family named *Danaidae* [də·nā/ĭ·dē], after a mythical Greek king.

Families are then divided into **genera,** and divided again to make the smallest group, the **species** [spē/shēz]. Find the *genus* and *species* of the monarch butterfly by looking at the following chart. Remember that the *genus* name and the *species* name put together make up the monarch's **scientific name:** *Danaus plexippus* [dăn/ā·ŭs plĕk·sĭp/əs].

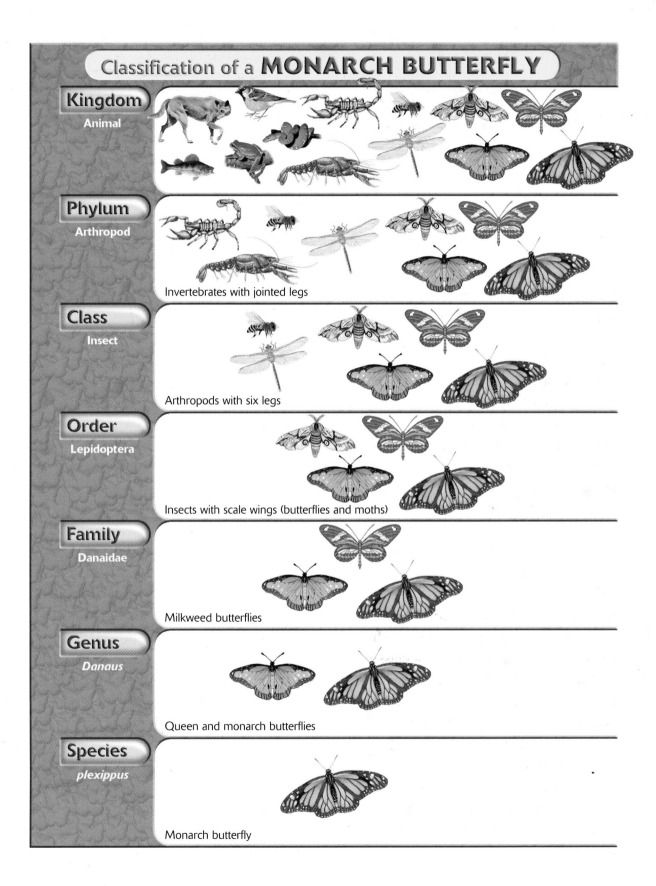

Classification of a MONARCH BUTTERFLY

Kingdom
Animal

Phylum
Arthropod

Invertebrates with jointed legs

Class
Insect

Arthropods with six legs

Order
Lepidoptera

Insects with scale wings (butterflies and moths)

Family
Danaidae

Milkweed butterflies

Genus
Danaus

Queen and monarch butterflies

Species
plexippus

Monarch butterfly

Comprehension Check 2.2

1. What type of invertebrate has an external skeleton, a segmented body, and jointed appendages?

2. Name the strong, lightweight covering that protects an arthropod while giving its body strength and support. What is this covering made of?

3. What are the three body regions of an insect?

4. What do we call the openings in the abdomen of an insect that are used for breathing?

5. Give the three uses for an insect's antennae.

6. What are the two kinds of metamorphosis?

7. List the four stages of complete metamorphosis.

8. List the three stages of incomplete metamorphosis.

2.3 Familiar Orders of Insects

Entomologists (scientists who study insects) know that insects belong to the animal *kingdom,* the *phylum* arthropods, and the *class* insects. Within the class insects, entomologists recognize 25 to 30 smaller groups or *orders.* You are probably quite familiar with the insects found in eight of these orders. Let's learn about the specific characteristics that cause the insects to be placed into these groups.

Crickets, grasshoppers, locusts, and **cockroaches** all belong to the same order because they have *straight, papery wings that fold in a straight line along their bodies* whenever they are not flying. The name of their order, **Orthoptera** [ôr·thŏp′tər·ə], is a Greek word meaning "straight wings." Grasshoppers and locusts are known for the damage they can do to farmers' crops.

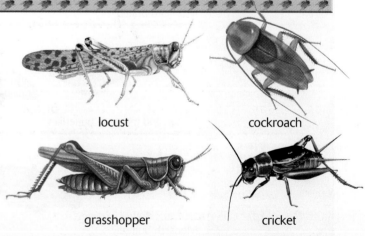

locust

cockroach

grasshopper

cricket

2 **Dragonflies** and **damselflies** are the only kinds of insects in the order **Odonata** [ō′dō·nā′tə: "toothed"]. The name comes from the toothlike projections these insects have on their mouths. You can easily recognize dragonflies and damselflies by their *long, slender bodies, huge eyes, and two pairs of equal-sized transparent wings*. Dragonflies can exceed 35 miles per hour in level flight and may reach 50 or 60 mph in a dive.

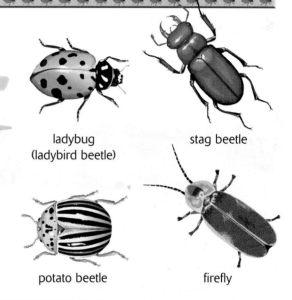

dragonfly   damselfly

3 **Beetles** are the most numerous of all insects. Did you know that one quarter of all the species of animals in the world are beetles? You can recognize them by the *hard forewings* that fit over their bodies like shells and form a *straight line down the back*. Their order name, **Coleoptera** [kō′lē·ŏp′tər·ə], means "sheath wings."

Although many beetles destroy crops, farmers are fond of the colorful ladybug, or ladybird beetle, because it preys on aphids and other garden pests. Some other members of this group are the June bug, the Colorado potato beetle, the stag beetle, and the firefly.

ladybug
(ladybird beetle)

stag beetle

potato beetle

firefly

4 A fourth order of insects includes **aphids, tree hoppers, leaf hoppers, cicadas** [sĭ·kā′dəz], **scale insects,** and the **lac** [lăk] **insect** of southern Asia. When these creatures are not flying, their *wings rest on their back in the shape of a tent*. Their order is named **Homoptera** [hō·mŏp′tər·ə], which means "same wings." They do much damage to plants and are therefore a nuisance to farmers. However, the lac insect is helpful to man because it secretes a substance we use to shellac wood products.

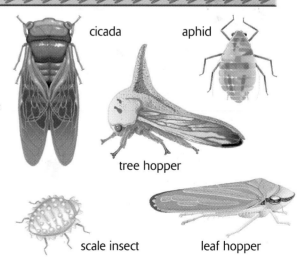

cicada   aphid

tree hopper

scale insect   leaf hopper

5 Another group of insects is made up of ***social insects*** such as **bees, ants,** and **wasps.** While most other insects prefer to stay alone, these insects live together in colonies. Many of them have *two pairs of filmy, membranelike wings,* giving the order its name **Hymenoptera** [hī′mə·nŏp′tər·ə], or "membrane wings."

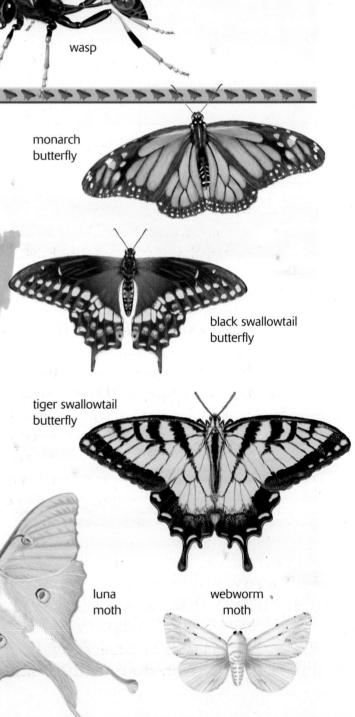

ant

honeybee

wasp

6 The wide variety of colors that **butterflies** and **moths** display is a result of God's wonderful design. When we classified the monarch butterfly, you learned that the order of butterflies and moths is called **Lepidoptera** [lĕp′ĭ·dŏp′tər·ə], or "scale wings." *Thousands of microscopic scales on each wing give butterflies and moths the interesting markings and colors we enjoy.*

Can you tell the difference between a butterfly and a moth? The time of day in which you observe the insect can give you a good clue. A butterfly prefers to fly about during the day, but a moth is **nocturnal**—active at night. You can observe the insect's wings, antennae, and body thickness for additional clues. Butterflies fold their wings together when they rest, whereas moths usually rest with their wings spread out. The butterfly's antennae are thin with a knob at each end; a moth's antennae are feathery. Finally, a butterfly's body is usually not as thick as a moth's.

monarch butterfly

black swallowtail butterfly

tiger swallowtail butterfly

luna moth

webworm moth

7 Members of the next order are really the only insects you can call "bugs." The **true bugs** are known for the way they suck sap from plants and body fluids from animals with their piercing-sucking mouth parts. Their order is named **Hemiptera** [hĭ·mĭp′tər·ə], or "half wings," because many true bugs have what looks like half wings for their second set of wings. Some true bugs do not have wings at all. Members of this group of insects include bedbugs, squash bugs, stinkbugs, and water striders. If you see an insect whose *front wings cross over to form an X or a V at the base of the abdomen,* you have probably found a true bug. If you do not see an X or a V, the insect is probably not a true bug, even though "bug" may be a part of its common name. You can look in a field guide to be sure, or you can look more carefully at the insect's characteristics. For instance, the ladybug has "bug" in its name, but what characteristics show you that it is a beetle rather than a true bug?

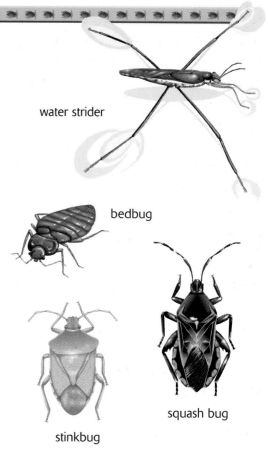

water strider

bedbug

squash bug

stinkbug

8 Perhaps the least popular of all insect groups is the one that consists of **flies, gnats,** and **mosquitoes.** Creatures in this group not only bother you on hot afternoons; they can also carry such diseases as dysentery, sleeping sickness, typhoid fever, encephalitis, and malaria. One characteristic common to these insects is that they all have only *two wings.* Thus they are called **Diptera** [dĭp′tər·ə], or "two wings." Some flies look very much like bees. If you can see how many wings the insect has, you can tell whether it is a bee or just a fly mimicking a bee. Here are two other clues: (1) Bees fold their wings over their backs when at rest; flies hold them slightly out to the side. (2) Bees' antennae are longer than their heads; flies' antennae are shorter than their heads.

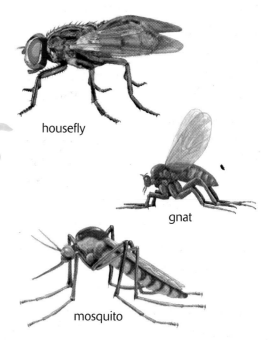

housefly

gnat

mosquito

How would you like to start your own zoo? In a city zoo, most of the animals are vertebrates. Of course many vertebrates, such as a lion or a bear, would be too big or too dangerous for your classroom or bedroom, but many invertebrates are small and easy to keep for observation.

Start your invertebrate zoo by trying to find representatives of the familiar orders of insects. You will not want to put dragonflies, butterflies, or moths in the zoo; these insects are created to fly free. A caterpillar that will turn into a butterfly or moth will make a fascinating exhibit, however.

To find many different types of insects, look for them in a variety of places. The brightly flowering plants in a garden or beside a road would be a good place to begin your search. By moving quickly, you can catch flying insects in a jar or a net. You can find other types of insects by digging up a little dirt and putting it in a box. If you sift through the dirt with your hands, you will find insects and perhaps other types of invertebrates that you will learn about later. An old sheet (or a newspaper) can also be a handy tool for collecting insects. Spread out a sheet on the ground beside a bush or some tall plants. Gently bend the stems and leaves of the plant over the sheet. Shake the

plant carefully. Insects and other small animals will land on the sheet. You will be able to see them clearly and choose the ones you would like for your zoo.

When you find an insect you would like to keep in your zoo, place it in a jar or clear plastic container (the bigger the better) along with a few leaves from the plant where you found it. Lids with holes punched in them make fine covers for bigger insects. Tiny insects, however, should be stored in containers covered with fine screen, gauze, or cheesecloth.

As an eyewitness reporter, you will need to learn some details about the insect. What is its name? Which order does it belong to? Checking its wings will help you answer this question. A field guide can help you to identify an insect, especially if the insect belongs to an order not mentioned

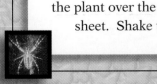

in this chapter. What is its scientific name? What is its natural habitat?

On a small piece of paper, write the common name of the insect, the scientific name, the order the insect belongs to, and its habitat (living place). Tape this information to the insect's new home. How many different insects can you find?

Comprehension Check 2.3

1. What do we call a scientist who studies insects?

2. Name three insects that belong to the order Coleoptera ("sheath wings").

3. Name three insects that belong to the order Hymenoptera ("membrane wings").

4. Name three insects that belong to the order Orthoptera ("straight wings").

5. Name three insects that belong to the order Homoptera ("same wings").

6. Name three insects that belong to the order Lepidoptera ("scale wings").

7. Name two insects that belong to the order Odonata ("toothed").

8. Name three insects that belong to the order Diptera ("two wings").

9. Name three insects that belong to the order Hemiptera ("half wings").

10. What term describes an animal that is active at night?

11. Label the correct insect in the space below.

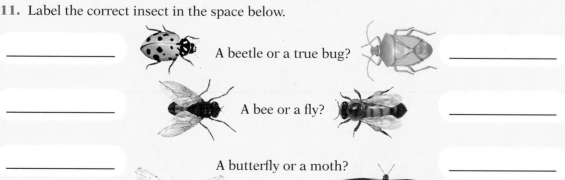

_____   A beetle or a true bug?   _____

_____   A bee or a fly?   _____

_____   A butterfly or a moth?   _____

Sketch it TO SEE IT

Good observers sharpen their skills by drawing what they see. Study the insect pictures on this page and draw them in the correct "cages." Think of the characteristics of each group as you draw.

beetles

true bugs

butterflies / moths

crickets / grasshoppers / locusts / cockroaches

flies / gnats / mosquitos

dragonflies / damselflies

social insects

aphids / hoppers / cicadas

2.4 Spiders: Arthropod Engineers

How spiders differ from insects

Spiders are arthropods, but they are *not* insects! They are insect eaters. Spiders belong to the animal *kingdom* and the arthropod *phylum,* just like insects; but they belong to a different *class* than insects and are known as **arachnids** [ə·răk′nĭdz]. Do you remember what body regions insects have? They have three—head, thorax, and abdomen. God created spiders with only *two distinct body regions,* an abdomen and a **cephalothorax** [sĕf′ə·lə·thôr′ăks]. The cephalothorax is like a head and thorax combined.

Another characteristic of spiders is that they have *eight legs.* How does this help you to distinguish them from insects? Spiders also have several *simple eyes* which are designed differently from the wonderful compound eyes of insects; most spiders have eight simple eyes. Although

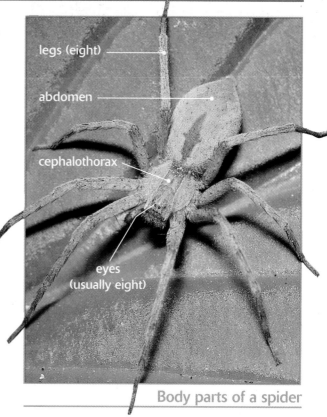

legs (eight)

abdomen

cephalothorax

eyes
(usually eight)

Body parts of a spider

most insects can see their surroundings quite clearly, many spiders have rather poor vision. Because they have *no wings,* spiders have to crawl from place to place. They have no antennae, but feel by means of **setae** [sē′tē] sensitive hairs that grow all over the body. Most spiders are *creative engineers,* making delicate *webs* to trap their food. Insects often get tangled up in these specially designed traps.

Spiders also differ from insects in *the way they breathe.* While insects breathe only through spiracles and tracheae, spiders breathe through spiracles, tracheae, *and* a special **book lung.** In this organ, several thin sheets of tissue filled with blood vessels are stacked like pages in a book.

closeup of wolf spider

setae

Female wolf spider carrying baby spiders

baby spider

When air enters the tiny openings at the front of the spider's abdomen and passes between these sheets, the oxygen in the air changes places with the carbon dioxide in the blood vessels. In this way, the oxygen passes into the blood much more quickly than if the spider had to depend upon the network of spiracles and tracheae alone.

Another way spiders differ from insects is in *the way they grow*. Baby spiders are tiny replicas of their parents. They do not go through metamorphosis. While baby insects are crawling around as caterpillars or other kinds of larvae, baby spiders are weaving miniature webs.

The male spiders of many species grow to only half the size of the female spiders. Some fully grown male spiders do not even look like their female partners. Because male spiders are smaller and weaker than female spiders, they sometimes run the risk of being eaten when they visit a female spider's web to mate.

The spider's silky specialty

Have you ever run into a spider's web? Perhaps you walked through one when you were hiking in the woods last summer. You felt the sticky silk against your face before you actually saw the almost invisible web. You may not have seen the tiny spider that hid nearby, waiting for an insect to fly into its trap. If you had taken the time to observe the torn web after walking through it, you might have seen the spider dart across the remaining silk lines in anticipation of a meal. Imagine the spider's surprise to find a huge, gaping hole instead!

Uses for silk. Spiders manufacture silk inside their abdomens and use it in various ways. They create elegant silk *webs* to trap insects. They rely on silk *safety lines* to keep from falling when they jump from place to place. A few spiders *camouflage* (disguise or conceal) their hideaways with silk. Others *decorate* their homes with webs of intricate design. Mother spiders protect their eggs by constructing silk *nests* where they leave the eggs to hatch on their own or by carrying their eggs in silk *pouches* attached to their abdomens. Many young spiders sail through the air on silk strands that carry them from their place of birth to new homes. This is called **ballooning.**

Female wolf spider carrying silk pouch (egg sac)

Kinds of silk. God has given spiders special **glands** that produce a variety of silks. One gland produces *strong, elastic silk*—far stronger than an equal weight of steel—that is able to support a spider weighing one thousand times as much as its web. A second gland

Garden spider wrapping cricket with silk

produces *sticky silk* that the spider weaves in with the strong, elastic silk in its web so that trapped insects are glued tight until the spider can reach them. Another gland provides *wrapping silk* for tying up insects and other victims that the spider may wish to save for a later meal.

The master weaver's techniques. The different silks from these and other glands are actually liquids while they are stored in the spider's abdomen. Whenever silk is needed, the spider applies pressure to special tubelike structures called **spinnerets.** The spinnerets squirt out long, thin streams of liquid silk from the spider's body. When the liquid silk leaves the spider's body, it hardens to become one solid thread. As long as the spider continues the pressure on the spinnerets, the thread lengthens. If the spider increases the pressure, the thread becomes thicker; if the spider decreases the pressure, the thread becomes thinner. The

spider can therefore control the type of thread and the size of the thread by applying the correct amount of pressure to its spinnerets.

Once the spun silk is hardened, the spider uses its feet to move the thread from place to place. Such a task would be impossible if it were not for the tiny claws that God has placed at the very tips of the spider's feet. The claws and the stiff hairs around them allow the spider to snag and reposition the silk without having to worry about the silk slipping out of its grasp. The spider's claws are therefore like hands that it can use to quickly weave its intricate web. No wonder God praises the spider's skill in His Word! Proverbs 30:28 tells us that "The spider taketh hold with her hands, and is in kings' palaces." Just as the spider turns its silk into beautiful webs, we also can do our best with whatever God gives us.

Observing a garden spider

You can become an eyewitness to the amazing way a spider captures its prey. You will first need to find a spider web in your back yard or in a nearby field. More than likely, the web you find will have the wheel-shaped design of an **orb web** like that of the **garden spider.** Notice how the web hangs like a paper-thin curtain.

If you look at the very center of the web, you might see the spider. Notice that it seems too large and heavy to be supported by the fragile strands of silk. If you cannot find the spider, it may be resting on a leaf or twig at the very edge of the web, waiting for an insect to get entangled in the silken trap. Gently touch the outer strands of the web with a small twig and watch the spider rush from its hiding place.

Observe the spider closely. Do you see the tiny hairs that help it feel? These setae are extremely sensitive to any vibration in the silk touching the spider. If a fly lands on the web, the spider senses not only the arrival of the fly, but also the fly's location. Almost immediately, the spider knows which way to go to find its meal.

To see how quickly the spider finds an entrapped insect, place an ant, a fly, or a small grasshopper on the web. (Do not place a moth on the web, because the tiny scales on the moth's wings would stick to the web and come off the moth, allowing it to escape.) As you watch the spider move across the web toward the insect, notice that it seems to skip some of the threads as

it travels. To insure that the insect will not leave, the spider has woven a spiral of sticky silk throughout its harmless-looking web. This sticky silk glues the insect to the web. As the insect fights to free itself, the spider races toward it, carefully avoiding the sticky threads. Upon reaching the insect, the spider pounces upon it and paralyzes it with a venomous bite. If the spider is hungry, it then injects digestive fluid into the insect, turning its body tissue into liquid. Once the digestive juices have taken effect, the spider sucks up the insides of its prey. If the spider is not hungry, it quickly wraps the insect with silk and saves it to be eaten later. More than likely, the spider will sense that you are watching it and will decide to wait until you leave before it eats its meal. Report your observations to the class.

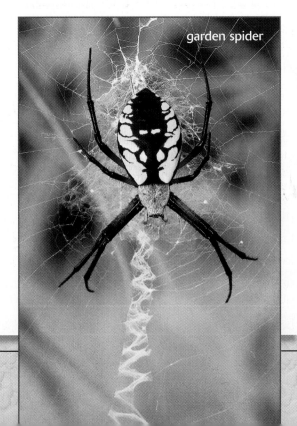

garden spider

Collecting web art

An orb web rarely lasts longer than a day. The web is soon destroyed by insects struggling to free themselves from the sticky thread. The spider is not dismayed, however, at the ruin of its web, because the purpose of the web is to catch insects. In fact, if insects do not bother the spider's web, the spider will destroy it and make a new one in a different location.

You can best study an orb web by capturing its precision on paper. To do this, you will need some *white spray paint, a 12 x 18-inch sheet of black construction paper, a pair of scissors,* and a friend. You will first need to find a perfect web. The best time to do this is early on a morning when there is no dew on the ground. In the morning, there is a good chance that you will find a new web that has not yet been disturbed by insects. When you have found a perfect web, lightly spray both sides of it with white paint. Do not worry about the spider; it will sense danger and escape to a safer place. When both sides of the web are painted, carefully place the black paper on the web. You and your friend should each hold one edge of the paper. Each should put his other hand in the middle of the paper so that when you both push the paper against the web, every strand will hit the paper at about the same time. The spider web will stick to the paper as soon as they touch each other. With your scissors, cut the threads that anchor the web to branches and leaves. Now you have your own spider web. Carry the web inside and lay it flat until the painted silk has dried. Once it has dried, you may want to use some plastic spray to preserve it for use as a decoration in your room. By going out and collecting several more webs, you can start a collection. You will notice that each one is somewhat different from the others.

spinning the first radial threads

spinning the sticky spiral thread

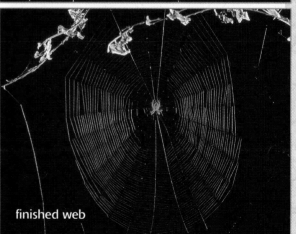

finished web

Science & GREAT CHRISTIANS

Jonathan Edwards
(1703–1758)

Jonathan Edwards was America's greatest preacher in colonial times. As a boy, young Jonathan would wander for hours in the woods after his chores were done, thinking about his father's sermons, praying, and enjoying the wonders of God's creation. Years later, Jonathan Edwards wrote these words about some of his thoughts during his boyhood wanderings: "God's excellency, His wisdom, His purity, and love, seemed to appear in everything; in the sun, moon, and stars; in the clouds and blue sky; in the grass, flowers, trees; in the water and all nature; which used greatly to fix my mind. I often used to sit and view the moon for a long time; and in the day, spent much time in viewing the clouds and sky, to behold the sweet glory of God in these things: in the meantime singing forth, with a low voice, my contemplations of the Creator and Redeemer."

At the age of eleven or twelve, Jonathan Edwards wrote an essay about ballooning spiders that revealed a keen observation of these tiny creatures. Jonathan also wrote essays on colors and the rainbow that suggest that he might have become an able scientist if he had been so inclined. Instead, he became a minister of the gospel, serving as pastor of three churches, working as a missionary to the Indians, and serving as a college president. His preaching helped to spark the Great Awakening, the revival that swept through the American colonies during the years before the War for Independence, and his writings mark him as Colonial America's greatest philosopher and theologian. In many of his sermons, Jonathan Edwards used illustrations from his boyhood observations as an amateur naturalist. For example, in his message from Proverbs 30:24–28, he portrayed the spider as one of the marvels of God's creation. Then, in his most famous sermon of all, *Sinners in the Hands of an Angry God,* Edwards told those in his congregation who were putting off coming to Christ for salvation that it was God's mercy that keeps a sinner from plunging immediately into eternal darkness: "God holds you over the pit of hell, much as one holds a spider over the fire. . . . Therefore, let every one that is out of Christ, now awake and fly from the wrath to come." Because of this powerful message, many of his hearers repented of sin and accepted God's gracious salvation in Christ.

Comprehension Check 2.4

1. In what class do spiders belong?

2. What body section of a spider consists of a combined head and thorax?

3. Give the name for the feeling hairs of a spider.

4. What is a book lung?

5. What term describes the action of young spiders sailing through the air on silk strands?

6. Name the tubelike structures that squirt out the spider's silk when it is needed.

7. List six differences between insects and spiders.

2.5 A Selection of Spiders

There are over 36,000 different species of spiders. Many weave orb webs. Many weave other kinds of webs. Some do not weave any webs at all. How many different kinds of spiders have you seen?

Trap-weaving spiders

The **platform spider** blankets a small section of ground with a flat maze of silk to form what is often called a *sheet web.* You may have seen this kind of web in a meadow or

platform spider with sheet web

on a football field. This spider preys on fleas, grasshoppers, and other insects found in bushes or grass.

funnel weaver with prey

The **funnel weaver** shapes its web like a funnel with the broad opening facing upward and the narrow opening pointing toward the ground. Across the broad opening, the funnel weaver spins a maze of almost invisible threads. When an overconfident insect wanders near the edge of the funnel, it trips over one of the threads and slides down through the hole at the bottom. The funnel weaver quickly pounces on the insect and eats it.

The **house spider** weaves those untidy cobwebs that your mother sweeps out of the corners of your house. She may not like having such a creature in her home, but this spider is much more successful in destroying tiny household pests than insect spray or any kind of insect trap.

Ambushing spiders

Some spiders trap insects, but not with intricate webs. The **ogre-faced spider** uses its silk to make a tiny net small enough to hold between its legs. As it hangs from a thin strand of silk by one or two feet, the ogre-faced spider waits patiently for its next meal. When an unsuspecting insect walks by underneath, the spider throws the net over the insect,

house spider wrapping insect with silk

ogre-faced spider with net

pulls the net taut, and then hoists the insect up into the air. The spider then covers the surprised insect with a blanket of silk. Once the insect is secure, the spider sucks out the insect's body fluids with its mouth while its feet busily construct another net. By the time it finishes its meal, the ogre-faced spider is ready to catch another insect.

trapdoor spider emerging from hole

spitting spider (top) with prey

Trapdoor spiders dig a hole in the ground and wait for their meal. They line the hole with silk and then build a silk trap door that fits snugly over the top of the hole. After sprinkling leaves and dirt over the door to hide it from view, a trapdoor spider lays silk threads across the ground around the hole. These threads let the spider know when food is near. The spider then settles down just beneath the trap door to wait. When an unsuspecting insect trips across the threads of silk, the trap-door spider throws open the trap door and lunges out of the hole in surprise attack.

Hunting spiders

Some spiders hunt for their prey instead of waiting for prey to fall into a trap. The **spitting spider** creeps to within firing range of an insect and spits out a pair of strong, sticky threads. The threads immobilize the victim long enough for the spider to move in and paralyze it with a poisonous bite.

jumping spider

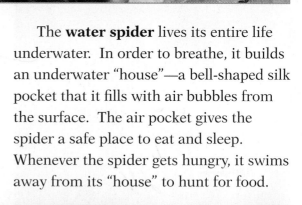

fishing spider

The **jumping spider** relies upon extraordinarily keen eyesight that enables it to skillfully hunt insects like a cat hunts mice. Look for this unique spider on plants, fences, and the sides of buildings as it jumps from place to place or prepares to pounce upon a nearby insect. God has also given the jumping spider a silk safety line to keep it from falling to the ground if it misses its target.

 ## Swimming spiders

Although most spiders prefer to live on land, two kinds are comfortable in water. The **fishing spider** can move across the surface of water as easily as across a rock. It can chase insects on the water surface or lure insects and small frogs within reach of attack by sitting quietly and vibrating its front legs to create a small ripple. The ripple on the surface of the water entices the prey to swim close enough for the spider to dive down and catch it.

The **water spider** lives its entire life underwater. In order to breathe, it builds an underwater "house"—a bell-shaped silk pocket that it fills with air bubbles from the surface. The air pocket gives the spider a safe place to eat and sleep. Whenever the spider gets hungry, it swims away from its "house" to hunt for food.

water spider leaving its "house"

InvertebrateZOO

A wolf spider makes a nice addition to the invertebrate zoo. To find one, you will probably have to go out at night, since that is when wolf spiders are most active. Ask an adult to accompany you, and be sure to remember your flashlight. A wolf spider might be found hunting in the open, or it might be resting under a rock. You can sometimes spot wolf spiders at a distance by the tiny green sparkle of their eyes in the beam of your flashlight.

If you find a wolf spider, keep it in a small terrarium (a container, similar to an aquarium, with a screen on top) with plants and rocks found in the area where you caught it. If you caught a female, she may have an egg sac. Watch as the young spiderlings emerge from the egg sac and climb onto their mother's back. Any insect that you can catch would make a fine meal for the spider.

Make a label stating the spider's scientific name, habitat, and eating habits, and place the label on the outside of the terrarium. Compare the spider to the members of the insect exhibit. How is it different? How is it similar? Some of your web art would make an attractive decoration for the exhibit.

All spiders are venomous, but few are dangerous to humans. Even the most poisonous spiders usually bite only when they are injured or threatened or when they must defend their eggs or their young. In the United States, two spiders you should avoid are the black widow and the brown recluse. The **black widow** may occasionally be found in dark basements, sheds, piles of sticks, and other sheltered areas. Just under an inch in length, it can easily be recognized by the red, orange, or yellow **"hourglass"** on its black abdomen. Its bite may not be noticed at first, but the venom soon causes a dull pain and then headaches, chest tightness, and shortness of breath. If the victim is left untreated, he may suffer paralysis, seizures, heart failure, or other serious conditions. Fortunately, because most hospitals have **antivenin** [ăn′tē·vĕn′ĭn: a medicine that deactivates venom] for such spider bites, it is rare for someone to die from a black widow bite.

Even though the **brown recluse** is half the size of the black widow, it is just as dangerous. You can identify this harmful spider by a dark **violin-shaped mark** on top of its light brown or tan body, and by its six tiny eyes grouped in three pairs. During the day, the brown recluse likes to rest in dark, quiet places, where it sometimes spins a loosely woven cobweb. At night, it comes out to hunt for insects. Although shy, the brown recluse will bite if it feels threatened; many bites occur when someone puts on a shirt or shoes in which the spider is hiding. The bite of a brown recluse is often painless, but the poison soon causes a large, red rash. Within a day or two, a very painful open sore develops at the bite; the sore is very slow to heal and usually requires medical treatment. Some of these effects can be prevented if treated early; therefore, it is important for the person who is bitten to receive medical treatment as soon as possible.

Prevent spider bites by keeping your hands away from places where spiders may hide. If you are cleaning behind furniture, in the cellar, or in the yard or shed, use a broom or brush to sweep out webs. Do not try to brush them away with your bare hands, because a spider may attack in self-defense. Some people who live where brown recluse spiders are common like to shake out clothes before putting them on to make sure a spider is not hiding inside.

black widow

brown recluse

Tarantulas: The hairy giants

All spiders are covered with hair, but none appear quite so hairy as the **tarantulas,** the largest spiders in the world. These giants among spiders do not see well, but rely upon a keen sense of touch to let them know when food is near. Although they feed primarily on insects, they may also eat small reptiles, mammals, and sometimes even frogs. Most tarantulas hide in burrows, under rocks, or on tree branches and wait for their prey to come by; when the spider senses that prey is near, it attacks with a sudden pounce and a poisonous bite. Other tarantulas hide during the day but come out to hunt at night.

You can find tarantulas in warm areas around the world. Although a tarantula bite can kill small animals, their venom is not dangerous to humans. Still, a tarantula bite may be quite painful, since the sharp fangs of an adult tarantula may be more

cobalt blue tarantula

than half an inch long. If they feel threatened, many tarantulas can also fling sharp, hooked hairs into the face of an attacker, causing painful itching and irritation.

Most tarantulas have a leg span of five to seven inches when full grown. The largest tarantula, the **Goliath birdeater** of South America, has a body length of three and one half inches and a leg span of ten inches. Such a spider would cover an entire dinner plate if it were to crawl into your kitchen cupboard. Despite its name, this giant spider rarely if ever eats birds, but instead lies in wait for insects, lizards, and other small animals.

Tarantulas not only grow larger than other spiders; they also live longer. A typical spider lives only a year, but a tarantula may live for six years before it even reaches adulthood.

Although male tarantulas often die soon after mating, female tarantulas have been known to live for twenty or thirty years.

Goliath birdeater tarantula

Comprehension Check 2.5

1. Name three "trap-weaving" spiders.

2. Name two spiders that "ambush" their prey.

3. What type of hunting spider is noted for its keen eyesight?

4. Name two swimming spiders. Which one lives under water its whole life?

5. What two poisonous spiders are mentioned in the text? Give the main identifying marks of both.

6. What is the largest spider in the world? To what group of spiders does this spider belong?

2.6 Spiders' "Classmates"

Spiders are not the only arthropods in the *class* of arachnids. ***Daddy long-legs, scorpions, ticks,*** and ***mites*** *are also arachnids, because they too have eight legs.* But these creatures lack the two distinct body sections characteristic of spiders. Some have the cephalothorax and the abdomen combined in one body section, while others have many distinct body sections.

Dancing daddy longlegs

The **harvestman,** sometimes called the *daddy longlegs,* has a round body suspended between eight long, scrawny legs. *The harvestman is not a spider, because it has only one body section.* However, like most spiders, it is a great friend to farmers. It feeds on plant lice and other pesky insects that destroy garden plants. Since the harvestman has no spinnerets to make webs, it must hunt for its food. This peaceful arachnid has no fangs or venom; its only defense lies in its ability to release an unpleasant musty smell.

Scorpions and their toxic tailpieces

A more dangerous arachnid, the **scorpion,** has *a long tail with a poisonous needlelike point on the end.* When it strikes, the scorpion whips its tail over its body and administers a quick stab. The scorpion uses its tail only in self-defense, or when its victim is too big to be crushed by its pincers or bitten by its mouth. Although a person stung by most scorpions is in

harvestman

little danger of dying, he may suffer much pain. However, like other poisonous stings and bites, scorpion stings are much more dangerous to young children than they are to adults.

There are over 700 different types of scorpions, ranging in length from less than an inch to eight inches. Although most scorpions live in tropical regions, a few kinds live in the southern and southwestern parts of the United States. Scorpions usually hide under rocks or in crevices or burrows during the day. They may even hide in empty shoes. At night, they hunt for spiders, cockroaches, and other kinds of food.

Unlike spiders and other arachnids, *the mother scorpion bears live young instead of laying eggs.* When the baby scorpions are born, the mother catches them with her feet. She then lets them climb onto her back, where they will ride for about two weeks until they are old enough to live on their own. Scorpions *breathe entirely through book lungs.* Unlike spiders and other arachnids, scorpions do not have tracheae and spiracles.

scorpion

ticks before and after feeding

Ticks: Greedy gorgers

While other arachnids are busy hunting or trapping insects, the **tick** spends its time riding about on an animal, a bird, or even a person. It is not just a hitchhiker, however. It actually buries its head in the host's skin and feasts upon the other creature's blood. If given the chance, the tick will swallow so much blood that its body will swell to two or three times its original size. Because ticks feed on living creatures, they are called parasites. The organism on which the parasite lives is called the *host.*

Mites: Burrowing banqueters

The smallest arachnids are the **mites,** tiny eight-legged creatures that can sometimes be seen only with a microscope. Some types of mites cause irritating skin diseases in humans, while other types harmlessly feed on dust in your carpet.

If you have ever walked through a field of weeds or tall grass and later found yourself scratching at mysterious red dots on your ankles, you know what it is to be attacked by mites. Each of those red spots was caused by a **chigger,** the immature form (larva) of the bright red *harvest*

adult harvest mite on leaf

mite. Adult harvest mites look like very tiny, bright red spiders, but the young chiggers are so small that you probably could not see one even if it were crawling on your hand. Usually, they can be seen only with the help of a microscope or a magnifying glass. When you are outdoors, chiggers may climb onto your skin and feed on your blood, leaving red, swollen areas that can last for several weeks. After feeding, the chiggers drop off, bury themselves in the soil, and emerge later as adults.

With the exception of a few giant mites that grow to the size of tiny ticks, mites are too small to be seen. Because of their small size, they are able to live almost anywhere without being noticed. Many mites are scavengers that live in soil or carpet; some live in the water; and some infest foods such as grains, fruits, and cheeses. Some of the most troublesome mites are those that feed on other living creatures. These mites may be found in some strange places—under snake scales, in sea lion nostrils, or even on the bellies of tiny insects.

A parasitic mite is an unpleasant guest, robbing its host of important body fluids. Even more harmful is the damage it does to the host's skin. Female mites of a few species dig tunnels in the skin and lay their eggs there. An animal serving as host to these mites may suffer great irritation. It may scratch vigorously in a useless attempt to get rid of them. Cows, horses, and other barnyard animals can lose their hair because of infestation by mites. The mites can cause a skin infection called **mange,** which can be fatal to the animal if not treated. People can develop a skin infection called **scabies** from certain mites. The best remedy is one of the mite-killing ointments that can be prescribed by a doctor.

Comprehension Check 2.6

1. What arachnid is sometimes called "daddy longlegs"?

2. Give three characteristics that distinguish scorpions from spiders.

3. Name two types of arachnids that are parasites.

4. What term describes the organism on which a parasite lives?

5. What are the smallest arachnids? Name two infections they can cause in animals and people.

Sketch it TO SEE IT

Study the arachnid pictures on this page and draw them in the correct "cages." Think of the characteristics of each group as you draw.

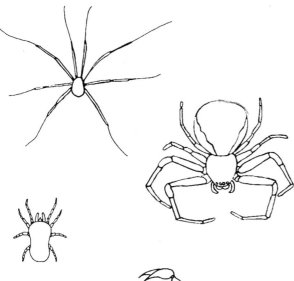

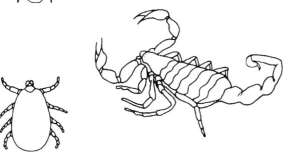

tick

spider

harvestman

scorpion

mite

2.7 Crustaceans

Crusty critters with ten legs

You have now learned about two *classes* of arthropods—insects and arachnids. Did you know that the shrimp, lobsters, and crabs you may have eaten for dinner also make up a class of arthropods? If you look at them closely, you can see that they have *jointed appendages, segmented bodies,* and *external skeletons* like other arthropods. These strange-looking creatures are called **crustaceans** [krŭ·stā′shənz]—arthropods with hard, crusty shells. Most of them crawl along the ocean floor in search of fish, mollusks, and other foods.

Special characteristics. The shells of crustaceans are made of chitin, like the external skeletons of other arthropods, and are hardened by calcium carbonate, the mineral found in limestone, chalk, marble, and seashells. Crustaceans continue to grow throughout their lives, and must therefore **molt,** or shed their shells, in order to make room for their expanding bodies. A molting crustacean is defenseless from the time when its old shell cracks open until its new shell hardens.

Like insects, most crustaceans have *three main body regions:* the *head,* the *thorax,* and the *abdomen.* In some crustaceans, the head and thorax are joined into a cephalothorax. *Each body region is further divided into several segments.* Many crustaceans have *ten jointed legs* and strong *pincers* [pĭn′sərz] used for crushing food and for self-defense.

Crustaceans have *four antennae*—one short pair and one long pair—which they use to touch, taste, and smell. Like insects, crustaceans use their antennae to search for food and to sense when danger is near. Most adult crustaceans also have *compound eyes,* which enable them to see clearly. The eyes of many crustaceans are positioned on the ends of movable *eye stalks* that allow the animal to see in any direction it chooses without turning its body.

Body parts of a crayfish

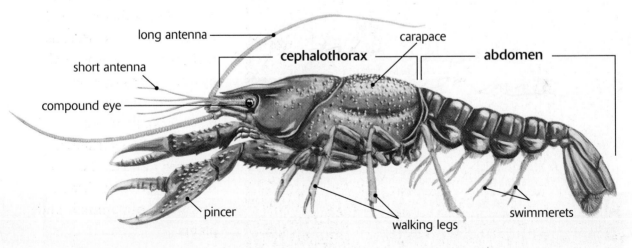

long antenna

short antenna

compound eye

cephalothorax

carapace

abdomen

pincer

walking legs

swimmerets

Because they must breathe underwater, most crustaceans have *gills* positioned just above where their feet connect to their bodies. Gills are thin structures with many blood vessels. As water flows over the gills, oxygen in the water is exchanged with carbon dioxide in the blood. (Fish also have gills, as do some mollusks.) Some very small crustaceans have no gills; they breathe directly through their skin.

The miracle of regeneration. If a crustacean loses a foot or antenna in battle, it hides itself until the *missing part grows back.* This amazing replacement of lost body parts, called **regeneration,** is a God-given ability few other animals enjoy.

Insects of the sea. There are over 30,000 different kinds of crustaceans. Although many types live on the ocean floor, certain small crustaceans float near the ocean surface staying close to and feeding on colonies of microscopic plants

krill

and animals called **plankton.** Some of the most important of these crustaceans are small shrimplike animals called **krill.** Krill are a favorite food of blue whales and other large whales; an adult blue whale may eat 40 million krill per day.

Some larger crustaceans are surf dwellers, living along sandy beaches or rocky coasts. Others prefer freshwater streams or lakes, and a few do not live near water at all. Crustaceans differ widely in shape, size, and natural habitat. They are so numerous that they are often called the "insects of the sea."

Crabs: The army tanks

Characteristics. *Crabs* are crustaceans that are easily recognized by their broad, flat bodies and their two large pincers. Because their bodies are protected by a single sturdy shell, called a **carapace** [kăr′ə·pās], they look somewhat like miniature armored tanks as they *run sideways* along the beach. Crabs eat both animals and plants.

Body parts of a blue crab

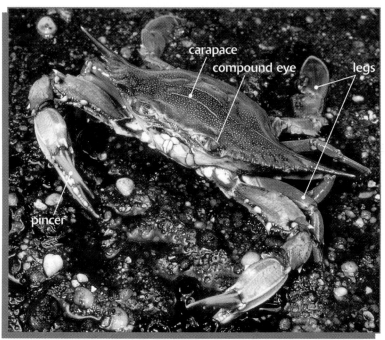

carapace
compound eye
legs
pincer

Kinds. Over 4,500 different kinds of crabs exist, ranging in size from the tiniest, the **pea crab,** which hides its quarter-inch body in the shell of a live clam or oyster, to the giant **Japanese spider crab,** which may weigh up to forty pounds and have legs nearly five feet long. The **fiddler crab** looks like any other crab except it has only one huge pincer or claw sticking out before it like a giant club. At first, you might think its other pincer had been torn away in battle. But it is there, dwarfed by its partner. The male fiddler crab uses its oversized claw not only as a weapon, but also as a show-piece to attract female fiddler crabs. The sand-colored **ghost crab** lives in burrows on Atlantic and Caribbean beaches, often hiding during the day and coming out at night to hunt for food. It is a fast runner, and its coloring is so similar to the color of the sand that it is difficult to spot at night. The **king crab** of Alaska and the **blue crab** of the eastern United States are popular seafoods.

Japanese spider crab

pea crab

fiddler crab

ghost crab

hermit crab

American lobster

The **hermit crab** has become a popular pet because of its interesting habit of living in discarded snail shells. Unlike true crabs, the hermit crab has a protective shell only on the front part of its body, leaving its much longer abdomen without defense. So it borrows a snail shell to protect its soft abdomen. The hermit crab backs into its borrowed shell, uses its small rear legs to lock itself in, and then uses its other, bigger feet to walk. When the hermit crab outgrows its shell, it simply finds a bigger shell to serve as its new home. Whenever the crab senses danger, it backs completely into the shell with only its large pincer sticking out. Protected by their shells, most hermit crabs can venture a great distance from the water, and some spend most of their lives on dry land.

 ## Lobsters: The tail bearers

Thick tail and swimmerets. While a crab has its abdomen hidden under a broad shell, the **lobster's** abdomen takes the form of a thick, muscular tail sticking out behind its narrow body. This tail, protected by crusty plates, is often used by the lobster to escape quickly from danger. When it sees that it is about to be crushed or eaten, the lobster flicks its tail underneath its body in order to lunge backward and out of the way.

Like the crab, the lobster has ten legs. The lobster also has a pair of **swimmerets** connected to the underside of each abdominal section. These swimmerets are leglike limbs that help lobsters move not only when they are swimming but also when they are walking along the ocean floor.

Kinds of lobsters. The **American lobster** or **Maine lobster,** which is prized by seafood lovers for its enormous pincers and meaty tail, hunts for clams and oysters in the frigid North Atlantic Ocean. If left alone over a period of many years, this lobster may grow to more than three feet in length and more than forty pounds. In the past, lobsters often lived long enough to reach this large size. Today, however, most American lobsters grow to a length of eighteen inches or so before they are trapped by lobster fishermen for sale to stores and restaurants around the world.

The **spiny lobster,** or **rock lobster,** has no pincers to use for self-defense, but it is not entirely weaponless. God has altered one pair of this crustacean's antennae by making them extremely long, with sharp edges that can slice into flesh. The spiny lobster uses these antennae as swords to ward off attackers. Because each antenna works independently of the others, the spiny lobster can feel for food with its two smaller antennae while its two larger antennae guard against attacks by fish. Like the American lobster, the spiny lobster is trapped and sold for food.

spiny lobster

A freshwater lobster. You do not have to visit the ocean to see a crustacean in its natural home. You might be able to find a **crayfish** (also called "crawfish" or "crawdad") in a lake, pond, stream, or drainage creek near your house. This small freshwater lobster feeds on worms, snails, and other small water animals, as well as on plants or anything else it thinks might be edible. Raccoons, birds, other animals, and some people eat crayfish.

Shrimp: The small fry

Small wonders. Because of their narrow bodies, crusty shells, and swimmerets, **shrimp** look like miniature lobsters. Although a few shrimp, which are often called **prawns,** can grow to ten inches in length, most shrimp grow no longer than two inches. Fishermen catch shrimp by dragging their nets on the ocean floor where they know shrimp feed on dead animals and decaying plants. In spite of their diet, shrimp are a popular seafood.

crayfish

prawn

brine shrimp

cleaner shrimp cleaning a fish

The **brine shrimp,** one of the smallest shrimp, has unique feet. These "gill-feet" are used for swimming, breathing, and filtering water for food. Brine shrimp are often collected by fishermen, dried, and sold to pet stores, where they are fed to fish in aquariums.

Interesting habits. Not all shrimp are defenseless. The **pistol shrimp** has one large pincer that it uses as a type of stun gun. When it feels threatened, it snaps its

pincer shut so forcefully that it sounds like a small firecracker, scaring off any predators. The shrimp also uses the loud noise to stun the tiny creatures that it eats.

Other shrimp get their food in a completely different way. Several species of **cleaner shrimp** use their long antennae to beckon passing fish. When a fish approaches, the cleaner shrimp climbs aboard to search for parasites and other things that may be harmful to the fish's skin. The fish patiently waits, even opening its gill covers to allow the shrimp to clean inside its gills. Once the shrimp has feasted upon all the parasites on the fish's skin, it drops off and the fish swims away.

pistol shrimp

grasping pincer

noisemaking pincer

🦋 The fortress-builder

Here is a riddle for you to solve. What animal may be a world traveler even though it stays in one place at all times? Can you guess? The answer is a barnacle. When a **barnacle** is young, it cements itself to an object and then builds a hard shell around itself so that it cannot be disturbed. This small crustacean may make its home on a rock or a pier. Or it may fasten onto a moving object such as a sailboat or ocean liner, or even onto a living creature like a whale or sea turtle. The barnacle can therefore tour the world simply because it made its home on a moving object. No matter where it lives, the barnacle simply waits for food to swim nearby. An opening in its self-made fortress allows the barnacle to stretch out its 24 long legs and grab tiny plants and animals that pass within its reach.

barnacles

pill bugs

🦋 The landlubber

You may never have watched a shrimp or lobster swim in the ocean or a crab scrabble across a barnacle-covered rock face. But you probably have seen a small crustacean crawling in your own back yard. Although most crustaceans live in the ocean, the **wood louse** lives on land in moist places under leaves and stones. It eats plants and rotting wood. Because it does not live in water like other crustaceans, the wood louse must rely upon moisture in the soil in order to breathe through its gills. Therefore, it does not usually venture out of its hiding place into daylight.

A wood louse is easily recognized by the number of legs it has. Instead of having five pairs like many crustaceans, or three pairs like insects, the wood louse has *seven pairs of legs*.

One type of wood louse, the **pill bug,** or *roly-poly,* gets its name from the way it rolls itself into a hard little ball whenever it senses danger. If the hard, crusty plates that protect the pill bug do not discourage a spider or insect from trying to attack, the pill bug can also expel an offensive odor.

InvertebrateZoo

A Customized Crayfish Aquarium

The crayfish can become an interesting pet for anyone who is quick enough to grab it behind its two sharp pincers. By dislodging stones on the bed of a creek or river, you may spy one scrabbling away from its discovered hiding place. Watch how the crayfish turns its body around and swims backward so its big pincers are facing you. The pincers are its form of self-defense. You can catch the crayfish by quickly grabbing it behind its pincers. Drop it in a half-filled bucket of creek water.

You can build a home for a crayfish in *an aquarium.* You will also need *a small board two or three inches wide, a half inch thick, and long enough to fit snugly between the front and back walls of the aquarium; some soil; and some creek water.* Before you put the soil and water into the aquarium, make sure the board fits snugly in the aquarium. Once you are sure the board divides the aquarium securely, place the soil on one side, piling it high enough to be level with the top edge of the board. Then pour the water into the compartment on the other side so that it is almost level with the top edge of the board. Place some plants, small stones, and grass seed on the dirt to create a natural habitat. A small feeding dish would be useful for holding mealworms, earthworms, snails, and other foods you might give the crayfish. The aquarium is now ready for a crayfish. Do not try to put more than one crayfish into the aquarium. Two crayfish will fight until one or both die.

Drop a pebble near the crayfish. How did the crayfish react? Now drop an insect or worm near the crayfish and watch how long it takes for the crayfish to respond. How does the crayfish differ from the other arthropods in your zoo? How is it similar? With the help of a field guide, make a label for the crayfish telling its scientific name, its habitat, and its eating habits.

The crayfish should be comfortable in its new home for several weeks. You will have to replenish the creek water often, but do not be concerned if the water in the aquarium becomes a little muddy. After three or four weeks, take the crustacean back to where you found it and let it go.

A Hermit Hideout

A hermit crab, which may be found along the seashore or purchased from a pet shop, is a good specimen for your invertebrate zoo. And it makes a great pet that you can keep long after all the other inhabitants of the zoo are gone. You will need *a small aquarium or a fishbowl filled with two inches of sand, two shallow dishes or jar lids, a piece of driftwood, two or three small stones, and a spray bottle filled with water.* Put the crab on top of the sand in the bowl as soon as you bring

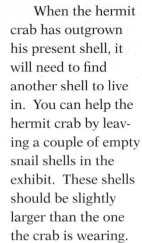

it home. It will hide completely in its shell or dig into the sand just far enough to leave its shell sticking out. Place the piece of driftwood on the sand so the hermit crab can crawl underneath it or climb onto it. Then arrange the stones around the driftwood. Next, place one of the dishes or lids where the hermit crab can easily get to it. The dish should contain about half an inch of non-chlorinated bottled water (or tap water that has been sitting out for a day; the chlorine in fresh tap water can prevent hermit crabs from absorbing the calcium they need for their exoskeletons). You may wish to press the dish into the sand a little so the crab does not have to climb over the edge to find the water.

Hermit crabs will eat small pieces of banana, apple, celery, or lettuce, as well as peanut butter, cornmeal, and brine shrimp. Put a few bits of such food into the remaining dish and set the dish into the exhibit. You may be surprised at how little the hermit crab will eat. Special hermit crab food is also available at pet stores.

Place the hermit crab's new home on a counter or table away from direct sunlight or heat. Change the water and food once a day to keep the crab healthy. (If your crab does not eat much, you may wish to feed him only every other day.) You should also spray a mist of water over the entire exhibit each day. The mist creates a humid environment for the hermit crab's home.

When the hermit crab has outgrown his present shell, it will need to find another shell to live in. You can help the hermit crab by leaving a couple of empty snail shells in the exhibit. These shells should be slightly larger than the one the crab is wearing. When the hermit crab is ready to change shells, it will move next to one of the new shells, crawl out of its old shell and back into the new one. The crab will move quickly from shell to shell, because it does not want to leave itself unguarded. If you have the opportunity to see this change of lodgings, be sure to look closely at the part of the crab's body normally tucked away inside a shell. Because hermit crabs will fight over a suitable shell, it is best to keep only one crab in your exhibit unless you have several shells available. If you do keep more than one crab, use an aquarium or other large habitat rather than a fishbowl so that your crabs have plenty of room to explore.

Most hermit crabs will tolerate gentle handling and enjoy being taken out of their cages. Observing the hermit crab can be very interesting even if you do not get to see it changing shells. How does it walk with a borrowed shell on its back? Why doesn't the shell fall off?

When you compare the hermit crab to the other members of your arthropod zoo, what makes it unique? How is it different from a crayfish? How is it similar? Report your findings to the class. Make a label for your hermit crab, telling its scientific name, its habitat, and its eating habits.

A Roly-Poly Representative

Perhaps the easiest crustacean to collect for your invertebrate zoo is the pill bug, or roly-poly. You should be able to find several of them by looking under vines, leaf piles, bricks, and stones. The picnic table you used in your yard all summer is the perfect place for pill bugs to hide. When you move the table, you may reveal pill bugs crawling in the ground right under the table legs. Cement blocks, logs, and debris in a field are also perfect hiding places for these tiny crustaceans.

A margarine container or a plastic cup half filled with soil and a few dead leaves is all you need to make a pill bug feel at home. Before picking up a pill bug, first touch it with your finger to make it curl up in self-defense. Drop several pill bugs into your container. Punch a few small holes in the container and cover it. Spray the container every day or two with a mist of water. Since pill bugs are more active in moist, dark places than in dry, light places, you may want to place a piece of black paper or cloth over the container.

Carefully observe a pill bug with a magnifying glass. How many sections does it have? How long are its antennae? How many legs does it have? Turn the pill bug upside down. What was its reaction? Report your findings to the class.

Make a label for the pill bug telling its scientific name, its habitat, and its eating habits.

Comprehension Check 2.7

1. List four characteristics of crustaceans.

2. What term describes the process in which a crustacean sheds its exoskeleton to make room for its expanding body?

3. What term describes the ability of crustaceans to replace lost body parts?

4. Which crustaceans run sideways?

5. Name the hard, protective shell that shields a crab's soft body.

6. What do we call the leglike limbs connected to a lobster's abdomen?

7. Which lobster does not have pincers?

8. What are the smallest shrimp mentioned in the text? What are the largest?

9. What crustacean lives in damp areas on land?

Study the crustacean pictures on this page and draw them in the correct jars. Think of the characteristics of each group as you draw.

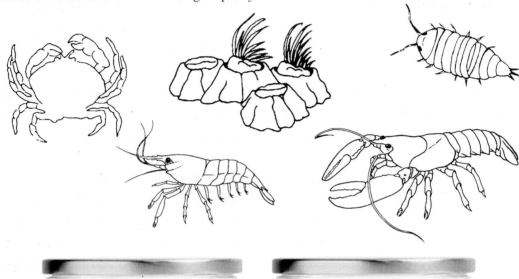

barnacle

wood louse

crab

lobster

shrimp

2.8 Centipedes and Millipedes

If an arthropod has six legs, it is in the *class* Insecta (insects). If it has eight legs, it is in the class Arachnida (arachnids). If it has ten legs, it is in the class Crustacea (crustaceans). But if it has 30, 70, or 150 legs, what is it? It cannot be an insect or an arachnid; it must belong to another class, the class of centipedes or the class of millipedes. Do you know how to tell the difference between a centipede and a millipede? The answer is found in the number of legs on each body segment.

Centipedes: Leggy wigglers

As you turned over stones in your search for pill bugs, you may have discovered one of these many-legged creatures. It resembles a caterpillar or a worm except it has a flattened body and numerous legs. Because of its many legs, it is called a **centipede** ("one-hundred footed").

Two legs per segment. The centipede has many body sections, each but the last two having one pair of legs; the last two sections have no legs at all. If the centipede has 17 body sections, it has 30 legs. How many legs does a centipede with 45 body sections have? As the centipede grows, it adds sections—and therefore legs—until it is an adult. Although the name *centipede* suggests 100 legs, the average adult centipede has 50 or less; the common house centipede has 30. A few kinds of centipedes, however, can grow more than 350 legs.

Poison and speed. The "legs" at the very front of the centipede (closest to the centipede's mouth) are shaped like jaws and are tipped with sharp points that resemble fangs. The centipede uses these poison jaws to kill and eat insects, arachnids, worms, and sometimes other centipedes. The South American **giant centipede,** over ten inches in length, is capable of killing larger animals such as lizards and mice. Although a centipede's poison is not strong enough to kill a person, it can cause a welt as painful as a wasp sting.

To catch its prey, the centipede must be able to move quickly. Fortunately for the centipede, its flexible body allows it to wriggle and twist, stretching its many legs for the largest stride possible. A centipede usually hunts at night. During the day, it hides in damp, dark places under leaves and stones to keep its body from drying out.

house centipede

Millipedes: Graceful gliders

Four legs per segment. A **millipede** ("one-thousand footed") looks similar to a centipede except the millipede's body is rounded instead of flat and has *two pairs of legs on each body section* instead of only one. (The first three sections and the last may be legless.) Although the name *millipede* suggests 1,000 legs, the most any millipede has is 750. Most common millipedes have fewer than 300 legs, and some have as few as 24.

Because it has so many legs, you might think that the millipede could move quickly from place to place. But it travels much slower than the centipede because it takes very short steps with each pair of legs moving together as a unit. While the centipede wriggles somewhat like a snake, the millipede glides slowly along its route, its body scarcely moving as small forward steps ripple along either side.

Placid herbivore. As far as the millipede is concerned, there is no reason to rush. It is not a **carnivore** (flesh-eater) like most centipedes. Rather, it is a **herbivore** (plant-eater), because its diet consists of rotting leaves and decayed plant matter. Consequently, it does not need to hurry to catch its food. The millipede's food just lies there and waits for the millipede to come.

millipede

Two means of defense. Since the millipede cannot move quickly to escape from danger, the Creator has given it a weapon of self-defense. *Stink glands* in two rows along the sides of its body release a poisonous substance capable of either harming or killing a potential attacker. If the poison does not work, the millipede can hastily *curl into a ball,* wrapping its hard external skeleton as a shield around its legs and tender belly. A mother millipede protects her eggs by curling around them and lashing out if a predator gets too close.

millipede in defensive posture

Comprehension Check 2.8

1. What fast, flat-bodied, carnivorous arthropod has one pair of legs per body segment? What does its name mean?

2. What slow, round-bodied, herbivorous arthropod has two pairs of legs per body segment? What does its name mean?

3. What does the term *carnivore* mean?

4. What does the term *herbivore* mean?

2.9 Worms and Mollusks: Invertebrates without External Skeletons

Not all invertebrates have external skeletons as the arthropods do. A tremendous variety of animals exist without the support of any skeleton at all. These animals are all invertebrates, but they do not all belong to the arthropod phylum like insects, arachnids, and crustaceans. After reading about these interesting wonders of creation, you may want to observe some of them on your own. You can learn more about invertebrates without external skeletons by visiting a library or a science museum, by collecting some specimens for your invertebrate zoo, or by observing them in their natural habitats.

Earthworms: Wriggling workers

One invertebrate you could study very closely is the **earthworm** that burrows in the soil of a flower garden. An interesting characteristic of the earthworm is that it swallows soil. Only decayed plant and animal matter is digested by the worm, however. The rest of the soil passes right through the earthworm's body. As the earthworm crawls from place to place, it is performing two important jobs. First, it is enriching the soil with its **castings,** the soil that has passed through its body. Second, it is keeping the soil light and loose so that rain can soak down to water the roots of plants.

earthworms digging through soil

Invertebrate Zoo

Preparing a worm farm can be fun. First, get *a small fishbowl or other transparent container such as a large jar* to use for your terrarium. You can gather some inhabitants and some soil for your farm by digging in the garden. Go down about a foot with the shovel, working carefully to avoid slicing through soft bodies. Put the soil in *a box or other temporary container* for transport to your zoo. Sift through the soil with your hands to loosen it and to make sure you have some worms. You may find a few other creatures that have been caught by surprise. Some of them could be kept in different containers as other invertebrate exhibits. If you need additional worms, look for them on the ground or on sidewalks after a hard rain. Earthworms often come out of the ground after it rains.

Before putting the worms into the terrarium, observe one or two of them closely. **Be sure to keep the worms moist** as you handle them. An earthworm breathes through its skin. If its skin is not moist, oxygen does not pass through into the body, and the worm dies. Keep a small container of water handy, and sprinkle the worms frequently.

First, find the head and the tail of the worm; the head is the end closest to the thicker, smooth section of the worm's body.

Measure the worm from head to tail. Now find out how many segments the worm has. You could estimate the number of segments by counting the segments in an inch and multiplying that number by the total length of the worm.

If you have ever tried to collect earthworms for fishing, you may have discovered that although an earthworm is slimy and legless, it is still able to hold onto the soil, making it hard for you to pull it loose. Look at the earthworm through *a magnifying glass,* and you will notice eight movable bristles, called **setae,** on each segment. These stiff hairs give the worm the ability to fasten itself to the soil as it crawls. If your worm is an adult, you should also notice the thicker, smooth section of the worm that produces the egg case. This egg case slips to the front of the worm's body and over the head when it is time to release the eggs. Why does each worm have an egg case? Among worms there are no males or females. Every worm lays its own eggs.

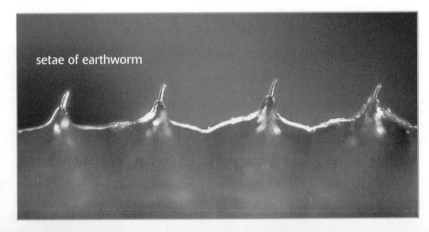

setae of earthworm

Put one of the worms on a table and watch how it uses the segments of its body to crawl. Then wrap the worm loosely in a damp paper towel and shut it into a shoebox. After 3 minutes, open the box and unwrap the worm quickly but carefully, and put it back on the table. Immediately shine a bright flashlight directly at the worm. Do you notice a difference in the way the worm moves? Describe its behavior. The earthworm reacted to the bright beam of the flashlight because its skin is sensitive to light. Do you think a worm is more likely to come to the top of the ground for food in the daytime or at night?

Now fill the terrarium almost to the top with soil, taking care not to pack the soil. Place the worms in the worm farm. Lightly stir some *small bits of lettuce, grass, dry leaves, and crushed cereal* into the top layer of soil so the worms have something to eat. If you cover this food with a layer of soil, the food will not become moldy. The exhibit should be cool and moist, but not wet. Earthworms need moisture to live but they cannot work well in mud. You may either spray your exhibit lightly every day or two, or put a damp sponge on top of the soil. To keep an energetic worm from escaping the terrarium, fasten a piece of cheesecloth over the top with a rubberband.

Because a worm's skin is sensitive to light, the worms in your terrarium may avoid coming to the sides of the transparent container. Covering the sides of the terrarium with black paper for a week or two will make the worm farm resemble the worms' natural, dark habitat and may encourage the worms to tunnel right up to the sides, where you will be able to see them. Once the tunnels have been made, remove the black paper. Using a 5-inch-long piece of string held against the glass, estimate how many inches of tunnel you can see. Can you find the castings at the tops of the tunnels?

head

leech

Parasitic worms

Because the earthworm enriches the soil, it is a friend to farmers. Other worms, however, are not quite so friendly. Three parasitic worms are **leeches, tapeworms,** and **roundworms.** A leech fastens to the skin of its host and feeds on the host's blood. A tapeworm grows inside the intestines of a host, robbing it of important nutrients. Roundworms can live in the lymph nodes, intestines, and even the muscles of their hosts taking their nourishment from the host's blood or partially digested food.

Mollusks

What do clams, oysters, slugs, snails, squids, and octopuses have in common? All of these soft-bodied invertebrates are classified in the *phylum* Mollusca **(mollusks).** Most mollusks make themselves beautiful, hard coverings called **shells.** We might think of the shell of a mollusk as a small castle that the creature builds for its protection. Like a crustacean, a mollusk makes its shell hard with calcium carbonate. The food that the mollusk eats provides all the minerals it needs to make its shell. The shell is produced in liquid form by a tissue called the **mantle.** In the mantle are small organs that give out special substances for hardening or coloring the shell. Many shells of dead mollusks are washed onto the seashore as "seashells." Not all mollusks live in the ocean, however. Some live in freshwater ponds or even in your back yard.

Snails and slugs. Have you ever tried to move around on just one foot? This form of travel would be difficult for you, but it is exactly what God designed for mollusks. He gave each of them one muscular foot. A **gastropod** [găs′trə·pŏd′: "stomach-foot"] moving along on its foot looks as if it were sliding on its stomach. A small gland at the bottom of the foot coats the surface with slime, which helps the foot slide forward. Without the slime, the foot could not move.

A common garden gastropod, the **snail,** is often considered the farmer's

banded forest snail

cowrie

whelk

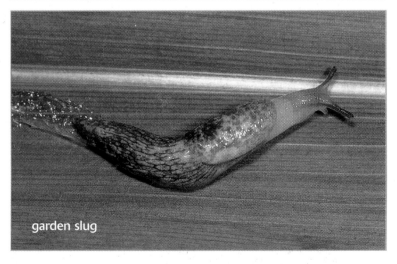
garden slug

enemy because it eats young plants. The snail is an interesting creature to observe. Its single slippery foot expands and contracts, pushing the snail forward. At the front of the foot are the snail's mouth, eyes, and antennae. The part of the body containing the snail's heart, stomach, and other important organs is protected by the shell on the back of the muscular foot. When the snail senses danger, it can pull back into its shell so that only the bottom of its foot shows.

Many snails live in salt water. They are part of a large group of sea-faring **univalves** (one-shelled mollusks). Many univalves manufacture beautiful shells that are highly prized by collectors. Some are smooth, like the glossy shell of the **cowrie;** others are ridged or bumpy, like the shell of the **conch** [kŏngk].

The **slug,** though a close relative of the snail, does not have a protective shell. But like the snail, the slug moves about by expanding and contracting its foot. The sea slug, or

nudibranch [noo'də·brăngk], is one of the most beautiful of sea creatures. This spectacular gastropod comes in an amazing variety of colors, from delicate pinks and purples to brilliant shades of yellow, blue, or red. Most nudibranches are decorated with a fringe of gills that resemble feathers, flower petals, or tiny branches.

nudibranch

gills

Bivalves. Mussels, oysters, clams, and **scallops** are *bivalves* [bī'vălvz]—mollusks having two matching, fan-shaped shells joined by hinges. When a bivalve is attacked by an enemy, strong muscles shut its shell tight to keep out the attacker. Some bivalves have a muscular foot that helps them to move slowly from place to place. This foot digs into the sand, then swells at the end to form a hatchet-shaped anchor. Once its foot is anchored in the sand, the bivalve can pull itself forward. If you live near the ocean, you could develop a fascinating collection of bivalve and univalve shells.

bay scallop

eyes

Clam burrowing into sand

1. Muscular foot is pushed into sand.

2. Blood is forced into foot, causing it to swell and form an anchor.

3. Using the foot as an anchor, the clam pulls itself down into the sand.

Invertebrate ZOO

If you can capture a few garden snails, you will have a fine addition to your zoo. To become a snail sleuth, go outside early in the morning while the grass is still wet with dew. Carry out your search wherever flowers or bushes are growing or leaves are rotting on the ground. Perhaps you can track a snail by the shiny slime trail it has left behind as it walked. (If you cannot find a snail, a slug would do just as well.) When you spy a snail, put it into *a fishbowl or other transparent container* along with some leaves from the plants near the place where you found it. Wash your hands with hot, soapy water after handling the snail.

You can make your exhibit permanent by adding *one or two inches of soil, some grass seed, and some leaves* for the snail to eat. Be sure to keep the snails in a shady place so that they do not dry out. Because snails are most active in damp surroundings, you will need to spray the exhibit lightly every day or two. Also provide *a jar lid with a little water* where the snail can soak itself. Some *wire screen* placed on top of the fishbowl will keep your snails from becoming runaways.

Cover your desk with *a piece of newspaper* and then pick up a snail so that you can observe it carefully. How large is the snail? Measure its shell from end to end. Do you have snails of various sizes? What happens if you touch a snail

lightly on the head? On one of its antennae? A snail's eyes are at the ends of its upper antennae. To find out how well the snail sees, slowly move your hand toward one of its eyes. How soon does the snail retract its antenna? Does it see your hand at a distance or only when you are very close? Now let the snail walk across the desk, and watch its foot expand and contract as it moves. What kind of path does your snail travel? If your snail does not want to move, a few drops of water may stimulate it to become active. To find out what your snail likes to eat, try feeding it *fresh or wilted lettuce, fruit rinds, celery leaves, and tree leaves.* Make a label for the snail telling its scientific name, its habitat, and its eating habits.

Cephalopods. A third kind of mollusk, the **cephalopod** [sĕf′ə·lə·pŏd′: "head-foot"], differs greatly from other mollusks because its foot and its head are not separate. Instead, the "foot" and head are combined into a single headlike structure. All of the vital organs of a cephalopod are found inside this "head foot." At the base of its "head," the cephalopod has two eyes and several tentacles that it uses to catch fish and other prey. Most cephalopods swim by sucking water into a chamber of their bodies and then forcing the water out. The released water pushes the mollusk forward in the same way that air escaping from a balloon pushes a balloon forward. This type of movement is called **jet propulsion.**

octopus

nautilus

The **octopus,** a rather shy cephalopod, has eight long tentacles, each with two rows of muscles that act like suction cups. An octopus has excellent vision thanks to its well-designed eyes, which are remarkably like the eyes of mammals and other vertebrates. Although it has no shell, the octopus can protect itself from danger by shooting a dark, inky substance into the water and swimming away before the water clears. The **squid** and the **cuttlefish** have ten tentacles with suction cups, and internal shells that help support and protect their "heads." When they meet an enemy, they are more likely than the octopus to attack, but they may also seek to escape under the cover of an inky blackness. The **nautilus** has a beautifully designed external shell that protects its body. It has as many as 94 tentacles, none of which has suction cups. The nautilus usually locks itself inside its shell whenever danger is present.

squid

cuttlefish

Comprehension Check 2.9

1. What invertebrates swallow soil and are beneficial to farmers?

2. Name three parasitic worms.

3. Identify the order of invertebrates whose name means "stomach-foot." Give two examples.

4. What is the name for a one-shelled mollusk? Give two examples.

5. What is the name for a two-shelled mollusk? Give two examples.

6. Identify the order of invertebrates whose name means "head-foot." Give two examples.

7. What are the main differences between an octopus and a squid?

2.10 Strange Sea Specimens

Some invertebrates do not look like animals at all. Most of these strange-looking creatures live on the ocean floor, where they could be easily mistaken for plants or rocks. You can observe many of these invertebrates yourself if you ever have the opportunity to snorkel along the coast of a tropical island or if you know someone who collects these creatures and displays them in a saltwater aquarium.

Artistic oddities

The **sea star** (starfish) lying on the ocean floor is perhaps the most unusual-looking invertebrate, because it does not resemble a plant, an animal, or a rock. It has five or more **rays** (arms) arranged around its center with such perfection that the sea star looks more like a motionless piece of art than a living creature. This spiny-skinned invertebrate is lively enough, however, when it finds a clam or oyster to eat. Grasping the bivalve's shell with its rays, the sea star attempts to pull the mollusk apart. Two rows of tiny **tube feet,** like little suction cups, are located on the underside of each ray and help the sea star keep a firm grip as the bivalve fights to keep its shell shut. If the mollusk

sea stars (starfish)

sand dollars

sea star eating a clam

shell opens just a little bit, the sea star will force its tonguelike stomach into the opening and begin to digest the still-fighting bivalve. Once it has overcome the mollusk, the sea star finishes its meal of soft flesh, loosens its grip on the now-empty shell, and returns to its position as an unusual work of art.

 ### Prickly pincushions

A close relative of the sea star is the spiny **sea urchin.** Looking something like a thorn bush or a porcupine, the sea urchin lies on the ocean floor and feeds on plant and animal matter that it finds in the water. The sea urchin uses its spines to protect the thin but rigid shell that surrounds its body and to right itself whenever it is turned over by a strong

water current or by another animal. The long tube feet stretching beyond its spines allow the sea urchin to move along the ocean floor, dig into the sand, or even climb rocks that get in its way.

Some sea urchins have short, flexible spines that resemble fur, whereas others have spines the size of pencils. A few have spines so small that they are hardly notice-able. One such sea urchin is the flat **sand dollar** that lives off the coasts of North America.

Three other relatives of sea stars and sea urchins are the flowerlike **sea lily,** the frilly **feather star,** and the long, bumpy

sea urchins

feather star

sea cucumber

sea cucumber. Each of these creatures has a design very different from the simple design of the sea star.

sponge

From ocean to bathtub

The **sponge,** another interesting creature living on the ocean floor, has a number of small openings, or pores in the sides of its body. These pores allow water to pass through the exterior of the sponge into its center, where the water flows up and out of a larger opening. Small hair-like structures, called flagella, keep the water moving along through the body and collect any microscopic food particles carried by the water.

Ranging from the size of a walnut to 12 feet in height, sponges look more like stones or bushes than animals. Some of the over 4,000 different kinds of sponges are harvested by commercial sponge fishermen. After these sponges are removed from the water, they are spread in the sunshine until their flesh is decayed and their skeletons are dried. Because the dried skeletons of sponges soak up and hold water, they have long been used for scrubbing floors, washing dishes, and even taking baths. However, most of the sponges we use today are not dried sea animals, but are man-made imitations.

Structure of a sponge

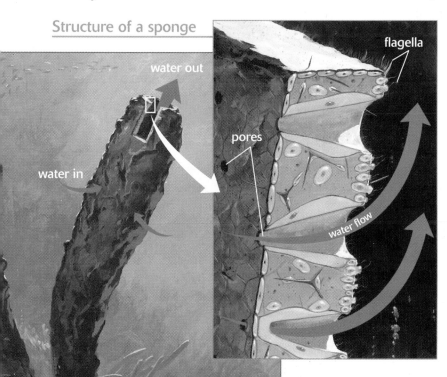
water out
water in
pores
flagella
water flow

sea anemones

Decorative deceivers

With petals circling a disk, the **sea anemone** [ə·nĕm′ə·nē] looks like a flower on the ocean floor. The sea anemone is not as harmless as a flower, however. Its "petals" are really tentacles, always ready to capture a fish or crab that comes too close. Special stinging cells on the tentacles paralyze the victim, permitting the sea anemone to eat it without a struggle. The deceptively peaceful-looking sea anemone quickly sucks the juices out of the victim, digests its flesh, then releases its shell or bones.

A colony of craftsmen

The **coral polyp** [pŏl′ĭp], a tiny relative of the sea anemone, builds a limestone cup at the base of its tubelike body. Whenever the coral polyp is disturbed, it pulls the rest of its body into the hard cup. Like the sea anemone, the coral polyp uses stinging tentacles to capture its prey. Most coral polyps make their homes in large colonies, where millions of live polyps rest on the emptied limestone cups of their ancestors. These emptied cups form coral rock. When ridges of coral rock lie at or near the surface of the water, they are called **coral reefs.**

Hopping hydras

Another animal similar to the sea anemone is the **hydra** [hī′drə], a tiny freshwater invertebrate with tentacles around its mouth. You might be able to find some hydras in pond water or lake water. You will have to use a magnifying glass to see them clearly because they are only 1/4 to 1/2 inch long. The hydra resembles a coral polyp in its appearance and in the way it captures its prey. It does not, however, build a limestone cup or stay in one place. Although it usually fastens to some under-

coral reef

closeup of coral polyps

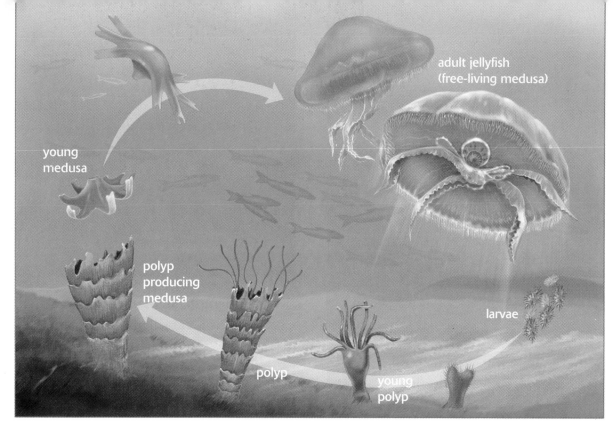

young medusa

adult jellyfish
(free-living medusa)

polyp
producing
medusa

larvae

polyp

young
polyp

Life cycle of a jellyfish

water object, it can change locations by sliding along its base or by turning "somersaults" with the help of its tentacles.

hydra somersaulting

 Floating fantasies

The **jellyfish** is a beautiful ocean invertebrate. Its delicately colored, bowl-shaped body floats near the surface of the sea, trailing long tentacles through the water. Swimmers who come in contact with its tentacles realize that the jellyfish can also be also a dangerous animal. Each tentacle contains **stinging cells,** which shoot a stinging poison into anything they touch. It is not safe to handle a jellyfish even when it is washed up on the beach, because the

stinging cells may still work even if the jellyfish is dead. Although painful, the sting of most jellyfish is not deadly. A moist paste of meat tenderizer rubbed on the site of the sting can help take away the pain.

A jellyfish goes through many changes during its life. A young jellyfish **larva** fastens to an object in the water and then grows to resemble a coral polyp. As the **polyp** matures, its body divides into many disklike sections stacked one on top of the other. Eventually each of these sections breaks away and becomes a young **medusa** [mĭ·dōō′sə]. A medusa is the free-floating, umbrella-shaped stage of a jellyfish. It has a mouth underneath in the center and tentacles dangling from around the mouth. At first, the medusa lives in a cloudy mass of plankton, where food is always plentiful. In time, the tentacles lengthen and the

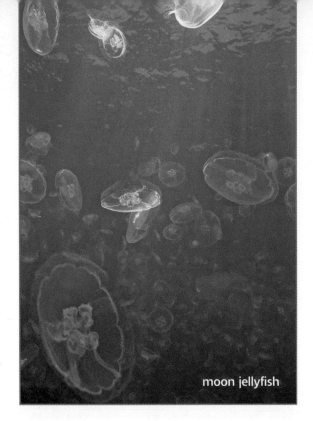

moon jellyfish

Portuguese man-of-war
(seen from below)

medusa grows to become more balloonlike in appearance. The jellyfish is now large enough to leave the plankton and swim by itself. Its tentacles protect the jellyfish from any sea creatures that might attack it. The tentacles also trap food and carry it to the mouth of the jellyfish.

The **Portuguese man-of-war** is actually a colony of several jellyfishlike creatures living and working together. Although all of the members of the colony are connected to one another, they have different jobs. Some catch the food, whether it be small fish or other prey, while others eat and digest it. The colony is supported at the ocean's surface by a large floating air bladder (actually one of the colony members). The tentacles of this amazing colony may grow to as long as 150 feet in length, although the tentacles of most colonies measure less than 50 feet.

EYEwitness reporter

Snorkeling for sea invertebrates

If you ever visit a tropical island, even in your imagination, be sure to find some flippers, a mask, and a snorkel so that you can study the amazing world of underwater invertebrates that lies along the island coast. You will want to swim with some friends or family members, not only for your own safety, but also so you can share the interesting discoveries that you make. As you swim along the surface of the water, you will notice a wide variety of exotic fish staring at you as they float slowly by. How many different shapes, sizes, and colors of fish can you find? Notice how close some of them come to you. They probably are just as interested in you as you are in them.

After taking a deep breath through your snorkel, dive down to the ocean floor, where you might find a conch or some other type of mollusk, or a crustacean scrabbling along the sand in search of food. If you see only some strange-looking rocks and plants, you may begin to wonder if the only animals in this giant aquarium are a bunch of nosy fish. Keep looking around as you return to the surface for more air. When you float back to the surface, do not forget to blow out of your snorkel until it reaches the open air. You do not want to swallow a mouthful of salt water.

The next time you dive down to the ocean floor, double-check the rocks and plants. You may actually be viewing an invertebrate. Perhaps a sea anemone will suddenly reach up and grab a fish that swims too close, or maybe a sea urchin with its spine sticking out everywhere will start to creep along. With one of your flippers, carefully turn the sea urchin over so you can see its mouth. (Avoid touching it with your hands since some sea urchins are poisonous.) Watch how it works to turn itself right-side-up.

By this time, you will probably need more air. As you are floating on the surface, look around the ocean floor for sea stars and sand dollars. These creatures would be safe to handle for closer study. If you spy a sea star, catch a quick breath and dive down to pick it up. You may be surprised at its rubbery feel, and you may be even more surprised as it begins to curl its rays around your hand.

If you show your snorkeling partners the sea star you found, you will probably start a race to see who can find the most sea stars. As you are collecting sea stars, notice the wide variation in color and size. How many different colors can you find? Did anyone find a sea star with more than five rays?

Snorkeling can be an exciting way to see the awe-inspiring world that God created beneath the surface of the sea. While you enjoy the beauty hidden along the beach, be careful not to swim too far away from shore or become too tired. Always go with a couple of friends.

You may be tempted to take a sea star or some other creature home. Remember that just as you do not belong in the ocean without proper equipment, the animal you want to take home does not belong on dry land.

inverte**brate**zoo

The ocean exhibit of the invertebrate zoo can include a wide variety of interesting objects. Mollusk shells are plentiful in many places. They can also be purchased or represented by pictures. Separate the mollusk shells into bivalves and univalves. You may also be able to include the shells of such sea urchins as the attractive sand dollar. A dried sea star or a rock with barnacles cemented to it would make fine specimens for the ocean exhibit. And don't forget to include a few skeletons, like a sponge and some pieces of coral.

After you have collected all the objects for the exhibit, decide on an attractive way to display them. By using field guides, learn the names of all the animals and label them.

Comprehension Check 2.10

1. Name the unusual invertebrate that feeds on mollusks by sticking its stomach into their shells.

2. What relative of the sea star is covered with spines?

3. Identify the flowerlike invertebrate found on the ocean floor, which uses its colorful tentacles to paralyze its prey.

4. What tiny animals are responsible for building underwater ridges and reefs?

5. Name the tiny freshwater invertebrate with tentacles around its mouth.

6. What beautiful, bowl-shaped animal floats near the surface of the water trailing stinging tentacles?

7. Which creature is like a floating colony of jellyfishlike animals?

Sketch it
TO SEE IT

Study the sea creatures pictured on this page and draw them in the correct places in the ocean scene. Think of the characteristics of each one as you draw it.

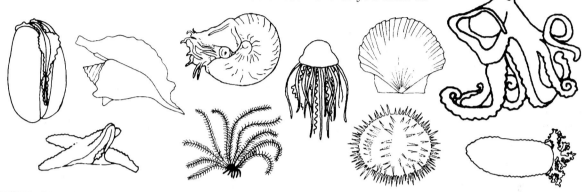

nautilus

octopus   jellyfish

feather star

sea cucumber   sea star

scallop

mussel   conch   sea urchin

Variety in the world of invertebrates

Beetles and barnacles, clams and crayfish, scorpions and sponges, pea crabs and pill bugs—who besides God could have thought up the wide variety of invertebrates we have been studying? Each creature displays God's creative imagination. For instance, let's consider the different ways in which invertebrates get from one place to another. Insects fly, spiders crawl, slugs slide, crabs scurry, millipedes ripple, worms wriggle, shrimp swim, and hydras somersault. Squids and octopuses squirt a jet of water out of their siphons to move about. Many invertebrates such as the coral polyp, sea anemone, and sponge never move at all; and the barnacle travels only as a hitchhiker.

We can see God's love for variety even in the number of legs given to each creature. To millipedes and centipedes God gave dozens of legs, to crustaceans ten, to spiders eight, to insects six, but to the gastropods and other mollusks He gave only a single foot. And He made worms to be contented with no feet at all.

The world of invertebrates is also a world of many colors. Beneath the surface of the waves, coral polyps mass together in formations of brilliant orange, yellow, purple, or green. Sponges, sea anemones, and nudibranches decorate the ocean floor with all sorts of spectacular hues. In addition to these sea dwellers, insects also come in a wide assortment of colors. Have you ever been outside on a summer night when thousands of fireflies were flashing their tail lights? Have you ever seen a sky-blue dragonfly? Many insects—especially beetles—are decked out in bright yellows, reds, blues, or greens. And while some insects like the wasp wear stripes, others such as the ladybug prefer polka dots.

Although not all invertebrates are necessarily colorful or beautiful in appearance, they all have interestingly shaped (and sometimes even humorous-looking) bodies. Whether knobby or smooth, hairy or slimy or prickly, each body is perfectly designed for the jobs God has given that creature to do. What design could be more efficient than the bulging compound eyes of a fly? Those remarkable architects—the spiders—were given bodies that would allow them to build complex webs. The armored plating of crabs and lobsters, although not especially attractive, is very serviceable.

Invertebrates display many different sorts of beauty. The shell of the conch is beautiful and solid, serving to protect the animal that made it. The butterfly, however, is beautiful and delicate.

God created invertebrates in a great many sizes as well. The giant squid is the largest of all invertebrates, weighing as much as a ton and measuring up to 60 feet in length, as long as a mobile home; its eyes can be as large as basketballs. In contrast to these large creatures is the tiny mite, which is no bigger than a speck of dust. But did you realize that invertebrates come in much smaller sizes than that of

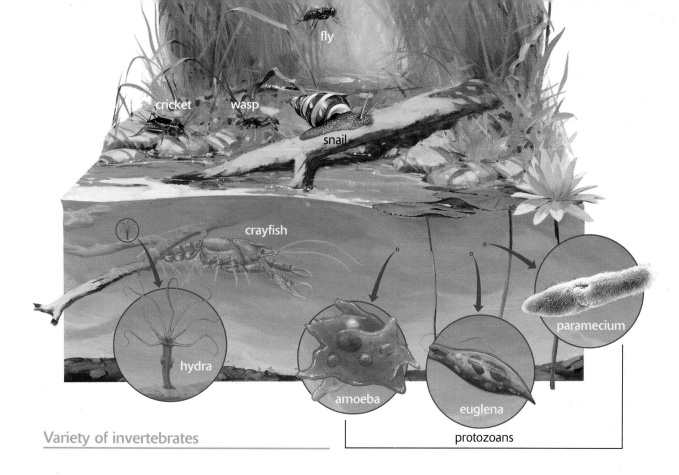

Variety of invertebrates

protozoans

the mite? To the smallest invertebrates, even the mite is a huge and bulky giant.

One-celled wonders

Scientists believe that there may be as many as 45,000 different types of miniature invertebrates known as **protozoans** [prō′tə·zō′ənz]. Most protozoans live in water, but they can be found all over—in ponds, seawater, damp soil, plants, animals, and even in people. Although protozoans are tiny, they show the wise design of the Creator as much as larger animals do. Each one is a complete individual, performing many complex functions.

Protozoans are the smallest possible animals because they are made up of *one single cell* that performs all the tasks ordinarily shared by many thousands of cells in larger animals. Most animals have thousands and millions of cells, and large groups of cells make up one single body part or specialize in one single task. But for the protozoan, one cell has to do it all.

People who choose not to believe that God created our wonderful world, but that it just happened over millions and millions of years, like to imagine that one-celled animals such as these are the simplest of living creatures from which all other creatures evolved. They believe that life originally started out as a one-celled organism. But when you see how complex and intricately built even these small creatures are, you will understand why it is foolish to think that even one of these tiny forms of life could have put itself together by chance.

CONCEPTS
IN SCIENCE

Tiny Units of Life

The smallest living unit in any living organism is a **cell.** (Molecules and atoms are smaller but not alive.) Some cells are complete little animals called protozoans. Others are only a tiny part of a larger organism. Cells are not all the same size. Although the largest cell, the yolk of an ostrich egg, is about the size of a baseball, most cells are so small that they can only be seen through a microscope. Among the smallest are bacterial cells so tiny that it would take 50,000 of them in a line to measure an inch. The human body contains as many as 60 trillion cells. If it were possible for you to count your own cells, and if you did nothing else but count them, you could hardly make a beginning before your life ended.

Cells do all of an organism's work. They produce growth, manufacture and transport essential materials, and respond to a wide variety of situations. Scientists once believed that the cell was a simple structure, but they are now beginning to discover that it is incredibly complex. With infinite wisdom, God has created the cell to be a wonderful, miniature structure that carries on the processes of life.

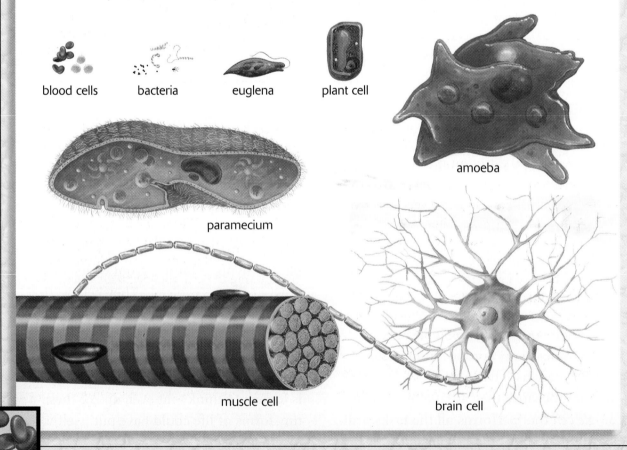

blood cells   bacteria   euglena   plant cell

amoeba

paramecium

muscle cell

brain cell

The Cell City

Many years ago, scientists thought that cells consisted of a simple, jellylike substance called "protoplasm." However, more recent discoveries have shown that a cell is actually more like a tiny, self-contained city with its own power plants, chemical factories, food warehouses, waste disposal facilities, and transportation systems.

Generally, scientists recognize **three main parts** of every plant and animal cell—the *cell membrane*, the *cytoplasm*, and the *nucleus*. **(1)** The **cell membrane** surrounds the cell and protects it. Everything that enters the cell, such as food and liquid, and everything that leaves the cell (wastes), must pass the cell membrane. It is impossible to overemphasize the importance of the cell membrane. Think of it as a wall protecting a city full of life and vitality, but surrounded outside by hostile forces that would bring about the death of the city if allowed to enter. The cell membrane must be very selective about what it allows to enter the cell. If the cell membrane malfunctioned, the cell would immediately die. **(2)** The volume of the cell is filled with a jellylike fluid called the **cytoplasm** [sī′tə·plăz′əm]. Many different types of tiny organs, called **organelles,** move around in the cytoplasm and carry on essential processes of life. If we continue to compare the cell to a city, we could think of organelles as chemical factories, food ware-

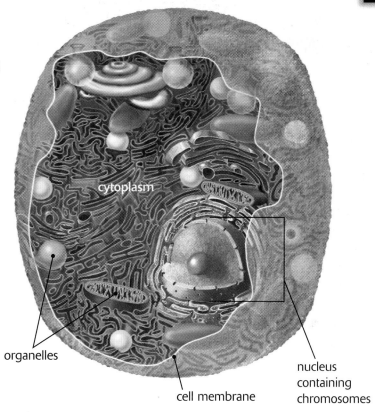

Animal cell

houses, waste disposal facilities, and power plants. **(3)** The **nucleus** [noo′klē·əs], often located in the center of the cell, directs the work of the cell. It is like the control center from which orders are given out to the factories. Within the nucleus are threadlike structures called **chromosomes** [krō′mə·sōmz] that contain the instructions for running the cell and for making needed parts. (Chromosomes also determine the characteristics of the organism as a whole. For example, whether you are male or female, or have light hair or dark, blue eyes or brown, is determined by the chromosomes within the nuclei of your cells.)

The amazing amoeba

A common and interesting protozoan is the **amoeba** [ə·mē′bə]. The amoeba cannot be said to be round, square, or oblong. It has no definite shape because its shape changes continually as it moves. In order to go from place to place, the amoeba pushes out projections called **pseudopods** [soo′də·pŏdz′], or "false feet." An amoeba usually has several pseudopods sticking out in different directions.

The amoeba has an unusual way of eating. Instead of swallowing food with a mouth as other animals do, the amoeba uses its pseudopods to encircle the tiny particle that it is going to eat. You might say that the amoeba eats with its feet! Once the food is within the amoeba's body, it is placed in a tiny storage container called a **food vacuole** [văk′yoo·ōl′], where it is digested and absorbed into the cytoplasm.

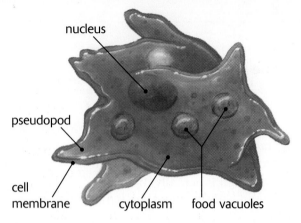

Structure of an amoeba

Although most amoebas live in water, some are parasites living inside the bodies of animals and people. You have some harmless amoebas living in your mouth right now. Some parasitic amoebas, however, cause diseases. One harmful species causes *amoebic dysentery*, a disease of the intestines that is common in parts of the world where good sanitation is not widely practiced. Fortunately, drinking water can be treated with heat or chemical disinfectants to kill dangerous amoebas and other microscopic organisms.

Amoeba engulfing food

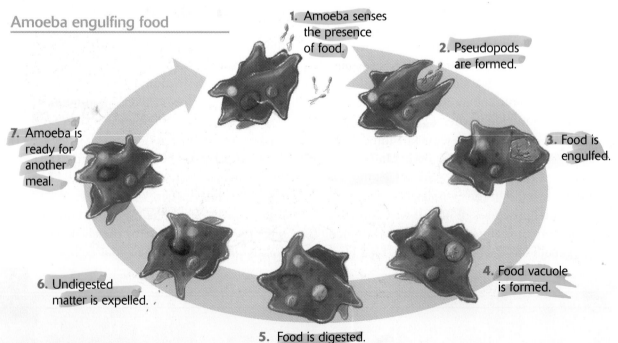

1. Amoeba senses the presence of food.
2. Pseudopods are formed.
3. Food is engulfed.
4. Food vacuole is formed.
5. Food is digested.
6. Undigested matter is expelled.
7. Amoeba is ready for another meal.

Paramecium: The shoe-shaped protozoan

The **paramecium** [păr′ə·mē′shē·əm] is a common protozoan with a unique shape; under a microscope, it often looks like a shoe or a slipper. The paramecium is covered with tiny, hairlike structures called **cilia** [sĭl′ē·ə]. The cilia act like tiny oars with which the paramecium propels itself through the water. Cilia around the paramecium's mouth cavity help the protozoan eat by sweeping food inside. Paramecia eat algae, yeast cells, and other protozoans. A food vacuole forms around the food and the food is digested. Food vacuoles circulate in the paramecium's cytoplasm, bringing digested food to the entire creature. Paramecia can be found in almost all bodies of fresh water.

Protozoans and man

Some protozoans are harmful to man because they cause diseases. We have already discussed amoebic dysentery. *Malaria* is a disease caused by protozoans that are carried by a mosquito of the genus *Anopheles* [ə·nŏf′ĕ·lēz′]. If the mosquito bites a person infected with malaria, some of the protozoans pass into the mosquito's stomach and then work their way to the mosquito's salivary glands. When the mosquito bites again, some of the protozoans are injected into a new host.

Many protozoans are useful animals. Paramecia are helpful because they consume algae. Some protozoans have shells that collect at the bottom of the ocean to form chalk. Untold millions of protozoans are part of the plankton that is an important source of food for ocean animals. There is much we do not yet understand about the role of protozoans in God's creation.

Structure of a paramecium

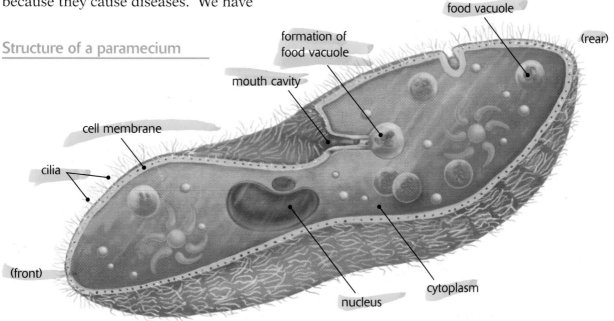

food vacuole

(rear)

formation of food vacuole

mouth cavity

cell membrane

cilia

(front)

nucleus

cytoplasm

Discovering microscopic mysteries

The famous Dutch naturalist Anton van Leeuwenhoek [lā′vən·hōok] was the first person to observe protozoans and write down what he saw. Leeuwenhoek was a storekeeper who studied nature in his spare time. His first step to discovery came when he decided to spend many hours learning from the best spectacle-makers how to grind lenses. Working with great care, Leeuwenhoek practiced this art until he was able to make the finest lenses in all of Europe. With his lenses, he made microscopes that would show him wonderful things no man had seen before. Leeuwenhoek was fascinated by the little things he could see with his microscope. He greatly admired the world of perfection that he saw in the brain of a fly or the stinger of a bee. But his greatest surprise came in 1675 when he looked at a drop of water and found it swarming with incredibly tiny animals! Leeuwenhoek later discovered these "beasties" or "animalcules," as he called them, inside the human mouth when he examined some of the tartar from his own teeth.

Leeuwenhoek looking through his microscope

InvertebrateZOO

It should not be difficult to collect protozoans for the zoo, but you will need *a microscope* to observe them. You can find amoebas and paramecia living in a nearby pond. Fill a bucket half full of pond water that has some pond weeds in it. Have an adult help you prepare a slide for the microscope, using a drop of slime from the leaf of a pond plant. Do you see any amoebas moving about?

If you place some of the weeds in a jar along with some pond water for several days, you should have hundreds of paramecia to look at. They move very quickly, but you should be able to see them darting about. If you view paramecia through a microscope, you should recognize their slipper shape and may be able to see the cilia.

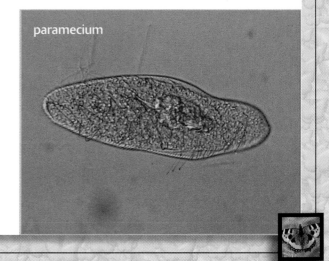

paramecium

Comprehension Check 2.11

1. What group of invertebrates are the smallest of all animals? How do they differ from larger invertebrates?

2. What is the smallest living unit in any organism?

3. Name the protective covering that surrounds a cell.

4. Which part of a cell directs the work of the cell?

5. Give the name for the jellylike fluid that fills a cell.

6. What threadlike structures contain the instructions for running a cell?

7. What word means "false feet"?

8. Name the tiny hairlike structures that help a paramecium move.

Chapter Checkup

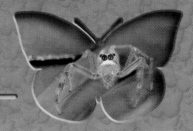

Part A

I. Define these terms.

entomologist
classification
scientific name
vertebrates
invertebrates
arthropods
exoskeleton
chitin
insect
antennae
spiracles
metamorphosis
complete
   metamorphosis
incomplete
   metamorphosis
molt
nocturnal

II. Define these terms regarding spiders.

arachnids
cephalothorax
setae
book lung
ballooning
spinnerets

III. Describe these arachnids.

platform spider
funnel weaver spider
house spider
ogre-faced spider
trapdoor spider
spitting spider
jumping spider
fishing spider
water spider
black widow
brown recluse
tarantulas
Goliath birdeater
harvestman
scorpion
ticks
mites

IV. Name two insects from each of the following orders.

Orthoptera
Odonata
Coleoptera
Hemiptera
Homoptera
Lepidoptera
Hymenoptera
Diptera

V. Identify the following.

two kingdoms of
   Linnaeus' classifi-
   cation system
three body regions of
   an insect
two types of
   metamorphosis in
   insects
two body regions of
   a spider

Part B

I. Define these terms.

crustaceans
regeneration
swimmerets
herbivore
carnivore
coral reef
mollusks
gastropods
univalves
bivalves
cephalopods
protozoan
cell
cell membrane
cytoplasm
nucleus
chromosomes
pseudopods
cilia

II. Describe these crustaceans.

Crab	Shrimp
pea	brine
Japanese spider	pistol
king	cleaner
blue	
hermit	**barnacle**
	wood louse
Lobster	**pill bug**
spiny	
crayfish	

III. Describe these invertebrates.

earthworm
leech
tapeworm
roundworm
sea star
sea urchin
sea anemone
coral polyp
hydra
jellyfish
Portuguese man-of-war
amoeba
paramecium

IV. List the differences between these arthropods.

centipede and millipede
octopus and squid

Our Fascinating Earth

Chapter 3

Human technology and architecture have resulted in some majestic and fascinating works. The graceful arc of a suspension bridge, the towering height of a skyscraper, and the thundering power of a huge dam are objects that people have built with the skills and resources that God has given them. But none of these works can compare with the majesty of God's own creation. If you have ever gone hiking or skiing in the mountains, looked out over a cliff at a deep valley, or visited a rocky seacoast, you have experienced some of the earth's natural wonders. The majesty and glory of God's creation is a reflection of its Creator.

The study of the earth and its structure is called **geology** [jē·ŏl′ə·jē]. **Geologists,** scientists who study the earth, have been able to uncover many of the secrets of our planet and its structure. However, there is still much more that we do not know.

3.1 Earth's Structure

The crust

An outer shell. Geologists divide the interior of the earth into three major sections: the *crust*, the *mantle*, and the *core*. The outermost layer of the earth is called the **crust.** Compared to the size of the earth (which is 8000 miles across), the crust is quite thin, averaging about 22 miles thick beneath the continents and only about 3 miles thick beneath the oceans. The crust is thickest beneath mountain ranges, where it may be as much as 40 miles thick.

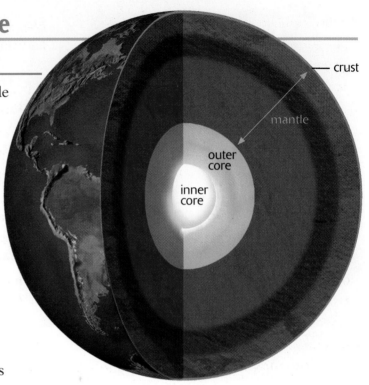

Over much of the earth, from the continental plains to the deep ocean, the rocks of the crust are covered by a thin layer of soil and a thick layer of sand and mineral fragments called **sediments;** most of these sediments were laid down by water, such as during the worldwide Flood described in Genesis 7 and 8. In many places, heat and pressure have compacted these sediments into solid rock. The sediments and sedimentary rock covering the crust average about 1 to

Earth's crust

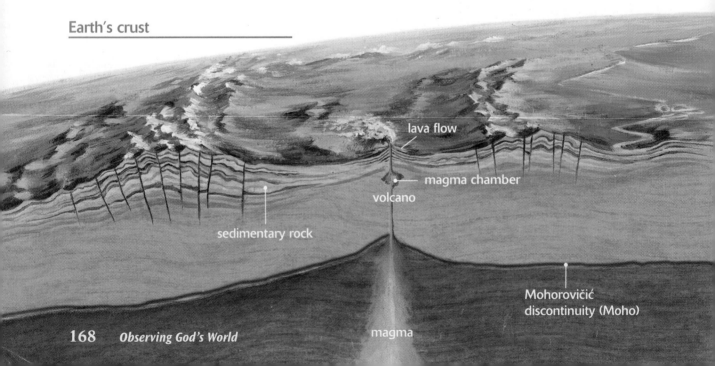

4 miles thick on land and about ¹/₂ mile thick beneath the oceans. In some places, this sedimentary covering has been worn away, or *eroded,* so that the actual rock of the earth's crust can be seen.

Warm rocks. The soil and sediments within a few feet of the earth's surface warm up during the day and cool off at night. However, the deeper rocks maintain a much steadier temperature; if you have ever been inside a cave in the summer, for example, you may have noticed that it was much cooler inside the cave than outside. Although the rocks within a few hundred feet of the surface often feel cool to the touch, ***the temperature of the rocks increases with depth;*** the deeper you go, the warmer it gets. At the bottom of the world's deepest gold mines, 2¹/₂ miles beneath the earth's surface, the temperature of the rocks is over 120 degrees Fahrenheit. At the bottom of the earth's crust, 20–25 miles beneath our

feet, the rocks are hotter than 900 degrees Fahrenheit.

 ## The mantle

Earth's middle layer. Beneath the earth's crust lies the **mantle,** the middle layer of the earth. The mantle is about 1800 miles thick and makes up the largest portion of the earth's interior. The boundary between the crust and the mantle is called the **Moho** [mō′hō], or *Mohorovičić discontinuity* [mō′hə·rō′və·chĭch dĭs′kŏn′tə·nōō′ĭ·tē], named after the Croatian geologist who discovered it. At the bottom of the mantle, the rocks are squeezed to a density nearly twice that of the earth's crust by the immense weight of the rocks above.

If you could somehow descend through the earth's mantle, you would find that the temperature continued to grow hotter as you traveled deeper. The temperature of the mantle rocks rises

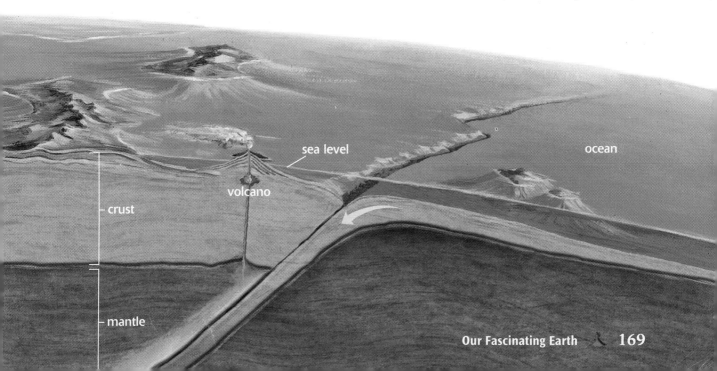

sea level

volcano

ocean

crust

mantle

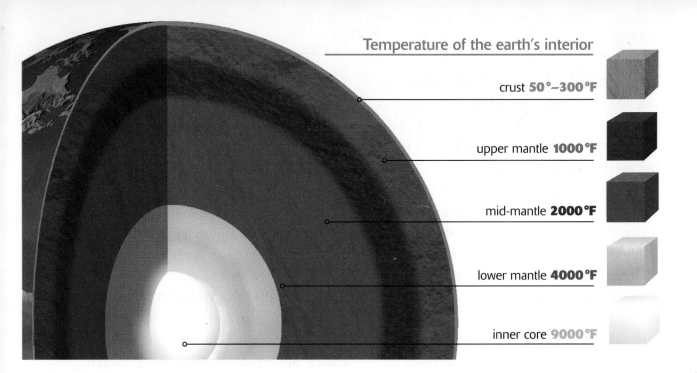

Temperature of the earth's interior

crust 50°–300°F

upper mantle 1000°F

mid-mantle 2000°F

lower mantle 4000°F

inner core 9000°F

from about 900°F at the top of the mantle to nearly 4000°F at the bottom—hot enough to melt steel! Like the crust, the mantle is made of solid rock. However, the high temperatures weaken the rock so that it is no longer firm and brittle, but can slowly flow under pressure like warm plastic. Interestingly, if a cave could somehow exist deep in the mantle, it would not be dark at all inside; the walls of the cave would glow red- or white-hot from the intense heat! Of course, no cave could ever exist at this depth because it would be instantly crushed by the weight of the rocks above.

 ## The core

Beneath the mantle lies the **core,** the innermost region of the earth. The core extends from the bottom of the mantle all the way to the center of the earth, 4000 miles beneath our feet. The sphere-shaped core is about 4400 miles across;

its outer boundary is located about 1800 miles beneath the earth's surface. Unlike the rocks of the crust and mantle, the core is composed of dense metals like iron and nickel. As you might expect, the earth's core is extremely hot, with a temperature of 9000°F or more at its center.

The earth's core is divided into two sections. The white-hot *outer core* consists of molten (melted) iron and nickel. Circulating electric currents in the liquid metal of the outer core generate the earth's magnetic field (discussed in section 3.10). The *inner core* is a mass of even hotter metal, but it remains solid instead of a liquid because of the much greater pressure upon it.

Although scientists have learned much about the earth's deep interior, the earth's crust is far more important to humans, plants, and animals. Most of this chapter will concentrate on the layer of the earth where we live—the earth's crust.

Soil is essential for all plant life. The small particles of rock and decomposed plants and animals that make up soil can easily be moved from place to place not only by man and animals, but also by natural elements such as wind and water. Although God undoubtedly made much of the earth's soil when He created the earth, He also ensured that new soil could be produced to replace any that was lost. New soil is formed by **weathering,** a process that causes rocks to gradually break or crumble into smaller pieces. Weathering takes place whenever rock is exposed to conditions on the earth's surface. Geologists classify weathering as either chemical or physical.

Chemical weathering occurs when natural acids slowly eat into a rock and break it apart. Natural acids are

soil

produced when rainwater mixes with oxygen and carbon dioxide gases in the air. Acids are also produced by mosses and lichens clinging to a rock. **Physical weathering** takes place when rock is broken down by water, ice, or windblown sand. The most rapid physical weathering occurs in areas where the temperature rises above freezing during the day and falls below freezing during the night. When water seeps into cracks and then freezes, it expands as it becomes solid. The pressure created by the frozen water widens the cracks in the rock, often causing the rock to split apart or crumble into smaller pieces.

Even a tender plant can exert enough pressure to split a rock apart as its roots slowly grow into the tiny cracks and crevices of the rock. Rushing water, creeping glaciers of ice, and scouring winds can also cause physical weathering.

Physical weathering

rock split by tree

sediments carried away by water

rocks worn down by windblown sand

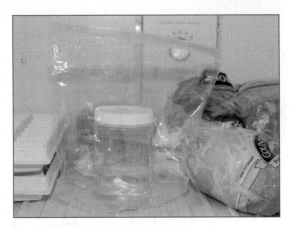

1. Weathering from water

To investigate the ability of freezing water to break rocks, you will need *a small glass jar* with a screw lid, *a recloseable plastic bag,* and *water.* Completely fill the jar with water and screw the lid tightly closed. Seal the jar in the plastic bag and place it in the freezer for at least eight hours. When you take the bag out of the freezer, carefully examine the contents. What happened to the jar? Do you know why? How do you think the forces that caused the jar to break affect the rocks?

2. Weathering from plants

You will need *a small plastic pill bottle, some soil,* and *two or three bean seeds* in order to observe how plants can cause physical weathering. Place the soil inside the pill bottle. Then plant the bean seeds in the soil. Be sure to sprinkle a little water on top of the soil as you wait for the seeds to germinate and for the new plants to grow.

As the beans grow, watch what happens to the pill bottle.

3. Weathering from chemicals

To see how chemical weathering takes place, you will need *vinegar, water, two small pieces of limestone or seashell, two pint-sized jars,* and *a hammer.* Pour about a half cup of water into one jar and an equal amount of vinegar into the second jar. With the hammer, crush a piece of limestone or seashell and drop the broken pieces into the water. Drop some other limestone or seashell pieces into the jar half-filled with vinegar. Do you notice any reactions taking place in the second jar? How are they different from the reactions of the limestone in the jar half-filled with water? The acid in the vinegar should make the limestone fizz as the calcium carbonate (the substance that limestone is made of) decomposes. The fizz lets you know that the acid is weathering the rock.

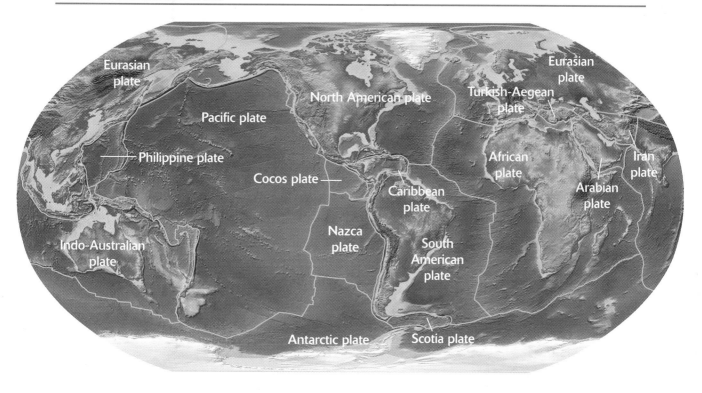

Movements of the earth's crust

Drifting plates. Most geologists believe that the earth's crust does not consist of one huge, unbroken shell of rock, but of several individual **plates** that "float" like rafts on the soft rock of the upper mantle. As heat rising from the earth's core causes the mantle rock to flow slowly from place to place, the plates resting on top of the mantle are dragged along. Careful measurements show that some of the earth's plates are drifting as much as eight inches per year.

In all, seven large plates and several smaller plates are thought to exist. Most of the United States is located on the *North American plate*, except for southwestern California, which lies on the *Pacific plate*. Locations and boundaries of other plates are shown in the illustration above.

Plate collisions. As different plates are dragged in different directions, they often collide or grind together at their edges. When two plates collide head-on, they may fold or buckle, producing mountains. Most of the world's large mountain ranges are located at or near plate boundaries. For example, the Himalayas, the highest mountains on Earth, lie on the boundary between the Indo-Australian plate and the Eurasian plate.

Moving plates are also thought to be responsible for many features of the ocean floor. For example, the earth's oceans contain underwater mountain ranges called **mid-oceanic ridges** where plates of the earth's crust are moving away from each other. As these plates move apart, they create a gap, or *rift,* between them that is quickly filled by molten rock rising from below, forming a ridge. In other places around the world, the edge of one plate is being forced beneath the edge of another. Where this occurs, a deep *trench,* like a muddy valley, is formed in the ocean floor.

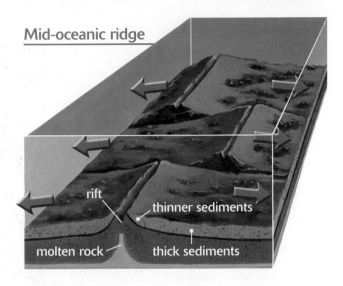

Mid-oceanic ridge

rift

thinner sediments

molten rock

thick sediments

These trenches are the deepest places in the ocean; in one trench in the South Pacific, the ocean is more than seven miles deep.

Comprehension Check 3.1

Clues. Give the word or term that best fits each clue.

1. The study of the earth

2. Scientists who study the earth

3. The outer layer of the earth

4. The boundary between the crust and the mantle

5. The innermost region of the earth

6. A mixture of broken-down rocks and decomposed plants and animals

7. The process by which new soil is formed

8. Type of weathering caused by ice, flowing water, or windblown sand

9. Underwater mountain ranges where plates of the earth's crust are thought to be moving away from each other

Explain.

10. Describe the earth's mantle.

11. Which part of the earth's core is a solid? Which part is a liquid?

12. Explain the difference between chemical and physical weathering.

3.2 Earthquakes

An earth-shaking event

The plates that make up the earth's crust move very slowly, but they do not always move smoothly. This is especially true when two plates are sliding against each other. As rough-edged plates grind together at their edges, they sometimes become stuck and temporarily stop moving. When this happens, the pressure upon the plates continues to build until finally the rocks give way under the strain, allowing the plates to suddenly jump forward. The sudden movement can cause the earth's surface to shake violently.

One place where this has happened is southern Alaska, where the edge of the Pacific plate is slowly being forced beneath the edge of the North American

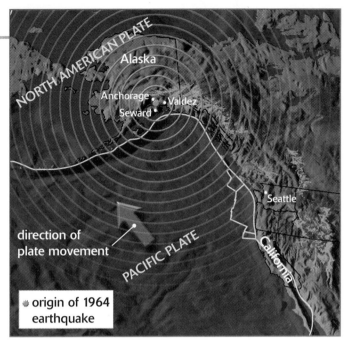

Alaska earthquake of 1964

plate. Hundreds of years ago, the plates became stuck and ceased to move. Over the next few centuries, the two plates stayed stubbornly locked together as the pressure built up. Finally, on a cold spring afternoon in 1964, a 500-mile-wide stretch of the Pacific plate suddenly broke free and slid forward several feet, causing over 100,000 square miles of earth to shake violently. The resulting earthquake was so powerful that buildings swayed 3000 miles away in Seattle, Washington. In the city of Anchorage, Alaska, 120 miles away from the rupture, buildings collapsed and streets ripped apart leaving huge, gaping holes.

school building broken in half by 1964 earthquake

old shoreline

new shoreline

island raised out of water by 1964 earthquake

In the next several months, as scientists studied the area surrounding the earthquake, they discovered that in just a few minutes, land 100 miles inland to the north and west of the earthquake fault had dropped between $2\frac{1}{2}$ and $7\frac{1}{2}$ feet, and islands 100 miles to the south and the east had risen about 6 feet out of the water. One island rose 33 feet in 4 minutes when the earthquake struck! In addition, over 25,000 square miles of land on the North American plate shifted south and east: Anchorage moved 6 feet; Valdez, 33 feet; and Seward, 47 feet.

The sudden movement of the Pacific plate under the ocean floor also created

tsunami damage in Seward, Alaska

monstrous waves known as **tsunamis** [tsōō·nä′mēz] that swept down the Pacific Coast, causing death and property damage as far south as California. Thankfully, although the earthquake destroyed large amounts of property, it claimed comparatively few lives because it struck a sparsely populated region on a holiday when schools and many businesses were closed.

Earthquakes and tremors

What is an earthquake? An **earthquake** may be defined as *any trembling or shaking of the earth's crust.* A weak earthquake, or **tremor,** may be felt as a slight vibration of the ground, accompanied by a low rumbling sound; in homes, dishes may rattle, and a picture or two might fall off the wall. A major earthquake, however, can be much more violent; the ground may heave and roll like a storm-tossed sea, throwing people and animals to the ground. Cracks often appear in the earth, and landslides and mudslides can occur in hilly regions as rocks and earth are shaken loose from steep slopes. In cities and other populated areas, the damage can be devastating as buildings and bridges come crashing down. After a major earthquake in a populated area, fires may break out from broken gas pipes and leaking fuel storage tanks.

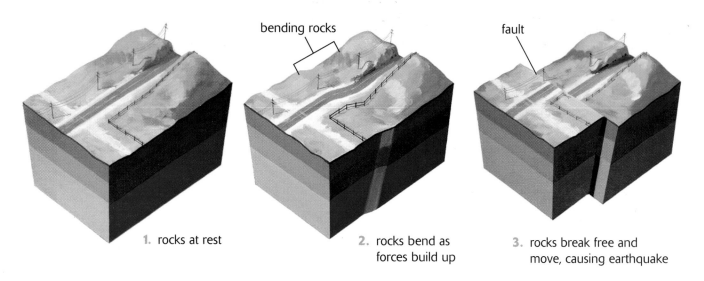

1. rocks at rest

2. rocks bend as forces build up

3. rocks break free and move, causing earthquake

Most large earthquakes last less than one minute, although the Alaska earthquake (the second largest ever recorded) lasted for four minutes. Smaller earthquakes or tremors called **aftershocks** may occur periodically for days or even months after a major earthquake, gradually decreasing in intensity.

mountain ridge made of folded rocks

What causes earthquakes? The study of earthquakes is called **seismology** [sīz·mŏl′ə·jē]. **Seismologists** [sīz·mŏl′ə·jīsts]—scientists who study earthquakes—believe that earthquakes are caused by movements of the crustal plates. Two plates in contact push against each other with tremendous force as they try to move in different directions. As long as the plates are free to move, major earthquakes do not occur. However, sometimes the edges of the plates become stuck and cease to move, allowing huge forces to build up.

For long periods of time, the plates may remain locked together. Rock near the boundary between the plates undergoes such extreme pressure that it may bend or crack. If the rock bends without cracking, the result is called a *fold*. Many hills and mountains were formed when rock folded under the pressure between moving plates. If the rock cracks, but does not move in any way, the result is called a *fracture*. Although some fractures reach up to ground level, most are confined to rock below the surface.

In general, folds and fractures do not relieve enough pressure to prevent the pressure between two plates from steadily building up. The force eventually becomes so great that the plates suddenly break free and slide against each other for several seconds. This movement produces a tremendous shaking of the earth—an earthquake. The 1964 Alaska earthquake was a dramatic example of this process. The break that appears in the rock at the boundary between two moving masses of rock is called a **fault.**

The famous *San Andreas* [săn ăn·drā′əs] *fault* in southwestern California has been the location of several well-known earthquakes. This fault forms part of the boundary between the Pacific and North American plates. Smaller faults may be found wherever rocks have been under great stress.

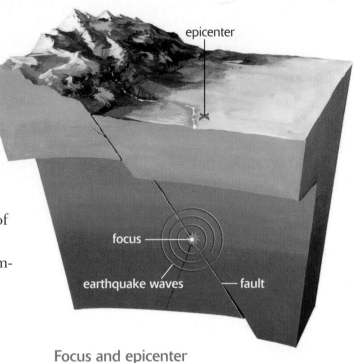

Focus and epicenter

The sudden movement of rocks during an earthquake can produce interesting land features. The rocks along one side of the fault may be lifted several feet higher than those on the other side, producing a short cliff. Rocks moving sideways can sever fences, highways, and stream beds and move the broken ends many feet apart.

The point underground where an earthquake begins is called the **focus.** The focus is usually less than 25 miles below the surface, although it may be as deep as 435 miles in some cases. The **epicenter** [ĕp′ĭ·sĕn′tər] of an earthquake is the place at ground level that is directly above the focus. The epicenter often receives the most damage during an earthquake.

fence broken by 1906 San Francisco earthquake

Magnitudes of some famous earthquakes

Year	Location	Magnitude	Number of Fatalities
1755	Lisbon, Portugal	8.8	70,000
1812	New Madrid, Missouri	8.0	unknown
1906	San Francisco, California	8.3	2,000
1923	Kwanto, Japan	8.3	143,000
1960	coastal Chile	8.6–9.5*	6,000
1964	Anchorage, Alaska	8.5	131
1976	Tianjin, China	7.8–8.2	500,000
1999	Izmit, Turkey	7.4	17,000
2001	Gujarat Province, India	7.7	20,000

*Depending on how it is measured.

Measuring earthquakes. Earthquakes vary greatly in their effects. A weak earthquake may be barely felt, whereas a strong earthquake may shake buildings and bridges so forcefully that they are badly damaged or even destroyed. Seismologists have devised scales of earthquake strength, or **magnitude,** in order to compare one earthquake with another. The most famous scale used to measure earthquake strength is the **Richter** [rik′tər] **scale,** invented by an American seismologist named Charles Richter.

Each unit on the Richter scale represents an increase in strength. For example, an earthquake with a magnitude of 8 is about 32 times stronger than one with a magnitude of 7, about 1,000 times stronger than an earthquake of magnitude 6, and about 32,000 times stronger than an earthquake of magnitude 5. The magnitudes of some important earthquakes are shown in the chart at the left.

Earthquakes with magnitudes less than 3 on the Richter scale are barely felt. Minor damage may occur to poorly constructed buildings during a magnitude 4.5 earthquake; an earthquake that registers a magnitude of 6 can cause more serious damage. Earthquakes of magnitude 7 or so are strong enough to destroy many buildings. An earthquake measuring 7 on the Richter scale releases as much energy as the explosion of one million tons of dynamite! Scientists estimate that of the more than one million earthquakes that occur worldwide per year, only about twenty reach a magnitude of 7 or greater. The most powerful earthquake ever recorded with scientific instruments occurred in the country of Chile in 1960. This devastating quake had a magnitude of between 8.6 and 9.5 (depending on how it is measured), although even stronger earthquakes are theoretically possible.

building damaged by 2001 Gujarat earthquake

Seismic belts

• location of earthquake

The location of earthquakes

Seismologists have discovered that most earthquakes take place where faults have already been established. Most faults lie along boundaries between the plates of the earth's crust. Since these faults produce most of the world's earthquakes, the regions where they are found are called **seismic belts.** About 80% of all earthquakes occur in the *Circum-Pacific Belt,* the region that circles the Pacific Ocean. About 15% of all earthquakes occur in the *Alpide Belt,* which cuts across southern Europe into Asia. The remaining 5% are scattered around the globe.

Most earthquakes in the United States occur along the West Coast from the Mexican border to Alaska, along the Circum-Pacific belt. However, earthquakes can also occur elsewhere in the United States. The Rocky Mountain region, New England, and New York experience occasional tremors, as well as many of the south-

eastern states. In 1811 and 1812, a series of violent earthquakes measuring about 8 on the Richter scale struck the town of New Madrid, Missouri, near the Tennessee border. Seismic waves from these earthquakes caused church bells to ring as far away as Boston, Massachusetts, and the shifting ground permanently changed the course of the Mississippi River.

Reducing earthquake damage

Most deaths from earthquakes result from the collapse of buildings and other structures, not from the shaking itself. Typical American houses are usually safe in an earthquake, although falling objects and broken glass can pose a hazard. The greatest dangers are found in cities, where people often live and work in large brick or stone buildings that are more prone to collapse. For this reason, buildings and bridges in earthquake-prone areas are often specially built to withstand earthquakes.

Comprehension Check 3.2

Clues. Give the word or term that best fits each clue.

1. Any trembling or shaking of the earth's crust

2. Giant waves that may be caused by earthquakes

3. The study of earthquakes

4. Scientists who study earthquakes

5. The break that appears between two moving masses of rock

6. The point under the ground where an earthquake begins

7. The strength of an earthquake

8. The regions of the earth's crust where most earthquake faults are found

9. Most earthquakes occur in this region

Explain.

10. How can the motions of the earth's plates cause earthquakes?

3.3 Volcanoes

A volcano is born

On February 20, 1943, a Mexican farmer was working in one of his fields when a large crack opened in the ground before him. Steam and smoke hissed from the crack, accompanied by a loud roar like a jet engine. The crack rapidly grew larger until it was twice as long as a football field and 10–16 feet across. Frightened, the farmer hurried to the village with news of the strange sight.

Before long, loud explosions were heard, hurling red-hot melted rock high into the air. As night fell, the explosions continued, lighting up the sky with a brilliant red glow. By the end of the next day, the farmer's corn field was

Paricutín volcano, Mexico

covered by a mound of steaming black rock as tall as a 13-story building. Ashes, gases, and molten (melted) rock gushing out of the earth caused the cone to grow to a height of nearly 500 feet by the end of the week. The volcano continued to grow in the months to come, spreading ashes and molten rock toward the villages of Paricutín [pä·rē′kōō·tēn′] and San Juan [sän wŏn′]. By June, the homes of the villagers were in the path of the advancing lava and had to be evacuated. The volcano reached a height of 900 feet by the end of the year and continued to sputter for the next nine years, until ash and lava were spread over 100 square miles of land. At the height of the volcano's activity, it produced 16,000 tons of steam and 100,000 tons of lava (molten rock) each day.

As suddenly as it began, however, the eruption ceased in February 1952. From the ground to the rim of its crater, the new mountain measured 1345 feet in height.

The volcano is now called *Paricutín*, after one of the destroyed villages.

The structure of a volcano

Scientists think that volcanoes begin with huge "bubbles" of melted rock that form deep in the earth's hot mantle. Because melted rock, or **magma,** is lighter than solid rock, such a "bubble" squeezes upward through the solid mantle toward the earth's surface. If a weak spot exists in the earth's crust, the magma may squeeze its way upward through the crust and form a large reservoir, or **magma chamber,** a few miles beneath the surface.

There, because of its intense heat, the magma melts the nearby rock and causes underground water to turn into steam. The large volume of gases produced in this way greatly increases the pressure within the magma chamber. As a result, the mixture of magma and gases pushes mightily against the surrounding rock,

Structure of a volcano

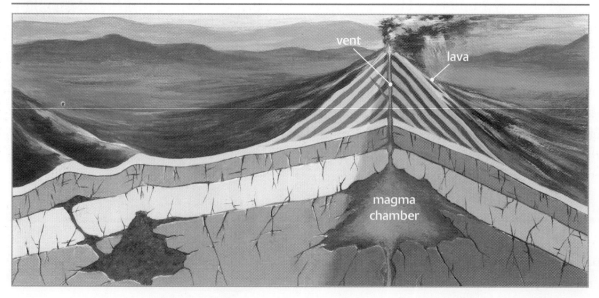

often causing it to bend or split apart. As pressure builds up inside the magma chamber, the magma may be forced higher through cracks in the rock, until finally the trapped gases blast an opening, or **vent,** through the earth's surface. This vent, which releases the pressure within the magma chamber, is what we call a **volcano.** Therefore, *a volcano is a vent that allows molten rock and hot gases to escape from within the earth.* Although the vent and cone are the most prominent features of a volcano to an observer, the underground magma chamber is the actual source of the eruption; the vent merely represents a "weak spot" in the earth's crust through which the magma or trapped gases can break through to the surface.

After reaching the earth's surface, molten rock is called **lava.** Since lava quickly cools and hardens, it collects around the mouth of the volcano. By the time the pressure in the underground magma chamber has subsided, the hardened lava left by the eruption may form a large mountain.

Major locations of volcanoes

Like earthquakes, volcanoes tend to occur in narrow belts that lie along boundaries between the plates of the earth's crust. More than a fourth of the world's active volcanoes are found in a volcanic belt that encircles the edge of the Pacific Ocean. This belt, which corresponds to the Circum-Pacific earthquake belt, is often called the **Ring of Fire.** Other belts of volcanoes are found along plate boundaries in southern Europe, the Caribbean, and southeast Asia.

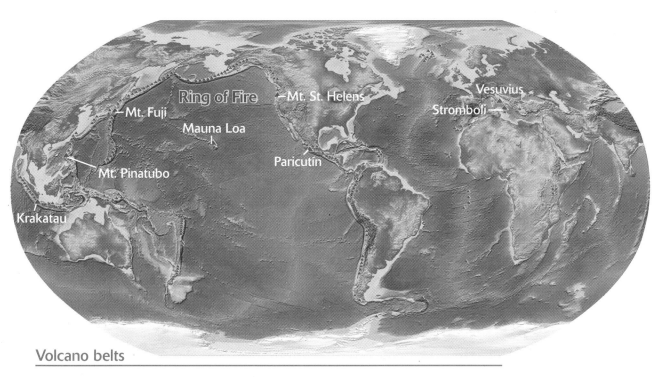

Volcano belts

Volcanoes are especially common where one plate of the earth's crust is being forced beneath the edge of another. As the weaker plate is forced downward into the hot mantle, it carries waterlogged sediments with it. These sediments quickly melt, forming "bubbles" of hot rock that may rise to the surface and form volcanoes. Mount St. Helens (p. 192), which erupted violently in 1980, is an example of such a volcano.

A few volcanoes, such as those of Hawaii, are located in the middle of crustal plates instead of at their edges. Scientists think that these volcanoes result from hot plumes of magma rising through the mantle that melt through the crust like a blowtorch, allowing the magma to more easily reach the surface. For this reason, these volcanoes are often called "hot-spot" volcanoes.

fumarole on Mt. Rainier, Washington

Fuming fumaroles

In some places where volcanoes are presently active or have been active in the past, the surface may be perforated by holes or cracks serving as escape vents for underground gases. Geologists call these vents **fumaroles** [fyo͞o′mə·rōlz]. Although some fumaroles emit harmful gases, they sometimes also enrich the soil with their vapors.

Fumaroles may continue to emit gases long after other volcanic activity has ceased. For example, most of Yellowstone National Park appears to be the remnants of a gigantic volcano. Although the ash and lava eruptions at Yellowstone must have ceased thousands of years ago, countless fumaroles and hot springs continue to dot the landscape.

Lava and tephra

When magma reaches the surface and is ejected from the volcano, it may take many different forms. If the magma is thin and runny, it may remain a liquid and flow down the sides of the volcano as molten *lava* before cooling and hardening into rock. If the magma is thick and pasty, on the other hand, trapped gases may cause it to explode into pieces as it leaves the volcano. Under these conditions, the lava fragments may solidify almost instantly into fragments of rock, called **tephra** [tĕf′rə].

Different sizes of tephra have been given different names. The smallest fragments are called **volcanic ash** and resemble dust or fine sand. Fragments more than $2\frac{1}{2}$ inches across are called **volcanic bombs** and **volcanic blocks.** The largest of these may measure several feet across! Fragments that are smaller than bombs and blocks, but larger than volcanic ash are called **lapilli** [lə·pĭl′ī: "little stones"].

volcanic ash

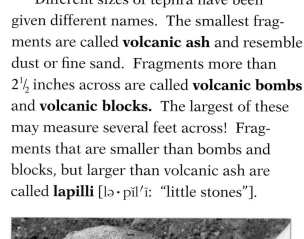
volcanic bomb

lapilli

EYE witness reporter

Making a volcano

You can see why volcanoes erupt by using *a clean pin* and *a small, half-empty tube of toothpaste*. Get permission before doing this experiment. With the pin, make a small hole near the top of the tube of toothpaste near the cap. Place the capped tube of toothpaste on the table and press as hard as you can on the bottom of the tube. What happens? In a similar fashion, liquid rock (magma) trapped under great pressure within the earth's crust will erupt from the surface.

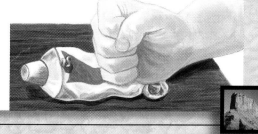

Comprehension Check 3.3

Clues. Give the word or term that best fits each clue.

1. A vent that allows molten rock and hot gases to escape from within the earth

2. Name given to melted rock while it is still underground

3. A reservoir of magma a few miles beneath the surface that may give rise to a volcano

4. Name given to melted rock that has reached the earth's surface

5. The belt of volcanoes that encircles the Pacific Ocean

6. Holes or cracks serving as escape vents for underground gases

7. Volcanic ash, lapilli, and volcanic bombs are examples of these rock fragments

Explain.

8. Some hikers on Mount Rainier were caught in a sudden blizzard, but they survived because of the fumaroles on the mountain. Why?

3.4 Classification of Volcanoes

At present, hundreds of volcanoes sputter and growl on the earth. Many more remain quiet, some never to erupt again, while others wait silently for the right moment to explode. Volcanoes also come in all shapes and sizes. Some consist of cones of loose rock a few hundred feet high, while others are giant mounds of solidified lava many miles across. Some volcanoes produce gentle flows of lava almost continuously, while others lie silent for hundreds or thousands of years before exploding with extreme violence.

Geologists classify volcanoes according to how they are formed, their level of activity, and the kind of eruption that they produce.

By how they are formed

Volcanoes can be divided into several cagetories based on how they are formed. Three common types of volcanoes are *cinder cone volcanoes, shield volcanoes,* and *composite volcanoes.*

Shield volcanoes. A **shield volcano** forms when large amounts of fluid, runny lava gradually build up a dome-shaped mountain. A typical shield volcano has a large **crater,** or depression, at its top. Lava erupts from fissures at the base of the mountain as well as from the vent at the top of the dome. If the mountain becomes too high for the lava to erupt from the crater, all eruptions come from

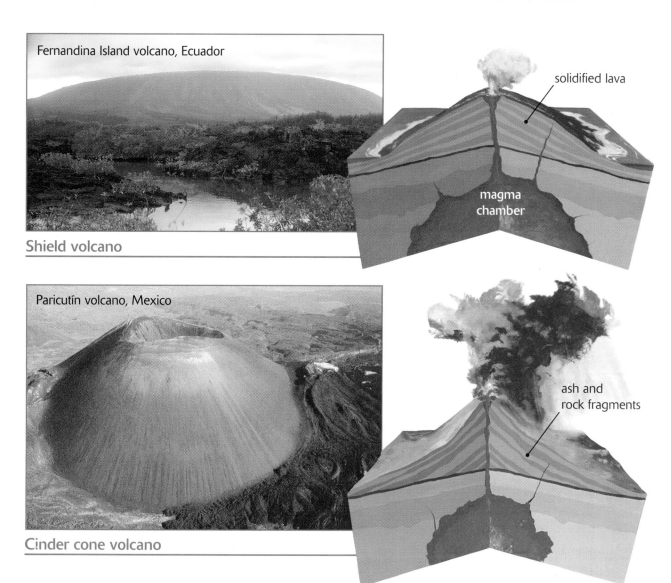

Fernandina Island volcano, Ecuador

Shield volcano

solidified lava

magma chamber

Paricutín volcano, Mexico

Cinder cone volcano

ash and rock fragments

fissures. From then on, the volcano no longer increases in height, but continues to broaden in diameter. If several shield volcanoes form in one area, their lava flows may join together to build a single huge mountain. The Hawaiian Islands are shield volcanoes.

Cinder cone volcanoes. A **cinder cone volcano** is formed by eruptions composed mostly of tephra, or small fragments of solidified lava (section 3.3). Eruptions of these volcanic solids build up cone-shaped mountains. Because cinder cone volcanoes are composed of loose materials, they do not grow as large as other volcanoes and are eroded away rather quickly. Most cinder cones are formed by a single eruption. Cinder cones usually occur in groups, but sometimes occur individually. One famous example of an individual cinder cone is the Paricutín volcano in Mexico, which grew from a flat corn field into a cinder cone more than 1300 feet high in only nine years. Sunset Crater in Arizona is a cinder cone volcano formed by an eruption in A.D. 1064 or 1065.

Mt. Mayon volcano, Philippines

solidified lava

ash and rock fragments

Composite volcano

Composite volcanoes. Some volcanoes produce both cinders and lava, creating a cone that has characteristics of both cinder cone and shield volcanoes. Such volcanoes, called **composite volcanoes,** form when alternating layers of fluid lava and tephra build up a steep, symmetrical mountain, perhaps with a small crater at the top. Mount Rainier and Mount St. Helens in the state of Washington, Mount Fuji in Japan, and Mount Vesuvius in Italy are good examples of composite volcanoes.

Calderas. If the magma chamber of a volcano is close to the surface, the empty chamber may "cave in" after the eruption is over, causing the ground to sink and forming a huge, bowl-shaped depression at the surface. Such depressions, called **calderas** [käl·dā′räz], may be later filled with rainwater to form large lakes. One of the most beautiful calderas in the United States is Crater Lake, formed by an eruption of Mount Mazama in Oregon thousands of years ago. The caldera later became filled with water, forming a lake 6 miles across and nearly 2000 feet deep.

Crater Lake

Volcanoes may also be classified by their activity. An **active** volcano is one that has erupted recently or is considered likely to erupt in the near future. Stromboli [strŏm′bō·lē] and Etna in Italy, Kilauea [kē′lou·ā′ə] in Hawaii, and Pinatubo [pē′nä-too′bō] in the Philippines are some famous active volcanoes. Mount St. Helens in the state of Washington has been considered an active volcano since its eruption in 1980.

active volcano (Mt. Etna)

A volcano which erupted many years ago and is now inactive, but which may erupt again, is classed as a **dormant volcano.** Paricutín in Mexico, Lassen Peak in California, and Mount Rainier in Washington are considered dormant volcanoes. A dormant volcano may become active again. Mount St. Helens was once considered a dormant volcano because it had not erupted since 1857. It became active again in 1980, however, and has erupted several times since.

dormant volcano (Mt. Rainier)

extinct volcano (Kilimanjaro)

Volcanoes that have not erupted in recorded history or are unlikely to ever erupt again are called **extinct** volcanoes. Mount Kilimanjaro in Africa is an extinct volcano. However, volcanoes can be extremely unpredictable, and it is sometimes difficult to determine whether a volcano is truly extinct or just dormant.

By kind of eruption

Not all volcanoes erupt in the same way. Some volcanoes produce lava flows so gentle that tourists and other sightseers can safely approach the vent, while others explode with such fury that the countryside is laid waste for miles around. Some volcanoes produce mostly liquid lava, while others produce mostly ash and other tephra. Some eruptions last for years, while others last for only a few days.

Geologists may classify a volcano by the kind of eruption that it produces. Many of these eruption types are named after a famous volcano that is noted for a particular style of eruption. Three common types of eruption are *Hawaiian eruptions,* Strombolian [strŏm·bō′lē·ăn] *eruptions,* and *Plinian* [plĭn′ē·ăn] *eruptions.*

Hawaiian eruption (Mauna Ulu)

Hawaiian eruptions. In a **Hawaiian eruption,** the volcano produces a large amount of fluid lava that surges from the volcano's vent like water from a fountain. If the lava gushes from a narrow conduit, it may shoot dozens of yards into the air, forming a vertical geyser of lava called a *lava fountain.* If the lava erupts from a long crack or fissure instead, it may produce a sheetlike fountain of glowing lava called a *fire curtain.* More commonly, the lava pools within the vent to form a "lake" of lava; if the lava overflows the sides of the vent, it will flow downhill until it cools and solidifies. Lava from Hawaii's Kilauea volcano sometimes flows all the way to the ocean, where it produces large clouds of steam as it enters the water.

Hawaiian eruption at night

Strombolian eruption (Mt. Stromboli)

Strombolian eruptions. Strombolian eruptions are named after a very active volcano in Italy called Mount Stromboli. Often called the "Lighthouse of the Mediterranean," Mount Stromboli erupts an average of once every 20 minutes. Its eruptions are noisy but usually quite mild. As gas bubbles up from the magma in the volcano's crater, globs of lava are flung into the air, where they harden into volcanic bombs. Occasionally, a more intense eruption causes lava to ooze down the side of the cone.

Plinian eruptions. Most **Plinian eruptions** come from volcanoes that have lain dormant for a long period of time. In a Plinian eruption, the volcano expels hot clouds of gas and dust high into the atmosphere, forming ash clouds that may travel completely around the world.

Plinian eruptions are usually quite violent. Even the moderate-sized Plinian eruption of

Mt. Stromboli erupting at night

Mount St. Helens in 1980 was 500 times more powerful than an atomic bomb; trees as far as 15 miles from the volcano were ripped from the earth, stripped of bark and branches, and tossed burning on the ash-covered ground. The 1883 explosion of the Indonesian island of *Krakatau* [krä′kə·tou′], also called Krakatoa, was 20 times more powerful than Mount St. Helens. The explosion was so loud that it was heard by people 2900 miles away, and houses 80 miles from the volcano had their windows shattered. Tsunamis (giant waves) produced by this eruption killed 36,000 people in the surrounding islands.

Plinian eruption (Mount St. Helens)

Comprehension Check 3.4

Clues. Give the word or term that best fits each clue.

1. Dome-shaped volcanoes formed by eruptions of fluid, runny lava

2. A depression at the top of a volcano

3. Relatively small, cone-shaped volcanoes formed mostly of tephra and quickly eroded

4. Steep-sided volcanoes formed by alternating layers of fluid lava and tephra

5. A large, bowl-shaped depression formed when an underground magma chamber caves in

Explain.

6. What is the difference between a dormant volcano and an extinct volcano?

7. Describe each of the following kinds of eruptions: Hawaiian, Strombolian, Plinian.

Swiss Alps

3.5 Fiery Rocks

Rocks: Earth's building blocks

Rock is the hard material that composes the earth's crust. God designed rocks to be the building blocks for our planet. With some rocks, He formed continents and islands of dry land, while others He made to crumble and wear away to provide nourishment for plants and animals. He crafted some rocks into beautiful landscape formations; in others He hid great stores of materials that could be used for man's benefit. Some rocks provide us with metals, building materials, and other useful substances. Other minerals, known for their beauty, are crafted into dazzling gemstones, jewelry, and works of art.

God created many of the earth's rocks when He created the earth, although the worldwide Flood of Noah must have worn away many of these rocks and formed new ones. Rocks are still being formed by natural processes today.

Types of rocks. Rocks come in all sizes, shapes, and colors. They may be smooth or rough, hard or soft, coarse-grained or fine-grained, extremely dense or light enough to float in water. Despite their great variety, rocks can be classified into three broad categories based upon how they appear to have been formed: *igneous* [ĭg′nē·əs] *rocks, sedimentary* [sĕd′ə·mĕn′tə·rē] *rocks,* and *metamorphic* [mĕt′ə·môr′fĭk] rocks.

All rocks are a mixture of many different substances. *The individual substances that make up rocks* are called **minerals.** A rock may be a mixture of just two or three minerals, or it may contain dozens of different minerals.

Composition
of granite

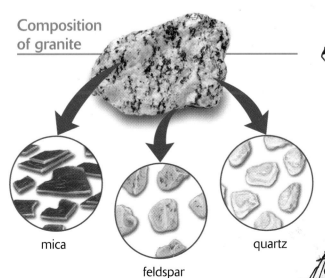

mica

feldspar

quartz

Igneous rocks: the "fiery ones"

You will recall that huge "bubbles" of hot, fluid rock, or *magma*, form deep in the earth's mantle and squeeze toward the surface. Occasionally, magma forces its way through the earth's crust by erupting out of a volcano. Once the magma flows from the volcano, it is called *lava*. As the lava cools, it eventually hardens into solid rock. Magma can also cool and harden into rock before it ever reaches the surface. *Rock that forms when molten rock solidifies*—whether above or below ground—is called **igneous rock.**

Igneous rock can be divided into two categories, depending on where the molten rock hardens into solid rock. Igneous rock formed at the earth's surface is called **extrusive igneous rock.** (*Extrusive* means "forced out"; most extrusive igneous rocks form when magma is forced out of a volcano.)

At other times, magma forces its way through the lower parts of the crust but does not reach the earth's surface. Instead, the

pumice

obsidian

magma remains in pockets below the surface and slowly cools and hardens while still underground, forming what is called **intrusive igneous rock.** (*Intrusive* means "forced into or between.")

Properties of extrusive rocks. Although all igneous rocks come from magma, they have different textures, based on how fast the original magma solidified. If a rock cools very quickly, the minerals in the magma solidify all at once without separating, giving the rock a smooth texture. Because molten rock cools quickly once it reaches the surface, extrusive rocks have a ***fine-grained appearance.*** One example is **obsidian** [ŏb·sĭd′ē·ən], a shiny black rock that resembles glass. **Pumice** [pŭm′ĭs] is not as smooth as obsidian because it is made from gas-filled lava. As the lava cools, the escaping gas leaves behind hollow spaces in the hardening rock, making the rock foamlike in appearance. The air trapped in pumice makes it light enough to float on water. A third type of extrusive igneous rock, **basalt** [bə·sôlt′], is formed from thin, runny lava and often solidifies in vast mounds or sheets. The Hawaiian Islands are formed from basalt. If basalt cools too rapidly, it may crack in a geometric

basalt

Giant's Causeway (basalt)

a result, the completely solidified rock contains crystals of many different kinds, giving it a speckled texture. If you look closely at an intrusive igneous rock, you should be able to see the individual mineral crystals. Because intrusive rocks are produced by slowly cooling magma, the mineral crystals have a long time to form and can grow quite large, giving intrusive rocks a ***coarse-grained appearance.***

A common intrusive rock is **granite,** a strong, light-colored rock that contains at least three different kinds of mineral crystals: glasslike *quartz,* dull white, gray, or pink *feldspar,* and black, shiny *mica.* Although much granite lies deep within the earth, some can be seen on the earth's surface. Because granite withstands weathering well, many monuments and famous buildings are made of granite. Granite is the most common igneous rock and can be found almost everywhere on land.

pattern, forming great columns. One of God's basalt masterpieces is the Giant's Causeway in Northern Ireland.

Properties of intrusive rocks. Like any other form of rock, magma is made of a mixture of different substances. When magma cools quickly, all of the individual minerals in the mixture harden at about the same time, giving the rock a fine texture. However, when magma cools very slowly, some minerals have a chance to harden before others do, forming solid crystals within the magma. As the temperature slowly drops, one mineral solidifies, then another, until finally all the minerals have solidified into solid crystals. As

granite

mica

feldspar

quartz

Half Dome (granite), Yosemite National Park

EYE witness reporter

Comparing magma fudge

You can get an idea of how magma cools to form different rock textures by making some old-fashioned fudge at home. Your mother or another adult will need to help you with this demonstration. The ingredients you will need are *2 cups of sugar*, *¾ cup of milk*, *2 squares of chocolate*, *2 tablespoons of light corn syrup*, and *two tablespoons of butter*. You will also need *a saucepan, a cake pan, a bowl, a spoon, a glass of water*, and *a burner*.

Turn the burner on to medium heat and pour the sugar, milk, chocolate, and corn syrup into the saucepan. Place the saucepan on the burner and gently stir the ingredients until the chocolate melts and the sauce begins to boil. This is your "magma." For the next four or five minutes, watch the "magma" as it boils. Do the bubbles remind you of a type of bubbly magma that becomes pumice? After about five minutes, take a spoonful of the "magma" and drop some of it into the glass of water. If the mixture seems to form a soft ball in the water, you are ready for your demonstration. If the mixture spreads throughout the water, wait a minute or two and try again.

Once the mixture forms a soft ball in the water, remove the saucepan from the hot burner. Gently stir the two tablespoons of butter into the hot chocolate "magma." Pour half of the "magma" into the cake pan and leave it alone until it hardens. Pour the other half into a bowl, quickly stirring it with the spoon until it becomes thick. Place the bowl of thickened "magma" in the refrigerator to cool.

Now compare the two types of hardened "magma," or fudge. Which type would be like intrusive igneous rock? Which type is more like extrusive igneous rock? Cut the "rocks" into squares so you, your teacher, and your classmates can enjoy them. Be sure not to eat too many. Although fudge is much more edible than real igneous rocks, you can still become ill if you try to eat the entire batch!

Comprehension Check 3.5

Clues. Give the word or term that best fits each clue.

1. The three broad categories of rock

2. The individual substances that make up rocks

3. Rocks formed when molten magma or lava solidifies

4. A well-known igneous rock that contains quartz, feldspar, and mica

5. List the differences between extrusive and intrusive igneous rocks. Give an example of each.

3.6 Layered Rocks and Changed Rocks

 Sedimentary rocks: the "layered ones"

You will recall from section 3.1 that most of the earth's crust is covered by a layer of sand and mineral fragments, or *sediments*. In many places, heat and pressure have compacted these sediments into solid rock. *Rock that is formed from sediments that have been pressed together into solid rock* is called **sedimentary rock.**

You may have visited the Grand Canyon in Arizona or the Badlands in South Dakota. Or perhaps you have viewed the Appalachian mountains in the

Badlands, South Dakota

eastern part of the United States or the Rockies in the west. You might have even seen such landmarks as Table Mountain in South Africa, the White Cliffs of Dover in England, or the Blue Mountains in Australia. These famous rock formations are all examples of sedimentary rock.

Over 75% of the earth's surface is covered with sedimentary rock. You can recognize sedimentary rocks by the horizontal lines marking the boundaries between layers of hardened sediment. Sedimentary rocks are formed from three different kinds of sediments: mechanical sediments, chemical sediments, and organic sediments.

Mechanical sediments. You recall that some rocks are broken down as a result of physical weathering—that is, as a result of their exposure to water, wind, or ice. The resulting sand, clay, or rock fragments may then be carried elsewhere by heavy rains, flooding, or strong winds and deposited in a thick layer elsewhere. The sediments that result are called **mechanical sediments** because they were physically carried away by the "mechanisms" of nature. These sediments may later be pressed together to form sedimentary rock. *Sandstone, shale, conglomerates* [kən′glŏm′ər·ĭts], and *breccia* [brĕch′ē·ə] are examples of rocks formed from mechanical sediments.

Sandstone, a rough, crumbly rock which consists of particles of quartz sand that have been fused together into rock, is sometimes used for making glass. In the past, sandstone was also a popular building material; the outer walls of many old buildings are made of sandstone. **Shale** is formed from mud or clay that consists of much smaller particles than sand, and is often found in layers of sandstone or limestone. It can easily be broken and ground up for use in making bricks.

sandstone

sandstone building

shale

conglomerate

breccia

Conglomerate rock and *breccia* both consist of pebbles embedded in hardened sand or clay. Conglomerate rock has rounded pebbles, while breccia has pebbles with sharp edges. Like sandstone, conglomerate rock was once popular in constructing the outer walls of buildings.

Chemical sediments. When water seeps through rocks, some minerals in the rocks may be dissolved by the water and carried elsewhere. These minerals may later crystallize or settle out of the solution, forming **chemical sediments.** One type of rock formed by chemical sediments is the crystal **halite,** or rock salt. Halite is mined and refined to be used in making chemicals, tanning leather, salting roads in the winter, and—of course— flavoring food! **Gypsum** [jĭp'səm], another rock formed by chemical sediments, is used in construction materials such as plaster of Paris and plasterboard.

gypsum

salt mine

halite (rock salt)

Organic sediments. Other sedimentary rocks are made from **organic sediments,** consisting of dead plants, shells, or animal skeletons. Most rocks made from organic sediments are types of **limestone. Chalk** is the cemented skeletons of microscopic sea animals. It is a soft white rock formerly used in the classroom to write on chalkboards. (Most classroom chalk today is manmade.) Discarded shells from snails, nautiluses, and other gastropods fuse together to form *shelly limestone.* The shells or their imprints are often preserved in the limestone rock. Any trace left in rock by a plant or animal is known as a **fossil.** *Reef limestone,* of which coral reefs are made, is the only stone formed by living animals. Do you remember what animals make coral reefs? Reef limestone has been discovered in the Canadian Rockies, the Guadalupe [gwŏd′ə·lōō′pā] Mountains of New Mexico, and the Alps in Europe.

shelly limestone

Shelly limestone also exists in mountains or plains far away from the ocean; much of this was probably laid down during the Flood of Noah. Miners extracting minerals from such deposits find many fossils. Fossils form when plants and animals are quickly buried by sediments that later turn into rock.

coal

Coal is a very useful material commonly found in sedimentary rock. It comes from decayed plants and is mined throughout the world for heating and industrial purposes.

chalk

White Cliffs of Dover (chalk)

1. Flood-formed fossils

Many fossils of sea animals have been discovered in layers of limestone found in mountain or desert regions far from any water. How did the fossils get there? Vast numbers of fossils were formed during the worldwide Flood described in Genesis chapter six. The raging waters that destroyed every living creature deposited fish, sea snails, and other creatures on the existing sea floor. These creatures were then covered by layers of sediment. The sediment turned into limestone after the waters subsided. Later, the sea floor was uplifted to form limestone mountains. To understand how limestone and fossils could be formed by a flood you will need *a quart jar and cover, sand, soil, pebbles, water, a pencil eraser,* and *a spoon.*

Put four tablespoons each of sand, soil, and pebbles into the quart jar. Place the eraser on top of the pile of dirt. The eraser represents a plant or animal. Fill the jar with water, screw the lid in place, and shake the jar vigorously. This action will create floodlike conditions within the jar. Place the jar on the table and observe what happens as the water becomes calm again. The pebbles settle to the bottom immediately. Sand and large particles of

soil settle next, and finally fine soil particles settle on top. Notice the distinct layers of materials. Which layer do you think contains the eraser? What kept it from settling on top? Do you see how the Flood could have buried dead sea creatures within the layers of sediment? The remains of these creatures would have become fossils.

2. Creating salt crystals

Minerals dissolved in water will collect and form solid crystals if the water is evaporated. This process is involved in the formation of rock salt, which geologists call *halite.* To see how rock salt is formed, you will need *a clear glass, a spoon, a pencil, a paper clip, a piece of string, salt,* and *some hot water.* Pour hot water into the glass until it is nearly full. Gradually dump a spoonful of plain table salt into the hot water. Stir the water as the salt dissolves. Add two more spoonfuls of salt and stir until all of the salt dissolves in the water. Fasten one end of the piece of string to the paper clip and tie the other end to the pencil. Drop the paper clip into the glass and lay the pencil across the top so that the string hangs in the salt water solution. The crystals will form on the string as

the water evaporates. Put the glass in a safe place, where it cannot be knocked over.

After two or three days, check to see if any crystals have begun to grow on the string. Study the string each day to watch the progress of the crystals. When the water has completely evaporated, you should see several salt crystals attached to the string. How are the salt crystals on the string different from the salt in the shaker?

How are they the same?

Metamorphic rocks: the "changed ones"

The change of a caterpillar to a butterfly or of a tadpole to a frog is called metamorphosis (meaning "to transform"). A similar term—**metamorphism**—is used to describe *the change of a rock into a new type of rock.* Such a change may be brought about by extreme heat or pressure. The rocks produced by metamorphism of igneous or sedimentary rocks are called **metamorphic rocks.**

Foliated rocks. Based on their appearance and texture, metamorphic rocks can be divided into two groups: *foliated rocks* (layered rocks) and *unfoliated rocks* (unlayered rocks). ***Foliated rocks are rocks made up of layers like the leaves of a book.*** One example of a foliated rock is **slate,** a weather-resistant, waterproof rock. Slate, which begins as shale, is very hard and smooth and splits into thin leaflike layers. In colonial and pioneer days, children used the smooth surface of a small piece of slate and some chalk instead of paper and pencil to do their schoolwork; the chalkboards in old schools were also made of slate. Slate tablets are still being used by school children in some countries today. You may also see slate-covered roofs on some older buildings.

Metamorphism

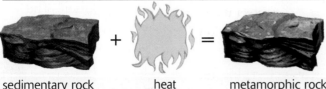

sedimentary rock   heat   metamorphic rock

slate

Unfoliated rocks. Many metamorphic rocks do not have a layered appearance and cannot be split into thin layers like slate and other foliated rocks. They are therefore called **unfoliated rocks.** Perhaps the most beautiful and most widely used unfoliated rock is **marble,** a rock that was once limestone but was hardened by extreme heat and pressure within the earth. Because it withstands weathering better than many other rocks, marble is often used to make statues and monuments. The finest deposits of marble are found in Italy, where the great artist Michelangelo carved his magnificent statues of David and Moses from large pieces of marble. Some marble statues still in existence today were made by ancient sculptors over 2500 years ago.

marble statue of Moses by Michelangelo

Earth Explorer

Rock hounding

You can begin a hobby that is interesting, inexpensive, and simple: rock collecting. To make your own rock museum, you will need *a notebook, a pencil, newspapers,* and *a field bag.* To classify and organize your collection, you will need *a field guide to rocks, a cardboard box* (an egg carton will also work well), *labels,* and *a glue that dries clear.*

You can find rocks near cliffs, outcroppings, and new road cuts as well as in rock pits. (Be sure to obtain permission from the property owner first!) Look for small, loose specimens that will be easy to display. Do not chip or pry specimens out of a cliff or rock formation unless you have explicit permission from the owner to do so. Wrap each specimen in old newspaper to protect it and mark the newspaper with an identification number. In your notebook, write the number and then note where and when you found the rock. Either in the field or once you get the rocks home, try to identify each rock you collect with the help of a field guide to rocks and minerals. Specimens of rare, beautiful, or hard-to-find rocks can also be purchased inexpensively from rock-collecting shops around the country. You may also have an opportunity to add to your collection when you go on vacation.

Some rock hounds (collectors) place their rocks in small display boxes. You can, if you prefer, display your rock specimens in an egg carton. If you wish, you can use clear-drying glue to secure each rock to the carton or box. Make a label for each rock, showing the type of rock, its identification number, and perhaps where and when you found the rock. You can spend many enjoyable hours adding to your rock museum.

Comprehension Check 3.6

Clues. Give the word or term that best fits each clue.

1. Rock formed from sediments that have been pressed together

2. A rough, crumbly rock sometimes used to make glass

3. Rock formed from mud or clay, often ground up and used to make bricks

4. Rock made of pebbles cemented together

5. Another name for rock salt

6. Soft, white rock formed from the cemented skeletons of microscopic sea animals

7. Any trace left in a rock by a plant or animal

8. An igneous or sedimentary rock that has been changed by extreme pressure or heat

9. A weather-resistant, waterproof rock formed by metamorphosis of shale

10. A beautiful rock that withstands weathering well and is commonly used for statues

British Crown Jewels

3.7 Hidden Treasures of the Earth: Gems and Metals

Hidden within igneous, sedimentary, and metamorphic rocks are deposits of minerals useful to man. When refined, these minerals are used to make a wide variety of products. Pots and pans made of copper, iron, or aluminum warm food on stove burners. Brilliant gems set in rings of gold or silver display great beauty. Coal, oil, and gas provide energy for factories and heat for homes. Cars, airplanes, plastics, cleaning solutions, toothpastes, many medicines, and concrete—all are made from mineral treasures taken from inside the earth.

Hidden gems

The beauty of God's creation is not limited to exotic animals, colorful plants, and majestic mountains and sunsets. Within the dull-colored rocks that cover the earth lie small deposits of igneous and metamorphic crystals called **gemstones.**

When cut and polished, these crystals gain a brilliance that can last for centuries. Because of their beauty, cut gemstones, or **gems,** have been used as symbols of wealth and power by rulers in almost every civilization.

Precious stones. The rarest, most durable and beautiful gems are considered **precious stones.** These gems have been prized throughout history for their hardness, their color, and the dazzling ways they reflect light.

The **diamond,** which is a hard, crystalline form of carbon, is *the hardest of all known minerals.* Thus a crystal of diamond cannot be scratched by any other material; it can be cut only by another diamond.

530-carat diamond in
British Royal Sceptre

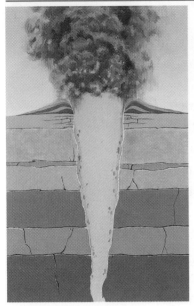

1. Diamond-bearing magma from upper mantle erupts through crust, forming volcano.

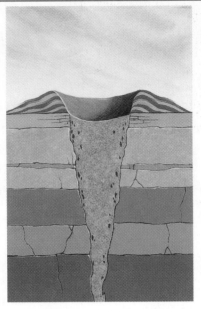

2. Eruption ceases; diamond-containing magma cools and solidifies.

3. Eroded volcano remnant is mined for diamonds.

Most diamonds used as gems are mined from mineral deposits in Brazil, India, and South Africa. These deposits are usually found in deep tubelike formations known as **diamond pipes** that appear to be the clogged vents of extinct volcanoes. Most diamonds shaped into gems are clear and colorless; your mother may have such a diamond on her wedding ring. Red, yellow, and blue diamonds are extremely rare and therefore even more valuable than colorless diamonds. Diamonds too small or with too many blemishes to be cut into gems are used in drills, saws, and surgical knives.

Although the common, opaque (not transparent) form of the mineral *corundum* [kə·rŭn′dəm], also called emery, is not particularly valuable, two colored forms of corundum are highly valued as precious stones. When pure corundum contains traces of the metal *chromium*, the resulting transparent red stone is called **ruby.** Some of the rarest and most valuable gemstones in the world are deep red rubies. Most of these rubies come from corundum deposits in the nation of Myanmar [män·mär′: formerly called Burma]. When corundum contains traces of *iron* or *titanium* [tī·tā′nē·əm] instead of chromium, it may have a blue, yellow, orange, or even purple color and is known as a **sapphire.** The most famous sapphires are bright blue. A bright blue sapphire is almost as rare as a deep red ruby.

ruby

sapphire

corundum

emerald

red spinel

turquoise

lapis lazuli

amethyst

tourmaline

Different forms of the mineral *beryl* are also prized as gems. The most famous form of beryl is the deep green **emerald**. The beautiful green color results from traces of chromium.

Semiprecious stones. Gems that are not as rare or as durable as precious stones are called **semiprecious stones.** These may be so beautiful that they are easily confused with more valuable stones. However, they are more easily scratched or chipped when placed in a ring or necklace. One semiprecious stone commonly confused with ruby is **red spinel** [spĭ·nĕl′]. One famous red spinel, known as the "Black Prince's Ruby," is the central stone in the British Imperial State Crown.

Other beautiful semiprecious stones include purple *amethyst*, green, yellow, or blue *zircon*, multi-colored *tourmaline* [to͝or′mə·lĭn], deep blue *lapis lazuli* [lăp′ĭs lăz′ə·lē], blue-green *turquoise*, milky gray *chalcedony* [kăl·sĕd′′n·ē], and green *jade*. The last four have been favorites of craftsmen who have used them throughout history to carve objects of lasting beauty.

Hidden metals

Among the many minerals found in rock are **metals** such as *gold, silver, copper, iron,* and *aluminum.* We use metals to make gold rings, silver platters, copper coins, brass fixtures, steel beams, and many other metal products.

Metals, in their natural state, are mixed with other minerals. Any rock containing a metal together with impurities is called an **ore.** Pure metal is obtained by mining an ore and then removing the impurities by heat or by chemical processes.

Precious metals. Like precious stones, **precious metals** are known for their durability, rarity, and beauty. The precious metal **gold** has been valued by man since earliest times (see Gen. 2:12). Gold is often mixed with other metals— such as silver, nickel, platinum, or

gold coin

gold nugget and bullion

Gold

copper—which increase its strength or alter its color. Although much refined gold is made into jewelry and other decorative items, most of it is formed into bars or coins and locked away as a financial investment. The desire for gold was a primary reason for exploration of the New World in the days of Columbus and Montezuma and for the sudden expansion of settlements in Alaska and California during the Gold Rush days.

gold coin from ancient Greece

Earth Explorer

Purifying metals in ancient times

Thousands of years ago, certain metals that exist in nature in a relatively pure form (such as gold and silver) were usually purified by a simple heating process. The impure metal was placed in an open container and heated until it melted, causing the lighter impurities to float to the top; the resulting layer of impurities was called *dross.* The impurities could then be simply scooped away, leaving the pure, white-hot metal behind which was then allowed to cool. This process is referred to several times in the Bible (Ps. 12:6; Prov. 17:3).

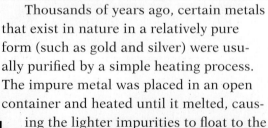

Although the precious metal **platinum** [plăt′ĭ·nəm] has been known since ancient times, it was only in the 1700s that it was discovered by Europeans. In recent years, platinum has become much more expensive than gold because of its rarity and its many uses. Platinum is used in fine jewelry; in making mechanical, electrical, and surgical tools; in refining oil; in reducing pollution from car exhausts; and as a financial investment. Most platinum comes from mines in South Africa, Russia, the United States, and Canada.

Silver, another precious metal, has been used for centuries to make jewelry, fancy trays, silverware, and other items that display its lustrous beauty. It is now mined primarily for industrial and technical applications. For example, it is an ingredient of photographic film. Because silver tarnishes and scratches easily, metalworkers often mix it with other metals for added durability. Like gold and platinum, silver is popular as an investment. Much of the world's silver has been molded into bullion and stored in vaults. Deposits of silver are often found in ores of zinc, lead, copper, or gold. Much silver is therefore mined as a byproduct of other metals. The most productive silver mines in the world are found in Mexico; these were started in the late 1500s and are still being worked today.

platinum coin

Platinum

car catalytic converter

clean air out

ceramic tubes coated with platinum

polluted exhaust in

Silver

silver tea set

camera film containing silver bromide

silver bars

silver coins

Practical metals. Not too many things around your house are made of precious metal. Although your family may have a few decorative items made of silver or trimmed with gold, it is very unlikely that you would barbecue hamburgers on a platinum grill, ride a bicycle made of silver, or eat with a solid gold fork! Other metals are much more practical for daily use.

One very practical metal, **iron,** has been fashioned into weapons and tools for thousands of years. Because it is strong and abundantly available, iron is *the most commonly used metal.* Some of these products are made of *cast iron,* as in the heavy skillet your grandmother may have used to cook eggs and bacon. Cast iron is also used for such items as manhole covers, sewer grates, and truck engines. However, most iron products are in the form of **steel,** an alloy [ăl′oi′: mixture of metals] of iron and carbon. A rust-resistant type of steel called *stainless steel* is an alloy of iron, chromium, and nickel. One easy way to learn which products in your home contain iron is to touch them with a magnet. A magnet sticks tightly to most metals that contain iron.

Iron

iron mine in Minnesota

steel locomotive

stainless steel

cast iron skillet

Iron ore can be found throughout the world in sedimentary rock. However, most iron comes from large deposits in China, Brazil, Australia, India, Russia, and the United States.

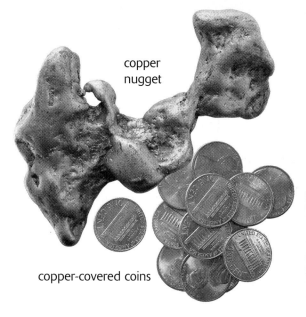

copper
nugget

copper-covered coins

aluminum-bodied car

aluminum
foil

aluminum
flashlight

aluminum
can

Copper, the reddish-orange metal that covers a penny, is a good conductor of electricity and is easy to shape into thin strands. It is commonly used for electrical wiring in homes. Some household water pipes are also made of copper. Most copper used worldwide comes from deposits in Chile and the United States; Indonesia, Australia, and Canada are also major producers. Two alloys containing copper are **brass** (made from copper and zinc) and **bronze** (made from copper and tin).

An important substitute for steel and copper is a silver-colored metal known as **aluminum.** Its light weight and strength make aluminum an excellent metal for airplanes, car and truck wheels, and high-voltage power lines. It is also used to make kitchen foil and soda cans. An ingredient of a common sedimentary rock called *bauxite* [bôk′sīt], aluminum is the most widespread of all metals in the earth's crust. The largest producer of aluminum ore is Australia.

Other important metals include *nickel,* an ingredient in stainless steel and rechargeable batteries; *zinc,* used to make batteries and to protect steel from rusting; and *uranium,* used as a fuel for nuclear power plants, naval ships, and submarines.

brass
coin

bronze
statue from
ancient Italy

Science & GREAT CHRISTIANS

Martin Luther
(1483–1546)

Martin Luther, the great German reformer, was born nine years before Columbus discovered America. From his parents, Martin learned the virtues of hard work, honesty, and thrift. Martin's father had left the family farm to make a living as a miner. By working hard and saving his money, he became the owner and operator of several copper mines. Martin grew up under the shadow of dark, wooded cliffs that were crowned by a great castle and pierced by mine shafts—symbols of the waning Middle Ages and of the new world of science and industry that was about to begin.

It was a time of deep spiritual darkness. Without the light of an open Bible in the language of the people, peasants and princes alike lived in superstitious fear of the unknown. They believed the forests to be populated by witches, hobgoblins, elves, fairies, sprites, trolls, and evil spirits of all sorts. Many people believed such false "sciences" as alchemy (the belief that ordinary metals could magically be changed into precious metals) and astrology (the belief that the position of the stars and planets at the time of one's birth determined a person's destiny). Magicians and fortunetellers deceived many people with their crafts of trickery. But worst of all, the people suffered in the bondage of a religious system that portrayed God as a distant Judge Who stood ready to condemn people to hell and who could only be approached through priests and sacraments said in a language understood by few of the common people.

In this dark world, Martin Luther spent his childhood. He grew up rightly believing that heaven was as real as the sky above him and hell as real as the earth beneath his feet. Yet Martin, like most people of his time, did not know the Lord as his Savior. After spending years as a Roman Catholic monk, he finally came to a saving faith in Christ through an intense personal study of the Bible. When God opened up the Bible to Martin Luther, He also opened up the book of nature for him. Although Martin had always been a keen observer of the wonders of God's creation, he began to see his Lord and Savior in every particle of creation and encouraged others to do likewise. Luther declared: "All creation is the most beautiful book or Bible; in it God has described and portrayed Himself."

Luther and his followers, the Protestants, began to encourage a new interest in the study of science. Luther wrote: "We now look deeper into creation than we did under the papacy. Before they did not care to know how a child grows in the mother's womb. We are beginning, however, to recognize the wonders of God in a little flower. They used to pass it by, looking at nature with the interest of a cow." Luther used images and examples from nature in all of his preaching and teaching. He believed that Christians should explore the natural world to learn more about God and to discover the secrets hidden there by God for man's benefit.

Luther had no use for astrology because he knew from God's Word (see Ps. 31:14–15) that his future was in his Savior's hands. He also rejected alchemy, commenting on one occasion when a ruler was cheated by an alchemist: "The princes deserve to be cheated because they think that a creature can be changed by human lies to something different from what it was created to be."

Intrigued by the mystery of light, Luther had an idea about the nature of light that was strikingly similar to that of modern physicists. But Luther's greatest contribution to science was his translation of the Bible into the language of the people and his other activities that helped dispel the spiritual and intellectual darkness of the time. He compared God's Word to a fiery shield made of a metal that is "purer than gold, which, tried in the fire, loses none of its substance, but resists and overcomes all the fury of the fiery heat. He that believes God's Word overcomes all, and remains secure everlastingly, against all misfortunes; for this shield fears nothing, neither hell nor the devil."

Martin Luther

Comprehension Check 37

Clues. Give the word or term that best fits each clue.

1. The rarest, most durable and beautiful gems

2. The gemstone that is the hardest of all known minerals

3. Metals such as gold, silver, and platinum that are known for their durability, rarity, and beauty

4. Any rock containing a metal together with impurities

5. The most commonly used metal

6. A reddish-orange metal that is a good conductor of electricity

3.8 Hidden Treasures of the Earth: Important Fuels

What do laundry soaps, plastic bowls, nylon jackets, car tires, wax candles, and sweet-smelling perfumes have in common? They are all made from two valuable materials hidden within the earth: coal and petroleum. These are commonly burned as **fuels** to run machines, heat homes, and cook foods. But they are also important ingredients in thousands of other products we use every day.

Coal: the fossil fuel

You read in section 3.4 that coal is formed from decayed plant matter and is commonly found in sedimentary rock. If you were to place a thin section of coal under a microscope, you might see dead algae, grains of pollen, and other tiny remains of plants. All these remains would be considered fossils. Miners often find within coal even bigger fossils such as imprints of entire leaves. Because coal is derived from the fossilized remains of plants, it is called a **fossil fuel.** Coal is especially useful as a fuel for generating electricity; it is also used as a

fuel in many types of factories. Over half the electricity produced in the United States is produced by coal-burning power plants.

A variety of coals. Not all coal is the same. Some coal is soft, dark brown, and crumbly, while other coal is pure black and very hard. The four major types of coal are *anthracite* [ăn′thrə·sīt′] *coal,* or "hard coal"; *bituminous* [bī·too′mə·nəs] *coal,* or "soft coal"; *sub-bituminous coal;* and *lignite coal,* also called "brown coal."

coal-burning power plant

Hard coal is another name for **anthracite,** a hard, shiny, black coal. Because it burns slowly, cleanly, and with a hot flame, anthracite was once the preferred heating fuel for many homes. It is the most expensive coal to mine, not only because it is the least common type of coal, but also because it is generally located deeper in the earth than other types.

anthracite coal

Bituminous coal, *the most common type of coal,* is often called **soft coal.** This black, shiny coal is most widely used by industry and is the major fuel used to produce electricity in power plants. Four features of bituminous coal make it attractive as an industrial fuel: it is plentiful, easily mined, relatively inexpensive, and produces high temperatures when burned. Soft coal contains *bitumen,* a tarlike substance that, when removed from the coal and refined, is called **coal tar.** Coal tar is used to make plastics, detergents, perfumes, and many other important products.

bituminous coal

Sub-bituminous coal, the second most common type of coal, is softer and more crumbly than bituminous coal. It is widely used for generating electricity. Large deposits of sub-bituminous coal are found in Wyoming, Montana, and other Western states.

sub-bituminous coal

Of the four types of coal, **lignite coal** or "brown coal" is the poorest in quality. Ordinarily, lignite gives off an offensive odor and large amounts of black, sooty smoke when burned. However, modern pollution-control technology has made it possible to burn lignite very cleanly in power plants to produce electricity.

lignite coal

overburden

coal bed

surface coal mine

A variety of coal mines. Coal is found in horizontal layers called *beds* or *seams*. These coal beds are usually buried beneath other sedimentary rock, such as sandstone or shale. The first coal mines were dug by men using picks and shovels; the coal was hauled out of the mine using carts pulled by people or draft animals. Later, to speed up the process of extracting buried coal, miners used explosives to break it into chunks. In modern mines, huge digging machines have replaced picks and shovels, and conveyor belts have replaced animal carts. Modern mining methods have made coal mining much safer and more productive.

Not all coal is extracted from the earth in the same way. Coal beds lie in different situations—some near the surface of flat land, others deep within hills and mountains. In order to extract coal from different locations, engineers have developed various types of mines. The situation determines what kind of mine is dug.

If a coal bed is located within 150 feet or so of the surface, the coal can be removed by **surface mining.** Large earthmoving machines strip away layers of rocks and soil, called **overburden,** to expose the coal. Huge excavators then load the coal onto conveyor belts or large trucks, which carry it to a processing plant where the coal is crushed and cleaned. After being processed, the coal is loaded aboard trains, ships, or barges and transported to power plants and other coal users. Nearly two thirds of all U.S. coal is produced by surface mining. After the coal is removed, the overburden is replaced and the land is restored as closely as possible to its original condition.

If a coal bed is located more than 150 feet or so beneath the surface, removing the overburden would be too expensive to allow surface mining. Instead, the coal is removed by **underground mining.** Large vertical tunnels, or *shafts,* are dug downward through the ground to the coal bed. Miners then use heavy equipment to dig out the coal and transport it to the surface.

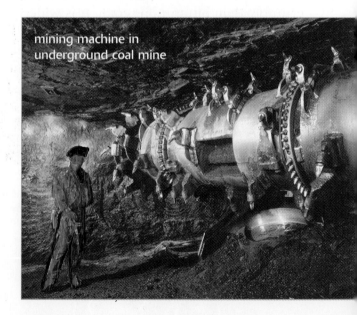

mining machine in underground coal mine

EYEwitness reporter

How were coal and petroleum formed?

Coal and petroleum are useful fuels that appear to have been formed from dead plants and animals, probably during or shortly after the worldwide Flood recorded in Genesis. During the Flood, large quantities of vegetation could have been swiftly uprooted, massed together, and buried to form the beds of coal we find today. Rapid and complete burial is essential to coal formation; otherwise, oxygen would cause the plants to decay in the usual manner. Petroleum could have come from marine plants and animals that were rapidly buried and later turned into oil by heat and the intense pressure of the overlying rocks. Although God's Word does not tell us specifically about how fuels were formed, it does declare that "in his hand are the deep places of the earth" (Ps. 95:4). Truly, God's provision for us is evident in the earth's vast deposits of coal and oil.

petroleum (crude oil)

Petroleum: the liquid fuel

Another fossil fuel that may have been formed from the remains of once-living creatures is **petroleum.** The word *petroleum* comes from two words that mean "rock oil." Petroleum in its natural form (the state in which it is pumped from the ground) is called **crude oil.** This thick, flammable liquid has a dark color and sometimes gives off an unpleasant odor.

Petroleum is actually a mixture of thousands of different substances called **hydrocarbons.** A hydrocarbon is a chemical substance made primarily of hydrogen and carbon. Chemists find hydrocarbons very useful for making new products because their molecules can be easily taken apart, rearranged, and put together again. Millions of different substances, from rubber tires to imitation leather, can be made from crude oil hydrocarbons.

Finding petroleum. Petroleum is found in certain sedimentary rocks that are full of tiny hollow spaces; such rocks are said to be *porous* [pôr′əs: full of holes]. The hollow spaces between the grains of porous rock allow oil, water, or gases to collect. Large amounts of petroleum are often found trapped where a layer of porous rock is surrounded by less porous rock.

You cannot tell by merely looking at surface rock whether a reservoir of petroleum lies below. Instead, oil geologists use a variety of sensitive instruments to allow them to "see" the rock formations that lie deep beneath the surface. Some of these instruments measure tiny variations in the earth's gravity and magnetism, while others measure the properties of rocks. Sound waves caused by explosives or heavy equipment can also be "bounced" off of deep rock formations, giving geologists a clue as to their shape and depth. Certain rock formations are more likely to contain petroleum than others. (For example, petroleum is often found in areas where rocks are squeezed upward from below by underground salt deposits.) Engineers drill holes into the most promising formations to see if they contain oil.

Recovering and refining petroleum. Petroleum is usually taken from the ground by drilling a narrow hole into a petroleum deposit and simply pumping out the oil.

After the crude oil is removed from the ground, it is transported by ship or pipeline to huge industrial complexes called *refineries* to be refined or processed so that different parts of it can be used in a variety of ways.

Remember that petroleum is actually a mixture of many different substances called hydrocarbons. At a refinery, a process called *fractional distillation* can be used to separate the hydrocarbons into different groups, or **fractions.**

Recovering petroleum

- drilling rig
- drill shaft
- nonporous rock
- porous rock containing natural gas
- salt dome
- petroleum
- petroleum

oil platform in Gulf of Mexico

Petroleum industry

gasoline truck

1. Oil wells produce oil.

2. Ships or pipelines carry oil to refineries.

3. Refinery products are transported to consumers.

In this process, the oil is heated until it is boiling and then injected into the bottom of a large, hollow tower. The tower, or *fractionating column*, is divided into several different compartments by perforated steel trays. The heavier residue settles to the bottom of the tower, while the hot vapors begin to rise up through the different trays, cooling as they rise. As each hydrocarbon cools enough to condense into a liquid, it condenses on the steel tray at that level and is drained off. The other vapors continue to rise until they, too, condense. At the very top of the tower, vapors that did not condense are taken off as gases.

The heaviest petroleum fractions (those that settle out at the bottom of the tower) are used to make tar and asphalt. Fractions that condense slightly higher in the tower are used to make grease, motor oil, or heating oil. Still lighter fractions are used to make diesel and jet fuel, paint thinner, and gasoline. The hydrocarbon gases that make it to the very top of the tower are commonly used as fuels; propane and "LP gas" (liquified petroleum gas) used for home heating are the result of this process.

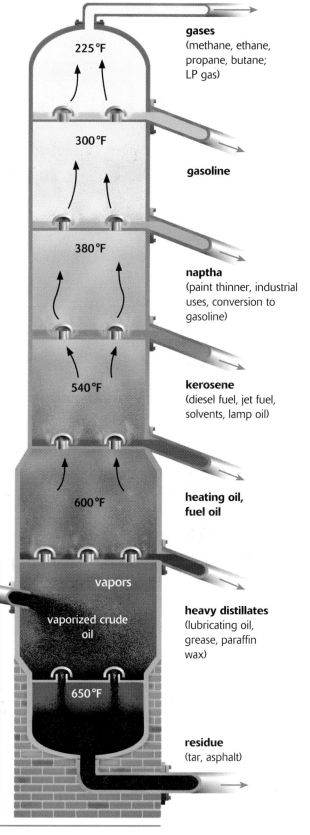

gases
(methane, ethane, propane, butane; LP gas)

225°F

gasoline

300°F

naptha
(paint thinner, industrial uses, conversion to gasoline)

380°F

kerosene
(diesel fuel, jet fuel, solvents, lamp oil)

540°F

heating oil, fuel oil

600°F

furnace (700°F)

vapors

heavy distillates
(lubricating oil, grease, paraffin wax)

boiling crude oil

vaporized crude oil

crude oil

650°F

residue
(tar, asphalt)

Fractionating column

Comprehension Check 3.8

Clues. Give the word or term that best fits each clue.

1. A hard, shiny, black coal that is expensive to mine

2. The most common type of coal, also known as "soft coal"

3. Two types of coal mining mentioned in the text

4. The poorest quality of coal, also known as "brown coal"

5. The thick, dark-colored, flammable liquid that is considered a liquid fossil fuel

Explain.

6. Why is coal called a *fossil fuel?*

7. Explain how oil geologists find buried petroleum.

Caves

Imagine entering a small hole in the ground and finding miles and miles of mysterious passageways and rooms. *Caves* are some of the most mysterious places of the earth's crust. A **cave** is any hollow space in the earth's crust that has formed naturally and is large enough for a person to enter. Very large caves are called **caverns.** A cave may consist of only one "room," or it may consist of a whole network of connected chambers and corridors. The scientific study of caves is called **speleology** [spē′lē·ŏl′ə·jē].

Caves are often damp, humid places; many contain streams or even large lakes. Caverns and passageways often run together into giant underground networks that stretch for miles in every direction;

Ogle Cave in New Mexico

the interconnected passages of Kentucky's Flint Ridge-Mammoth-Joppa cave system, for example, total at least 350 miles in length. Individual caverns may also attain tremendous size. One cave in Malaysia opens into a huge chamber a third of a mile long and a quarter mile across, with a ceiling more than 20 stories above the floor.

Formation of a cave

1. Rainwater penetrates cracks in limestone.

2. Acidic water dissolves limestone, enlarging crack.

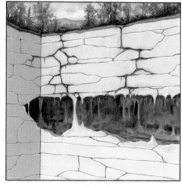

3. Water recedes, leaving cave.

Kinds of caves

Sea caves and lava caves. Caves form in a variety of ways. When the ocean beats upon a weak area of a cliff and erodes a hole into the rock, the result is a **sea cave.** When molten lava flows out from beneath a hardened surface of lava, it often leaves behind an underground chamber called a **lava cave.** Another type of cave forms when earthquakes cause deep fissures in the earth's crust.

Solution caves. Most large caves are *solution caves* that form in a sedimentary rock called **limestone.** (A **solution cave** is a cave formed by the dissolving of underground rocks by water.) Limestone, a sedimentary rock, is made of a mineral called **calcium carbonate**—the same material mineral that is found in seashells. Calcium carbonate is easily dissolved by acids.

As rainwater passes through the air and the soil, carbon dioxide gas from the air dissolves in the water, making the water slightly acidic. If the rainwater then seeps downward through cracks in the rock into a deposit of limestone, the acid in the water will slowly eat away and dissolve the calcium carbonate in the limestone. Soon, the trickle of water becomes an underground stream. Eventually, after many years of erosion, the underground stream may have eaten away enough rock to form a large cavity, or cave.

sea cave in Santa Cruz Island, California

lava cave in California

Earth Explorer

To discover what rocks contain calcium carbonate and would be most likely to dissolve in water, you can do this simple acid test. You will need *vinegar, seashells,* and *a variety of rocks.* Try to include samples of limestone, marble, coral, concrete, granite, and coal as well as of any other rocks available.

Geologists use hydrochloric acid to test for the presence of calcium carbonate in rocks. Vinegar, a weak acid, will also work. Pour a small amount of vinegar on the limestone and notice what happens. The fizzing indicates that the rock contains calcium carbonate. Now pour some vinegar on the granite. Notice that nothing happens. Granite does not contain calcium carbonate. Try the other rocks and record your observations.

Cave formations

Although huge chambers and dizzying vertical shafts may be the most dramatic cave features, many caves also contain beautiful and unusual rock formations formed as water containing dissolved minerals evaporates, leaving the minerals behind. You may already be familiar with stalactites and stalagmites, which are two of the formations you might see in a cave. Other bizarrely shaped formations may also be present.

Soda straws and stalactites. Thin, hollow tubes that hang from the ceiling of many caves are called **soda straws.** Soda straws are formed when drops of water hang one after another from the ceiling of the cave and evaporate, leaving a ring of crystallized calcium carbonate where the rim of each drop touched the ceiling. As water continues to fall through the ring and evaporate, the ring gradually becomes a hollow tube a few inches long.

Eventually, the center of the soda straw may become plugged, forcing the water to flow over the outside of the soda straw instead. This process forms a thicker, icicle-shaped formation known as a **stalactite.** (The word *stalactite* comes from a Greek word meaning

soda straws

stalactites

stalagmites

"drop by drop.") You can remember that a stalactite grows down from the ceiling when you think that a stalac**tite** has to hold **tight** to keep from falling.

Although we associate stalactites with caves, stalactites can form wherever water carrying minerals drips and evaporates. Stalactites have been found under cliffs and bridges, as well as in mines, tunnels, and subways.

Stalagmites. Water dripping from the ceiling of a cave sometimes falls to the floor and evaporates there, depositing a steep mound or spike of calcium carbonate on the floor. Such a structure on the cave floor is known as a **stalagmite.** If a stalagmite grows tall enough to reach the ceiling of the cave (or to join with a stalactite hanging from the ceiling), the result is called a **column.**

EYE witness
r e p o r t e r

Growing stalactites

To see how stalactites grow, you will need *two one-quart milk cartons, an 18-inch piece of cotton string* (cord or yarn will also work), *a paper plate, two small nails, water, Epsom salts,* and *food coloring* (optional)

First, cut the tops off the milk cartons. Then make a solution of Epsom salts and warm water, in the proportion of 5 table-spoons of Epsom salts to every 2 cups of water. Be sure the Epsom salts are thoroughly dissolved in the water. You may wish to add a little food coloring to the solution. Make enough solution to fill each carton about 2/3 full; then soak the string in the solution. After the string has soaked, tie each end of the string to a nail (the nail will serve as a weight to keep the string in the solution). Drop one of the two nails into each carton. Set the cartons about one foot apart in a place where they will not be disturbed. Be sure that the midpoint of the string hanging between the cartons is lower than the level of water in the cartons. Put the paper plate between the two cartons and below the midpoint of the string.

Within a couple of weeks, stalactites should begin to form on the string.

draperies

flowstone

Draperies and flowstones. If a trickle of water runs down an angled ceiling or wall of a cave instead of falling straight to the floor, calcium carbonate crystals may form **draperies**—thin, wavy sheets of hanging rock—instead of stalactites. Water may also flow over broad areas of the wall or floor of a cave, depositing a sheet of minerals; the resulting formation is called **flowstone.** Flowstones along a cave wall may look rather like a frozen waterfall.

Moon milk. If the air of the cave is very humid, calcium carbonate may not be able to crystallize as the water evaporates. Instead, the mineral is deposited on the cave's surface as a soft paste sometimes called **moon milk.**

Rafts and pearls. In some caves, underground pools of water containing a large amount of dissolved minerals may be found. If the pool lies undisturbed, evaporating water may leave behind thin, floating disks of calcium carbonate that may range in size from less than an inch to nearly a foot across. These formations are known as **cave rafts.** Cave rafts eventually sink when they become too heavy to be supported by the water or when the surface of the pool is disturbed.

Some of the most unique rock formations are found in shallow pools that

cave pearls and moon milk

are constantly agitated by dripping water. When calcium carbonate particles become attached to a grain of sand in such a pool, layers of the mineral build up around that grain of sand in the same way that a pearl is produced by an oyster. Because the water is in constant motion, these **cave pearls** do not stick to one another or to the side of the pool.

guacharos (oilbirds)

 Life in a cave

A variety of animals make their homes in caves. Some visit caves regularly but cannot live there for long periods; they must always return to the surface to find food. Animals of this kind are known as **trogloxenes** [trä′glō·zēnz], or "cave guests." Trogloxenes include bats,

pack rats, frogs, and even certain birds, such as the guacharo [gwä′chə′rō′], or oilbird, of South America. The guacharo builds its nest in a cave.

Some animals are designed in such a way that they can live their entire lives either in a cave or above ground; if circumstances allow, they may regularly go from one place to the other. These animals are called **troglophiles** [trä′glō·fīlz], or "cave lovers." Certain types of fish, insects, and crustaceans are troglophiles.

Other animals live only in caves and cannot survive above ground. Animals of this type are known as **troglobites** [trä′glō·bītsl, or "cave dwellers." Although they may be very similar to certain troglophiles, they are usually colorless and blind. The troglobites include various kinds of fish, insects, and crustaceans, but no birds or mammals. The food supply available in caves is not sufficient to support warm-blooded animals.

cave fish

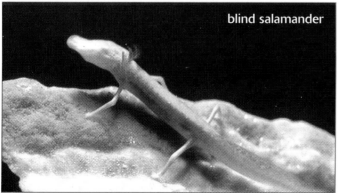
blind salamander

Comprehension Check 3.9

Clues. Give the word or term that best fits each clue.

1. Any hollow space in the earth's crust that was formed naturally and is large enough for a person to enter

2. The study of caves

3. The kind of rock in which solution caves usually form

4. The basic mineral that makes up limestone

5. Animals that visit caves regularly but have to return to the surface to find food

6. Label each cave formation.

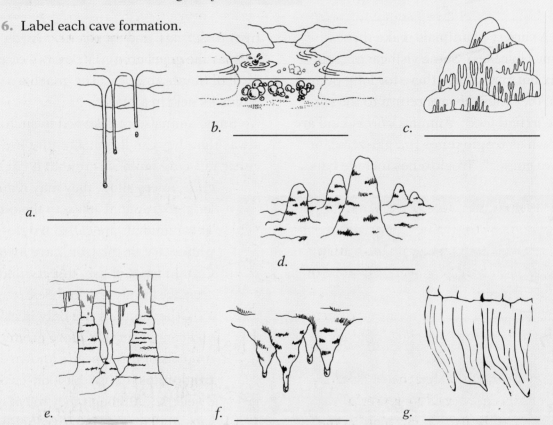

a. _____

b. _____

c. _____

d. _____

e. _____

f. _____

g. _____

Explain.

7. Are solution caves formed mostly by chemical weathering or by physical weathering? (see section 3.1)

8. Some caves have an abundance of green plants growing at or near the entrance. However, once you pass a certain point as you are entering a cave, green plants disappear. Why?

3.10 A Giant Magnet

You have probably played with small magnets by using them to pick up tacks and pins or by placing two magnets close enough together that they attract or repel each other. But magnets also have many practical uses. They are an important part of electric motors, loudspeakers, computer disk drives, and most televisions. Around the house, small magnets hold cabinet doors shut and fasten calendars and memos to the refrigerator door. But did you realize that you live on a magnet? More than 400 years ago, an English scientist named William Gilbert discovered that the earth is a gigantic magnet.

The earth's magnetic field

Magnetism is the force that pulls magnets apart or pushes them together. If you have ever picked up nails with a magnet, you have seen what the force of magnetism can do. The area surrounding a magnet in which the force of magnetism affects other objects is called a **magnetic field.**

Scientists think that the earth's magnetic field is produced by powerful currents of electricity that circulate in the earth's core. Compared to the small magnetic field produced by an ordinary bar magnet, the earth's magnetic field is huge, stretching tens of thousands of miles into space. However, because the earth's surface is thousands of miles away from the outer core, the earth's magnetic field may seem weak compared to the field of an ordinary bar magnet. To demonstrate this truth, hold a compass in one hand. Notice that the earth's magnetic field attracts the compass needle, causing it to point to the north. Now, using your other hand, bring a bar magnet close to the compass. The needle will swing toward the bar magnet because its field is much stronger at such close range, even though the earth's magnetic field is actually far more powerful. The earth's magnetic field just *seems* weaker because its source is millions of times farther away from the compass than the bar magnet.

Magnetic poles

You may have noticed that the magnetic field of a bar magnet seems strongest at the two ends, or **poles,** of the magnet. The earth's magnetic field also has two poles. The earth's northern magnetic pole is located in northern Canada, several miles northwest of Ellef Rignes [ĕl'ĕf rĭng'nās] Island and about 1000 miles from the geographic north pole. The earth's southern magnetic pole is presently located in the ocean off the coast of Antarctica, about 1600 miles from the earth's geographic south pole.

The earth's magnetic poles do not remain in fixed locations, but wander over a small region of the earth's surface. The northern magnetic pole is presently moving north at an average speed of 9.3 miles per year, or about 135 feet per day. It also moves several miles back and forth each day as the earth rotates.

The source of earth's magnetism

Where does the earth's magnetic field come from? At first, you might think that the earth has a giant metal magnet buried at its core. However, this cannot be true because the earth's magnetic field seems to originate in the earth's outer core, which is a white-hot mass of liquid metal (section 3.1). Any magnet there would quickly lose its magnetism and melt! Also, the magnetic poles of a buried magnet would not wander around like the earth's magnetic poles do. For these and other reasons, scientists believe that the earth's magnetic field is produced by currents of electricity rather than any sort of buried magnet. But how can electricity produce a magnetic field? Whenever an electric current flows through an object, the current produces a magnetic field around the object. If you have ever

Compass in Earth's magnetic field

A compass aligns itself with the earth's magnetic field so that it always points toward the northern magnetic pole.

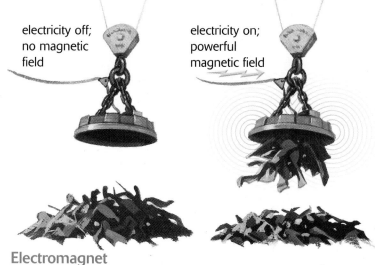

electricity off; no magnetic field

electricity on; powerful magnetic field

Electromagnet

seen an **electromagnet**—a magnet that becomes magnetized only when it is hooked to a battery or some other source of electric current—you have seen one way that electricity can produce a magnetic field. As powerful currents of electricity circulate in the earth's outer core, they produce a similar magnetism that makes up the earth's magnetic field. *The earth remains "magnetized" because of the unceasing electric currents deep within its core.*

The magnetosphere

The magnetic field that is produced in the earth's core extends many thousands of miles into space. The region of space affected by the earth's magnetic field is called the **magnetosphere** [măg·nē′tō·sfīr]. Imagine an enormous invisible doughnut surrounding the earth, with the northern and southern magnetic poles sticking out of the hole. This doughnut is what the magnetosphere would look like if we could see it with our eyes.

However, the earth's magnetosphere is not perfectly round like a real doughnut. Instead, it is bunched up on the side that faces toward the sun and stretched out on the side that faces away from the sun.

The magnetosphere is yet another example of the Creator's loving care in making the earth safe for man. A stream of harmful particles called the **solar wind** flows constantly from the surface of the sun. If it were not for the magnetosphere, these potentially harmful particles would enter our atmosphere. The solar wind is not able to penetrate the magnetosphere, however, because the magnetosphere deflects (pushes aside) the harmful particles so that they pass around the earth.

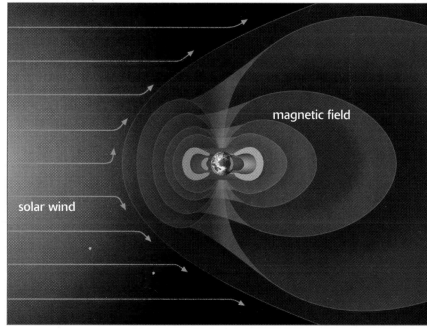

magnetic field

solar wind

Solar wind and Earth's magnetosphere

A few solar wind particles do become trapped in the earth's magnetic field and are funneled toward the magnetic poles. When they collide with molecules of air in the atmosphere near the poles, they create breathtaking displays of light known as **auroras** [ô·rôr′əz] but do not cause any harm.

aurora borealis over Manitoba, Canada

The **aurora borealis** [bôr′ē·ăl′ĭs: "northern light"] appears in the Northern Hemisphere and is seen most often in Alaska, Canada, the Scandinavian countries, and northern Russia. Occasionally, people living in the northern United States can see it. On rare occasions, it can be glimpsed as far south as Mexico. The *aurora australis* [ô·strā′lĭs: "southern light"] appears in the Southern Hemisphere. If you live in an area where an aurora can be seen, remember that it is evidence of earth's magnetosphere, part of God's wise design for our planet.

EYEwitness reporter

The force of magnetism

1. Making a magnet

You can turn a simple nail or a straight pin into a temporary magnet. All you need is *a bar magnet, a nail or straight pin,* and *a collection of paper clips.* Rub the nail with the end, or pole, of the magnet, in such a way that you stroke the nail in the same direction every time. Once you have given the nail about fifty strokes with the magnet, place the magnet aside and hold the nail over a paper clip. The paper clip should stick to the nail. Now see how many paper clips your new magnet can hold.

Make a second temporary magnet by rubbing a nail a hundred times with the magnet. How many paper clips can this magnet hold? Does the number of strokes affect the strength of the magnet?

2. Observing a magnetic field

For this demonstration, you will need the following equipment: a *bar magnet and/or a horseshoe magnet; iron filings or fine steel wool cut into small pieces; a piece of poster board, glass, or clear plastic;* and *a pencil.*

Place the bar magnet on a flat surface and lay the poster board (or other material) on top of the magnet. Sprinkle iron filings (or steel wool pieces) on top of the poster board. Notice the pattern that forms around the magnet. Gently tap the top of the poster board with the pencil. Watch as the filings form an even more definite pattern. You are observing the magnetic field of the magnet.

The earth's magnetic field has a similar pattern on a much larger scale. A compass, which is a small magnet balanced so that it can turn freely, is affected by the earth's magnetic field in such a way that the north-seeking pole of the compass points to the earth's northern magnetic pole.

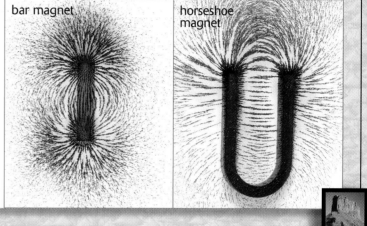

bar magnet   horseshoe magnet

Comprehension Check 3.10

Clues. Give the word or term that best fits each clue.

1. The area surrounding a magnet in which the force of magnetism affects other objects

2. The places on a magnet (usually at the ends) where its magnetism is the strongest

3. A magnet that becomes magnetized only when it is hooked to a battery or some other source of electric current

4. The region of space affected by the earth's magnetic field

5. A stream of harmful particles that flow constantly from the surface of the sun

Explain.

6. What causes the breathtaking displays of light called *auroras?*

Chapter Checkup

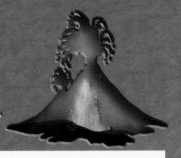

Part A

I. **Define these terms.**

geology

crust

mantle

Moho

core

weathering

chemical weathering

physical weathering

geologist

seismologist

mid-oceanic ridge

II. **Know these terms about earthquakes.**

tsunami

earthquake

seismology

fault

focus

epicenter

magnitude

seismic belts

III. **Identify the following.**

3 kinds of volcanoes (by how they are formed)

3 kinds of eruptions

IV. **Know these terms about volcanoes.**

magma

magma chamber

vent

volcano

lava

Ring of Fire

fumaroles

tephra

volcanic ash

crater

active

dormant

extinct

Part B

I. Define these terms.

rock
fossil
gemstones
precious stones
ore
precious metals
iron
copper
fossil fuel
petroleum
cave
speleology
solution cave
magnetic field
poles
electromagnet
magnetosphere
solar wind

II. Identify the following.

4 types of coal
2 types of coal mining
3 main categories of rock
3 categories of animals that live
   in caves

III. Know these terms about rocks.

extrusive and intrusive igneous
   rocks
mechanical sediments
chemical sediments
organic sediments
foliated and unfoliated rocks

IV. Describe these cave formations.

soda straws
stalactites
stalagmites
columns
draperies
flowstones
cave pearls

V. Give the characteristics of
   these rocks.

granite
sandstone
shale
conglomerate
halite
chalk
coal
slate
marble
diamond
limestone

God's Great Universe

People have always been fascinated by the unexplored vastness of outer space. From ancient times, people have gazed in awe at the canopy of stars, seeing in their arrangement the shapes of humans and animals. Wondering at the motion of the planets, ancient astronomers charted their courses through the skies. The changing phases of the moon were used to determine the months. Dramatic eclipses and the appearance of mysterious comets in the heavens inspired awe and even fear.

Man has always desired to understand the mysteries of the heavens. What force propels the planets along their heavenly paths? What are the planets like? How far away are the moon and stars? What are comets made of? Although people have pondered such questions for thousands of years, it has only been in the last few centuries that we have found some of the answers. The study of the stars, planets, and all other heavenly bodies is called **astronomy. Astronomers,** scientists who study outer space, try to understand what the stars, planets, and all other heavenly bodies are like and what affect they have on each other.

Although there are many things about the universe that we do not understand, two things are very clear. First, God created it. Genesis 1:1 tells us that "In the beginning God created the heaven and the earth." Second, it tells us of His glory. Psalm 19:1 says, "The heavens declare the glory of God; and the firmament showeth His handiwork."

No air

Have you ever wondered, as you gazed up into the blackness of the night sky, what outer space is like? If you were to travel there, you would find the environment rather unfriendly. Conditions in space are much different than they are on the surface of the earth where we are surrounded by the layers of air known as the *atmosphere.* If you could ride in a spacecraft as it traveled upward from the earth's surface, the surrounding air would soon become so thin that you could not breathe unless your spacecraft was pressurized with its own supply of oxygen. Soon you would reach the *exosphere,* that topmost region of the atmosphere in which molecules of air travel for miles without encountering other air molecules. Between 300 and 900 miles up, even these last lonely air molecules would be left behind you. In space there is no air at all, other than a stray molecule here and there. Space is almost a **vacuum,** *an area containing no air or any other matter*—space is mostly pure emptiness! Even the huge planets, the countless numbers of stars, and other heavenly bodies fill up only a very, very small fraction of the space in the universe.

No air friction

Because there is no air in space, there is no friction caused by air, either. Remember that **friction** is *the force that resists motion.* If the engines on an airplane zooming through the earth's atmosphere were to stop running even for a short time, the plane would be quickly slowed down by the friction caused by air molecules colliding with the plane. But in outer space, your spacecraft would be able to travel *unimpeded by friction* due to air. The only friction it would encounter would be caused by collisions with tiny fragments of rock or particles of space dust. You could fire the spacecraft's rockets for a few minutes, turn them off, and continue traveling almost forever, or until your ship ran into some other heavenly body. To slow down, you would have to fire rockets in the other direction.

Mostly black

While looking out the porthole of your spacecraft, you would be amazed at the brilliance of the fiery stars, the nearby moon, and the shining blue earth below

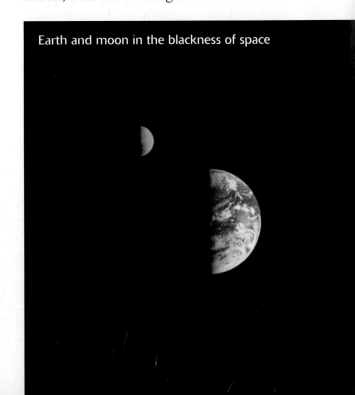

Earth and moon in the blackness of space

you. But it also would be difficult not to notice the blackness that frames the heavenly bodies and contrasts so strongly with their brightness.

Have you ever wondered why space is black? Blackness is the absence of light. Because space is mostly emptiness, it cannot radiate or reflect light. The bright stars, tiny pinpoints of light separated by vast regions of blackness, are the only sources of light in a universe that would otherwise be completely dark.

Unusual activities

As a traveler in space you would notice some unusual things happening. Once your engines were turned off and the spaceship was coasting through space, you would be free to float here and there about the ship as you desired. There would be no up and no down, and you would feel as though you did not weigh anything at all. Living in this condition would require some adjustment, though. Many daily routines that are simple enough on earth, such as brushing your teeth or eating breakfast, would become quite a challenge. You might find that your breakfast orange juice had left your glass only to become an orange ball floating, like a miniature sun, in the middle of the room.

Extremes of temperature

If you wanted to go on a space walk outside your ship, you would have to wear a space suit. Besides furnishing

you with oxygen, this space suit would protect you from *extremes of temperature.* On the earth, the atmosphere moderates temperature both by shielding the surface from the sun's potent heat radiation, so that daytime is not too hot, and by blocking heat loss from the surface after the sun goes down, so that nighttime is not too cold. But in space, if your space walk were on the sunny side of the spaceship, the outside of your space suit could gradually heat up to a temperature of more than two hundred degrees *above*

Skylab astronauts demonstrating weightlessness

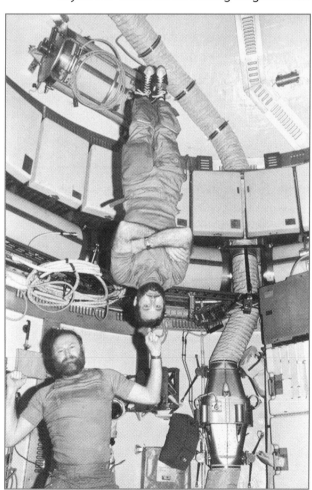

zero. If you were to go around to the shady side of the ship, however, the temperature of your suit would gradually drop to far *below* zero. In deep space, far from the sun and other stars, the average temperature is coldest of all—more than four hundred and fifty degrees below zero.

astronaut working outside space station

EYE witness reporter

Observing friction

1. Although a spaceship speeding through space does not encounter friction due to air molecules, air friction can be easily observed right here on earth. To demonstrate how air friction resists movement, you will need *two pieces of scrap paper, paper clips, rocks, a quarter, a nickel or other coin,* and *other small objects of different weights.*

You already know that if you allow objects to drop out of your hands, they will fall to the ground. But when different objects are dropped together, do they hit the ground at the same time? To find out, hold a paper clip, a rock, and a quarter out over an open floor space. Let them drop out of your hand. Which one hits the floor first? You will notice that even though

the objects differ in weight, they reach the ground at the same time. Try several more objects. You may wish to stand on a chair to see if the extra height makes a difference.

Now take one of the sheets of paper and wad it up into a ball. Drop it along with a few other objects. Does the wadded paper hit the floor at the same time as the other objects? Drop the flat sheet of paper along with the wadded piece. What happens? Even though the two pieces have the same weight and are made of the same substance, they do not fall in the same way. The flat sheet of paper seems to float to the ground, taking more time as it drops. What causes this to happen? The flat sheet of paper encounters more air resistance than the wadded piece of paper. In other words, its broader, flatter shape makes it run into more collisions with air molecules on the way down. These collisions greatly slow its descent. What other things might encounter more air resistance than you saw when you dropped such objects as paper clips, rocks, and coins?

You have now demonstrated that the speed at which an object falls depends not on its weight but on the air resistance it encounters as it falls. What do you think would happen if a feather and a cannonball were raised to equal heights in a vacuum and released at the same time?

2. Friction occurs not only when air resists the motion of a falling object, but also whenever two solid surfaces rub against each other. For this demonstration you will need *a small block of wood, a screw eye, string, a rough wooden board, a sheet of glass,* and *a heavy stone*. (Have an adult help you screw the screw eye into the block of wood before you do this demonstration.) Tie the string to the screw eye in the small block of wood. Place the block of wood on the rough wooden board. Next, place the heavy stone on top of the block. Pull the block so that it slides over the rough board. Then place the block and the stone on the sheet of glass and pull.

Does the block slide more easily on the board or on the glass? Why do you think the one produces more friction than the other?

Comprehension Check 4.1

Clues. Give the word or term that best fits each clue.

1. The study of the stars, planets, and all other heavenly bodies

2. Scientists who study outer space

3. An area containing no air or any other matter

4. The force that resists motion

5. A space suit not only provides oxygen to an astronaut outside his spacecraft, but also provides protection from extremes of __?__.

Explain.

6. Write a paragraph about what it would be like to travel in space. Be sure to include at least four of the characteristics discussed in class to show how traveling in space differs from traveling on Earth.

Milky Way in night sky

distant galaxies

This photo covers a patch of sky the size of a grain of sand held at arm's length. Nearly every point of light you see is a distant galaxy.

4.2 Galaxies: Giant Groups

Each night, a multitude of stars twinkle above us. Although these stars appear to be scattered randomly throughout space, they actually belong to an ordered structure known as a galaxy. A **galaxy** is *a star system containing from millions to billions of stars.* The **Milky Way,** the galaxy in which we live, is the home of over 400 billion stars, including our own sun.

Until the early 1900s, most astronomers thought that the Milky Way was the only galaxy in the universe. However, we now know that the observable universe contains countless galaxies; astronomers presently estimate that there are over 120 *billion* of them! To put this number

in perspective, imagine holding a dime at arm's length so that it is silhouetted against the nighttime sky. Nearly 12 million galaxies are found in the patch of sky covered by the dime!

Super structures

Galaxies are not spread at random throughout the universe, but are grouped together in orderly, complex structures. For example, our Milky Way galaxy (which we can see as a hazy band of light across the sky on a very dark night) is one of about 40 galaxies in a cluster known as the **Local Group.** The two largest galaxies in this group are the Milky Way and a slightly larger galaxy called the

Andromeda galaxy

Andromeda [ăn·drŏm′ĭ·də] **galaxy,** visible with the naked eye on a dark night. Most of the galaxies in this group are clustered around these two largest members. The three galaxies closest to ours are the **Sagittarius** [săj′ĭ·târ′ē·əs] **Dwarf galaxy,** the **Large Magellanic** [măj′ə·lăn′ĭk] **Cloud,** and the **Small Magellanic Cloud.** Both of the Magellanic Clouds are visible with the naked eye from the Southern Hemisphere.

Astronomers believe that our Local Group is part of a larger grouping known as a *supercluster,* and that the universe is filled with superclusters joined together so as to form the walls of vast bubble-shaped structures, like a sink full of soap bubbles, which appear to be completely empty in the middle. Astronomers are amazed at the order and regularity that exist even on such a large scale.

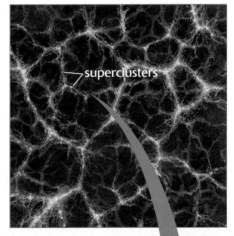

superclusters

arrangement of superclusters in the universe

Local Group (galaxy cluster)

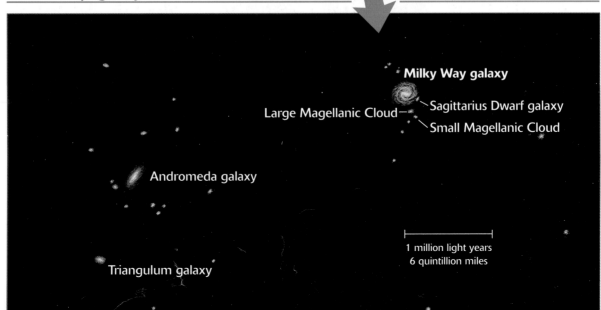

Milky Way galaxy

Sagittarius Dwarf galaxy

Large Magellanic Cloud

Small Magellanic Cloud

Andromeda galaxy

Triangulum galaxy

1 million light years
6 quintillion miles

Sombrero galaxy

Galactic shapes

Spiral galaxies. Astronomers classify galaxies according to shape. **Spiral galaxies,** including the Milky Way and the Andromeda galaxy, look like giant pinwheels spinning through the void of space. All spiral galaxies have a central *nucleus* that resembles a flattened ball, to which are attached long, curved arms. The arms seem to spiral closely about the nucleus if it is large, and they seem to spiral rather loosely if the nucleus is small. In addition to billions of stars, spiral galaxies also contain vast amounts of gas and dust.

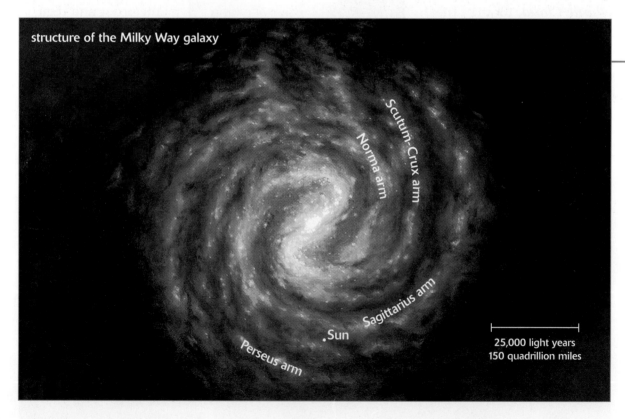

structure of the Milky Way galaxy

Scutum-Crux arm

Norma arm

Sagittarius arm

Sun

Perseus arm

25,000 light years
150 quadrillion miles

In some spiral galaxies, called **barred spirals,** the spiral arms are attached to a straight "bar" that runs through the center of the galaxy.

Because astronomers live inside the Milky Way galaxy, their view of the remoter parts is blocked by a thick veil of stars and dust; therefore, they are not completely sure what the whole galaxy looks like. Presently, astronomers think that the Milky Way is a large barred spiral galaxy with two major arms and several smaller arm segments surrounding a nucleus shaped like a flattened football. Our sun is not in the center of the galaxy, but is found among the spiral arms.

elliptical galaxy

Elliptical galaxies. When viewed from the side, **elliptical** [ĭ·lĭp′tĭ·kəl] **galaxies** resemble eggs or footballs. Some elliptical galaxies are almost spherical. Compared to spiral galaxies, elliptical ones are not as structured, and do not contain as much free gas or dust.

Barred spiral galaxies

Irregular galaxies. Irregular **galaxies** are composed of stars clumped together in no definite shape. Two of the galaxies closest to ours, the Large Magellanic Cloud and the Small Magellanic Cloud, are both irregular galaxies.

irregular galaxy

Celestial clouds

In addition to stars, many galaxies also contain **nebulae** [nĕb′yə·lē] (singular: *nebula*), large clouds of gas and dust floating in space. Nebulae are most common in spiral and irregular galaxies. Our own Milky Way galaxy contains many beautiful nebulae, but most are too faint to be seen with the unaided eye, even though some of them would appear larger in the sky than the full moon if we could see them. A large telescope is needed to show the majesty of these giant clouds.

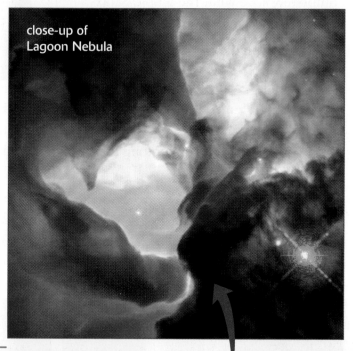

close-up of Lagoon Nebula

Nebulae

Lagoon Nebula

Trifid Nebula

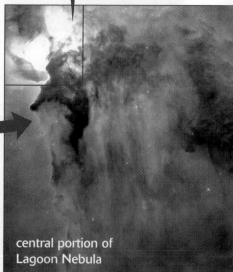

central portion of Lagoon Nebula

Comprehension Check 4.2

Clues. Give the word or term that best fits each clue.

1. A star system containing from millions to billions of stars

2. The name of our galaxy

3. The cluster of about 40 galaxies that the Milky Way belongs to

4. Three small galaxies closest to the Milky Way

5. The three basic types of galactic shapes

6. A spiral galaxy in which the spiral arms are attached to a straight "bar" that runs through the center of the galaxy

7. Large clouds of gas and space dust

4.3 Constellations: Figures in the Stars

The starry dome

On a dark, cloudless night, we can see thousands of stars scattered across the black vault above. If you look at the stars long enough, you might imagine that you can see simple pictures of people, animals, weapons, and other earthly things. The stars outlining such an imaginary picture are called a **constellation.** Many such groups of stars have names that have been used since ancient times.

If you live in the Northern Hemisphere, you will notice that there are certain constellations that never completely disappear below the horizon. These stars appear to revolve around the North Star, or *Polaris* [pə·lăr′ĭs], the Pole Star.

The "rotation" of the stars around Polaris is an illusion caused by the actual rotation of the earth. The North Star does not appear to move in the sky, but remains in the same position each night. Neither does it rise nor set, because it is located directly above the northern end of the earth's **axis of rotation** (an imaginary line that stretches

stars revolving around Polaris

Polaris

axis of rotation

North Pole

from pole to pole through the interior of the earth, around which the earth rotates). If you were to stand at the North Pole, the North Star would be directly above you; from other places in the Northern Hemisphere, the North Star would be closer to the horizon but still to the north of you. If you were south of the equator, you could not see the North Star at all.

Figures in the stars

The sky is currently divided into 88 constellations recognized by astronomers all over the world. Some of these constellations, such as Fornax [fôr'năks: the Furnace], are fairly recent members of the sky family. But many of the constellations were recognized in the sky thousands of years ago. People in ancient times spent long hours gazing at the heavens, and many of the figures they saw there are still remembered today.

A parade of stars

Some constellations can be seen only at certain times of the year. The constellation Orion, for instance, is hidden from our view in the late spring and summer because the sun comes between the earth and those particular stars, and they are invisible in the bright daytime sky. But several months later, after the earth has traveled around to the other side of the sun, the constellation appears in the night sky.

When the sun sets at night, assorted constellations reveal themselves against the black background of space. As the night progresses, some of these constellations set below the horizon, and others rise to take their places. The parade of constellations continues all night long until the sun rises and its light again obscures the stars from our sight.

If you were to stay up all night long, you could see many different constellations, each one rising slowly in its turn from below the eastern horizon. But the most easily observed constellations are those above the horizon shortly after sunset, before most people go to bed. The constellations that can be seen in the early evening during spring are referred to as *spring constellations*. The ones that can be viewed best in the autumn are called *autumn constellations*. The constellations described in this book are those most easily observed in the late fall and early winter.

Constellations of the Northern Hemisphere

The Great Bear. Of all the constellations in the northern sky, few are more easily recognizable than **Ursa** [ûr′sə] **Major,** the Great Bear. This constellation contains the *Big Dipper,* one of the most familiar groupings of stars. To locate the North Star, imagine a straight line drawn through the two outer stars in the dipper's bowl, which are known as the *Pointers,* and follow this line from the top of the bowl to Polaris. The Big Dipper is often used to mark the seasons as well as to locate other northern constellations.

The Little Bear. The constellation containing Polaris is **Ursa Minor,** or the Little Bear. Polaris is located at the end of the bear's tail. The Little Bear is more commonly called the *Little Dipper.* Because most of the other stars in this constellation are fainter, Polaris is sometimes the only star that is easily visible,

especially if you live near bright city lights. However, both the Little Dipper and the Big Dipper can be seen on very dark nights almost year around from most of the United States.

Queen Cassiopeia. Although the constellation **Cassiopeia** [kăs′ē·ə·pē′ə] was named after a mythical queen of Ethiopia, it really looks more like a letter of the alphabet than a person. Made up of five bright stars, the constellation seems to have the shape of a huge *M* or *W,* depending on which way it is turned in the heavens.

King Cepheus. The five-sided constellation **Cepheus** [sē′fē·əs], named after Cassiopeia's husband, looks like a house with a sharply pointed roof. If you imagine that the roof is actually a tall hat, you can see the profile of the king's face below it. To find Cepheus, look again at the line that goes from the Pointers to Polaris. If you follow this line beyond Polaris, it will pierce the king's hat like an arrow.

Draco (The Dragon)

Cepheus

Little Dipper (Ursa Minor)

Big Dipper

Polaris

Cassiopeia

Pointers

Ursa Major (Great Bear)

galaxy is *the most distant object that can be seen with the naked eye.* On a dark, moonless night, this galaxy can be glimpsed as a fuzzy patch about twice as wide as a full moon. A pair of binoculars reveals a seemingly oval shape, but a telescope is needed to see the galaxy clearly.

To the rescue. In the early evening sky of winter, the constellation **Perseus** [pûr′sē•əs] will be located almost directly above you. Perseus was a mythical hero who killed the whale, saved Andromeda from the rock, and later married her. One of the brightest stars in this constellation is *Algol* [ăl′gŏl′], actually a binary star (a group of two stars). Every three days, Algol dims for ten hours as the fainter star passes in front of the brighter star. If you look at Algol for several nights in a row, you may notice this change in brightness.

A flying horse. A flying horse named **Pegasus** is another famous character of Greek mythology. Three of the stars in the Great Square between Andromeda and Pegasus make up the horse's wing. If you find its wing first, you can see the rest of its body more easily.

The lady in chains. According to mythology, Cassiopeia and Cepheus had a daughter named **Andromeda.** Because her beauty made others jealous, Andromeda was chained to a rock to be devoured by a huge whale. (For most of the year, the stellar constellation Whale is too far below the horizon for us to see him). The stars in Andromeda seem to depict the figure of a lady bound with a chain. Her head is one of the bright stars in the **Great Square,** not a constellation in itself, but a group of stars in the constellations Andromeda and Pegasus [pĕg′ə•səs].

Near Andromeda's "knee" is the spiral Andromeda galaxy (p. 241). Roughly 15 quintillion miles away, the Andromeda

The Lion. The constellation **Leo,** the Lion, can be seen close to the eastern horizon on winter nights. **Regulus** [rĕg′yə·ləs], the brightest star in the constellation, marks one of the lion's front paws. To find Regulus, draw a line through the back of the Big Dipper's bowl and out the bottom of the Dipper. The bright stars that outline part of the lion's head are called the **Sickle.**

The Swan. On the other side of the Big Dipper is **Cygnus** [sĭg′nəs], the Swan, which is located in the Milky Way. **Deneb** [dĕn′ĕb], the Swan's brightest star, is located at the top of the **Northern Cross,** a magnificent sight formed by the five brightest stars in the constellation. To find the Swan, extend a line out the top of the Big Dipper through the two stars at the back of the bowl until you reach Deneb.

The Twins. Gemini [jĕm′ə·nī] resembles twin brothers holding hands. The brightest stars in Gemini are **Castor** [kăs′tər] and **Pollux** [pŏl′əks], the heads of the two boys. In the winter and spring sky, you can see the twins walking on the Milky Way. To find this constellation, imagine a line drawn diagonally through the Big Dipper's bowl and outward from the bottom right corner. The line will lead you to Pollux.

The Dragon. Curving around the Little Dipper is the long tail of **Draco** [drā′kō], the dragon. Draco has a rather thin body and a large, somewhat diamond-shaped head. The constellation is best seen during the summer, when it is highest above the northern horizon, on a very dark night.

Cygnus
(The Swan)

Deneb

Northern
Cross

Draco
(The Dragon)

Ursa Major
(Great Bear)

Castor

Pollux

Gemini
(The Twins)

Sickle

Leo
(The Lion)

Regulus

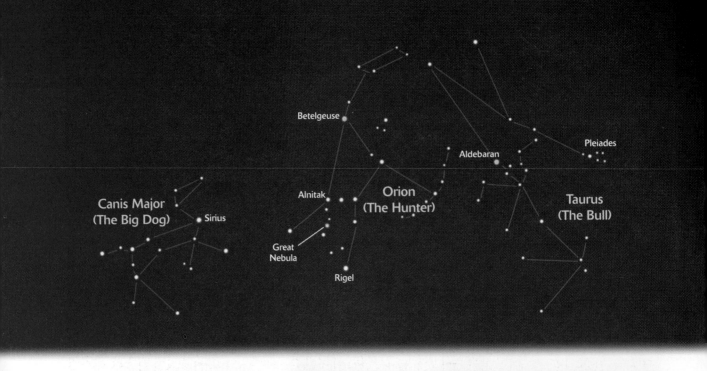

Betelgeuse

Pleiades

Aldebaran

Canis Major
(The Big Dog)

Sirius

Alnitak

Orion
(The Hunter)

Taurus
(The Bull)

Great
Nebula

Rigel

The Hunter. If you look toward the south on a winter night, you will see **Orion,** *the brightest of all constellations.* In one hand, this mighty hunter seems to hold a shield, and in the other he raises a club. A bright sword hangs at his side. Orion's brightest stars are *Betelgeuse* [bēt′′l·jōōz], his right shoulder, and *Rigel* [rī′jəl], his left foot. Reddish-orange Betelgeuse is such a large star that if it were placed in the middle of our solar system, the planets Mercury, Venus, Earth, and possibly Mars would be inside it! The most spectacular part of the constellation, however, is Orion's shining belt, made up of three bright stars that seem to wrap around the hunter's

Great Nebula in Orion

waist. Using binoculars, can you locate a glow among the stars of Orion's sword? This great mass of glowing gas and dust is known as the *Great Nebula.* Orion, mentioned in the Bible in Job 9:9 and 38:31, is hidden from view in the Northern Hemisphere summer because the sun comes between it and the earth.

Pleiades

The Bull. One of the fiercest characters in the sky is **Taurus,** the Bull. Although his horns are long and threatening, and his eye, the large orange star *Aldebaran* [ăl·dĕb′ər·ən], is red with rage, he retreats before the shield and upraised club of Orion the hunter. One of the most spectacular sights in Taurus is the star cluster known as the *Pleiades* [plē′ə·dēz′], located in our drawing at the tip of one of Taurus's horns. Although we can see the six brightest stars in this group even with the unaided eye, binoculars reveal much more of their beauty and allow us to see many of the dimmer stars also. The Pleiades are mentioned in Job 9:8, 9 and 38:31, and in Amos 5:8.

The Big Dog. The constellation **Canis** [kā′nĭs] **Major** (the Big Dog) stands below

and slightly to the east of Orion and appears to accompany Orion in the hunt. The brightest star in this constellation, named **Sirius** [sĭr′ĭ·əs], is *the brightest star in the night sky.* Although Sirius is very bright, the rest of the constellation can be difficult to see in North America because it is low in the sky, close to the horizon.

Constellations of the Southern Hemisphere

Although the northernmost constellations, such as Ursa Major, are hidden from much of the Southern Hemisphere, other northern constellations are visible from below the equator. Likewise, northern observers can see many southern constellations as well.

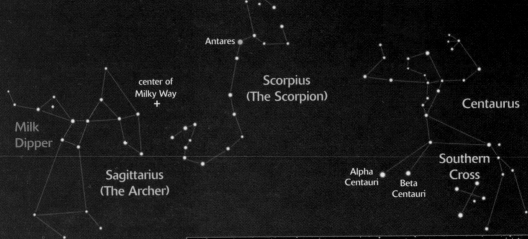

Antares

center of
Milky Way
+

Scorpius
(The Scorpion)

Centaurus

Milk
Dipper

Alpha
Centauri
Beta
Centauri

Southern
Cross

Sagittarius
(The Archer)

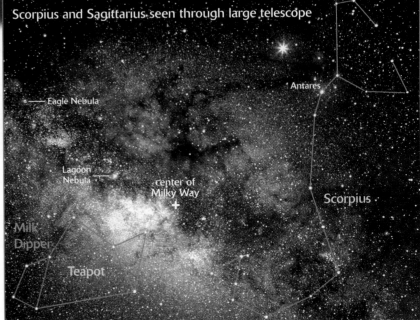

Scorpius and Sagittarius seen through large telescope

Eagle Nebula

Antares

Lagoon
Nebula

center of
Milky Way
+

Scorpius

Milk
Dipper

Teapot

The Scorpion. The large claws and long body of the constellation **Scorpius** [skôr′pē·əs: the Scorpion] weave their way through the sky. The brightest star of the Scorpion is *Antares* [ăn·târ′ēz], whose name means "rival of Mars." This star's brightness and fiery red color often cause people to confuse it with the planet Mars.

The Archer. Near Scorpius, the constellation **Sagittarius** [săj′ĭ·târ′ē·əs: the Archer], aims his bow and arrow at Scorpius as if about to slay him. The brightest stars in this constellation form a figure sometimes called the *Milk Dipper* or the *Teapot* that extends partially into the Milky Way. The spout of the Teapot points toward the center of the Milky Way galaxy.

A strange creature. The large constellation **Centaurus** [sĕn·tôr′əs] is said to resemble a centaur, a mythical creature with the body of a horse and the chest, arms, and head of a man. The two front feet of the creature are the stars *Alpha Centauri* and *Beta* [bā′tə] *Centauri.* Alpha Centauri is actually a group of three stars; the smallest member of the group, *Proxima Centauri,* is the closest star to Earth besides our sun. Centaurus is too far south to be seen by most northern observers.

Between the legs of Centaurus shines the **Southern Cross,** a group of four very bright stars. The Southern Cross is the most familiar sight in the southern sky, but is hidden from northern observers. Although the Southern Hemisphere has no pole star, the upright bar of the cross points nearly due south.

Comprehension Check 4.3

Clues. Give the word or term that best fits each clue.

1. A group of stars which seems to outline the shape of a person, an animal, or something else is called a __?__ .

2. Star often confused with the planet Mars because of its brightness and reddish color

3. The North Star, found in the constellation Ursa Minor

4. The two stars in the Big Dipper that direct us to the North Star are called the __?__ .

5. The most distant object that can be seen with the naked eye

6. The brightest star in the night sky

7. The most familiar group of stars in the southern sky

8. Label the constellations pictured below.

princess chained to a rock

a. _____

mythical queen of Ethiopia

b. _____

half man and half horse

c. _____

a swan

d. _____

a dragon

e. _____

known as a mighty hunter

f. _____

winged horse

g. _____

hero who rescued a princess from a whale

h. _____

the archer

i. _____

a raging bull

j. _____

Northern Constellations

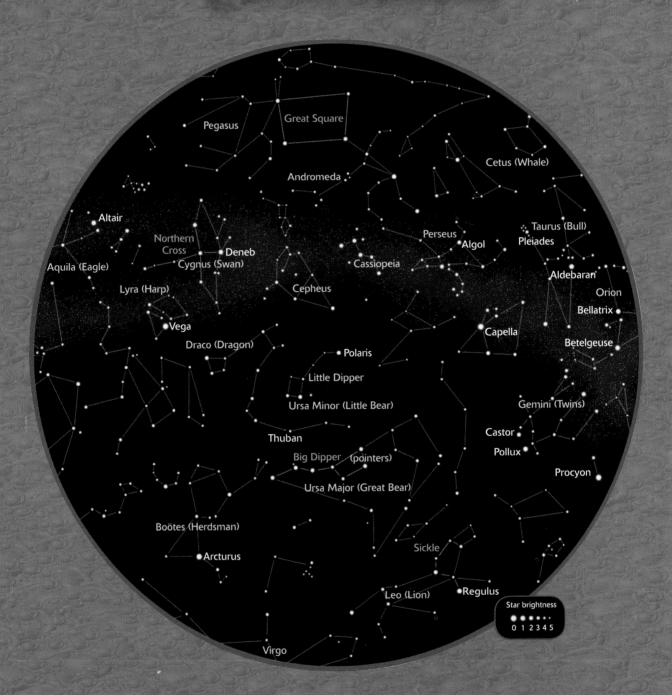

Pegasus
Great Square
Andromeda
Cetus (Whale)
Altair
Northern Cross
Deneb
Perseus
Algol
Pleiades
Taurus (Bull)
Cygnus (Swan)
Cassiopeia
Aquila (Eagle)
Lyra (Harp)
Cepheus
Aldebaran
Orion
Bellatrix
Vega
Capella
Betelgeuse
Draco (Dragon)
Polaris
Little Dipper
Gemini (Twins)
Ursa Minor (Little Bear)
Castor
Thuban
Pollux
Big Dipper (pointers)
Procyon
Ursa Major (Great Bear)
Boötes (Herdsman)
Sickle
Arcturus
Leo (Lion)
Regulus

Star brightness
0 1 2 3 4 5

Virgo

Southern Constellations

Cetus (Whale)

Fomalhaut

Achernar

Rigel

Orion

Canopus

Sirius

Canis Major
(Big Dog)

South Celestial Pole

Sagittarius
(Archer)

Milk Dipper

Shaula

Alpha Centauri

Antares

Southern
Cross

Scorpius
(Scorpion)

Centarus

4.4 Stars: Distant Wonders

The sun: Our closest star

The beneficial star. The most important star to us on Earth is the **sun.** Although the sun is a fairly typical star in size and temperature, it benefits the earth every day, providing the heat, light, and energy that we need to survive. By studying the sun, the closest star to Earth, we can learn more about the billions of other stars which God created and about His provision for life on Earth.

Structure of the sun. The sun is a huge ball of extremely hot gases, mostly hydrogen and helium. The sun's strong gravity pulls the hot gases together and keeps the sun from blowing apart. Surrounding the sun is a very hot *atmosphere* that stretches many thousands of miles into space. The sun does not sit still, but slowly spins, completing one rotation in slightly less than a month.

Although it appears small in the sky, the sun is by far the largest object in the solar system. In fact, the sun is so big that if it were hollow, more than a million planets as large as the earth would fit inside. The sun is also located at an immense distance from the earth—**93 million miles.** Can you imagine how long it would take to *drive* 93 million miles? If you drove at 70 mph and never stopped for food, gas, or rest, it would take 150 years!

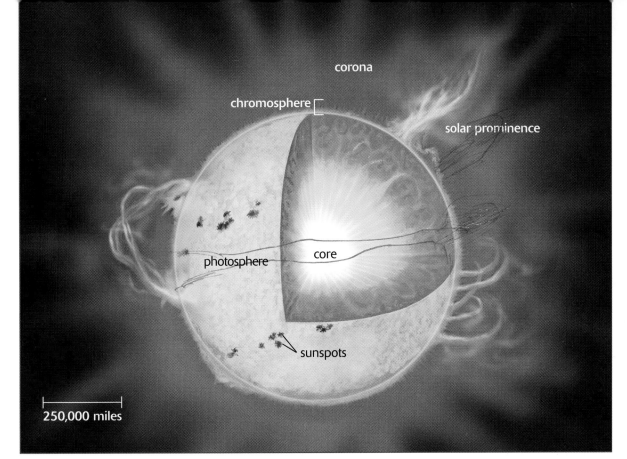

Structure of the sun

A fiery furnace. The hottest region of the sun is the central part, or **core,** where temperatures are thought to exceed 27,000,000 °F. Scientists think that the intense heat and pressure in the sun's core squash hydrogen atoms together so tightly that they combine to form helium atoms, releasing much energy.

As heat moves outward from the blazing core of the sun, it causes gas closer to the surface of the sun to boil like water being heated on a stove. Gigantic currents of hot gas churn in these layers, allowing heat from deeper within the sun to come to the surface. Near the surface, these large currents break up into smaller "bubbles" of rising gas that rise to the surface, giving the sun's face a speckled or granulated look. Each "bubble" or **granule** is about six hundred miles across (about the size of the state of Montana) and lasts five or ten minutes before cooling and sinking back into the sun.

The sun's visible surface is called the **photosphere** [fō′tə·sfĭr], or "sphere of light." Although it looks solid from a distance, the sun's surface would look more like a brilliantly glowing cloud or mist if you could somehow view it up close. Like the filament of a 100-watt light bulb, the photosphere glows with an intense light because it is very hot (10,000 °F). This temperature is more than twice as hot as any light bulb filament, making the sun's surface far brighter than any ordinary bulb.

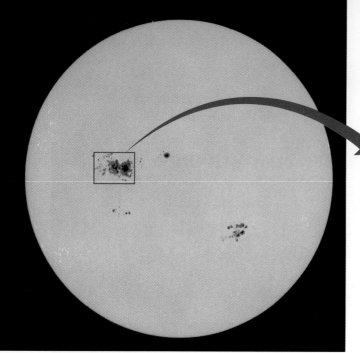

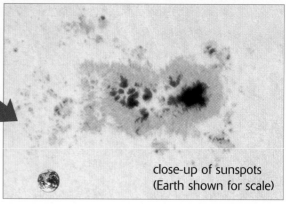

close-up of sunspots
(Earth shown for scale)

Sunspots

Not all of the photosphere is this hot, however. The sun's surface often contains patches of gas that are cooler than the rest of the sun and therefore not as bright. These patches, called **sunspots,** are visible in special telescopes as darker spots or blotches that slowly move across the face of the sun as the sun rotates. Scientists think sunspots occur when the sun's magnetic field slows down the currents of hot gases that bring heat to the sun's surface. In the places where these hot currents are hindered, the sun's surface cools, creating a sunspot. Sunspots range in size from as small as a state to much larger than the earth. Even though sunspots are darker and cooler than the rest of the sun, they would still be very bright if viewed separately. The center of a sunspot is only about one fourth as bright as other regions of the sun's surface, but still far brighter than the filament of a 100-watt bulb.

Scientists have discovered that sunspots follow a cycle of about eleven years.

For a brief portion of the cycle, the face of the sun is practically empty of sunspots. Then the sunspots appear and begin to move diagonally across the face of the sun. As many as two hundred sunspots may appear on the sun in a single cycle. Gradually, the sunspots disappear and the sun is blank again.

The sun's atmosphere. Above the sun's blazing surface (the photosphere) is a thin atmosphere of very hot hydrogen and helium. Although even hotter than the sun's surface, the sun's atmosphere is so thin and transparent that it usually cannot be seen because of the photosphere's glare. However, if the earth's moon passes in front of the sun—a **solar eclipse**—it can block this glare, allowing the sun's atmosphere to be clearly seen.

Atmosphere of the sun

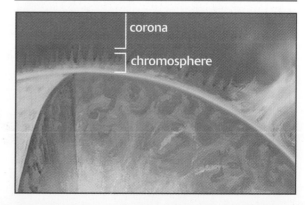

corona

chromosphere

spicules

Astronomers often divide the sun's atmosphere into two regions. The part of the sun's atmosphere closest to the sun's surface is called the **chromosphere** [krō′mə·sfîr], or "sphere of color," because it has a delicate pink or orange color when seen during an eclipse. The temperature in the chromosphere rises from 10,000 °F near the sun's surface to as much as 50,000 °F at a distance of 1000 miles from the sun. Faint "spikes" of hydrogen gas called **spicules** commonly rise from the chromosphere to a height of several thousand miles, but can only be seen using sensitive instruments.

Using special telescopes, scientists can occasionally see huge loops of cooler gas, called **solar prominences,** erupting thousands of miles from the chromosphere, suspended gracefully in space by the sun's powerful magnetic field. Occasionally,

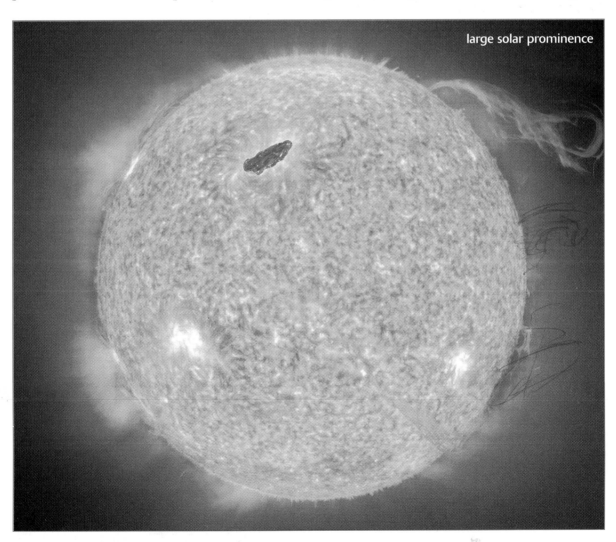
large solar prominence

tremendous bursts of energy called **solar flares** occur in the chromosphere; scientists think that these abrupt flashes of energy are caused by sudden changes in the sun's magnetic field. Solar flares are immensely powerful; the explosion of a large flare can release more energy than 100 billion atomic bombs. Streams of tiny particles (radiation) produced by solar flares can disrupt radio communication and electrical power transmission on the earth.

solar flare erupting from sun's surface

The colossal corona. The hottest region of the sun's atmosphere, called the **corona,** is a haze of very hot gases that extends hundreds of thousands of miles from the surface of the sun. The corona, like the chromosphere, is visible to the human eye only during a total solar eclipse. Heated by the sun's powerful magnetic field, the corona is far hotter than the sun's surface, reaching a temperature of more than 6,000,000 °F. The corona is an ever-changing layer of solar action. Solar flares and prominences often spew out into the scorching gases of the corona, forcing it to stretch even farther into space. It is often punctured by giant "holes" which expand and shrink according to changes in solar magnetism.

At the outer fringes of the corona, particles of gas escape into space at high speed (up to 2 million miles per hour), forming a faint "wind" of high-speed particles called the **solar wind.** Scientists estimate that every second, more than a million tons of gases escape the corona as the solar wind. The sun's strong magnetic field causes the solar wind to "blow" more strongly from some portions of the corona than from others; it blows most strongly from the holes that commonly occur. The colorful auroras sometimes seen in the night sky in the far north are caused by particles of the solar wind beating against the earth's atmosphere.

sun's corona seen during solar eclipse

Long-distance measurements

Although the sun is a long distance from the earth, most stars are so far away that we cannot measure the vast distances between them in everyday units. Even though 93 million miles seems like a long distance, the sun is actually very close to the earth compared to the distant stars we have already studied. In fact, stars such as Betelgeuse, Sirius, and even Proxima Centauri [prŏk′sə·mə sĕn·tôr′ī] are so far away that it is difficult to imagine the vast gulf separating us from them. These vast distances may be referred to in Job 22:12, "Is not God in the height of heaven? and behold the height of the stars, how high they are!"

Understandable units. If someone asked you how far it is from New York to Los Angeles, would you give your answer in inches or in miles? Obviously, you would answer in miles. In a similar way, it would be awkward to express the enormous distances to the stars in miles. The only star close enough to measure in miles would be the sun, and it is 93 million miles away; the next closest star, Proxima Centauri, is about 25 trillion miles away. But even this mind-boggling distance is only a smidgen of the distance across our galaxy—an amazing 590,000,000,000,000,000 (590 quadrillion) miles.

These huge distances are easier to understand if measured in units much larger than a mile. One unit that can be used for measuring such large distances is the **light year**—*the distance light travels in one year.* Light travels at a speed of

more than 186,000 miles per second—about 5.9 trillion miles every year. The distance from our sun to Proxima Centauri is about 4.2 light years; thus, light seen today on the earth from Proxima Centauri has been traveling about 4.2 years. The Andromeda galaxy, the most distant object visible to the unaided human eye, is thought to be about 2.6 million light years away. The distance across the Milky Way galaxy is about 100,000 light years.

For measuring distances within our solar system, however, the light year is too large; for example, the earth is only 0.000016 light years from the sun. It is easier to say "93 million miles."

SPACE**X**PLORER

One way to picture the enormous distances to objects in the solar system or to distant stars is to compare them with everyday objects. For example, if we imagine that the earth were shrunk to the size of the period at the end of this sentence (0.5 millimeter), the moon would be a tiny speck just over half an inch from the earth. On this scale, the sun would be reduced to the size of a tennis ball and would be located 19 feet away from the "earth." The most distant planet in the solar system, Pluto, would be about 250 yards (2½ football fields) from the tennis ball. The speed of light in our imaginary solar system would be reduced to about ½ inch per second.

At this scale, we have managed to shrink the solar system down to the size of a baseball stadium or a large parking lot. At this scale, how far away do you think the stars would be? You might be surprised to learn that even Proxima Centauri, the nearest star other than our sun, would be located nearly *1000 miles away!* The bright star Sirius would be nearly 2000 miles away, and the star Rigel in Orion would be more than 200,000 miles away.

This comparison also helps us imagine the huge size of some celestial objects. If the earth were a period and the sun were a tennis ball, the star Betelgeuse in Orion would be a giant sphere as large as a 10-story building!

Can we apply this size comparison to galaxies? Yes, but the sizes and distances are so large that they are still difficult to grasp. If the earth were a period and the sun a tennis ball 19 feet away, the Andromeda galaxy (the closest large galaxy to us) would be 60 million miles across and 670 million miles away. The most distant galaxy visible with the largest telescopes is thought to be at least 4000 times farther away than the Andromeda galaxy.

Star magnitude

Astronomers refer to the brightness of a star as its **magnitude.** However, there are two ways to describe the magnitude of a star: its *actual* brightness, or how much light it actually produces, and its *apparent* brightness as seen from Earth. For example, a small flashlight seen from a few feet away *seems* brighter than a car's headlights seen from two or three miles away, even though the car's headlights actually produce more light. In the same way, the star Rigel in the constellation Orion produces thousands of times more light than the star Sirius, but Sirius seems brighter in the night sky because it is much, much closer (50 light years instead of 900 light years).

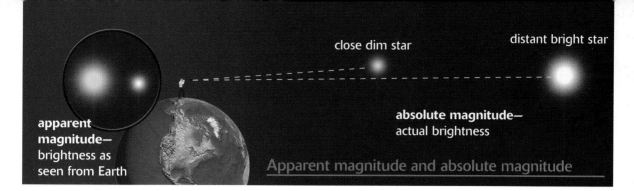

apparent magnitude— brightness as seen from Earth

close dim star

distant bright star

absolute magnitude— actual brightness

Apparent magnitude and absolute magnitude

The actual brightness of a star—how much light the star produces—is called the star's **absolute magnitude.** The absolute magnitude of a star does not depend on the star's distance, but on the amount of light it produces. By contrast, the apparent brightness of a star as seen from earth is called the **apparent magnitude.** The apparent magnitude of a star depends on two things: its *actual brightness* and its *distance from the earth.*

Analyzing appearance. More than a hundred years before Christ lived on the earth, a Greek astronomer and mathematician named Hipparchus [hĭp·pär′kəs] developed a system of classifying stars by their brightness. Hipparchus called the brightest stars *first-magnitude* stars. He classified the faintest stars that were just visible to his unaided eyes as *sixth-magnitude* stars, and he assigned all other stars magnitudes within this range. His basic system was later modified for added precision, and is still in use today. The most important thing to remember about this system is that *the lower the apparent magnitude number, the brighter the object.* Some objects in the sky are so bright that their apparent magnitudes are negative numbers.

The brightest appearing star in the night sky (Sirius) has an apparent magnitude of –1.5. The very bright star *Betelgeuse,* in the constellation Orion, usually has an apparent magnitude of about 0.4. On a very dark night, a person with good eyesight can just barely see stars of magnitude 6. The faintest stars that can be seen with binoculars have magnitudes of 8 or 9. The most powerful telescopes in the world can detect stars as faint as 30th magnitude—dimmer than a glowing coal from a dying campfire seen from 10,000 miles away.

Apparent Magnitude

	Object	Apparent magnitude *(at brightest)*
Visible with the unaided eye	sun	–27
	moon	–13
	Venus	–4
	Jupiter	–2.5
	Sirius	–1.5
	Saturn	0
	Rigel	0.15
	Betelgeuse	0.4
	Mars	1
	Polaris	2.5
	Andromeda galaxy	4–5
	Uranus	6
Visible with binoculars	largest asteroids (in main belt)	6–10
	Neptune	8
	Barnard's Star	9.5
	spiral galaxy on p. 242	10–11
Visible with large telescope	Pluto	14
	faintest stars and galaxies on p. 240	29–30

star temperature, color, and brightness

5000 °F   10,000 °F   20,000 °F   40,000 °F

✐ *Color and categories*

From red to blue. Although a star's apparent magnitude depends largely on its distance, a star's absolute magnitude (the amount of light it produces) depends on two things: its *surface temperature* and its *size*. The star's surface temperature also determines the star's color. Relatively cool stars—those with surface temperatures of 5500 °F or so—appear reddish-orange to the eye (like a campfire or a dim light bulb). Warmer stars, like our sun with its 10,000 °F surface, shine with a much brighter yellow hue. Hot stars shine pure white or blue-white, and the hottest of them all blaze brilliant blue with surface temperatures of 70,000 °F or more.

Generally, the hotter a star's surface, the brighter it will be. However, some cooler stars, like Betelgeuse, manage to outshine smaller, hotter stars simply by being much bigger. The light from a red star the size of our sun, for instance, would be rather feeble; but if you were to multiply that star's surface area ten thousand times, it would be very bright. A tiny white star, on the other hand, could be very hot but so small that it would produce less light than an average-sized yellow star. The brightest stars are both large and hot, such as Rigel, also in Orion; even though it is about twice as far away as Betelgeuse, Rigel actually appears slightly brighter to the eye.

Giants and dwarfs. Stars whose temperature and brightness fall into an average range are called *main sequence* stars.

Classifying stars

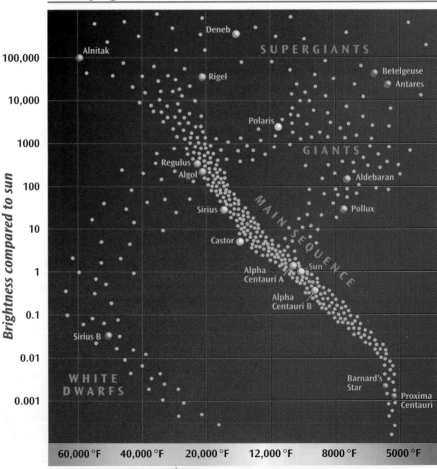

Brightness compared to sun

Surface temperature

Betelgeuse
500,000,000 mi.

Sun
865,000 mi.

diameter of Earth's orbit
186,000,000 mi.

Sirius
1,700,000 mi.

Polaris
40,000,000 mi.

Rigel
60,000,000 mi.

Deneb
150,000,000 mi.

Earth
8000 mi.

Sirius B
6000 mi.

Crab Pulsar
12 mi.

Our "average" sun is a main sequence star, as are most stars in the universe. However, some stars do not fit in the main sequence because they are much brighter than other stars of the same temperature. These stars are called *giants* and *supergiants* because their greater brightness is due to their larger size. The largest supergiants are the red supergiants like Betelgeuse and Antares; some of these stars are so big that if they were placed where the sun is now, the planets Mercury, Venus, Earth, Mars, and Jupiter would be inside them! Some of the most powerful stars are hot supergiants like Deneb; although much smaller than red supergiants, they are much denser and produce far more light for their size.

A few white-hot stars are much dimmer than average stars of the same temperature. Because their dimness is due to their very small size, these stars are called *white dwarfs*. Some white dwarfs are as small as the earth, but contain as much matter as the sun. The matter of these stars is packed so tightly that a single teaspoon of it would weigh more than a full-grown elephant. (Even smaller stars than white dwarfs exist, but we will talk about these in chapter 5.)

Stellar siblings. Astronomers have discovered that many stars in the galaxy do not travel through space alone, but rather in groups of two stars that circle around each other just as the moon circles around the earth. Such a star system is called a **binary star,** or *double star.* For example, Sirius, the "Dog Star," has a companion, called Sirius B (nicknamed "the pup"), so faint that a large telescope is needed to see it at all. Even with a telescope, you can spot the tiny star (a white dwarf) only when it is far enough away from Sirius that it is not blotted out by the glare of its namesake. Sirius B revolves around Sirius once every 50 years.

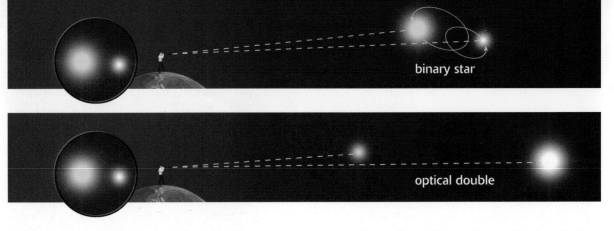

binary star

optical double

Binary stars are very common, but you cannot assume that two stars make up a binary star just because they appear to be very close together. A pair of stars that *appear* very close together from our perspective on the earth, but which are actually far apart, are called an **optical double.** For example, a person with good eyesight can tell that the second star from the end of the Big Dipper's handle is really two stars. Although they look like one binary star, one of the stars is actually far behind the other; the two stars are actually over 30 light years apart. Binary stars can be distinguished from optical doubles by watching the two stars over several months or years; if the stars are seen to circle each other, they obviously form a binary star.

Stellar explosions. Most stars in the sky have shone unchanged ever since people started observing them. However, a few stars have undergone definite changes that have been observed by astronomers. The most dramatic changes are caused by huge explosions that make the star seem far brighter than it

was originally. When the explosion fades, the star may remain seemingly unharmed by the experience, or it may have disappeared into a gigantic cloud of flaming gas.

Occasionally a star will suddenly flare up to many times its original brightness. Such an occurrence is called a **nova** [nō′və]. The star continues to be very bright for some time and then eventually returns to its original magnitude. All novas discovered so far seem to be white dwarf stars orbiting other stars; astronomers speculate that hydrogen gas from the larger star collects on the surface of the white dwarf and occasionally explodes, resulting in a temporary outburst of energy. After the extra hydrogen is burned up, things return to normal. A few novas flare up as often as every 20 years.

In violent contrast to a nova, which leaves the star unharmed, a **supernova** is

Supernova (exploding star)

star before explosion

supernova

the actual explosion of a star—a cosmic catastrophe of amazing violence. From a once-faint star quickly develops one of the brightest stars in the heavens; one supernova in the year 1054 was so bright that it could be seen on earth even during the daytime. In a short time, however, the light fades, and all that remains is the hot, dense core of the star surrounded by an expanding nebula of gas.

Crab Nebula (remnant of A.D. 1054 supernova)

Comprehension Check 4.4

Clues. Give the word or term that best fits each clue.

1. The hot central part of the sun

2. The sun's visible surface

3. Dark patches on the sun's surface caused by the sun's magnetic field

4. Huge loops of cooler gas erupting thousands of miles from the chromosphere that are suspended in space by the sun's magnetic field

5. Tremendous bursts of energy caused by sudden changes in the sun's magnetic field

6. The hottest region of the sun's atmosphere, extending hundreds of thousands of miles from the sun's surface

7. A faint "wind" of high-speed gas particles that stream into space from the sun's corona

8. Unit used to measure great distances, such as the distances between the stars; equal to about 5.9 trillion miles

9. A group of two stars that circle around each other

10. The violent explosion of a star

Explain.

11. How far is the sun from the earth?

12. What is the difference between absolute magnitude and apparent magnitude?

13. Which is brighter, a star with a magnitude of 0, a star with a magnitude of 1.5, or a star with a magnitude of 6?

CONCEPTS
IN SCIENCE

The heavens have always played an important part in the lives of people here on earth. But some people, in their sinfulness, have worshiped the heavenly objects rather than the Creator, God. They turned away from God to idolatry, the worship of false gods, and to astrology.

Do not confuse the science of astronomy with the false belief of astrology. *Astronomy* is the scientific study of the stars, planets, and all other heavenly bodies to discover their size, makeup, motion, and position. *Astrology* is a false belief, or superstition, which claims to tell people's futures by studying the influence of the sun, moon, and stars on people's lives.

God warns us against believing in astrology. Read Isaiah 47:13, 14, and Daniel 2 to find out what God thinks of this false belief. When we look up at the heavens, we should think about God, not about fortunetelling and luck. *"The heavens declare the glory of God; and the firmament showeth His handiwork"* (Psalm 19:1).

4.5 Early Ideas in Astronomy

Ancient astronomers spent many hours studying the night sky, noting the brightnesses of the stars, and plotting their positions on maps of the constellations. They knew that most stars remain in a fixed location relative to other stars, but they also observed five "stars" traveling on independent courses across the sky. Because these unusual stars moved from constellation to constellation as the months passed, astronomers called them *planets*—the "wanderers."

A matter of perspective

Every day, the sun seems to rise above the eastern horizon, journey across the sky, and sink below the horizon in the west, only to reemerge in the eastern sky some twelve hours later. At night, the stars, planets, and moon make similar journeys across the sky, although their actual rising and setting may be hidden by the light of the sun. What happens to the sun, moon, and other heavenly bodies when they vanish below the horizon? In ancient times, some people believed that the earth was flat and that the heavenly bodies journeyed underneath the earth before reappearing in the east.

Astronomers in ancient Greece discovered, however, that the earth is not flat but round. Yet as they watched the rising and setting of the heavenly bodies, many of these astronomers were led to the erroneous view that all heavenly bodies—stars, planets, sun, and moon—revolve around a stationary earth. In their model of the universe, the moon moved in the closest circle of revolution, followed next by the planets Mercury and Venus in their own circles, then by the sun, and then by the planets Mars, Jupiter, and Saturn. Farthest away were the body of fixed stars, thought to be attached to a giant rotating sphere surrounding the rest of the universe. One Greek astronomer named Claudius **Ptolemy** [tŏl′ə•mē] wrote a book in which he presented this idea of an **Earth-centered universe** so convincingly that his theory became the accepted viewpoint for more than 1400 years.

Today, of course, we know that the earth is not a flat surface under which the heavenly bodies must pass before rising again into view. Neither is the earth a stationary sphere around which all heavenly bodies revolve. Rather, the earth is a sphere in motion. Heavenly bodies only *appear* to rise above and sink below the horizon. Their motion as seen from our perspective on the earth is actually a result of the earth's rotation on its axis. The sun, the moon, a planet, or an individual star gradually comes into view as our side of the earth turns to face it. Then it dips below the horizon as our side of the globe turns away. But because we cannot see or feel the earth rotating, you can understand why people in ancient times thought that the other bodies were in motion around the earth.

Although the motions of the sun and moon were easily explained by the theory of an earth-centered universe, the motions

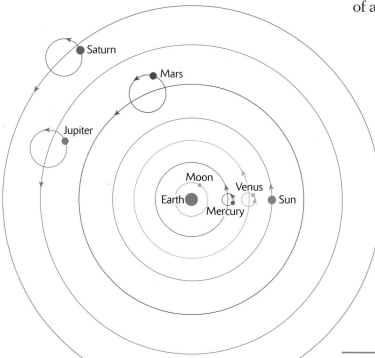

Earth-centered system of Ptolemy

of the five planets were much more perplexing. Planets do not move through the sky in straight lines, as do the sun and moon. In fact, every so often they appear to reverse direction, travel backward for a while, then turn around and go the other way again. To explain the motions of the planets, Ptolemy assumed that the planets traveled in small circles set in bigger circles. However, this made his theory very complicated.

A central sun

In the 1500s, a Polish astronomer named Nicolaus **Copernicus** [nĭk′ō·lā′əs kō·pûr′nə·kəs] was led to question Ptolemy's theory when he realized that, over hundreds of years, Ptolemy's predictions of planetary positions had become rather inaccurate. Copernicus felt that there must be a better way to explain the motions of the planets through the sky. He decided to assume that all the planets **orbit** (revolve around) the sun. Of all the heavenly bodies, only the moon orbits the earth.

The most unusual aspect of Copernicus's theory was his belief that *Earth itself is also a planet.* Like other planets, Earth is in motion around the sun. According to Copernicus, day and night are caused by the earth's rotation on its axis.

With Copernicus's model of a **sun-centered system,** the occasional backward motions of the planets are easily explained. These motions exist only in the perspective of an observer on the earth. The observer is himself moving through space on a planet, and his planet is traveling at a speed different from that of any other planet. The path traced in the night sky by each planet is the combined result of its actual motion and the earth's actual motion. While proceeding through its orbit, Earth races past all planets farther from the sun,

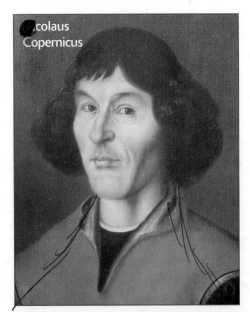

Nicolaus Copernicus

Sun-centered system of Copernicus

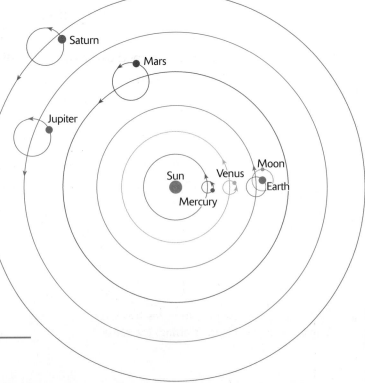

Saturn
Mars
Jupiter
Sun
Mercury
Venus
Moon
Earth

and in turn is outrun by the two planets nearer the sun: Venus and Mercury. Thus, as the earth passes Mars, Mars seems to travel backward for a time, much in the same way that a slow-moving car on the freeway seems to move backward as the car you are riding in passes it.

Unfortunately, Copernicus (like Ptolemy) assumed that the orbits of all of the planets had to be perfect circles. As a result, he was forced to add additional, smaller circles to the orbits in order to explain the planets' motions. This made his theory nearly as complicated as Ptolemy's.

For many years, the model proposed by Copernicus was not popular. After all, people could not feel the earth moving beneath their feet. Other scientists such as Galileo were ridiculed for agreeing with Copernicus, even though they had evidence to suggest that Ptolemy's theory was wrong. Galileo, for instance, saw moons orbiting Jupiter, a discovery indicating that not all bodies in the solar system circle the earth. As science developed after the Protestant Reformation of the 1500s, more and more astronomers began to question the truth of Ptolemy's earth-centered view of the universe.

Somewhat out of round

A short time after Copernicus, a German astronomer named **Johannes Kepler** [yō·hän′ kĕp′lər] began to study the orbital motions of the planets. Kepler was a godly Lutheran whose goal was "finding the mathematical harmonies in the mind of the Creator." After examining very careful records of the planets' tracks across the skies, he made an astounding discovery: the path of a planet around the sun is not a circle with the sun at the center, as Copernicus had thought, but rather is a special type of oval called an ellipse [ĭ·lĭps′].

An **ellipse** is *a symmetrically shaped oval*. Inside an ellipse are two points known as **foci** [fō′sī: plural of *focus*]. The sum of the distances from each of the two foci to any point on the ellipse is always the same. For example, let's say that the distance from one focus to a certain point on an ellipse is 5 inches, and the distance from the other focus to the same point is 2 inches. The sum of these distances is 7 inches. If you move to another point on the ellipse, the distance from the first focus to that point may have decreased to only 4 inches, but the distance from that point to the second focus will have increased to 3 inches, for the same total of 7 inches. The distances from both foci to every point on that particular ellipse must total 7 inches; otherwise, the shape is not an ellipse.

Shape of an ellipse

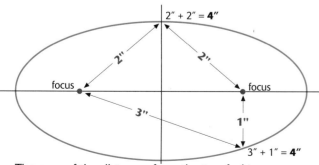

The sum of the distances from the two foci to any point on the ellipse is always the same.

AMATEUR ASTRONOMER

Drawing ellipses

You can draw an ellipse using the following equipment: *a sheet of poster board or a piece of cardboard, two tacks (six if you use the poster board), a length of string,* and *a pencil.* To do the experiment at school, tack the poster board (one tack in each corner) to a bulletin board in your classroom. Then place the other two tacks in the middle of the poster board. These will be the foci of your ellipse. At home, you can perform the experiment by placing two tacks in a piece of cardboard. (You may want to double the cardboard up so that you do not stick the tacks into the tabletop beneath.)

The next step is to tie the ends of the string together. Then place the string around the two tacks and the tip of your pencil, and pull the string tight so that it forms a triangle. (Do not pull too hard or you may pull out the tacks.) As you keep the string taut, move the pencil point

all the way around the two foci, drawing a shape on the poster board or cardboard. This shape will be an ellipse, because your pencil point always stays the same total distance from the two foci. When the pencil moves closer to one of the foci, it moves farther away from the other so that the total distance (determined by the fixed length of the string) remains constant. Try spreading the foci farther apart. How does this change affect the shape of the ellipse? Try putting them right next to each other. What shape would be made if both foci were located at exactly the same point?

Planets on the move

Having discovered the elliptical shape of the planets' orbits, Kepler was able to formulate **three laws of planetary motion.** The **first law** states that *every planet orbits the sun in an ellipse, with the sun as one of the foci of the ellipse and an empty point in space as the other.* The shape of each planet's elliptical orbit is

different. For instance, the orbit of Mars is much more elliptical than that of Earth. In fact, Earth's orbit is nearly round. Our planet is never farther than 94.5 million miles away from the sun, and never closer than 91.4 million miles. The average distance between Earth and the sun is **93 million miles.** Can you imagine how the earth's climate would be affected if the earth's path had the shape of a longer, narrower ellipse?

The **second law** states that *as a planet moves closer to the sun, it travels faster; and as it moves farther away, it slows down.* For instance, Earth travels about 2200 miles per hour faster when it is closest to the sun than when it is farthest from the sun.

The **third law** *shows the relationship between a planet's distance from the sun and the time it takes the planet to complete one orbit.* Although Kepler did not know the actual distances in miles between the sun and the planets, he was able to use this law to calculate the planets' *relative* distances from the sun; that is, their distances in comparison to each other. He measured these distances in astronomical units, one **astronomical unit** being *the distance between the earth and the sun.* Mars, for instance, is about 1.5 astronomical

units from the sun, just slightly farther away than Earth. Saturn is about 9.5 astronomical units away from the sun. Although modern astronomers have been able to calculate these distances in miles, the astronomical unit—equivalent to ***93 million miles***—is such a useful measuring rod that it is still used today.

One consequence of Kepler's third law is that ***the inner planets travel around the sun at a much faster pace than do the outer planets.*** Even at its slowest speed, Mercury—the planet closest to the sun—moves along much faster than distant Saturn ever does. Because the outer planets move more slowly and travel

Johannes Kepler

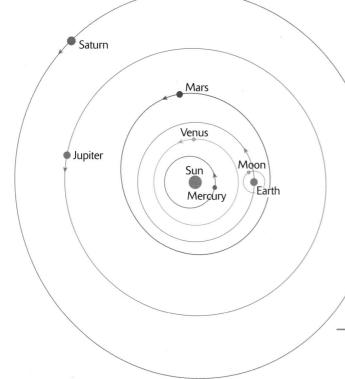

Kepler's system of elliptical orbits

farther while completing one revolution around the sun, their years are much longer than those of the inner planets. Mercury's year is only as long as 88 days on Earth, but Saturn's year is equal to 29½ Earth years.

Gravity: glue for the universe

Kepler's three laws describe the motion of the planets, but they do not explain why the planets orbit the sun. What keeps the planets in their elliptical orbits? Why do they not leave the solar system to travel on their own through the universe? These questions were answered by **Sir Isaac Newton.** His greatest scientific achievement was the discovery of **gravity,** *the force of attraction that exists between any two objects*. His **law of universal gravitation** states that *the strength of the gravitational force between two objects depends on their masses (the amount of matter they contain) and the distance between them.* Two dimes in your pocket have such a small force of gravity between them that it is not noticeable or measurable, but large objects such as the moons, planets, and stars have a strong gravitational attraction for each other even over the great distances separating them in space. Gravity holds the planets on their courses around the sun. It causes stars to clump together into galaxies and galaxies to cluster together in groups. On a smaller scale, the earth's gravity pulls a high fly ball back to the ground and makes you fall when you trip on a tree root.

If the gravitational force of the sun is strong enough to affect the motion of planets millions of miles away, what keeps the sun from pulling the planets in toward itself until they collide with the sun? Newton proposed that if any object (whether a planet or a cannonball) were completely free from the influence of all outside forces, it would travel in a straight path through the universe without slowing down or changing direction. But the sun's gravity pulls on the moving planets and bends their courses into ellipses. Their speed is fast enough for them to maintain their distance from the sun, yet not fast enough for them to escape from the sun's gravity and plunge headlong into deep space. To avoid collapsing inward toward the sun, the planets closest to it must travel faster than those farther away, because the sun's gravity pulls on them more strongly.

Sir Isaac Newton

Science SPEAKS

Great Scientists Give Glory to God

Johannes Kepler (1571–1630)

"We may behold how God, like a master-builder, has laid the foundation of the world according to order and law."

"I give Thee thanks, Lord and Creator, that Thou hast given me joy through Thy creation."

Galileo (1564–1642)

"A hundred passages of holy Scripture teach us that the glory and greatness of Almighty God are marvelously displayed in all His works and divinely read in the open book of the heaven."

Sir Isaac Newton (1642–1727)

"The motions which the planets now have could not spring from any natural cause done but were impressed by an intelligent agent."

"The universe was rightly designed a Temple of God. This Being governs all things . . . as Lord over all."

"If all the great books of the world were given life and brought together in convention, the moment the Bible entered, the other books would fall on their faces as the gods of Philistia fell when the ark of God was brought into their presence in the temple of Dagon."

Comprehension Check 4.5

Clues. Give the word or term that best fits each clue.

1. Ancient Greek astronomer that is known for his theory of an earth-centered universe

2. Polish astronomer who proposed a sun-centered system, in which the earth and the other planets revolve around the sun

3. German astronomer who formulated the three laws of planetary motion

4. A symmetrically shaped oval

5. Two central points of an ellipse

6. The distance between the earth and the sun, or 93 million miles

7. English scientist who formulated the law of universal gravitation

Explain.

8. The three laws of planetary motion

9. The Law of Universal Gravitation

4.6 Exploring the Solar System

Our sun is the center of a vast system many billions of miles across. Around the sun are found all the smaller heavenly bodies that orbit the sun, their movements governed by the sun's powerful force of gravity. The largest heavenly bodies that orbit the sun are known as **planets.** Many of the planets, in turn, are surrounded by smaller bodies called **moons** that orbit the planet. Moons orbit their planets while the planets themselves follow larger orbits around the sun. In addition to the planets and moons, there are other heavenly bodies that orbit the sun yet are independent of the planets. These smaller bodies can be divided into three groups: *asteroids, meteoroids,* and *comets.* (You will read about these three groups in a following section.)

The sun's "kingdom" of planets, moons, and smaller bodies is called the **solar system.** *The solar system is made up of the sun and all the heavenly bodies that orbit it.* The known solar system consists of nine

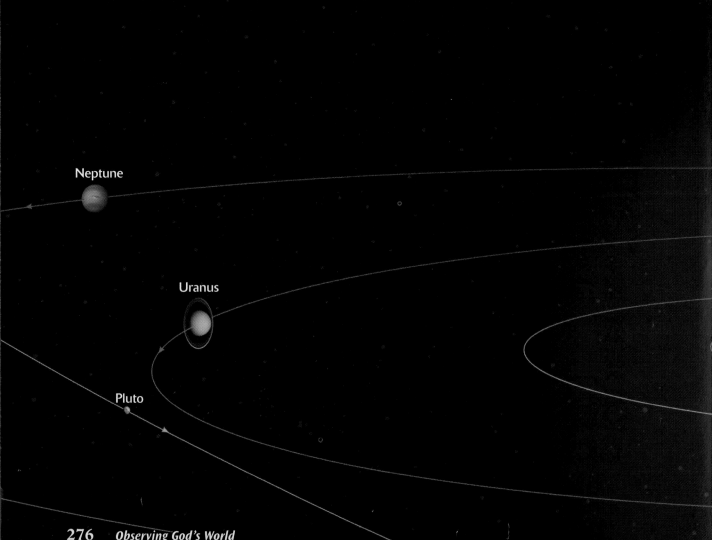

Neptune

Uranus

Pluto

planets, more than one hundred moons, and countless asteroids, comets, and meteoroids.

 ## Newfound members of the solar system

Ancient astronomers tracked seven wanderers in the heavens: the sun, the moon, and five starlike bodies—*Mercury, Venus, Mars, Jupiter,* and *Saturn.* After the time of Copernicus, Earth itself became recognized as a sixth planet. The known solar system, then, consisted of six planets, the earth's moon, and the sun.

The invention of the telescope opened the door for many new discoveries. Galileo found moons orbiting the planet Jupiter, just as our moon orbits the earth. And it was not long before astronomers discovered that there were more than six planets orbiting the sun. In 1781, a seventh planet, *Uranus* [yŏŏ′rə·nəs] was discovered by an English astronomer and his sister; 65 years later, in 1846, astronomers discovered an eighth planet, *Neptune.* The ninth and final planet, a tiny world named *Pluto,* was discovered in 1930.

Mars Earth Venus Mercury sun

asteroid belt

Jupiter

Saturn

Planets and moons

Inner and outer planets. The nine planets can be divided into two groups. The four planets closest to the sun—*Mercury, Venus, Earth,* and *Mars*—are the **inner planets.** They are made mainly of rocks and metals. Earth is unique because it is the one planet perfectly suited for life.

The **outer planets** are *Jupiter, Saturn, Uranus, Neptune,* and *Pluto.* Except for Pluto, these planets are much larger than the inner planets. They are not made of solid rocks or metals, but are composed mainly of gases, liquids, or ice. Although the inner planets are separated from each other by "only" tens of millions of miles, most of the outer planets are spaced roughly a *billion* miles apart. Pluto is over 100 times farther away from the sun than Mercury is. (You will read more about what the planets are like in chapter 5.)

Multiple moons. We normally use the word *moon* to refer to the heavenly body that revolves around the earth. But just as Earth is one planet among many, so is Earth's moon just one of many moons in the solar system. In a more general sense, the word *moon* can refer to any natural satellite of a planet. (The individual fragments making up a ring around a planet would not, however, be considered moons.)

Most of the planets in the solar system have more than one moon. In fact, *only two planets—Venus and Mercury—have no moons,* and only two planets—Earth and Pluto—have just one moon. It is hard to keep track of the exact number of moons orbiting some of the planets in our solar system, because additional moons orbiting such planets as Uranus and Saturn are continually being discovered. In 2002, Jupiter had 39 known moons, Saturn had 30, and Uranus had 21. Neptune has 8 known moons, while Mars has 2.

Some of the solar system's moons are large spheres bigger than Earth's moon or even larger than some of the smallest planets. Other moons are small chunks of rock only a few miles across.

Other solar systems? Is our sun the only star in the universe surrounded by planets, or did God create other "solar systems" in addition to our own? The Bible is silent on this question. Astronomers have long speculated that other stars might have planets and solar systems just as the sun does, but it was not until the development of more sensitive telescopes in the 1990s that astronomers could study the question in a scientific way. By 2000, it appeared that several dozen nearby stars were surrounded by at least one planet. However, we can say for certain that whatever these planets are like, they are not like the earth; we know from the Scriptures that Earth is *the* special planet that God designed especially for the people, animals, and plants that He created. As Psalm 115:16 states, "The heaven, even the heavens, are the Lord's: but the earth hath He given to the children of men."

Comprehension Check 4.6

Clues. Give the word or term that best fits each clue.

1. The largest heavenly bodies that orbit the sun
2. The sun and all the heavenly bodies that orbit it
3. The inner planets
4. The outer planets
5. The two planets that do not have any moons

4.7 Our Earth

Would you like to be a space traveler? To ride in a spaceship would certainly be an exciting opportunity. Actually, you already are a space traveler, even though your feet may have never left the solid ground. Your mom and dad, your brothers and sisters, your friends at school—everyone you know—is a space traveler, because the earth we live on is itself traveling through space. It is an enormous spaceship, and you have been riding on it through space all your life.

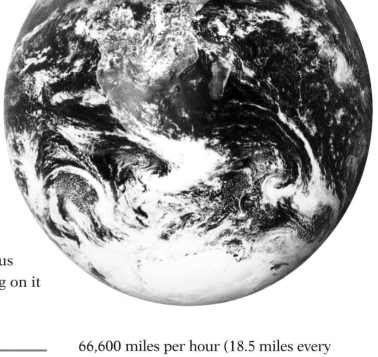

Earth on the move

Revolution. Speeding around our sun are many bodies of matter. Our spaceship, the earth, is one of the largest of these heavenly bodies. In each **revolution,** or trip around the sun, the earth travels about 590,000,000 miles at an average speed of 66,600 miles per hour (18.5 miles every second). It takes the earth only **365 ¹/₄ days,** or one **solar year,** to complete one revolution. If you are 12 years old, you have journeyed about 7 billion miles around the sun in your lifetime, even if you have never left your hometown!

Rotation. Not only does the earth revolve around the sun, but at the same time it also spins on its axis, rather like a top. As the earth spins, any given point on the equator travels around at a rate of over 1000 miles per hour. This rapid spinning allows the earth to complete one **rotation** in 24 hours. The earth's rotation is what causes the sun to rise and set.

Even though the earth is spinning like a top, we do not have to worry about falling off. Gravity keeps us from being flung into outer space. In fact, we do not even get the least bit dizzy. Because all of our surroundings are moving at exactly the same rate we are, we do not perceive the motion of our planet.

Designed for life

When we contemplate the vastness of the universe, we cannot help but be amazed at God's great power. We are also reminded of just how small we humans are. After all, our galaxy, though very large to us, is only a tiny corner of the universe. The stars are nothing more than small dots in this galaxy, and in comparison with the stars, the earth is merely a tiny speck of rock. Tucked away between two arms of the Milky Way galaxy, the

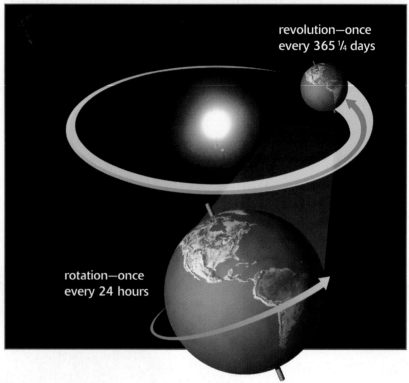

Rotation and revolution of the earth

revolution—once every 365 ¼ days

rotation—once every 24 hours

earth seems like an insignificant addition to the universe. You might start to think that the earth is not all that important. But the earth is actually very special. Although our God is big enough to make the vast universe, He is especially concerned about the earth, because it is the place where people live. God designed the earth to be our home.

The atmospheric filter. God designed the earth with a protective **atmosphere,** or blanket of air, that makes the earth hospitable for living things. When we compare the earth to the moon, which has no atmosphere, we can see how important the earth's atmosphere is. For example, the moon's airless surface is baked at more than 200 °F during the long lunar day, but becomes bitterly cold shortly after the sun finally sets. Harmful particles from the solar wind and solar flares (section 4.4) and rock fragments traveling at bulletlike speeds continually shower the moon's airless surface. The moon is also bombarded with other forms of invisible radiation from the sun, such as ultraviolet rays (which cause sunburn and skin cancer) and X-rays (which can be harmful in large doses). In contrast to the moon's inhospitable environment, the earth's atmosphere makes our planet a very hospitable place indeed. Even more importantly, the atmosphere provides us with oxygen to breathe.

God has given to the atmosphere the job of keeping harmful radiation from reaching the earth. For example, ultraviolet radiation is filtered out in the **ozone** [ō′zōn] **layer,** a region of the atmosphere between 10 and 30 miles above the

surface of the earth. Although most of the sun's ultraviolet radiation is absorbed in this layer, some does get through to the earth's surface. The small portion that gets through is what causes your skin to burn when you stay outside unprotected too long on a summer day. Although

Earth's protective atmosphere

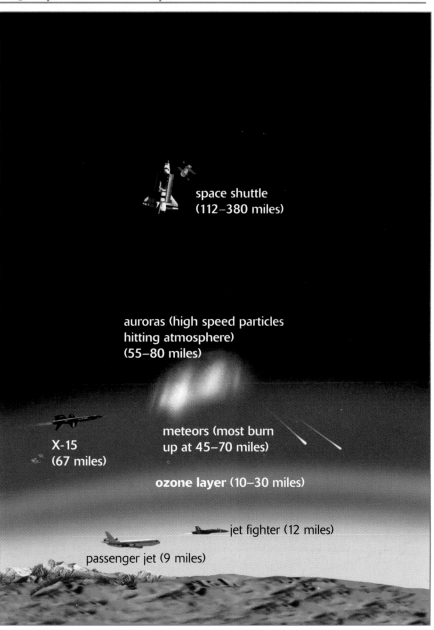

space shuttle
(112–380 miles)

auroras (high speed particles hitting atmosphere)
(55–80 miles)

X-15
(67 miles)

meteors (most burn up at 45–70 miles)

ozone layer (10–30 miles)

jet fighter (12 miles)

passenger jet (9 miles)

most harmful radiation is absorbed by the air above us, the atmosphere is designed to let beneficial radiation through to reach the surface. For example, infrared (heat) radiation and visible light are both able to pass through the atmospheric filter to the earth's surface, where they furnish us with warmth and light.

A delicate balance. The earth's atmosphere also helps protect us from harsh temperature extremes like those found on the moon. When the sun goes down on the moon, the moon's hot surface quickly radiates its heat back into space and grows bitterly cold. On the earth, however, God designed the atmosphere to hold in heat like a thick, insulating blanket. This ability of the atmosphere to retain heat around the earth is known as the **greenhouse effect.** The greenhouse effect helps the earth to stay warm at night, preventing temperatures from rapidly dropping below freezing every night as soon as the sun goes down.

The coldest temperatures in the universe—those that exist in the black voids of outer space far from any stars—can be as low as –454 °F. On the other hand, the temperature in the core of a star may reach several hundreds of millions of degrees. But in order for life to survive on Earth, temperatures on its surface must be kept within a very limited range. Most plants and animals cannot tolerate temperatures much over 100 °F or far below 0 °F. Earth's temperatures are prevented from swinging far above or below these limits not only by the atmosphere, but also by other features of the earth's design. For instance, God placed the earth at an ideal distance from the sun— not too close, or living things would burn up, and not too far away, or they would freeze. Also, God gave the earth a broad covering of surface water—the oceans. Because water holds heat much better than does solid ground, the oceans help to keep temperatures mild all over the globe.

Comprehension Check 4.7

Clues. Give the word or term that best fits each clue.

1. 365¼ days long

2. The earth completes one every 24 hours

3. Harmful ultraviolet radiation is filtered out in this region of the earth's atmosphere

4. The ability of the earth's atmosphere to retain heat around the earth

5. Help to keep global temperatures mild because water holds heat so well

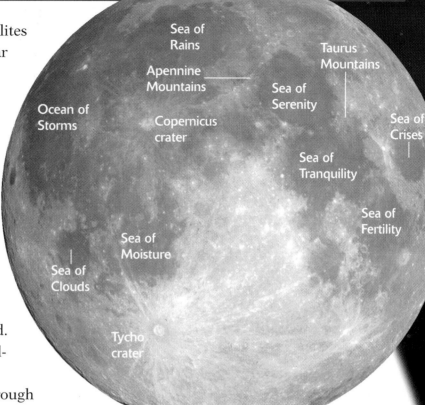

Sea of Rains

Apennine Mountains

Ocean of Storms

Copernicus crater

Taurus Mountains

Sea of Serenity

Sea of Crises

Sea of Tranquility

Sea of Fertility

Sea of Moisture

Sea of Clouds

Tycho crater

Of the thousands of satellites that orbit the earth, one is far larger than any of the rest. Glistening a soft silver-white in the nighttime sky, this satellite reflects enough light for you to see by even when the sun is shining on the other side of the earth. It was put into orbit by God long before man ever thought of launching satellites into space, and even before man had been created. What is this mysterious satellite? The **moon,** of course!

If you view the moon through a telescope or a pair of binoculars, you may think that it looks like a giant sponge. Its surface is pockmarked with countless craters, some smaller than tennis balls and others hundreds of miles across and several miles deep. Mountain ranges similar in size to the Rockies and the Himalayas rise up in some areas of the moon, while other areas, called **maria** [mä′rē·ə], or *seas,* resemble rolling plains. These maria are the dark patches on the moon you can see even with the unaided eye. They were named *maria* because people used to think that they were bodies of water on the lunar surface. Scientists later discovered that the maria are not nearly as smooth as they appear from Earth and that they contain no water.

The traveling moon

Orbiting the earth. Revolving around the earth at a speed of about 2300 miles an hour—faster than a speeding rifle bullet—the moon takes 29 days, 12 hours, and 44 minutes to complete a full cycle. This period of time is called a **lunar month.** The moon completes one rotation in about the same amount of time. Because the moon's periods of rotation and revolution are of equal length, the same side of the moon faces the earth all the time. When we see moonlight, we are seeing the rays of the sun reflected from the near side of the moon.

Phases of the moon. As the lunar month progresses, the moon seems to change size and shape. It does not really change, however; it just appears that way as different parts of it reflect the sun's light or are hidden in shadow as the moon circles the earth. The lunar month begins when the sunlit side of the moon is turned away from Earth and completely hidden from view. The moon at this time is called the **new moon.** As the moon revolves around the earth, we next see a tiny sliver, or *crescent*, of the moon. The visible moon then gradually **waxes,** or grows larger, until it is half light and half dark. The moon in this position is called the **first-quarter moon.** When the visible moon is waxing from the new moon to the first-quarter moon, it is said to be in the **crescent phase.**

As the moon continues its revolution, what we see gradually increases in size until the whole sphere is illuminated. When we see the entire sunlit side of the moon, we are viewing what is called the **full moon.** Because the visible moon seems to bulge as it waxes from first quarter to full, it is then said to be in the **gibbous** [gĭb′əs: bulging] **phase.**

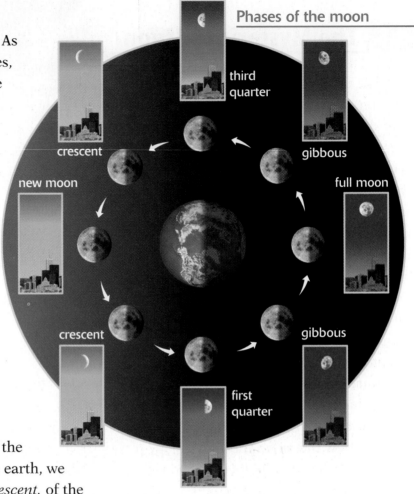

third quarter

crescent

gibbous

new moon

full moon

crescent

gibbous

first quarter

A second gibbous phase occurs when the visible moon **wanes,** or shrinks, from the full moon. When the moon is half dark and half light again it is called the **third-quarter moon.** The moon continues to wane, passing through a second crescent phase, until it again becomes invisible and a new lunar month begins.

Eclipses. You will remember that a solar eclipse occurs when the new moon moves directly between the sun and the earth for a few moments and blocks the sun's photosphere from our view. A **lunar eclipse** occurs sometimes when the moon is full. As the moon passes directly behind the earth, the earth briefly

lunar eclipse

blocks sunlight from the moon, causing the moon to appear darkened. If you go outside at night to watch a lunar eclipse, you can easily see the earth's curved shadow slowly move across the face of the moon.

Large appearance. Although the moon's diameter is only about one quarter as large as the earth's, the moon appears much larger than any other heavenly body you see in the nighttime sky. Even the sun, which is thousands of times larger than the moon, is covered by the moon during a solar eclipse. The great apparent size of the moon is a result of its closeness. The moon is only about 240,000 miles from the earth, whereas the sun is 93 million miles away.

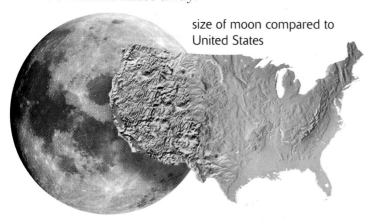
size of moon compared to United States

The moon's closeness to the earth creates quite a "stir" on the earth's surface. Ocean waters rise and fall as the moon passes overhead, and even the land feels the moon's gravitational pull. Those who live near the ocean are familiar with the changing of tides. These tides are caused by the moon's gravity, which pulls the water toward itself. Two high tides and two low tides occur every day as the earth slowly rotates through the pull of the moon's gravity.

High tide and low tide. The water of the ocean rises, or moves up the shore, until it reaches its highest point, called **high tide;** then it falls, or moves away from the shore, until it reaches its lowest point, called **low tide.** Coastlines on the earth experience high tide when they are in line with the moon. The pull of the moon's gravity creates a bulge in the water on that part of the earth's surface closest to the moon. At the same time, places on the opposite side of the earth are also at high tide. Those areas in between and

Tides

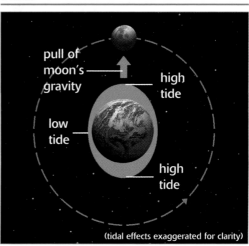

pull of moon's gravity

high tide

low tide

high tide

(tidal effects exaggerated for clarity)

low tide

high tide

not in line with the moon experience low tide. As the earth rotates, the tides at any particular coastal location change every six hours.

For instance, a particular beach may experience a low tide at eight o'clock in the morning. An early morning swimmer can place his towel a few yards from the water's edge without any fear of it getting wet. As the day progresses, however, the earth rotates so that by two o'clock in the afternoon, the beach is directly in line with the moon. By this time, the tide would be high on the shore—so high, in fact, that the swimmer's towel would be soaked by the waves. At eight in the evening, the tide is as low as it was at eight in the morning. Because the earth has made half of its rotation, the beach is as far away from being in line with the moon as it was

when the swimmer placed his towel on the beach. At about two in the morning, the tide at the beach is high once again. This time the towel should remain dry, however, because by now the swimmer has probably picked up his towel and gone home.

Spring tide. When the sun and moon are in line with the earth, the gravitational pull of the sun teams up with the gravitational pull of the moon. The combined forces create **spring tides,** which are higher or lower than normal tides. Spring tides occur twice in a lunar month, once during the new moon and once during the full moon.

Neap tide. Neap tides occur when there is a first-quarter moon or a third-quarter moon. At these times, the gravitational forces of the sun and the moon work at right angles, against each other. As a result, the tides are weaker than usual.

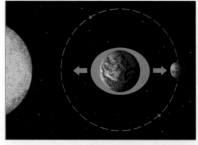
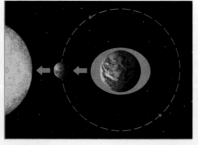

spring tides—stronger than usual

neap tide—weaker than usual

Spring and neap tides

Comprehension Check 4.8

Clues. Give the word or term that best fits each clue.

1. When the moon is in line with the earth and sun, rather far up the beach do the high tides run.

2. This phase displays the most light of all, because it is shaped like a big round ball.

3. From new to a quarter and three quarters to new, this phase may appear like a sliver to you.

4. This lunar phase is quite easy to sight, when the waxing moon is half dark and half light.

5. When the sun and the moon are at right angles to the earth, the result is a tide of little worth.

6. Twice in a lunar month this phase is found when the moon's shape bulges but is not quite round.

7. The moon in this phase seems to hide, because you cannot see its sunlit side.

Explain

8. Why does the moon appear to change shape as the month progresses?

9. Why does the moon seem to be bigger than any star?

10. Why do we have tides?

11. What is the difference between a solar eclipse and a lunar eclipse?

4.9 Smaller Space Travelers

The planets and their moons are not the only travelers in our solar system. Icy comets whiz around the sun before heading back into deeper space. Groups of odd-shaped asteroids glide along more slowly, resembling pebbles scattered between the giant planetary spheres. Meteoroids, whether chunks of rock or microscopic particles of dust and other debris, speed aimlessly through space until they are swept up by the gravity of an approaching planet or moon. Each of these tiny travelers—asteroid, comet, or meteoroid—has its own unique characteristics.

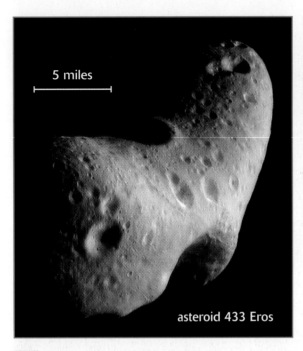

5 miles

asteroid 433 Eros

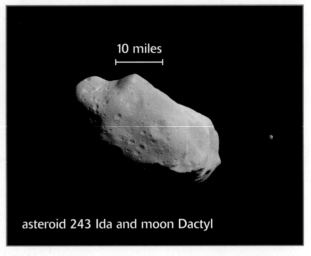

10 miles

asteroid 243 Ida and moon Dactyl

Asteroids: Odd orbiters

The amazing asteroid belt. On January 1, 1801, a dull gleam between Mars and Jupiter caught the attention of an Italian astronomer. As he continued to study the light through his telescope night after night, he noticed that it was moving, and that it was going in the same direction as were the nearby planets. He therefore concluded that the object, which he called *Ceres* [sĭr′ēz], was actually a planet. Shortly after his discovery, other astronomers determined that Ceres is too small to be classified as a planet; it measures only about 600 miles in diameter—about ¼ the diameter of the earth's moon. As more astronomers began to study the area around Ceres, they discovered many even smaller objects. Instead of a new planet, they had discovered a whole region of little "planets." So far, over 100,000 tiny worlds known as **asteroids** [ăs′tə·roidz]

are known to be traveling around the sun, and dozens more are discovered every day. Asteroids range in size from a few hundred miles across (like Ceres) to as small as a house. Scientists estimate that there may be more than 1 million asteroids larger than ⅔ of a mile in size, and an even greater number of smaller asteroids. If all of the asteroids were assembled together into a single planet, the planet would be somewhat smaller than earth's moon.

Asteroid names. Although the first asteroids were given names from Greek and Roman mythology, there are so many asteroids that other sources of names have had to be used. For example, one asteroid is named Beethoven, and another is named Africa. Since there are so many asteroids, astronomers also assign each asteroid a number to prevent confusion. When referring to an asteroid, astronomers usually use both the number and the name, such as *1 Ceres* or *1193 Africa*.

An assortment of asteroids. Most asteroids do not have the spherical shape that is common among planets and moons. For instance, one asteroid called 433 Eros [ĕr′ŏs] is 21 miles long, 8 miles across, and shaped like a bent potato. It slowly tumbles end over end as it orbits the sun. Some asteroids even have little "moons"—smaller asteroids that slowly orbit the larger asteroid.

Asteroid locations. Although most asteroids are found in a region called the **asteroid belt,** located between the orbits of Mars and Jupiter, a large number are found elsewhere in the solar system. A group called the *Trojan asteroids* shares the same orbit as the planet Jupiter; a few hundred Trojan asteroids travel millions of miles in front of Jupiter as it orbits the sun, while hundreds more tag along millions of miles behind the planet.

A very important group of asteroids located outside the main belt are the **near-Earth asteroids.** These asteroids are located in the inner solar system, and most of them cross paths with the earth. Every day, several small near-earth asteroids pass closer to the earth than the moon does, and one explodes high in the earth's atmosphere about once per month. Once every century or so, a small near-earth asteroid collides with the earth to produce a soccer-field-sized crater, as we shall see later.

Locations of asteroids

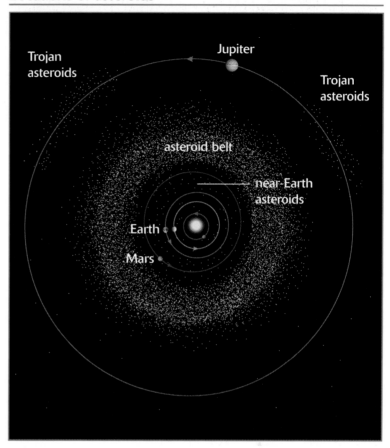

Comets: Icy travelers

A comet's parts. Some of the most spectacular objects in the night sky are **comets,** asteroid-sized objects that develop a huge, bright tail when they come near the sun. It is because of the characteristic tail that the term *comet,* meaning "long-haired star," came about. Ancient stargazers in Asia dubbed comets "broom stars" for the same reason. A comet is usually named for the person who first discovers it (or first calculates its orbit). One of the most famous comets is **Halley's comet,** named for Edmund Halley, a friend of Sir Isaac Newton.

solid mass of rock and ice

gas and dust clouds

5 miles

The heart of a comet is the **nucleus,** a frozen chunk of rock, dust, and ice about the size of a small asteroid. The nucleus of Halley's comet, for example, is about 10 miles long and 5 miles wide, a little shorter and wider than Manhattan Island.

As it approaches the sun, the frozen surface of the nucleus begins to warm up. The ice near the surface begins to melt, and particles of dust and ice are carried away by jets of steam and other evaporating substances. The gas and dust form a cloud called a **coma** [kō′mə] around the nucleus.

As the comet moves still closer to the sun, particles of dust in the coma begin to feel the pressure of the intensifying sunlight. They begin to drift away from the sun. The atoms and molecules of gas are affected in a similar manner by the *solar wind,* the stream of fast-moving particles that continuously flows from the sun's corona. Just as embers and smoke are blown downwind of a campfire by a gentle breeze, dust particles and gases are wafted away from the coma in a blazing streamer called the **tail,** which may be millions of miles long. Because of the different ways that the dust particles and gases are affected by the sun's gravity, they often separate into two tails of different colors. The stream of dust particles is white or slightly yellow, the color of the sunlight it reflects, while the stream of gases reacts with the charged particles of the solar wind to produce a bluish tint.

A comet's course. Although comets circle the sun as do the planets, their orbits are much more elliptical than those of most other heavenly bodies. Some comets make

comet Hale-Bopp in 1997

gas tail

dust tail

voyages of several billion miles, drifting out past the orbit of Pluto only to return and whip around the sun well within the orbit of Mercury. Others may get caught in the gravitational pull of one of the giant planets and spend the rest of its existence volleying back and forth between the planet and the sun. Yet another may move too close to the sun and quickly melt away, leaving only scattered fragments of ice and dust to tread its former path among the heavens. A few comets end their days by colliding dramatically with a planet, such as when comet Shoemaker-Levy 9 collided violently with the planet Jupiter in 1994.

The amount of time it takes a comet to complete an orbit is called its **period.** The period of one comet may be only a

explosion of comet in Jupiter's atmosphere, equal to 300 million atomic bombs

Comet impact on Jupiter

earth-sized impact scar left by explosion

few years, while the period of another may be measured in thousands of years. **Encke's** [ĕng′kəz] **comet** has the shortest recorded period— three years and four months. This comet's orbit is so small and so close to the earth that its entire path can be tracked by a trained observer. Halley's comet, on the other hand, takes about 76 years to

Orbits of selected comets

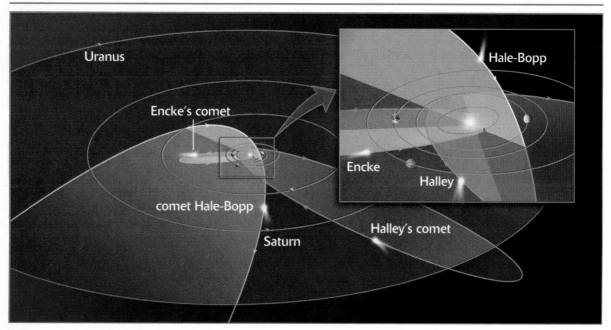

Uranus

Encke's comet

comet Hale-Bopp

Saturn

Halley's comet

Hale-Bopp

Encke

Halley

journey from beyond Neptune to around the sun and back. It came into view most recently in 1986. Can you determine when Halley's comet will pass by the earth again? The 1997 appearance of comet Hale-Bopp, seen by billions of people around the world, was the first visit by this comet in over 4000 years.

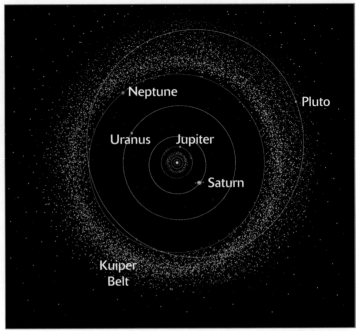

The comet belt. Since the late 1990s, astronomers have discovered hundreds of small, icy objects orbiting farther from the sun than the planet Neptune. These objects, which resemble comet nuclei, appear to be part of a vast "belt" similar to the asteroid belt called the **Kuiper** [ko͞o′pĕr] **belt.** Some objects in the Kuiper belt are as large as the largest asteroids.

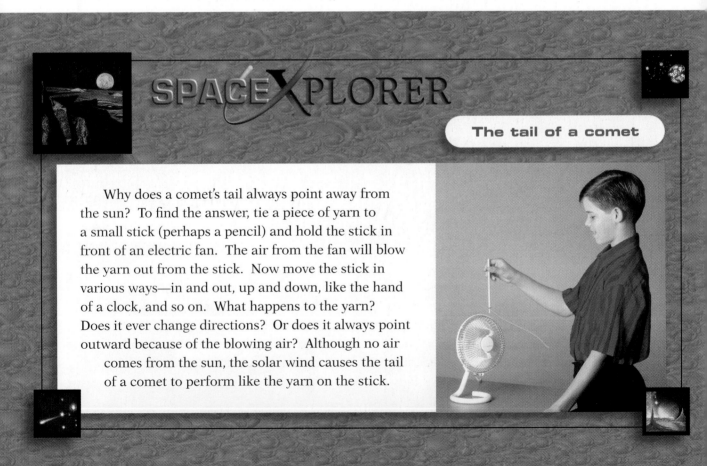

SPACEXPLORER

The tail of a comet

Why does a comet's tail always point away from the sun? To find the answer, tie a piece of yarn to a small stick (perhaps a pencil) and hold the stick in front of an electric fan. The air from the fan will blow the yarn out from the stick. Now move the stick in various ways—in and out, up and down, like the hand of a clock, and so on. What happens to the yarn? Does it ever change directions? Or does it always point outward because of the blowing air? Although no air comes from the sun, the solar wind causes the tail of a comet to perform like the yarn on the stick.

Meteors: Momentary intruders

Drifting meteoroids. Although asteroids are tiny when compared to the planets, they are not the smallest travelers in space. Other heavenly bodies known as **meteoroids** [mē′tē·ə·roidz′] also orbit the sun. Meteoroids are pieces of space debris that are smaller than the smallest asteroids. Although meteoroids come in a wide range of sizes—from microscopic specks of cosmic dust to boulders several feet across—most meteoroids are smaller than a person's fist. Like asteroids, meteoroids are pulled on by the gravity of any planet or moon nearby. Those that enter earth's atmosphere are called **meteors.**

Shooting stars. If you have ever watched a "falling star" dart across the sky for a few seconds and then disappear from view, you have seen a tiny piece of cosmic rock or ice meet a fiery end. As it rushes through the outer layers of the earth's atmosphere, friction with air molecules causes it to glow white-hot. The meteor usually burns up completely in a fraction of a second, long before it is able to reach the earth's surface. The dust that remains slowly settles through the atmosphere to the earth's surface, where it becomes part of the soil.

A **meteor shower** occurs when the earth passes through a cluster of meteoroids. During a meteor shower, hundreds of meteors may be seen shooting through the sky in an hour. Meteor showers, named after the constellation from which they appear to radiate, take place when the paths of meteoroid clusters cross the orbit of the earth. These clusters are usually debris trails left by comets.

SPACEXPLORER

Shower schedules

Check your school or local library to find out when meteor showers take place each year. You can look in an encyclopedia, an almanac, a book on meteors, or a space magazine to find a schedule. Once you discover when the next meteor shower will occur, ask your parents if you can either stay up late or wake up early to view it. Be sure to mark your calendar so you do not forget to look up in the sky when the meteor shower is scheduled to take place.

meteorite showing charred surface

nickel-iron meteorite cut in half to show structure

Meteorites

Reaching the ground. Not all meteors burn up in the earth's atmosphere. An occasional meteor is too large and dense to be completely destroyed by air friction. Although much of it burns away, some of it passes all the way through the atmosphere and hits the ground. A meteor that has landed on the earth's surface is called a **meteorite.**

A meteorite may be a pebble weighing only a few ounces, or it may be a huge boulder weighing several tons. Of the thousands of meteorites that hit the earth each year, almost all are so small that you would never even notice them. Only a few are large enough for scientists to collect and study.

The largest known meteorite still in one piece was found in Africa. It is a great hunk of rock weighing about 66 tons—equal to the weight of eight bull elephants or two tractor-trailer trucks.

To avoid confusing meteoroids, meteors, and meteorites, remember that *meteoroids* are space particles that have not entered the earth's atmosphere, *meteors* are space particles traveling within the earth's atmosphere, and *meteorites* are space particles that have passed through the earth's atmosphere and landed on the surface of the earth.

Explosive events. When small meteoroids enter the atmosphere, friction with the air slows them down so much that they are traveling only a few hundred miles per hour by the time they hit the ground (if they reach the ground at all). However, if a metallic asteroid the size of a football field were to enter the atmosphere, it would hardly slow down at all.

Barringer Crater, Arizona (¾ mile across)

1000 feet

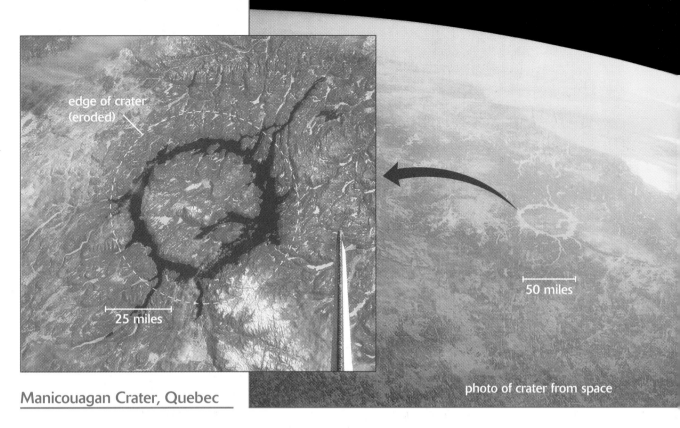

edge of crater
(eroded)

25 miles

50 miles

Manicouagan Crater, Quebec

photo of crater from space

Instead, it would slam into the ground while still traveling 20 times faster than a rifle bullet, producing a tremendous explosion. After the debris settled and the smoke cleared away, all you would see would be a huge hole in the ground, thousands of feet across and hundreds of feet deep. Just such an asteroid struck the desert near Flagstaff, Arizona, thousands of years ago; all that remains from the collision between this speeding rock and the earth is a huge crater over three quarters of a mile wide and 570 feet deep. Even larger impact craters are found elsewhere on the earth; for example, Lake Manicouagan in Canada is thought to be the eroded remnants of a crater more than 60 miles across. To date, more than 150 impact craters as large as the Arizona crater or larger have been discovered on the earth. Smaller craters

are still being formed on a regular basis; a small asteroid blasted a 380-foot-wide crater in the Saudi Arabian desert in the 1800s, and several small craters were formed by another asteroid that hit Russia in 1947.

If the asteroid were made of weak rock instead of strong metal, the result would be much different. Instead of slamming into the ground in one piece, the asteroid would break up and explode a few miles above the ground, producing intense heat and a powerful shock wave. In 1908, such an event leveled and burned hundreds of square miles of forest in a remote region of Russia; similar events in South America in 1930 and 1935 may also have been asteroid "airbursts." Military satellites detect dozens of smaller, harmless airbursts in the earth's atmosphere every year.

Comprehension Check 4.9

Clues. Give the word or term that best fits each clue.

1. Little "planets" ranging in size from a few hundred miles across to as small as a house

2. An asteroid-sized chunk of rock, dust, and ice

3. Three parts of a comet

4. Pieces of space debris that are smaller than the smallest asteroid

5. A meteoroid that enters earth's atmosphere and one that hits the earth

6. What happens when earth passes through a cluster of meteoroids?

7. The amount of time it takes for a comet to complete its orbit

8. Band of asteroids located between the orbits of Mars and Jupiter

9. The name of the largest asteroid

10. Group of asteroids found in the inner solar system, many of which cross paths with the earth

11. Band of cometlike objects located beyond the orbit of Neptune

Chapter Checkup

Part A

1. **Define these terms.**

astronomy	barred spiral	solar eclipse
astronomers	nebulae	chromosphere
vacuum	constellation	corona
friction	axis of rotation	solar wind
galaxy	photosphere	light year
Milky Way	core (of sun)	nova
Local Group	sunspot	supernova

II. Be able to recognize the constellations discussed in this chapter.

III. Name the constellation in which each star is found.

Polaris   Betelgeuse
Algol   Rigel
Regulus   Aldebaran
Deneb   Sirius
Castor   Alpha Centauri
Pollux

IV. Identify the following.

3 galaxies closest to ours

3 main types of galaxies

the North Star

the brightest star in the night sky

the most distant object visible with the unaided eye

the closest star to Earth besides our sun

the distance from the earth to the sun

V. Distinguish between the following.

solar prominence and solar flare

apparent magnitude and absolute magnitude

binary star and optical double

Part B

I. Define these terms.

orbit

ellipse

foci

astronomical unit

gravity

planets

solar system

solar year

atmosphere

ozone layer

greenhouse effect

maria

lunar month

lunar eclipse

near-Earth asteroids

period

meteor shower

II. Tell why these people are important.

Claudius Ptolemy

Nicolaus Copernicus

Johannes Kepler

Sir Isaac Newton

III. Know the order of the nine planets.

IV. Identify the following.

3 laws of planetary motion

the phases of the moon

3 parts of a comet

V. Distinguish between the following.

revolution and rotation

two types of tides

solar eclipse and lunar eclipse

asteroid and comet

asteroid belt and Kuiper belt

meteoroid, meteor, and meteorite

Exploring Space

God spoke light into the universe on the first day of Creation with the majestic command, "Let there be light." Everything we know about the distant stars and galaxies, we have learned by studying their light, which has traveled across the vast expanse of space to Earth. Therefore, our scientific understanding of the universe depends upon our understanding of the nature of light.

Chapter 5

5.1 Understanding Light

Sir Isaac Newton paved the way for our modern understanding of light when he discovered that sunlight is a combination of many colors. In the mid-1600s, he passed a beam of white light through a glass prism and demonstrated that white light is actually made up of the combined colors of the rainbow: red, orange, yellow, green, blue, and violet—often abbreviated ROY G. BV (pronounced "roy-jee-biv"). This color sequence makes up the **visible spectrum.**

Sir Isaac Newton

Making waves. A **wave** is a movement of energy from one place to another. Probably all of us have at some time dropped a pebble into a pool of water. As soon as the pebble hits the surface, ripples begin to move outward in expanding circles. Suppose a cork is sitting in the water nearby. What happens to the cork? Do the waves carry it across the pond? If you do an experiment to answer this question, you will find that the cork merely bobs up and down in its original spot.

The cork nicely illustrates what happens to the water at the surface of the pool. It may appear that each wave is an outward rush of water. But no water actually travels with a wave. Rather, the water at the surface simply moves a short distance back and forth, or *oscillates* [ŏs′ə·lāts]. **Oscillation** is a back and forth motion that repeatedly follows the same path.

The fact that each bit of water moves only a short distance when disturbed by waves, but does not travel from the center of the pool to the edge, shows that a wave is not a movement of matter from place to place. What, then, is a wave? It is the spread of *energy* from the water in one place to the surrounding water. When you drop a pebble into the water, the water where the pebble lands is briefly pushed out of the way in a back and forth motion. This motion spreads as a sort of domino effect to

the water farther away. As the back and forth motion spreads, we see a wave moving outward in all directions.

You do not need water to make waves. Simply take a long piece of rope, tie one end to a hook on the wall or to the knob of a closed door, pull the rope nearly taut, and then shake the rope up and down. You will see waves whipping along the rope from your hand to the far end. If we could take a stop-action photo of these waves, they would look like the illustration at the bottom of this page.

Wave anatomy. A wave has several features. A single rise or depression in a series of waves is a wave *pulse.* On the wave-carrying rope, each pulse is either an upward hump or a downward scoop. Any two consecutive pulses, one a rise and the other a depression, make up a wave. The high point of a wave is the **crest** and the low point is the **trough.**

Every wave is carried by something. Whatever carries the wave is called the wave **medium.** The wave media (*media is* the plural of *medium)* you have encountered so far in this chapter are water and a rope. The speed of a wave is simply how far the wave moves through the wave medium in a unit of time.

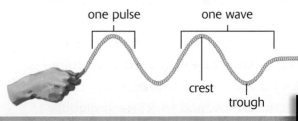

one pulse   one wave

crest

trough

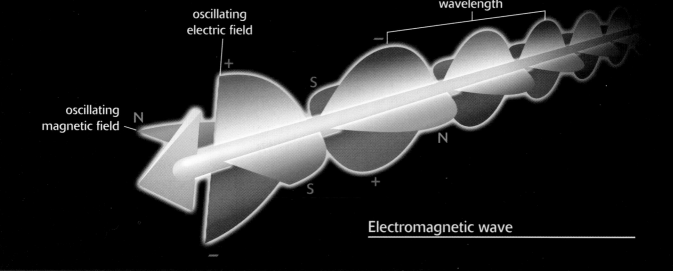

oscillating
electric field

wavelength

oscillating
magnetic field

Electromagnetic wave

Waves of light

Though Newton believed that light consists of streams of tiny particles, other experiments soon revealed that light behaves like waves. However, unlike water waves or sound waves, light waves do not travel by means of particles that oscillate (move back and forth). Rather, light consists of oscillating *fields*—an electric field and a magnetic field.

Understanding fields. If you have ever used a magnet, you know how magnets are able to attract or repel other objects by an invisible force. The region of space surrounding the magnet contains an invisible **magnetic field**—a region in which certain objects are attracted or repelled by the magnet.

You may also have experienced "static cling," such as when a sock in the dryer becomes charged with static electricity in the dryer and sticks to other clothes. When a sock (or any other object) is electrically charged with "static electricity," it is surrounded by an invisible

electric field—a region in which certain objects may be attracted or repelled. Electric fields are similar to magnetic fields in many respects.

Vibrating fields. Scientists have discovered that magnetic fields and electric fields affect each other in special ways. In particular, vibrating electric and magnetic fields can combine in a special way to form an **electromagnetic wave**—a wave consisting of an electric field and a magnetic field vibrating at right angles to each other. Electromagnetic waves are similar in some ways to sound waves or water waves, but with an important difference: because they are composed of vibrating *fields* instead of vibrating *particles*, electromagnetic waves *do not need a medium.* An electromagnetic wave can even travel through empty space.

Electromagnetic waves were discovered in the 1800s by a brilliant Scottish scientist named **James Clerk Maxwell.** Maxwell also realized that *light is a type of electromagnetic wave.*

Speedy waves. In a vacuum, where their motion is not hindered by matter, electromagnetic waves travel at the amazing speed of *186,000 miles per second,* or about 670 million miles per hour. This important number is commonly referred to as the **speed of light.** This is an amazing speed—in only one second of travel, an electromagnetic wave could circle the earth seven times! A light wave can travel farther in just one second than a jet airplane could go in a week.

It takes about 8½ minutes for light to travel the 93 million miles from the sun to the earth. At present, the fastest man-made spacecraft would take at least 3 months to travel the same distance. Light is by far the fastest of all travelers through space.

 A wave lineup

The behavior of an electromagnetic wave depends on its **frequency,** how fast the wave oscillates, and its **wavelength,** the length of one complete wave or cycle of oscillation (measured from crest to crest or trough to trough). The higher the frequency, the shorter the wavelength.

James Clerk Maxwell discovered that visible light is a form of electromagnetic wave. However, other types of electromagnetic waves exist; these waves behave much differently from visible light.

Electromagnetic waves with a frequency *lower* than visible light include *radio waves, microwaves,* and *infrared rays.* Electromagnetic waves with a frequency *higher* than visible light include *ultraviolet rays, X-rays,* and *gamma rays.* Together, the different types of electromagnetic waves, when arranged according to frequency and wavelength, make up the **electromagnetic spectrum.** It is important to remember that these different forms of radiation are all exactly the same kind of wave, differing only in frequency and wavelength.

Electromagnetic spectrum

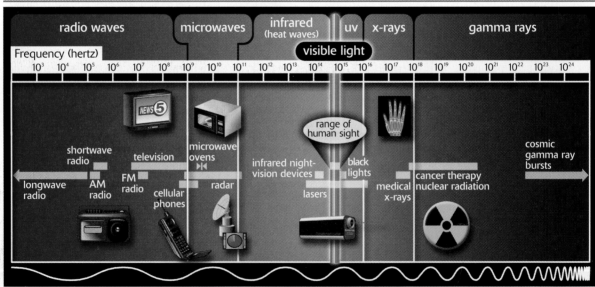

Comprehension Check 5.1

Clues. Give the word or term that best fits each clue.

1. The scientist who paved the way for our modern understanding of light when he discovered that white light is made of many colors

2. The colors of the visible spectrum

3. A movement of energy from one place to another

4. A back and forth motion that repeatedly follows the same path

5. The high point of a wave; the low point of a wave

6. Whatever carries a wave

7. Waves that consist of vibrating electric and magnetic fields

8. Speed of light

9. How fast a wave oscillates

10. The length of one complete wave or cycle of oscillation, measured from crest to crest or trough to trough

5.2 Instruments of Astronomy

Before 1600, the job of an astronomer was difficult, because his observations were limited to what he could see with the unaided eye. But the invention of the **telescope**—a device to make distant objects appear clearer or closer—greatly increased the ability of astronomers to study the skies. The first astronomer to make extensive use of a telescope in his study of the heavens was an Italian named **Galileo** [găl′ə·lā′ō]. He built his own telescope in 1609, and with it made many fascinating discoveries. He found out that

Galileo

the surface of the moon is not smooth but covered with mountain ranges, flat plains, and many craters of all sizes. He gazed at the band of the Milky Way and saw that it is made up of countless individual stars, each too small to be seen with the naked eye. He noticed dark spots on the sun, and discovered moons orbiting (revolving around) the planet Jupiter. He observed that the planet Venus has phases much like the phases of our moon. The invention of the telescope was the beginning of a new era in astronomy. The telescope was the key that unlocked the heavens and opened them up to the examination of scientists. Today, the telescope remains the chief tool of an astronomer.

There are two basic types of optical (visible light) telescopes: the **refracting telescope** like Galileo's, which uses lenses to gather light and form an image, and the **reflecting telescope,** which uses mirrors to produce an image.

EYEwitness reporter

Reflection and Refraction

Reflection. When you step into a bathtub filled with water, you start a wave that races outward in all directions. The wave cannot go far, however, before it hits the sides of the tub. It then turns around and closes inward toward your foot. The turning back or turning aside of any wave when it hits an obstacle is called **reflection.**

Refraction. Have you ever watched big white-capped waves when they were not coming straight in toward the beach but rather were coming in at an angle? Did you notice that when each wave broke across the sand, it changed direction? The reason is that the wave could not move as rapidly in shallower water. Because waves travel more slowly in shallow water than in deeper water, deeper water and shallower water act as if they are two different wave media. Whenever a wave comes at an angle into a new medium where it must change speed, the result is a change in the direction of the wave. This bending of any wave's direction at the boundary between two wave media is called **refraction.**

refraction of waves at a beach

deep water

shallow water

Refraction in action

How do light rays bend? Let's find out. Besides *a flashlight* and *a deep glass dish*, you will need *water, 4 or 5 drops of milk, 2 chalkboard erasers,* and *a small piece of cardboard with a narrow slit cut in it.*

Fill the dish about three-fourths full of water and add the milk, one drop at a time, until the water looks cloudy. Then darken the room. While you shine the flashlight through the slit and into the water at an angle, have a friend clap the erasers together above the dish. The chalk dust will outline the path of light so that it can be seen. What happens to the light beam when it hits the water at an angle?

To reflect the refracted light, place a *mirror* in the bottom of the dish. When the light beam reflects from the mirror, which way does it bend?

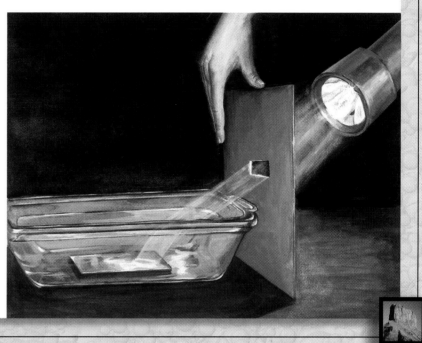

Refracting telescopes

Have you ever used a magnifying glass? If so, you know that the convex lens (⬣) of a magnifying glass produces an image of an object that appears much larger than the object really is. However, it only works for very close objects; a magnifying glass is useless for viewing distant objects. However, if you combine *two* magnifying glasses (two convex lenses) in a certain way, they produce a magnified image of distant objects.

The lens that faces the object being studied is called the *objective lens;* the purpose of the objective lens is to collect as much light as possible and bring it to a focus somewhere between the two lenses. The lens closer to your eye is called the *eyepiece;* it collects the light from the objective lens and directs it into your eye. In order for a telescope to produce a clear image, it must first be *focused* by carefully moving the eyepiece closer to or farther from the objective lens until the image is sharp.

This simple combination of two convex lenses is the ***simplest possible telescope.*** It is called a *refracting* telescope because the lenses bend, or *refract,* the light in order to form an image. (Modern refracting telescopes have additional lenses to produce a clearer image.) Binoculars can be considered a special type of refracting telescope.

By changing the shape of the two lenses, we can change the the way the telescope magnifies the image. Generally, making the objective lens wider produces brighter and sharper images. The largest refracting telescope ever built (in 1897) had an objective lens more than three feet in diameter. Changing the eyepiece has a different effect; using a stronger lens for the eyepiece does not make the image any brighter or sharper, but it does make it appear larger.

Reflecting telescopes

Sir Isaac **Newton** *developed the reflecting telescope,* which uses a large, curved mirror in place of an objective lens. Because lenses bend, or refract, different colors of light at different angles, it is difficult to keep the images they produce perfectly sharp. Mirrors, on the other hand, reflect all colors at the same angle, thus producing a much sharper image. Newton understood that if a parallel beam of light falls on a specially curved mirror, the rays of light are reflected and brought into focus at a point in front of the mirror. The image formed by the curved mirror can then be reflected into an eyepiece lens by a small, flat mirror, and enlarged by the eyepiece.

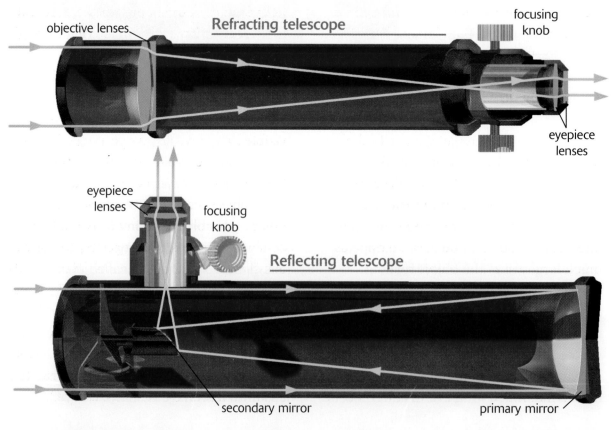

objective lenses
Refracting telescope
focusing knob
eyepiece lenses

eyepiece lenses
focusing knob
Reflecting telescope
secondary mirror
primary mirror

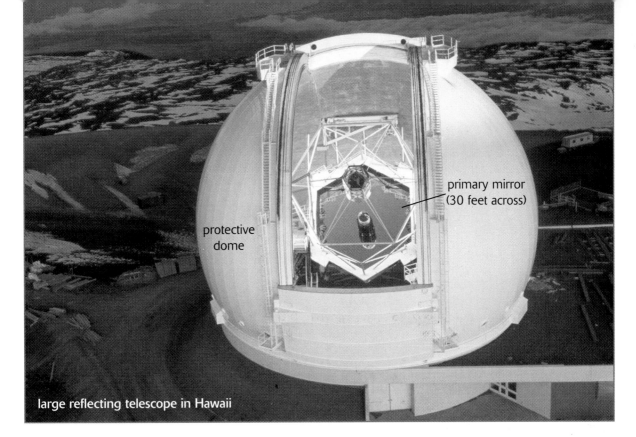

primary mirror
(30 feet across)

protective
dome

large reflecting telescope in Hawaii

Astronomers usually prefer reflecting telescopes instead of refracting telescopes because mirrors are cheaper and can be made much larger than lenses. Many improvements have been made to the basic Newtonian reflector since it was invented, resulting in several different types of reflecting telescopes in use today. The largest reflecting telescopes in the world have main mirrors more than 30 feet across; both of these telescopes are located at an observatory in Hawaii.

Astronomers use telescopes to study the heavens not only because telescopes magnify the *size* of the object being observed, but also because they increase the object's *brightness* by gathering more light than the unaided human eye. To increase their ability to detect faint objects, most large telescopes today are also equipped with sensitive video cam-eras instead of simple eyepieces. Because cameras are much more sensitive to dim light than the human eye, they can reveal faint details that a person looking through the telescope could not see.

Overcoming obstacles

Astronomers probing the heavens with visible light have always contended with several obstacles to their observations. One of these hindrances is the extreme faintness of the light from most distant objects; this obstacle may be overcome by simply making telescopes bigger, or by using more sensitive cameras. A more dif-ficult problem to overcome is the *distortion* caused by the earth's atmosphere, which causes pictures taken by even the largest telescopes to be blurry. (This same distor-tion causes the stars to appear to twinkle even when seen by the unaided eye.)

photo of Eagle Nebula taken by *Hubble*

Hubble space telescope

One way to avoid the interference of Earth's atmosphere is to place a telescope in space, where there is no air to distort the telescope's "vision." In 1990, a reflecting telescope with an 8-foot-wide main mirror was launched into orbit around the earth. Known as the **Hubble space telescope,** this medium-sized telescope can "see" without any atmospheric interference, producing images of great clarity.

In the late 1990s, the vision of ground-based telescopes was also dramatically sharpened. Instead of just trying to avoid atmospheric distortion, a technique called *adaptive optics* allows ground-based telescopes to overcome the distortion caused by the atmosphere. This technique involves computer-controlled mirrors that constantly flex and bend to correct for atmospheric distortion. Developed by the American military in the 1980s to allow powerful lasers to shoot down nuclear missiles, adaptive optics technology allows a large telescope on the ground to see almost as clearly as if it were in space.

Adaptive optics

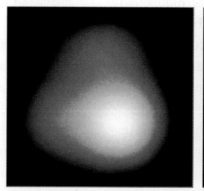

planet Neptune as seen by ground-based telescope

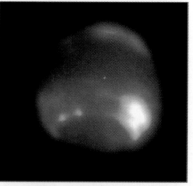

same image with adaptive optics system switched on

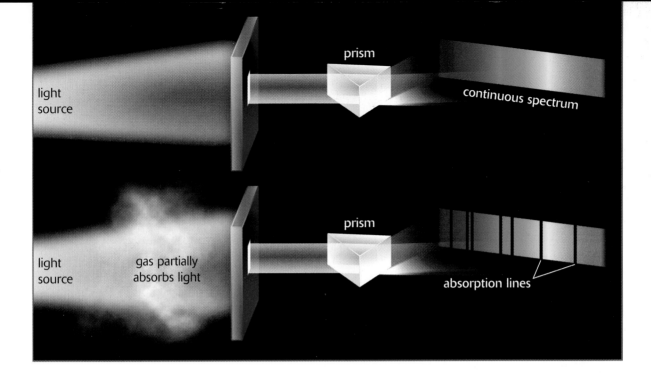

light source

prism

continuous spectrum

light source

gas partially absorbs light

prism

absorption lines

The spectroscope

When white light shines through a gas, light of certain colors is absorbed in patterns that are unique to that particular gas. If the light is then passed through a prism, the broad spectrum of color will show narrow, dark lines called *absorption lines* where particular colors were absorbed.

Instead of a simple prism, astronomers can use a special device called a **spectroscope** to split light into a spectrum for analysis. The invention of the spectroscope in the mid-1800s gave scientists an important tool with which to study the heavens. By comparing the absorption lines in sunlight with those of sample elements in the laboratory, scientists can determine what substances a distant object is made of and how hot it is. It was the spectroscope that allowed astronomers to discover that the sun is mostly hydrogen. Using spectroscopes, astronomers have determined the composition of other stars' atmospheres

and their surface temperatures; a star's size can then be estimated by comparing its temperature to its absolute magnitude.

A spectroscope can also reveal whether a star is actually a double-, triple-, or multiple-star system, even if the stars are too close together to be distinguished visually. By studying spectra (plural of *spectrum*), it is even possible to measure how fast a star is moving toward or away from Earth or how fast it is rotating. Large telescopes equipped with spectroscopes allow astronomers to study the spectra of even very faint stars.

The spectroscope has been useful in the study of the planets, as well. When a planet passes in front of a star, a spectroscope can record the changes in the star's light as it begins to be obscured by the planet's atmosphere. The presence and composition of Pluto's atmosphere and that of Saturn's moon Titan were discovered by long-distance spectroscopy.

Radio wave astronomy

radio telescopes in New Mexico

Earth's weather often poses problems for optical telescopes. Clouds, smog, and haze hinder visual studies, and atmospheric scattering of sunlight, moonlight, or city lights can obscure faint objects. Even if skies are clear and dark, interstellar clouds of dust and gas may lie squarely in the way of what the astronomer wants to see.

These problems can be avoided by using radio waves, which penetrate cosmic clouds and Earth's atmosphere with equal ease. Therefore, **radio telescopes,** instruments that collect radio waves from space, have some advantages over other types of telescopes; they allow us to study the heavens using portions of the electromagnetic spectrum that are invisible to the human eye. Radio telescopes can be thought of as large reflecting telescopes that detect radio waves and microwaves—electromagnetic waves with a frequency lower than that of visible light.

Radio astronomy had its beginnings in the 1930s when a Bell Telephone engineer studying static and its effect on communications discovered that some static was caused by radio waves from space. Initially, astronomers

were skeptical; but eventually the great advantages that radio astronomy offered and the new areas of exploration it opened up made the radio telescope a key instrument for studying the heavens.

Although the first radio telescopes could produce only rough maps of radio

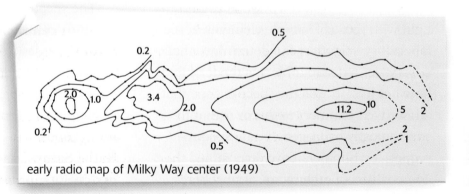

early radio map of Milky Way center (1949)

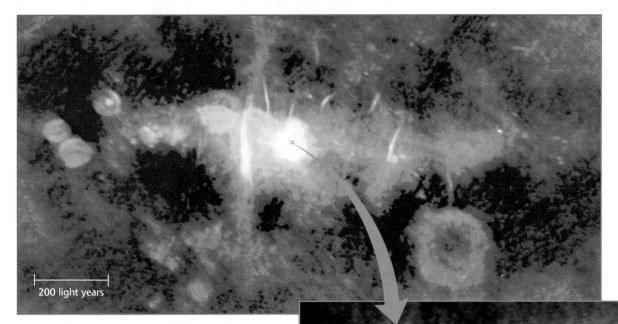

200 light years

Radio telescope images of Milky Way center

close-up of Milky Way center
2 light years

sources in the sky, modern radio telescopes can produce pictures of distant objects that are even sharper than photos taken with the best optical telescopes. Radio telescopes produced the first maps of the hidden surface of Venus and of distant asteroids, and have been used to study small but extremely massive objects located at the center of many galaxies (including the Milky Way).

Some of the most interesting objects that were discovered by radio telescopes are **pulsars** [pŭl′sârz]—stars producing rapid bursts of radio waves, in some cases hundreds of times per second. Pulsars are tiny but extremely dense rotating stars that emit directional beams of radio waves. Scientists believe that pulsars are examples of perhaps the smallest stars known—thousands of times smaller than the white dwarfs we studied in chapter 4. Even though an average pulsar contains more matter than the sun, its matter is squeezed so tightly that the star is less than 12 miles across—as small as a typical asteroid. Some pulsars spin so fast that they rotate 30,000 times in a single minute. Pulsars are thought to be the collapsed cores of stars that have exploded (supernovas).

You do not have to be a professional scientist to enjoy astronomy. Gazing at the heavens is a fascinating hobby that can be pursued by anyone. Many of the wonders of the night sky can be seen even using binoculars or a small telescope.

Even if you do not have access to an expensive telescope, you can use other instruments to observe the night sky. In fact, for the beginning astronomer, an ordinary pair of binoculars is often better than a telescope. Unlike telescopes, binoculars provide a wide, bright field of view and allow you to use both eyes. In fact, most binoculars will give you a better view of the night skies than Galileo had looking through his telescope! Quality binoculars are also much less expensive than quality telescopes and are much easier to carry. Later, when you become more practiced at viewing the night sky and have seen what there is to see with binoculars, you can "move up" to a telescope. (If you do buy a telescope, many amateur astronomers suggest avoiding inexpensive department-store telescopes, which often have inferior optics and flimsy bases.)

One excellent way to look at the sky through binoculars is to lie on your back in a reclining lawn chair; you can steady the binoculars by propping your elbows on the armrests and resting the rubber eyecups gently against your face. You can use your binoculars to see many interesting sights: double or multiple stars, nebulae, galaxies, and planets.

You may wish to start by exploring the cratered surface of the moon;

refer to the map of the moon's surface on page 283 to help you identify prominent landmarks. Other fascinating sights to see include the Pleiades cluster in the constellation Taurus; only six stars are visible to the unaided eye, but how many can you see through binoculars? Find the galaxy in Andromeda, the "sister galaxy" to our own Milky Way. View the spectacular Great Nebula in the sword of Orion, or compare orange-red Begelgeuse to blue-white Rigel; you might also try to distinguish the quadruple star known as the Trapezium [trə·pē′zē·əm].

Binoculars also allow you to see the planets more clearly. Bright Venus looks even brighter through binoculars; if the skies are clear and your binoculars are steady, the planet may even appear as a tiny crescent as it goes through the same phases as the moon. Jupiter and Saturn are also good targets for observation; if you have a steady rest, you may even be able to spot Ganymede and Callisto, two of Jupiter's largest moons. If you have powerful binoculars and a steady rest, you *might* even be able to make out the rings of Saturn, although a telescope is usually necessary to see them clearly.

In all your astronomical observations, a good field guide to the heavens will help you find your way around the skies and locate many other interesting sights visible through your binoculars. Many areas have local astronomy clubs that can be a big help to the beginning astronomer.

To see faint objects, you will need to allow plenty of time for your eyes to fully adjust to the darkness, a process which takes at least 15 to 30 minutes. Turn off all outdoor lights; if you have to use a flashlight to see your field guide, cover the end with several layers of red plastic wrap to avoid spoiling your night vision, or use a dim red "astronomers' flashlight." Also, if you do your observing in the winter, be sure to dress warmly!

Comprehension Check 5.2

Clues. Give the word or term that best fits each clue.

1. The first person to make extensive use of the telescope to study the heavens

2. The turning back or turning aside of any wave when it hits an obstacle

3. The bending of any wave's direction at the boundary between two wave media

4. The type of telescope that uses only lenses to collect light and form an image

5. The type of telescope that uses mirrors to collect light and form an image

6. A device that splits light into a spectrum for analysis

7. An instrument that collects radio waves from space

8. Tiny but extremely dense rotating stars that produce rapid bursts of radio waves

9. Scientist who developed the reflecting telescope

Discussion.

10. Why do most professional astronomers use reflecting telescopes rather than refracting telescopes?

11. Discuss two ways in which astronomers can overcome the distortion of starlight that is caused by the earth's atmosphere.

5.3 Principles of Space Flight

🛰 *Up, up, and away*

People have always wondered what it would be like to voyage out into the unknown reaches of space. But *how* could a person journey into space? Would-be space voyagers pondered that question for many centuries. Clearly some device was needed to propel people away from the earth, overcoming the force of gravity. What sort of device would do?

Some people suggested that a person might get into space by launching himself upward by means of a huge spring, or by harnessing the power of rising water vapor or flocks of birds. Others imagined that travelers to outer space could be carried into the skies by a huge balloon, or that a space capsule could be shot out of the atmosphere by a giant cannon. Many other interesting and rather fanciful ideas were proposed. But it was not until the late 1800s that anyone began to realize that the device by which space travel could be accomplished had been around for hundreds of years—the rocket.

Today, spacecraft routinely escape Earth's atmosphere and maneuver in space with the help of rockets. Rockets are also used to launch new satellites into orbit and to alter the orbit of various satellites as they circle the earth. Although spacecraft and rockets represent modern technology, they follow the same laws of motion stated by Sir Isaac Newton in the 1680s.

Satellite and rocket technology have had a huge impact on the science of astronomy. Fuzzy pictures of distant planets have been replaced by close-up photos from space probes. Unhindered by Earth's atmosphere, telescopes in orbit have enabled astronomers to see fascinating objects never seen before. **Astronauts,** people who journey into space, have orbited the earth and even walked on the moon. In the last four decades, mankind has learned more about the solar system than in all of previous history. Thanks to the technology and materials God has given us, we are better able to understand and appreciate His amazing creation.

British military rocket, 1815

Titan II rocket carrying Gemini spacecraft, 1965

Pioneers in rocketry

Although there were several men who could be considered pioneers in the science of astronautics, the two most important figures in the history of rocketry were Robert H. Goddard and Wernher von Braun [vĕr′nĕr fôn broun′].

Robert H. Goddard. The American scientist Robert H. Goddard is known as *the "Father of Modern Rocketry."* As early as 1902, when just a young but imaginative high-school student in Worcester, Massachusetts, Goddard was convinced that the rocket could be used to lift people off our planet and into space. After becoming a professor of physics, he continued to study how rockets could be developed for this purpose. Unfortunately, many scientists considered him foolish for dreaming of space flight, and for years Goddard struggled without recognition or financial support. But he persisted, and in 1926, Goddard *built and launched the first liquid-fueled rocket.* He also proved that rockets could fly in a vacuum, and he developed instruments for controlling rockets in flight. He even proposed a plan for a trip to the moon. When Goddard died in 1945, his dream was beginning to come true. Other Americans were becoming interested in the potential use of rockets for space travel, and the United States was starting a rocket development program of its own.

Wernher von Braun. Until his death in 1977, Wernher von Braun was generally

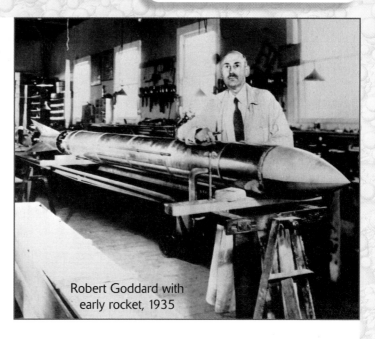

Robert Goddard with early rocket, 1935

considered to be the most knowledgeable astronautical engineer in the world. Even as a boy, von Braun was fascinated by fictional stories about space travel, and he was also very interested in rockets. One day he wondered whether rockets could push his coaster wagon. Being an adventuresome lad, he decided to find out. He fastened a number of rockets onto the sides and back of his wagon. Then he lit the rockets. But before he could manage to climb aboard, his wagon shot off down a crowded street in Berlin, Germany. As the *thrust,* or push, from the rockets made the wagon go faster and faster, Wernher dashed along behind, trying desperately to catch up with his runaway contraption. Smoke and flames came shooting out behind the wagon. Pedestrians scampered out of the way. Finally the rockets burned out, and his wagon rolled to a stop. After a stern lecture from the police and a warning not to do such a foolish stunt again, Wernher was sent home to his parents.

When he was only twenty years old, Wernher von Braun was appointed chief of the German army's rocket corps. Although he worked on military rockets during World War II, space travel remained his primary goal. At the end of the war, he was invited to come to America to participate in starting the space program of the United States. *With his help, the United States became the world leader in space exploration.* From 1960 to 1972, he was the director of NASA's Marshall Space Flight Center in Huntsville, Alabama. He was the man in charge of developing the Saturn V ("Saturn five"), the largest rocket ever built, used to carry men to the moon.

Wernher von Braun

Wernher von Braun speaks about design. Some scientists look at the universe and conclude that it is all the result of an accident. They say that order and evidences of design are just coincidences. But can these claims be true? No one would claim that the Saturn V rocket was the result of chance or accident, because it clearly shows the work of many intelligent human beings. Compared to the universe, a rocket is very simple. Dr. von Braun, himself a design engineer, had no difficulty recognizing that our universe is the handiwork of the Great Designer. He wrote, "One cannot be exposed to the law and order of the universe without concluding that there must be a divine intent behind it all. . . . The Creator is revealed through His creation."

Objects in orbit

A **satellite** is any object that orbits a larger object. The earth, for instance, is a satellite of the sun. The moon is a satellite of the earth. But in addition to the moon, there are numerous man-made objects that revolve around our planet. These artificial satellites are positioned at various distances from the earth— anywhere from 100 miles to more than 20,000 miles away. Although the word "satellite" is usually used to refer to

unmanned artificial satellites, manned spacecraft orbiting the earth can also be considered a type of satellite.

Hubble telescope in orbit

Making the rounds

Rocket engines burn only long enough to carry a satellite up into space. They do not continue to operate all the time the satellite remains in orbit. Why then does a satellite not fall back to the ground after the rocket engines are shut off? How does a satellite manage to stay in its orbit around the earth?

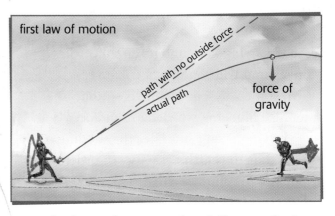

first law of motion

path with no outside force

actual path

force of gravity

Sir Isaac Newton discovered three laws of motion. One of these laws can help us to understand what keeps a satellite in orbit around the earth. The **first law of motion** states that *an object in motion will continue moving in the same direction and at the same speed unless an outside force acts upon it.* For instance, a spaceship traveling through space will continue to move in a straight line forever, unless it fires a rocket to change its course, or runs into something, or is pulled by the gravity of some heavenly body.

At first, you might question whether the first law of motion is really correct. After all, when you hit a baseball, it does not continue to travel in a straight line forever. If it did, every fly ball would be a guaranteed home run. But no matter how hard the ball is hit, it eventually falls back to earth.

A baseball is not, however, free from the influence of outside forces. What forces act upon a baseball in flight? First, the earth's force of gravity pulls the baseball downward. Also, the force of friction between the ball and air molecules slows the ball down in flight.

The motion of the baseball, then, is indeed governed by the first law of motion, which can be restated as follows: *if a force acts on an object, the object will change its velocity (speed and/or direction).* The baseball undergoes several changes in velocity between the time it leaves the pitcher's hand and the time it lands in the fielder's glove. First, the pitcher's arm applies a force to the ball and accelerates it toward home plate. When the ball encounters the force of the swinging bat, the ball's speed and direction change suddenly. Then, as it shoots through the air, the forces of gravity and friction start to influence its motion. Friction reduces the ball's speed to some extent, and the pull of gravity on the ball gradually bends its course back to the earth. Finally, the force applied to the ball by the fielder's glove brings the ball to a quick stop.

Satellites in orbit

The first law of motion also describes the motion of an orbiting satellite. Imagine that you have tied a tennis ball to a length of string and are swinging the ball rapidly round and round at arm's length. What happens if you let go of the string? The ball shoots away in a straight line. What happens if you gradually slow down the speed at which you are swinging the ball? Eventually, the ball will not travel fast enough to

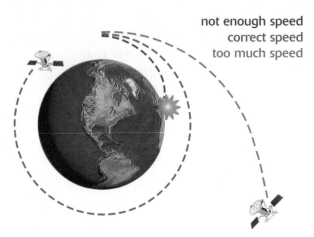

not enough speed
correct speed
too much speed

keep the string taut, and its circular rotation around your hand will collapse.

In some ways, a satellite is similar to a tennis ball being whirled around on a string. The "string" that ties the satellite to the earth is the earth's gravity. In order for a satellite to orbit the earth, its speed must fall within a certain range. If it goes too fast, it will "break" the string and shoot off into deep space, never to return. (Actually, the satellite would simply orbit farther and farther from the earth as it increased its speed, until it finally escaped altogether.) If the satellite does not travel rapidly enough, the earth's gravity will pull it downward, causing it to burn up in the atmosphere. Within the correct speed range, however, the satellite can continue orbiting the earth for many years. The pull of the gravitational "string" is just strong enough to bend the satellite's path from a straight line into a circle, but not so strong that it pulls the satellite back to the earth.

A rocket's job, then, is not just to carry a satellite the correct distance into space, but to accelerate it to the speed required to keep it in orbit. Because the speed required to maintain orbit around the earth is over 17,000 miles per hour, rockets must be very powerful.

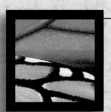

Science Speaks

Sir Isaac Newton: Discoverer of God's Laws

One night in 1654, some of the townspeople of Grantham, England, became frightened by a strange light flashing back and forth across the sky. They thought they were watching a comet as it passed by overhead. In those days, when there were many superstitions, a passing comet meant that something terrible was about to happen.

But the light was not a comet. It was merely a torch on the back of a kite made by twelve-year-old Isaac Newton.

As a schoolboy, Isaac Newton spent much of his time trying new experiments and making models of mechanical things he read about or watched being used. He built a water clock that told the time by allowing water to drip through a small hole from one container to another. He mixed certain chemicals together to create different colors of paint. Newton also made a miniature windmill that looked exactly like a large one being built near his school. The tiny windmill was even able to grind small amounts of corn! Young Isaac trained a mouse to run the mill so people could see how it worked.

When Isaac Newton was sixteen, he left school for a while to help his mother manage the family farm, but his overwhelming curiosity about God's creation finally convinced his mother that he needed to go back to school. So Isaac Newton returned to town to finish his classes. He then went to Cambridge University to study science and mathematics.

In one of Newton's classes, a professor taught what was then the common notion that sunlight was colorless. But when Newton later held a prism to the sunlight streaming in from his window, he noticed a rainbow of colors on the wall across the room. How could "colorless" light create rainbows? Isaac Newton concluded that sunlight actually contains a whole spectrum of colors. He wrote a paper proving his theory. This paper was read with interest by the scientists in the Royal Society, a special group of the greatest minds in England.

Newton was elected a member of the Royal Society a few years later when he developed a new kind of telescope called the Newtonian reflector. This telescope had a specially formed mirror that reflected light from the stars to the eyepiece at the side of the telescope. Newton, by this time a professor at Cambridge, made the mirror himself by pouring molten metal into a mold, letting the metal cool, and then grinding it and polishing it until it shone like glass. Newton's telescope was easy to use because the side-mounted eyepiece allowed the astronomer to see the stars without having to strain his neck in order to look through the lens, and also because it was much shorter than other telescopes of equal magnifying power.

Isaac Newton was surprised at all the attention his telescope received from the Royal Society, the nobility of London, and even the king of England. As far as Newton was concerned, there were many more important things to ponder.

Newton's greatest achievement was a book called *Principia Mathematica* that scientifically explained the laws of motion that govern the universe. In this book, Newton provided mathematical proof that a single force of attraction (gravity) binds all of physical creation together, both on earth and in the heavens, and that we live in a universe governed by a single set of laws given by the Creator. Newton wrote:

This most beautiful system of sun, planets, and comets could only proceed from the counsel and dominion of an intelligent and powerful Being. . . . This Being governs all things, not as the soul of the world, but as Lord of all.

Isaac Newton believed in the Lord of Creation and spent much time studying His Word. Many of his writings discussed important lessons he had learned in the Bible.

In 1705, Isaac Newton became the first Englishman to be knighted for his work as a scientist. When he died in 1727, he was buried at Westminster Abbey in a plot that had been reserved for a king. His discovery of the laws of motion and the law of gravity enabled later scientists to send astronauts to the moon and satellites into orbit. His study of light and his reflector telescope allowed astronomers to build larger and stronger telescopes in order to chart the stars.

Sir Isaac Newton

Comprehension Check 5.3

Clues. Give the word or term that best fits each clue.

1. People who journey into space

2. The "Father of Modern Rocketry"

3. Scientist who built and launched the first liquid-fueled rocket

4. The astronautical engineer who helped make the U.S. the leader in space exploration

5. An object that orbits a larger object

Explain.

6. State Newton's first law of motion.

5.4 Race to the Moon

Although simple solid-fueled rockets similar to modern fireworks have been used since the 1200s, it was the invention of the liquid-fueled rocket in 1926 that brought space within reach. The Germans made great advances with liquid-fueled rocketry during World War II. At the close of the war, the Soviets (Russians) captured the German research center, but many of the scientists escaped to the United States. Building upon German technology, both the United States and the Soviet Union began efforts to develop better rockets.

Sputnik *and* Explorer

The space race began in October of 1957, when the Russians launched **Sputnik** [spoot'nĭk] **1,** the first artificial object to orbit the earth. Less than a month later, a dog named Laika [lī'kə] was launched aboard a thousand-pound spacecraft named *Sputnik 2,* becoming the first living creature to orbit the earth. The United States responded

in January 1958 with its first satellite, a tiny 31-pound craft named **Explorer 1.** Although far smaller than the Russian satellites, *Explorer 1* carried scientific instruments onboard that led to a major discovery—the existence of a large belt of trapped solar wind particles around the earth. The Russians responded in 1959 with the first unmanned spacecraft to fly past the moon *(Luna 1)* and the first to crash-land on the moon *(Luna 2).*

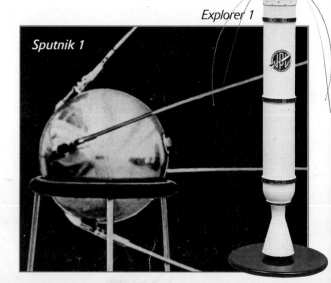

Explorer 1

Sputnik 1

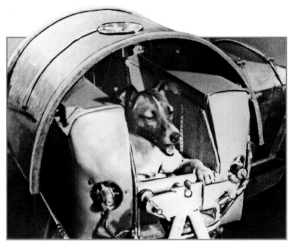
Laika in cabin of *Sputnik 2*

🪐 Vostok and Mercury

Vostok 1

Valentina Tereshkova · Yuri Gagarin

In 1961, Russian cosmonaut (astronaut) **Yuri Gagarin** [yo͞or′yĭ gə·gär′yĭn] became *the first person to travel in space* when he made a single orbit around the earth in his *Vostok* [vŏs·tōk′] *1* spacecraft. One month after Gagarin orbited the earth, **Alan Shepard** became *America's first person in space* with a fifteen-minute hop in a Mercury spacecraft. A year later, in 1962, **John Glenn** became *the first American to orbit the earth.* In 1963, **Valentina Tereshkova** [vəl′yĭn·tēn′ə těr′əsh·kô′və], the pilot of *Vostok 6,* became *the first woman to fly in space.*

Alan Shepard

John Glenn

Gemini and Apollo

In 1964, the Russians scored another first by launching three cosmonauts aboard a single spacecraft, *Voskhod* [vŏs·khōt′] *1*. America responded in 1965 with the Gemini program, a series of ten manned spaceflights. Unlike the clumsy space capsules used in previous Russian and American missions, the two-person Gemini spacecraft had a cockpit like a fighter plane and was very maneuverable. Gemini astronauts maneuvered from one orbit to another, docked with other objects in space, and even practiced working outside the spacecraft. With the Gemini program, the United States began to catch up to the Russians.

America finally took the lead in the space race with the Apollo program. Much larger than Gemini, the Apollo

astronauts in cockpit of Gemini spacecraft

spacecraft was designed to comfortably accomodate three astronauts.

The first manned Apollo flight, Apollo 7, tested the new spacecraft's systems as it orbited the earth for eleven days. The following flight, Apollo 8, was the *first manned spacecraft to orbit the moon.* As they circled the moon, the three astronauts celebrated Christmas by reading the first ten verses of Genesis to millions

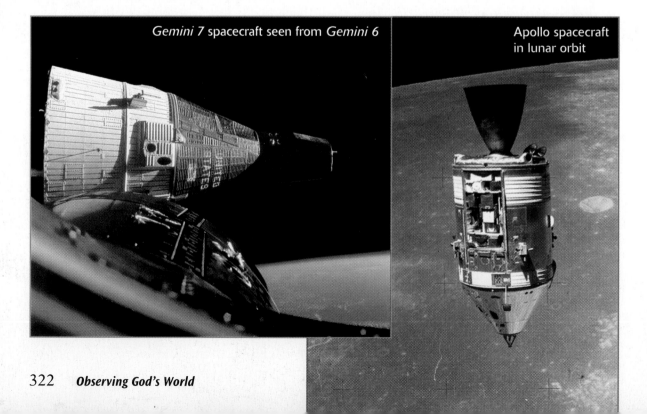

Gemini 7 spacecraft seen from Gemini 6

Apollo spacecraft in lunar orbit

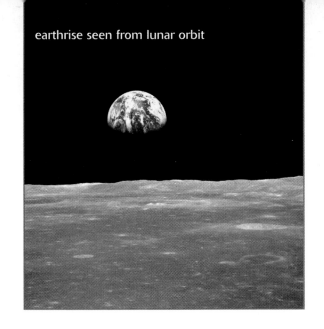

earthrise seen from lunar orbit

100 miles away from the Apollo spacecraft before returning. Meanwhile, the Russian space program stalled as scientists worked to fix problems with the giant N-1 rockets built to launch Russian missions to the moon.

During the Apollo 10 mission, American astronauts went back to the moon, this time with two spacecraft instead of one. As the Apollo spacecraft orbited the moon, two astronauts entered the lunar lander and descended to within 48,000 feet (9 miles) of the moon's surface, performing one last rehearsal before the flight which would involve an actual moon landing.

The first mission to actually land on the moon was **Apollo 11.** On July 20, 1969, as the Apollo spacecraft *Columbia* orbited the moon, two of the three astronauts boarded the lunar lander named

of television viewers. The rocket that launched the Apollo 9 mission also carried a second spacecraft, identical to those that would later transport astronauts to the moon's surface. Once in orbit around the earth, two astronauts crawled into the second spacecraft and tested it thoroughly, flying more than

launch of Apollo 11

323

Apollo 15 astronaut with lunar lander *Falcon* and Lunar Rover

Eagle and descended toward the moon's surface. After *Eagle* landed on the Sea of Tranquility, astronaut **Neil Armstrong** became the *first human being to set foot on the surface of the moon.* His words, "That's one small step for [a] man, one giant leap for mankind" summed up the feelings of Americans as by television they watched him step onto the lunar surface. After 21½ hours on the moon, *Eagle* took off to rendezvous with *Columbia.* The three astronauts set course for Earth, safely landing in the Pacific Ocean 2½ days later. Despite a slow start, America had won the race to the moon, demonstrating that her technology and industry were second to none.

The United States conducted several Apollo missions to the moon between 1969 and 1972. Astronauts spent a total of 12½ days on the lunar surface, collected over 800 pounds of rocks, and set up scientific instruments that would continue sending information to earth for many years. On the last three Apollo moon landings, a carlike vehicle called the Lunar Rover allowed the astronauts to travel several miles away from their spacecraft.

The final mission to the moon was Apollo 17, during which two astronauts spent a record three days exploring a deep valley in the Sea of Serenity. On December 16, 1972, the last astronauts to visit the moon boarded the lunar lander *Challenger* and took off from the moon's surface. To this day, the United States remains the only nation that has landed a man on the moon.

SPACEXPLORER

Mission to the moon

Many different teams of astronauts were involved in the Apollo missions. Learn about one of these teams and give a report to the class. In your report, discuss the names of the astronauts, the number of the Apollo flight, and the date of the mission.

You should also give some details of the mission by explaining what the astronauts did in space and what problems they encountered. Also share any other interesting information that you may find about the astronauts themselves. For instance, one astronaut has become active in politics, and another was an evangelist.

Comprehension Check 5.4

Clues. Give the word or term that best fits each clue.

1. The first artificial object to orbit the earth

2. The first U.S. satellite

3. The first person to travel in space

4. America's first person in space

5. The first American to orbit the earth

6. The Apollo flight that landed the first men on the moon

7. The first person to set foot on the surface of the moon

5.5 Space Stations

The Salyut *program*

After it became clear that the United States had won the race to the moon, Russian scientists turned their attention to building orbiting **space stations** in which two or three people could live and work for weeks or months at a time. In 1971, Russia launched the first space station, named *Salyut* [səl·yo͞ot′] *1*. Although *Salyut 1* was used only briefly, five more Salyut space stations were successfully operated. Two of these were orbiting military outposts, designed with spy cameras, defensive cannons, and missiles; the other three were orbiting science laboratories with telescopes and other scientific instruments. When each space station reached the end of its useful life, it was allowed to enter Earth's atmosphere and burn up. The last of the *Salyut* stations entered the atmosphere and burned up in 1991.

Skylab

The United States launched its first space station, **Skylab,** in 1973. In contrast to the cramped *Salyut* stations, *Skylab* contained a huge laboratory, spacious living quarters, and even a shower for the astronauts. Three different crews (of three astronauts each) traveled to the space station during 1973 and 1974 and conducted valuable astronomical experiments, including studies of our sun and a comet with special telescopes. After the last crew left *Skylab* in 1974, the station orbited unmanned for several years. Although NASA had intended to preserve the station for continued use, it was unfortunately allowed to reenter Earth's atmosphere in 1979 and burned up.

Skylab

Mir

In 1986, Russia launched a new space station, named **Mir** [mēr]. Unlike previous space stations, *Mir* was designed so that extra "rooms" (modules) could be added to the station after it was launched. Over the next several years, cosmonauts conducted astronomical studies, military projects, Earth observations, materials processing, and medical research. One cosmonaut spent a year and two months in space aboard *Mir,* a record that still stands. Robotic spacecraft met and docked with the station to bring supplies and to return materials from experiments conducted by the cosmonauts onboard. After the collapse of the Soviet Union, a number of American astronauts also visited the space station. After fifteen years in space, *Mir* finally entered the earth's atmosphere and burned up in 2001.

Mir

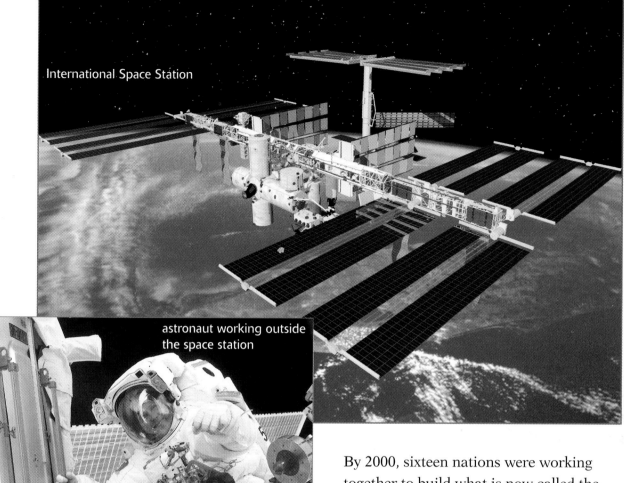

International Space Station

astronaut working outside the space station

The International Space Station

In 1984, President Ronald Reagan called on the United States to construct a new space station by 1990. Although the program was delayed by changes in plans, the proposal eventually took hold, and several other nations joined the effort.

By 2000, sixteen nations were working together to build what is now called the **International Space Station** (ISS), often called *Alpha*. The first module of the station was launched in 1998. The station consists of many modules that are assembled on the ground and then attached to the portion of the station already in orbit. When complete, the ISS will be as large as a football field and may weigh as much as 400 tons, with several laboratories for research and living quarters for three to seven crew members from various nations.

Comprehension Check 5.5

Explain. Tell what you know about each of the following space stations: *Salyut 1*, *Skylab*, *Mir*, and International Space Station.

5.6 The Space Shuttle

On April 12, 1981, the 20th anniversary of Yuri Gagarin's historic flight, the United States launched a new type of spacecraft, known as the **space shuttle.** The space shuttle was *the first spacecraft designed to be reused;* it is launched like a rocket and lands like an airplane. The space shuttle consists of four large components: the orbiter, which resembles a large airplane; the external liquid fuel tank; and the two solid-fueled booster rockets.

 ## A typical flight

Space shuttle missions are launched from the Kennedy Space Center on the east-ern coast of Florida. To prepare for a mission, the orbiter and solid-fueled booster rockets are first attached to the external fuel tank, and any necessary equipment is stowed aboard the orbiter. The vehicle is then transported from the assembly building to the launch pad (the same pad used by the Apollo program). After several days of preparation, the countdown begins, the shuttle's tanks are filled with fuel, and the astronauts climb aboard. Three seconds before liftoff, the shuttle's main rocket engines are ignited, followed by the solid booster rockets seconds later. The shuttle slowly climbs off the pad, gradually accelerating and turning toward the east. The solid booster rockets burn out and drop away 2 minutes after liftoff; 6½ minutes later, when the shuttle has climbed to 75–100 miles and accelerated to 17,400 miles per hour, the main engines

external fuel tank

solid-fueled booster rockets

orbiter

space shuttle liftoff

space shuttle *Discovery* in orbit

shuttle then uses its wings to glide through the atmosphere like an airplane, finally landing on a runway near the launch pad that it left several days before. After a few months of maintenance and repair, the orbiter is ready to fly once again. In addition to the first space shuttle, named *Columbia*, three other space shuttles— *Challenger, Discovery,* and *Atlantis*—were built to bring NASA's fleet to four. Tragically, the *Challenger* was destroyed by an accident shortly after takeoff in 1986, killing all seven astronauts onboard. After this disaster, a fifth shuttle named *Endeavour* was built to take *Challenger's* place.

are shut off and the empty external tank is released as well. After achieving orbit, the crew unfastens their seat belts and begins their mission.

The typical space shuttle mission lasts between 1 and 2 weeks. During the mission, the crew may launch or retrieve satellites or conduct scientific experiments. When the work is complete, the shuttle fires its rockets to slow down, causing it to descend into the atmosphere. The

On the horizon

Even though America's space shuttles are mostly reusable, they are still tremendously expensive to operate. Hundreds of people are required to ready the shuttle for launch and to monitor the mission, and each shuttle requires months of work before it can fly again. In this way, the shuttles are much different from regular airplanes, which can fly several times in one day and require only a few people to maintain

space shuttle *Columbia* landing

them. As a result, it costs only a few hundred dollars to fly a person and his luggage to a distant city, but it costs millions of dollars to fly a person into space aboard a shuttle.

In contrast to the shuttle, the ideal cargo rocket would be a spacecraft that could carry its payload (cargo) to orbit and return to the landing site in one piece without extensive ground support. It should require little maintenance after each flight and should be ready to fly again on short notice, as if it were a space-going commercial airliner.

At present, several private companies, the U.S. Air Force, and NASA are all working to create more practical spacecraft. Some proposals would land vertically like the lunar landers after each mission, while others would take off vertically but land horizontally like the space

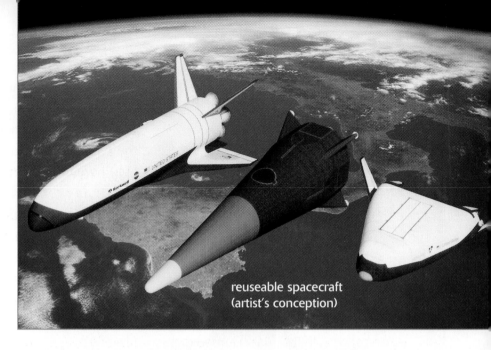

reuseable spacecraft
(artist's conception)

shuttle (except that they would not need booster rockets). Some proposed spacecraft take off and land horizontally like an ordinary airplane; such craft could either fill up their fuel tanks from a refueling plane at high altitude (like military airplanes do) before accelerating into space, or could be towed fully fueled into the air by a large airplane. Work has also been done on very fast, high-flying aircraft that could launch small rockets from the edge of space. Such spacecraft could greatly reduce the cost of getting into orbit, making space travel more practical.

Comprehension Check 5.6

Explain.

1. How is the space shuttle different from the manned spacecraft of the 1960s and early 1970s?

2. Briefly describe the events in a typical shuttle mission.

3. Why are shuttle flights still very expensive even though the shuttle is reused?

5.7 Satellites and Space Probes

Earth-orbiting satellites do just about everything. They can be used to gaze at distant galaxies, to search for buried minerals, and to relay telephone conversations or television broadcasts around the world. They can track hurricanes, make maps, find downed airplanes, and help sailors, pilots, and hikers navigate to where they want to go. Ever since the first satellite was launched in 1957, scientists and engineers have devised new uses almost every year.

Communications satellites

One of the most important uses of satellites is long-distance communication. News certainly travels faster in the age of satellites than it did in the days of sailing vessels, when a message might take weeks to cross the Atlantic Ocean from Europe to the New World. Today, friends and relatives are only a phone call away, and events taking place on the other side of the planet can be viewed on television as they happen. We enjoy the benefits of communications satellites every day.

Some **communications satellites** relay telephone conversations between the continents, and others transmit television broadcasts to TV stations around the globe; many homes are equipped with small satellite dishes to receive satellite TV broadcasts directly. Many of the programs you might hear on the radio are carried to your local radio station by means of satellites, and some satellites are even equipped to broadcast radio programs directly to listeners in their cars! Business executives who travel to remote areas sometimes carry "satellite phones"—portable telephones that allow calls to be placed from anywhere on earth, even the most remote desert or jungle. Satellites can even be used to provide e-mail and Internet access. Communications satellites also save the lives of many sailors and pilots every year by allowing people in distress to call for help. There are even communications satellites that do nothing but relay signals to other satellites!

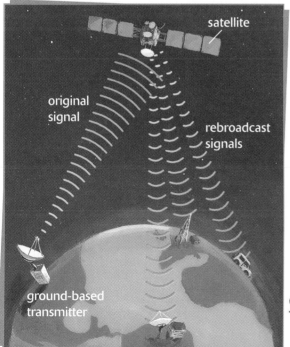

satellite

original signal

rebroadcast signals

ground-based transmitter

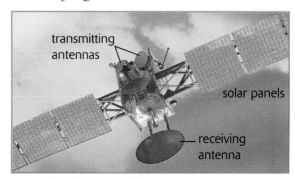

transmitting antennas

solar panels

receiving antenna

Communications satellite

Many communications satellites are placed in **geostationary orbits** directly above the equator. In such an orbit, a satellite follows the direction of the earth's rotation. Although traveling much faster than the surface below, the satellite is positioned so far away—at a distance of 22,370 miles—that it never outruns the point directly beneath it on the earth's surface. Because the satellite stays in one location in the sky, it can easily be found by transmitters and receivers on Earth. In effect, a geostationary communications satellite is like a broadcasting tower 22,370 miles tall.

Weather satellites

Before the age of satellites, meteorologists had to rely on the reports of planes and ships to learn about storms at sea. If no one encountered a storm, it could go completely undetected until it struck land, when it would be too late for people to prepare or evacuate. Today, weather satellites can detect a storm while it is still far from land, long before it threatens coastal areas.

Weather satellites provide forecasters with photographs of the cloud patterns that cover the globe, allowing them to study the weather around the world. You may be familiar with the satellite photos shown during the weather report on the evening news. In addition to photographing cloud patterns, advanced weather satellites measure cloud and ground temperatures, cloud heights, wind speeds, and relative humidity. At night, they use infrared cameras to detect patterns of heat distribution on the earth's surface. They can even track icebergs and locust swarms.

Weather satellite

satellite photo of hurricane

Polar and geostationary orbits

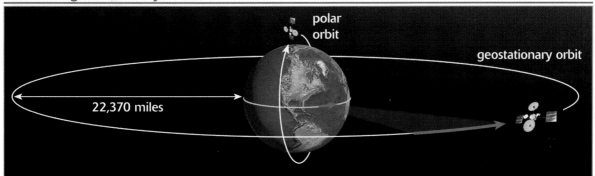

polar orbit

geostationary orbit

22,370 miles

Although weather satellites can be placed in geostationary orbits to provide a continuous view of the earth, they may also be placed in **polar orbits.** Satellites in polar orbits travel perpendicular to the equator, passing over the polar regions as they circle the earth. Because these satellites orbit at an altitude of only 500 to 600 miles, their photos show a smaller area than pictures taken from geostationary satellites, but reveal much more detail. These lower-orbiting satellites take less than two hours to travel around the earth, providing broad photo coverage of the planet.

Navigational satellites

Airplanes, ships, and other vehicles can obtain information about their position and speed from **navigational satellites.** A navigational satellite is basically an orbiting radio beacon that constantly transmits information about its position. Any vehicle that is equipped with the proper receiver can pinpoint its own position on the earth within a few yards using the signals from several of these satellites. The most famous network of navigational satellites is the *Global Positioning System,* or **GPS.** Compact GPS receivers are extremely popular with boaters, pilots, and hikers; many new cars also have built-in GPS receivers.

Navigational satellite

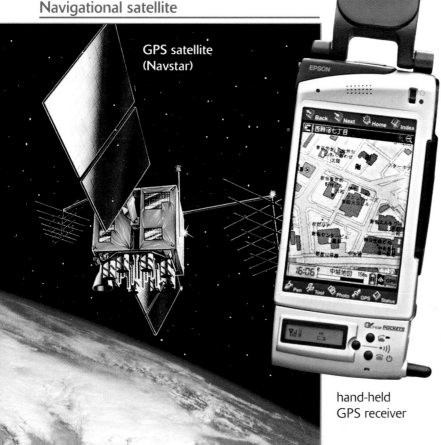

GPS satellite (Navstar)

hand-held GPS receiver

Earth resources satellite

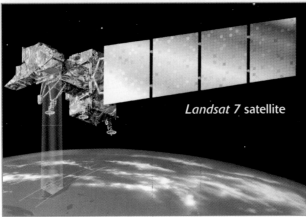
Landsat 7 satellite

Landsat photo of
Alexandria, Egypt

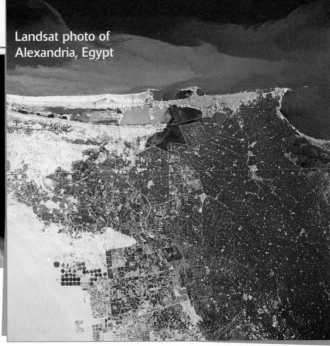

Earth resources satellites

Although most satellites are designed to carry out one or two principal tasks, an **Earth resources satellite** may perform a variety of functions, such as making maps, forecasting crop production, spotting forest fires, and surveying cities. These satellites also track fish migrations, measure wave heights, plot the terrain of the ocean floor, observe water levels in reservoirs, reveal faults in the earth's crust, and help discover deposits of coal, oil, or valuable ores.

Military satellites

Many satellites are operated by the military and help defend the United States against attack. Some satellites constantly scan the earth for missile launches or large explosions, while larger satellites equipped with large telescopes and sensitive cameras (sometimes called "spy satellites") can photograph foreign military installations on short notice, even at night. During a battle, satellites can monitor the movements of enemy ships, planes, and tanks and provide this information to generals and soldiers alike. The military also operates many navigation and communications satellites, including those of the Global Positioning System.

satellite photo
(simulated)

Military satellite

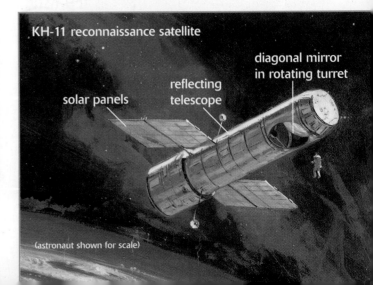
KH-11 reconnaissance satellite

solar panels

reflecting
telescope

diagonal mirror
in rotating turret

(astronaut shown for scale)

Astronomical satellites

Some satellites are designed as orbiting astronomical observatories, assisting astronomers in their study of the heavens. The Hubble Space Telescope (page 308) is a famous example of an **astronomical satellite.** Other astronomical satellites launched in recent years include large telescopes sensitive to X-rays; satellites designed to measure distances to nearby stars; and satellites equipped to study the sun.

Space probes

Using satellites, scientists have discovered many things about our own planet that we never knew before. But similar spacecraft have also been sent to study other planets, revolutionizing our knowledge of the solar system. An unmanned spacecraft that is launched specifically to explore the unknown is called a **space probe.** The very first earth-orbiting satellites were space probes, for they carried scientific instruments to learn more about the space near Earth. Later probes gave us our first photos of the far side of the moon. The sun, the moon, Halley's comet, eight of the nine planets, and even several asteroids have been surveyed by unmanned space probes.

Methods of investigation

Some space probes carry specialized cameras and instruments in order to gather information about the planets as the probes pass near them. *Voyager 2,* for example, carried television cameras, infrared and ultraviolet sensors, and instruments that measured radiation and magnetic fields with which it studied Jupiter, Saturn, Uranus, and Neptune. Others, such as the *Galileo* spacecraft sent to Jupiter and the *Cassini* spacecraft sent to Saturn, have carried smaller instrument pods which they can drop down into a planet's atmosphere. These pods allow scientists to learn about the mixture of gases in the planet's atmosphere and the air pressure and temperature of the atmosphere at different altitudes. The space probe *Magellan,* which orbited the planet Venus and mapped it in great detail, resembled the earth resources satellites that circle Earth. Other probes, such as the *Viking* and *Pathfinder* landers that touched down on

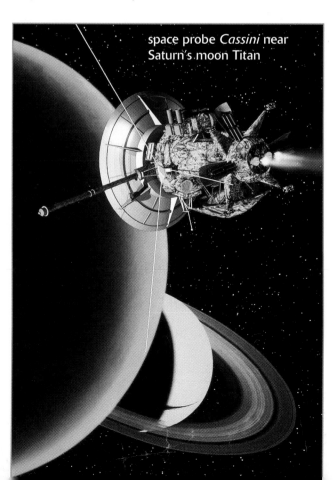

space probe *Cassini* near Saturn's moon Titan

Mars rover from *Pathfinder* spacecraft examines a Martian rock

Mars and the *Venera* spacecraft that landed on Venus, are equipped to land on other planets and take pictures, analyze soil samples, detect seismic tremors, and measure weather conditions at the surface. Through space probes, we have been able to discover many fascinating facts about the other planets in our solar system.

Comprehension Check 5.7

Clues. Give the word or term that best fits each clue.

1. Satellites that are used to relay telephone messages, television broadcasts, and other signals around the world

2. Orbit that allows a satellite to be always located above the same location on the earth

3. Satellites that help meteorologists study weather patterns around the world

4. An orbit that allows a satellite to travel around the earth, from pole to pole, in a short time to provide broad photo coverage of the planet

5. Satellites that allow airplanes, ships, and other vehicles to pinpoint their location

6. Satellites that make maps, forecast crop production, spot forest fires, etc.

7. Satellites that assist astronomers in their study of the heavens

8. An unmanned spacecraft that is launched specifically to explore the unknown

9. List three space probes mentioned in the text and tell which planets they explored.

5.8 Exploring the Inner Planets

The planets are among the most spectacular objects in the heavens. Most appear to shine more brightly than the stars. The planets, however, do not produce their own light. Like the moon, they reflect the rays of the sun. The four small planets nearest the sun—*Mercury, Venus, Earth,* and *Mars*—are called the **inner planets.** Scientists believe that all of them are made mostly of rocks and metals. The **outer planets** are *Jupiter, Saturn, Uranus, Neptune,* and *Pluto.* With the exception of Pluto, these planets are much larger than the four inner planets. And instead of being made out of solids like the inner planets, the outer planets are composed mainly of liquids and gases.

The solar system

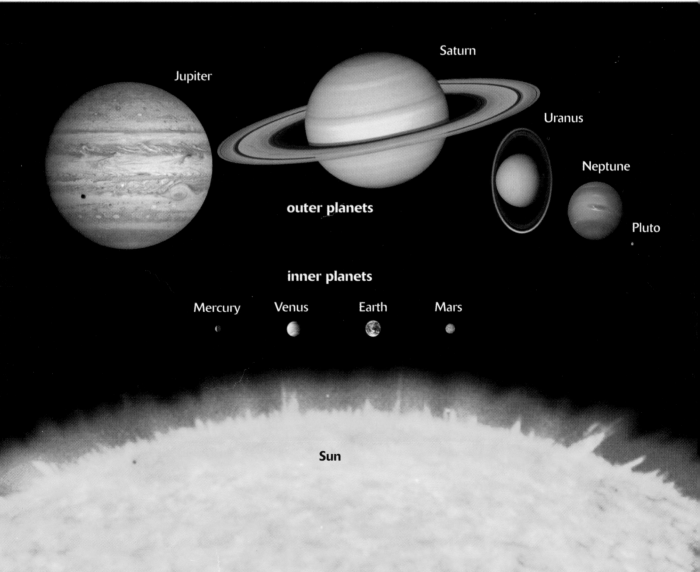

Jupiter

Saturn

Uranus

Neptune

outer planets

Pluto

inner planets

Mercury   Venus   Earth   Mars

Sun

Mercury: The moonlike planet

Small and speedy. **Mercury,** the *closest planet to the sun,* is similar to our moon in that it is rocky, barren, and pocked with craters. Because Mercury is so close to the sun, it is visible only in the bright twilight glow after sunset or just before sunrise. Mercury is the second smallest of the nine planets and only slightly larger than the earth's moon. Mercury's gravity is much weaker than Earth's gravity; if you weigh 100 pounds on Earth, you would weigh only 38 pounds on Mercury.

Traveling at a speed of approximately 30 miles per second (108,000 miles per hour), Mercury is also *the speediest planet.* It has the shortest "year" of any planet, orbiting the sun in only 88 Earth days. During its orbit of the sun, Mercury slowly rotates on its axis, completing one rotation every 59 Earth days. Because of Mercury's slow rotation and fast orbit, each "day" (period of daylight and darkness) lasts 176 Earth days, or 2 Mercury years. Mercury is one of only two planets that do not have moons.

An inhospitable world. Mercury's orbit is not as circular as the paths of most of the planets. The planet's distance from the sun varies from 43 million miles to 29 million miles at its closest approach. Because Mercury's period of daylight and darkness is exactly twice its year, the same two regions on opposite sides of the planet take turns enduring the high-noon sun at Mercury's closest approach each

Mercury

orbit. Because these are the only two regions on Mercury that experience the sun's greatest fury, they are called Mercury's "hot poles."

With hardly a trace of an atmosphere, Mercury receives little protection from the nearby sun's intense radiation and solar wind. The temperatures on Mercury rise and fall to great extremes due to the planet's slow rotation and its inability to produce a greenhouse effect. At high noon at the hot poles, the temperature can soar to 797 °F, which is nearly 250 °F hotter than the highest temperature setting on most kitchen ovens! On the opposite side of the planet, heat is quickly radiated outward from the surface and lost into space. Nighttime temperatures may drop to nearly –275 °F—more than a thousand degrees colder than the peak daytime temperature.

Venus: Earth's nearest neighbor

Starlike planet. The planet **Venus,** sometimes called the **morning star** or the **evening star** (depending on what time of day the planet is visible in the sky), shines upon the earth much more brightly than even the most brilliant stars. It is, in fact, the brightest object in the night sky except for the moon. The planet is bright not only because it is close to the earth, but also because it is covered with a dense blanket of highly reflective clouds that reflect about ¾ of the sunlight that falls upon them.

Venus orbits the sun once every 225 Earth days. But it takes the planet 243 Earth days to rotate on its axis, making Venus the only planet that takes longer to rotate than it does to travel around the sun. Venus is also unusual in that it rotates from east to west, so that the sun seems to rise in the west and set in the east. Each "day" (period of daylight and darkness) on Venus lasts 117 Earth days, or just over half a Venus year.

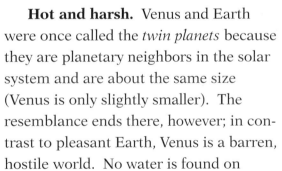

Venus

Hot and harsh. Venus and Earth were once called the *twin planets* because they are planetary neighbors in the solar system and are about the same size (Venus is only slightly smaller). The resemblance ends there, however; in contrast to pleasant Earth, Venus is a barren, hostile world. No water is found on the planet's rugged surface; only a corrosive drizzle of acid falls from the clouds above. These thick clouds covering Venus are not formed of water vapor, as are clouds on Earth, but of sulfuric acid—the same kind of acid found in a car battery. Thousands of volcanoes dot the surface of Venus, and at least some of these may be active.

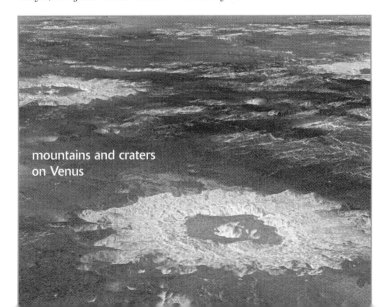

mountains and craters on Venus

surface of Venus as seen by *Venera 13* lander

The planet's heavy atmosphere—more than 95% carbon dioxide—presses down on the surface with a pressure 90 times greater than normal air pressure on Earth. If astronauts were ever to explore Venus, they would have to remain inside a strong protective shelter to keep from being squashed by the pressure of the atmosphere. The planet's thick atmosphere also traps the heat of the sun, making Venus *the hottest planet in our solar system.* Even at night, the surface temperature can be over 890°F—nearly a hundred degrees hotter than on Mercury! Because of this tremendous greenhouse effect, nighttime temperatures do not drop much lower than daytime temperatures.

CONCEPTS
IN SCIENCE

Seasons, Days, and Years

The year and the day

God has caused the earth to move in two different ways in regard to the sun. First, the earth revolves around the sun in 365¼ days, the period which we call a **year.** (We have an extra day in February every four years during *leap year* to use up the extra quarter of a day left over each year.) Second, the earth rotates on its axis every 24 hours. During this rotation, the sun shines on the earth, giving periods of light and darkness which we call **days** and **nights.** Ancient people often told time by using an instrument called a *sundial.*

The position of the sun's shadow on the dial told them what time it was.

God has caused us to have a day and a year of exactly the right length. If our day were as short as Jupiter's day (less than ten hours), we would not have time for all the things we wanted to do. If it were as long as Mercury's day (59 Earth days), we would have to sleep many times before the day was over. Instead, we have a 24-hour day, which gives us just enough time to work or play and just enough time to sleep. Similarly, if our year were as short as Mercury's (88 days), we would not have adequate growing seasons. If it were as long as Mars's (687 days), some countries would suffer from very severe winters. Everywhere we look, we see evidence of a loving God Who created the world. He knows what is best for us.

Months and seasons

The moon passes from new to new again approximately every 30 days, 12 times a year. Therefore we have **12 months** ("moonths") in a year. Ancient peoples could determine the time of the month by watching the phases of the moon. Often, these people considered the beginning of the month to be the appearance of the first thin sliver of moon after a short time when the moon could not be seen.

Our seasons occur because of the tilt of the earth's axis as it orbits the sun. Another way for our ancestors to determine months and seasons was by watching the stars. As the seasons change, different constellations become visible. Twelve important constellations called the *zodiac* encircle the earth as it orbits around the sun. As the earth travels its pathway around the sun, the sun appears to pass through these constellations, one per month. In the past, farmers knew that when the sun "entered" a particular constellation, it was time to plant a particular crop. They could tell which constellation the sun was in by watching to see which one was above the eastern horizon when the sun rose.

Weeks

There is no orbit of planets or heavenly bodies that gives us the **seven-day week.** That was given to us directly by God to help us remember that He is the Creator of all the marvels of the universe. God created our world in only six days, and on the seventh day, He rested.

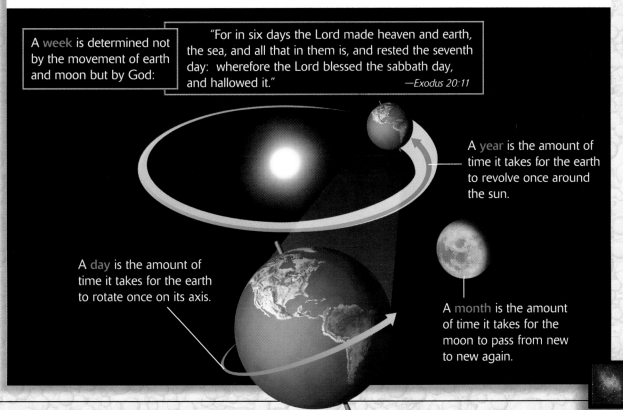

A week is determined not by the movement of earth and moon but by God:

"For in six days the Lord made heaven and earth, the sea, and all that in them is, and rested the seventh day: wherefore the Lord blessed the sabbath day, and hallowed it."
—*Exodus 20:11*

A year is the amount of time it takes for the earth to revolve once around the sun.

A day is the amount of time it takes for the earth to rotate once on its axis.

A month is the amount of time it takes for the moon to pass from new to new again.

Mars: The red planet

Mars, Earth's other planetary neighbor, is the fourth planet from the sun—the outermost of the four inner planets. Because it glows with a strong reddish light in the evening sky, Mars is often called the **"red planet."** Mars is about half the size of Earth, and its gravity is weaker; an object that weighs 100 pounds on Earth would weigh 38 pounds on Mars (the same as on Mercury). A day on Mars is only 38 minutes longer than a day on Earth.

Desert planet. Mars is completely barren, covered by rocky, windswept deserts of reddish sand; violent dust storms frequently rage across its surface. Polar caps composed of frozen water and dry ice (frozen carbon dioxide) are also conspicuous features of the planet because their white color stands out starkly against the red sand. The polar caps shrink and grow with the seasons as carbon dioxide evaporates and refreezes.

Mars

The atmosphere of Mars, which is about 95% carbon dioxide with only slight traces of water vapor and oxygen, is very thin. In fact, the earth's atmosphere at an altitude of 100,000 feet (3 times higher than Mount Everest) is thicker than the Martian atmosphere at the surface. Although summer temperatures on

surface of Mars as seen
by *Pathfinder* lander

Mars can sometimes exceed 80 degrees Fahrenheit, the lack of a greenhouse effect (chapter 4) causes temperatures to quickly plunge to 80 degrees *below* zero at night. During the winter in polar regions, it gets so cold (–190 °F) that a portion of the air actually freezes, forming a thick layer of dry ice (frozen carbon dioxide) on the ground.

Rugged terrain. The planet Mars abounds with deep canyons, large craters, and towering volcanoes. Some regions of the planet are covered by windswept sand dunes, while others are more rocky. Winding valleys resembling dry riverbeds are common in the southern hemisphere of Mars.

The Tharsis [thär′sĭs] Bulge, so called because it is raised several miles above the level of the surrounding areas, is the location of some of the most gigantic mountains and valleys in the solar system. Four huge extinct volcanoes tower upward from the Bulge. The largest, Olympus Mons [ə·lĭm′pəs mänz: "Mount Olympus"], is almost three times as tall as Mount Everest, the tallest mountain on Earth, and its base is nearly as large as the state of Arizona. The canyon known as Valles Marineris [văl′ĕs măr·ĭ·nĕr′ĭs: "Mariner Valley"] is 2500 miles long, as much as 62 miles wide in some places, and nearly 4 miles deep, making it much deeper and longer than Arizona's Grand Canyon.

Ice and fog. The crust of Mars is thought to contain significant quantities of water ice, known as *permafrost*, mixed with the soil; the thin atmosphere also contains water vapor. In the summer, Martian valleys occasionally fill with fog as water vapor in the air condenses into tiny ice crystals. Wispy ice clouds are also visible in the photo of Mars on page 342.

Martian moons. Two small, asteroid-like moons named *Phobos* [fō′bəs] and *Deimos* [dā′məs] revolve around Mars, each of them measuring only a few miles across. Phobos is a dark, heavily-cratered moon, and Deimos, the smaller of the two, is much smoother because dust covers all but the deepest craters. Both moons orbit rather close to Mars. Phobos, the closest, takes only 8 hours to travel around the planet. As a result, this unusual moon rises in the west, races across the sky, and sets in the east twice each Martian day.

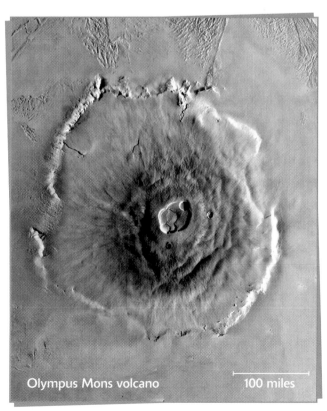

Olympus Mons volcano

100 miles

Comprehension Check 5.8

Clues. Give the word or term that best fits each clue.

1. The planet that revolves around the sun every 365¼ days

2. The planet nearest to Earth

3. The "red planet"

4. The planet with two moons, Phobos and Deimos

5. The planet often called the morning star or evening star

6. The planet closest to the sun

7. The "speediest" planet

8. The hottest planet in the solar system

5.9 Exploring the Outer Planets

As you can tell from the diagram on pages 276 and 277, the inner planets make up only a very small portion of the solar system. Beyond the orbit of Mars, the planets are much more spread out. Jupiter is nearly twice as far from the sun as Mars is, and Saturn is about twice as far away as Jupiter. Lonely Pluto is so distant from the sun (nearly 40 astronomical units) that the sun appears only as a very bright star.

In the past, very little was known about the outer planets—Jupiter, Saturn, Uranus, Neptune, and Pluto—because of the great distances separating them from the earth. But beginning in the 1970s, several space probes began to visit the outer planets, enabling scientists to learn many things about these remote members of the solar system.

Jupiter: King of the planets

Big and beautiful. Mighty **Jupiter,** the fifth planet from the sun, is *the largest planet in our solar system* and is bigger than all of the other planets put together. If Jupiter were hollow, it could swallow 1300 planets the size of Earth! The planet is composed mostly of hydrogen and helium; because of this, it is known as a *gas giant*. In addition to its enormous size, Jupiter also boasts the fastest rotation of any planet, only 9 hours and 50 minutes. At its equator, this translates into a rotational speed of over 28,000 miles per hour (mph). Jupiter's gravity is stronger than Earth's; a person who weighs 100 pounds on Earth would weigh more than 250 pounds on Jupiter.

Jupiter is clearly visible from Earth with the unaided eye, appearing far brighter than the star Sirius and nearly as bright as Venus. Jupiter is one of the most colorful planets in the solar system; its atmosphere swirls with red, cream, orange, and brown clouds. Swift wind currents whip these colorful clouds into bands and swirls that encircle the planet.

The **Great Red Spot,** a gigantic rotating storm twice as wide as the earth, has churned its way around Jupiter for centuries. Huge thunderstorms hundreds of miles across send forth lightning bolts with power ten thousand times that of lightning on Earth.

The monarch's moons. At least 28 moons, as well as a faint ring, whirl around the huge planet in a miniature of the solar system. Four of Jupiter's moons are big enough that they could be seen from Earth with the unaided eye if it were not for the brightness of the planet that overshadows them. **Ganymede** [găn′ĭ·mēd], *the largest moon in the solar system,* is bigger than the planet Mercury and only slightly smaller than Mars; it is covered with a mixture of ice and dark dust. Due to its icy surface, *Europa* [yo͞o·rō′pə] is smooth and white; measurements from the *Galileo* space probe suggest that an ocean of water dozens of miles

deep may exist beneath the thick ice layer. *Callisto* [kə·lĭs′tō] is icy and covered with craters like Ganymede. Red-orange *Io* [ī′ō] has the first active volcanoes ever discovered on another world; the moon's bright coloring comes from sulfur and other chemicals spewed out by Io's many volcanoes.

Jupiter

Moons of Jupiter

| Io | Europa | Ganymede | Callisto |

Saturn: The ringed planet

Radiant rings. The sixth planet, **Saturn,** is perhaps best known for its rings, for Saturn has *the most glorious rings of any planet in our solar system.* Directly above the planet's equator, the rings extend 170,000 miles from one end to the other, spanning an area of space 20 times as wide as the earth. Composed mostly of snowball-sized chunks of ice, the rings reflect sunlight in a dazzling display. The gravitational attraction of Saturn's inner moons helps keep the ring particles in their proper bands.

Windy world. Like Jupiter, Saturn is a gas giant composed mostly of hydrogen and helium. Saturn is large enough to

Saturn

sunset on Saturn (artist's conception)

contain 750 planets the size of Earth, but is only 95 times as heavy—Saturn is the least dense of all the planets. As a result, Saturn's "surface" gravity is only slightly stronger than Earth's. At first glance, Saturn's weather seems much milder than Jupiter's but its weather patterns are partly obscured from view by a hazy atmospheric layer. In fact, Saturn has winds that blow continuously at speeds of 1100 mph at the equator, a speed considerably faster than the speed of sound on Earth.

Many moons. Saturn also boasts at least 30 moons. Saturn's largest moon, called **Titan** [tī′tən], has *its own atmosphere,* composed mostly of nitrogen, that is even thicker than Earth's atmosphere. As a result, you could survive on

Titan as seen by
Voyager 2 spacecraft

surface of Titan (artist's conception)

Titan by wearing a simple oxygen mask instead of a whole space suit. However, you would have to wear *very* warm clothing—the surface temperature on Titan averages −290°F! Thick orange clouds obscure the surface from our view, but Titan is so cold that lakes and pools of liquid methane and ethane (the chemical components of natural gas) may exist on its hidden surface. Almost as large as Jupiter's moon Ganymede, Titan is larger than the planets Mercury and Pluto.

Mimas

Although Titan is the second-largest moon in the solar system, Saturn's other moons are only a fraction of the size of Earth's moon. One of these moons, called *Mimas* [mī′măs], revolves around Saturn [about 30,000 miles] beyond the outermost ring; its most prominent feature is a giant crater nearly a third as wide as Mimas itself. Other moons like *Iapetus* [ī·ăp′ə·təs] and *Phoebe* [fē′bē] follow paths that take them several million miles away from Saturn. Saturn's smallest moons are about the same size as the moons of Mars.

Uranus: An unusual planet

Mysterious planet. In 1781, Sir William Herschel and his sister Caroline discovered **Uranus,** the first new planet to be discovered in thousands of years. Uranus, the third-largest planet in the solar system, is nearly twice as far from the sun as Saturn. To a spacecraft orbiting Uranus, the planet would appear as a featureless turquoise sphere surrounded by a set of very dark rings; a haze of bluish crystals in the upper atmosphere hides much of the windblown clouds below from view. But it seems that Uranus consists of dense gases and perhaps an ocean of liquid water, ammonia, and methane covering a solid core the size of Earth. Although Uranus is surrounded by at least 21 moons, they are all rather small; Earth's moon is larger than all the moons of Uranus put together. Most of the moons are named after characters in William Shakespeare's plays.

Sideways system. The most unusual thing about the Uranus system is not its moons, or rings, or even Uranus itself, but that *the entire system is turned on its side.* The planet's equator, its ring system, and the orbits and equators of fifteen moons are all set on its edge in relation to the rest of the solar system.

Because of its odd tilt, Uranus has some very extraordinary days during its 84-year orbit. When the planet's north pole faces the sun most directly, the sun never sets in the northern hemisphere, but simply makes a circle in the northern sky every 17¼ hours (the time Uranus takes to rotate). As Uranus revolves about the sun, the sun makes a larger circle in the sky every day until it begins to dip below the horizon. At this point in its orbit, Uranus begins to experience a normal day-night cycle like the other planets. This continues for several earth years, while the days grow shorter and the nights grow longer. In time, the sun disappears below the horizon completely,

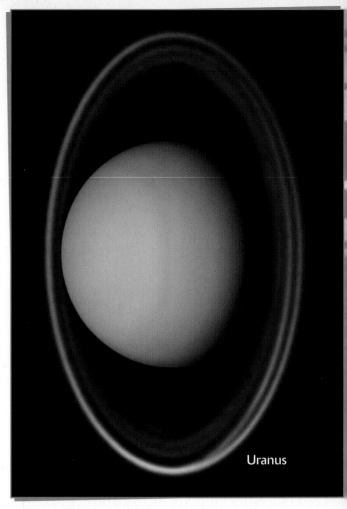

Uranus

and the northern hemisphere is lit only by the stars. After a few years of this "winter," the process is reversed, until the sun is again circling over the northern hemisphere.

Uranus's odd tilt poses a problem for evolutionists. The most popular evolutionary theory requires that all of the planets spin in the same direction and be more or less aligned, but Uranus foils that hypothesis. Some evolutionists argue that perhaps a now-destroyed planet collided with Uranus billions of years ago, but it is more difficult to explain why fifteen moons and a ring system are also aligned with the tilted planet. Uranus stands (or leans) as a silent witness to the creative hand of God.

SPACE**X**PLORER

The Herschels: Explorers of the Night Sky

William and Caroline Herschel

What does your family do for fun? One family may play baseball together in the back yard, while another might spend a day at the beach. Others make visits to museums or watch plays and sporting events or even hike in the mountains. Perhaps your family goes camping or travels across the country. Or maybe you prefer to stay at home as a family and do special projects together. It could be that your family does something extraordinary like the Herschel family did back in the 1700s. The Herschels spent their free time making telescopes and charting the stars in the heavens. In the process, they discovered a planet.

William, Caroline, and Alexander Herschel grew up in Germany, where their father was an army musician and an amateur scientist. When he was not playing music, Mr. Herschel tried to learn all he could about science by reading books. Because of Mr. Herschel's interest in music and science, the children also became musicians and amateur scientists like their father.

William Herschel moved to Bath, England, where he worked as a music teacher, composer, and church organist. Once while looking for information about music, William discovered a book that discussed the art of telescope making and viewing the heavens. After reading the book, he decided to build a telescope that would be capable of focusing on the moon, the nearby planets, and distant stars.

William designed a reflecting telescope similar to that of Isaac Newton, but on a much larger scale; in fact, no one had ever built such a large telescope before. William then enlisted the help of his sister Caroline and brother Alexander, who had joined him in England. Like Newton, the Herschels had to cast their own metal disks and then grind and polish them into mirrors. The first mirror cracked before it was completed, and the metal for the second mirror oozed all over the basement floor before it had a chance to cool in its mold. After over two hundred more attempts, the Herschel family finally succeeded in making a mirror that would work in William's special telescope design. Once the mirror was completed, William, Caroline, and Alexander were able to finish what became the largest telescope ever made to that point. It was over six feet in length and was capable of revealing

the Herschels' 40-foot telescope

the light of stars fainter than any that had been studied before. With this telescope, William and Caroline carefully recorded all the stars they could see in one small section of sky.

But William was not satisfied with this telescope, even though it displayed stars that had not been revealed before. He wanted to see the heavens more clearly. So he and his brother and sister continued to grind and polish larger mirrors for even larger telescopes. William and Caroline built one telescope in 1789 that was over 40 feet long and had a mirror that was 48 inches (4 feet) across. This telescope became known as one of the technical wonders of the 18th century.

In 1781, while the Herschels were busily grinding telescope mirrors and charting the stars, William discovered a faint, slowly moving object that neither he nor Caroline had noticed before in their previous studies of the skies. This object was the planet we now call Uranus. The discovery of a new planet created a sudden interest in William Herschel's work as an astronomer. Soon astronomers from all over England were stopping by the Herschel home to study the sky charts and to look through the giant telescopes the family had made. William was elected a member of the Royal Society, and William and Caroline were hired to be the king's personal astronomer and the astronomer's assistant. With the extra wages from the king, William was able to stop giving music lessons in order to spend more time studying the stars. What had once been a family hobby suddenly became the family occupation!

In 1788, William Herschel married a widow named Mary Pitt, and in 1792 they had a son, John Herschel. As John grew, he became an assistant to William and Caroline as they charted the skies with their telescopes.

The Herschels were especially interested in some heavenly objects they called *nebulae*. Some of these tiny, faint "clouds"—barely visible to the naked eye on a clear, dark, moonless night—were actually huge clouds of gas. Many of the nebulae, however, were too faint for the Herschel telescope to show their true structure. At that time, the Herschels did not know that these clouds were really galaxies—gigantic star systems or "island universes" in space much like our own Milky Way. William and Caroline spent 20 years looking for nebulae, and the three star catalogs they published listed 2500 nebulae and star clusters as well as 848 double stars. William was knighted by the king of England for his scientific achievements and became known as Sir William Herschel, the greatest English scientist since Sir Isaac Newton.

John Herschel continued his father's work, discovering 500 additional nebulae and charting the stars and nebulae of both the Northern and Southern Hemispheres. He, like his father and aunt, was convinced that each star or nebula he discovered was more proof that God is in control of the universe. John Herschel, who was also knighted by the king for his discoveries, once said that "all human discoveries seem to be made only for the purpose of confirming more and more strongly the truths come from on high and contained in the sacred writings."

Neptune: The nomadic planet

Two plus two equals Neptune.
Years after the Herschels discovered Uranus, astronomers analyzing that planet's motion made a disturbing discovery: the planet's course through the sky was unpredictable. Evidently the gravity of some unseen planet was pulling on Uranus just enough to produce noticeable changes in Uranus's orbital path around the sun.

Because the unknown planet was so far away, it would be no brighter than a very faint star, and very difficult to find unless astronomers knew where in the sky to look for it. Using information about the variations in Uranus's motion, two mathematicians predicted the position of the mystery planet. This eighth planet, named **Neptune,** was discovered in 1846, precisely where the mathematicians predicted.

A blue world. Neptune travels a long, lonely path around the sun, taking 165 Earth years to complete a single revolution in its orbit; if you were born on Neptune, you would die of old age long before your first birthday! In contrast to its long years, Neptune's days are rather short—just a little over 16 hours. The presence of methane in its atmosphere makes Neptune a beautiful royal blue. Thin, white cirrus clouds of methane ice crystals drift high above the azure cloud deck several miles below. Despite its seemingly peaceful atmosphere, however, Neptune has the strongest winds measured anywhere in the

Neptune

solar system. Powerful winds blast along at more than 1200 mph, over 1½ times the speed of sound on Earth. Giant rotating storms as large as the earth occasionally form in Neptune's atmosphere, churning their way around the planet for several years before dissipating.

cirrus clouds in Neptune's atmosphere

Scientists believe that, like Uranus, Neptune consists of dense gases and an ocean of water, ammonia, and methane surrounding a hot, rocky core as large as the earth. The "surface" gravity of both Uranus and Neptune is similar to Earth's gravity.

Neptune's moons. Eight known moons and five faint rings encircle Neptune. Neptune's largest moon is named *Triton* [trī'tŏn]; even though it is slightly smaller than Earth's moon, Triton has its own magnetic field and faint traces of an atmosphere. The temperature on this moon is the coldest measured anywhere in the solar system: −390°F. Powerful geysers on Triton's surface spout liquid nitrogen as much as 5 miles into the atmosphere.

Triton is very unusual in that it orbits Neptune in a clockwise direction (as viewed from the planet's north pole)—the opposite direction of every other large moon in the solar system. This poses a problem for evolutionists, whose theory of our solar system's origin would predict that all moons formed with a planet should revolve in the same direction. Although smaller moons formed elsewhere and captured by a planet's gravitational pull could possibly revolve in a different direction, Triton's large size rules out most evolutionary explanations.

Pluto: The pigmy planet

A frozen planet. Years after Neptune was discovered, some astronomers became convinced that still another planet, dubbed "Planet X," might lurk in the outer reaches of the solar system. After years of unsuccessful searching by several scientists, a 24-year-old American astronomer named Clyde Tombaugh [tŏm'bô] discovered a ninth planet, which he named **Pluto.**

Much about Pluto, *the outermost planet in the solar system,* remains a mystery. All that astronomers know about the planet has been learned through telescopes. Pluto is by far the *smallest planet,* measuring only ⅔ the size of Earth's moon; it is actually closer in size to the asteroid Ceres than it is to Mercury, the next smallest planet.

Triton

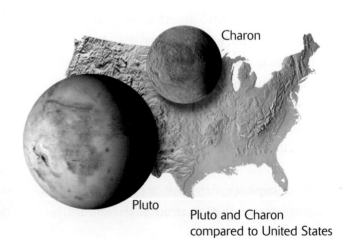

Charon

Pluto

Pluto and Charon compared to United States

Pluto and Charon
(artist's conception)

Although it is the only solid outer planet, Pluto is only about twice as dense as water. Because of its low density, many scientists believe Pluto consists mostly of frozen water, ammonia, and methane; its surface appears to be covered with frozen nitrogen. It is probably very much like Neptune's moon Triton in appearance. Pluto also has the weakest gravity of any planet; a person weighing 100 pounds on Earth would weigh less than 7 pounds on Pluto. If you can jump 3 feet off the ground on Earth, the same effort would send you sailing 45 feet in the air on Pluto!

A surprising moon. In 1979, astronomers were surprised to discover a moon orbiting the tiny planet. This moon, named *Charon* [kâr′ən], is half as large as Pluto and is almost as big as the largest moons of Uranus. Although it orbits only about 12,000 miles from Pluto, Charon moves rather slowly, taking a week to make one complete revolution around the planet.

Like Earth's moon, Charon always keeps the same side turned toward Pluto. Unlike Earth, however, Pluto always keeps the same side turned toward Charon. Because of this unusual situation, Charon never rises or sets as seen from Pluto, but seems to remain stationary in Pluto's sky as the stars move behind it. Also, Charon can be seen from only one side of Pluto; if you were to travel to the other side of the planet, you would never see the moon at all. Like Uranus and its moons, Pluto and Charon are tipped over sideways compared to the rest of the solar system.

Pluto's path. Pluto's year is the longest of all the planets'—248 Earth years. It follows the most elliptical orbit of all the planets. At the most remote point in its orbit, Pluto is more than four billion miles from the sun. But at another point in its orbit, Pluto crosses Neptune's path. For about 20 Earth years, Pluto is closer to the sun than Neptune is. Then Pluto crosses Neptune's path and once again becomes the outermost planet in our solar system, a distinction it will hold for more than 220 years.

Comprehension Check 5.9

Clues. Give the word or term that best fits each clue.

1. The largest planet in the solar system

2. Planet discovered by the Herschels

3. Planet with the moons Titan, Mimas, Iapetus, and Phoebe

4. The outermost planet

5. Large planet turned on its side in relation to the rest of the solar system

6. The smallest planet in the solar system

7. Planet with the moons Ganymede, Europa, Io, and Callisto

8. Planet with a moon named Charon

9. Planet with the Great Red Spot

10. Planet best known for its rings

11. Planet with a moon named Triton

12. The largest moon in the solar system

5.10 The Origin of the Universe

Think of the earth, our home, and of all the things—living and nonliving—that are on it. Then think of the sun and the moon, the lights that rule the day and the night, the innumerable stars in the billions of galaxies. Remember the variety that is seen among the nine planets of our solar system. Where did all these things come from? Do you think that scientists can tell us?

Scientists can prove some things by observation and careful experiments; we can learn many wonderful things through a study of science, and we have learned many such things as we have studied this book. If something cannot be observed, however, scientists cannot tell us much about it. If a hypothesis cannot be tested by experiments, then scientists cannot prove that it is true.

Science cannot tell us about the beginning of the world and the beginning of life. Was any scientist present to observe what happened when the universe came into existence? Can we send spaceships back in time to find out what happened? Can we do experiments to show where the first life came from? Is there any way to make and to test a hypothesis about how something happened so long ago? No! Scientists cannot really prove what happened before there were any people.

Some things that we cannot learn through science we learn by believing someone we can trust. Do you know the date of your birth? You probably do, but not by your own observation. You know it by trusting someone who was there or by reading written medical records. We can know about God's creation of the universe because He has told us about it in His Word. No other person was there in the beginning; the Bible contains God's true and reliable written record

of what happened at Creation, and we accept this record by faith (Hebrews 11:3). Genesis 1:1 says, *"In the beginning God created the heaven and the earth."* Before the creation of the universe, there was only God. God made matter and energy out of nothing. He spoke, and it was so. God also made the waters, and His Spirit *"moved upon the face of the waters"* to bring into existence the wonderful world that we know today.

On the first day of Creation, God created light and divided the light from darkness, making day and night. What special characteristics of light can you recall? Why do we have day and night?

On the second day, God created the firmament, which He called *heaven.* The firmament is the atmosphere that surrounds the earth.

God gathered the waters together to make the dry land appear on the third day. On that same day, God also commanded the earth to bring forth in abundance the wonderful variety of

plants we enjoy today, each with the ability to reproduce new plants of the same kind. What do you remember about photosynthesis, root systems, fruits, and the plant families that you studied earlier this year? The Bible tells us that twice on the third day—after God separated the seas and the land, and after He created the plants—God saw that His work was good.

The sun, moon, stars, and other heavenly bodies appeared on the fourth day. God made them to divide day from night, to give light to the earth, and to be for signs, seasons, days, and years. Can you remember what determines a day on Earth? A month? A year? How many heavenly bodies can you name? Again, God saw that His work was good.

On the fifth day, God created the birds and all the animals that live in water. He created each bird and each water animal with the ability to reproduce after its own kind, and He commanded them to fill the earth and the seas. At the end of the fifth day, God again pronounced it good.

The sixth day was the last day of Creation. God made the land-dwelling animals, from the largest dinosaur to the smallest insect. For His final act of Creation, God made man, the only creature that He made in His image (Genesis 1:24–31). God made man's body from the same matter He had used to create the earth, but man received his soul and spirit directly from God. All the living things upon the earth were made to benefit man; it was part of God's wise design for man to rule over the rest of creation. At the end of the sixth day when God surveyed all that He had made, He saw that it was very good.

On the seventh day, God rested. He blessed the seventh day and sanctified it; that is, He set it apart as a special day. God could have created everything at once, but He chose to do it in six days and to rest on the seventh in order to give us a pattern for the way He wants us to do our work (Exodus 20:9–11). Scientists have discovered that people are healthier if they rest for one day each week. How wise is our God, Who formed us for Himself!

Throughout history there have been people, even scientists who have thought up their own stories of how things came to be. Many myths, hypotheses, and theories of creation have been developed and discarded, but no one but the Designer and Creator of the universe is qualified to tell us how our magnificent universe *really* came into existence. From the time of Adam to the age of the astronauts, people who have earnestly wanted to know how our great universe came to be have looked to the Creator for the answer. And those who have searched for Him sincerely have found Him. Jesus said, *"Blessed are the pure in heart: for they shall see God"* (Matthew 5:8). Have you seen Him as you have sought to understand more about God's great universe?

Chapter Checkup

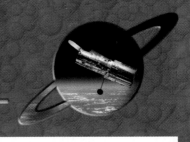

I. Tell why these people are important.

Sir Isaac Newton

James Clerk Maxwell

Galileo

Robert H. Goddard

Wernher von Braun

Yuri Gagarin

Alan Shepard

John Glenn

Valentina Tereshkova

Neil Armstrong

William and
    Caroline Herschel

II. Define these terms.

visible spectrum

wave

oscillation

crest

trough

medium

magnetic field

electric field

electromagnetic wave

speed of light

frequency

wavelength

electromagnetic spectrum

pulsars

astronaut

space station

space probe

satellite

polar orbit

geostationary orbit

Global Positioning System

III. Define these terms about telescopes.

telescope

refraction

reflection

refracting telescope

reflecting telescope

Hubble space telescope

spectroscope

radio telescope

IV. Distinguish these spacecraft and space stations.

Sputnik 1

Explorer 1

space shuttle

Apollo 11

Skylab

Mir

International Space
    Station

V. Know the following planets and moons and their distinguishing characteristics.

Mercury

Venus

Mars

Jupiter

Saturn

Uranus

Neptune

Pluto

Ganymede

Titan

VI. List two uses of each type of satellite.

communications

weather

navigational

Earth resources

military

astronomical

Matter and Chemistry

What do you think of when you hear the word *chemistry*? If you think of a chemistry set, test tubes, and colored, smoking liquids, you are seeing only a small part of the picture. Chemistry actually touches every aspect of our lives. Eating food involves chemistry; so does breathing, thinking, or using your muscles to ride a bike. The dishes you eat from, the clothes you wear, and the house you live in all required a knowledge of chemistry to make.

Chemistry can be thought of as the study of what substances are made of, and how one substance can be changed into another. Chemistry is one of the most important sciences. The field of medicine is based largely upon chemistry; so is the field of agriculture. Without chemistry, we would not have concrete, steel, glass, rubber, or nylon. Even such items as bread and soap require a basic knowledge of chemistry to make.

Definition of matter

Did you know that you have something in common with a fish, a cloud, a sock, a flea, and a flower? Your body and all of these things are made of matter. **Matter** can be described as ***anything that takes up space and has weight.*** Water, rock, wood, animals, people, the largest galaxies, and the smallest atoms—all are examples of *material* things—things made up of matter. Even invisible air is made of matter: you can feel air as it moves through your nostrils or as it rushes through the window of a fast-moving car. Can you think of some things that are not made of matter? Such things are said to be *immaterial*. Light is immaterial, although it is part of the physical world. Also immaterial are things like your thoughts and feelings, your soul, and God Himself.

Concept Check

Check the items that are made of matter.

- ✓ granite
- a dream
- an idea
- ✓ water
- love
- ✓ Mercury
- light rays
- ✓ soap bubbles
- time
- ✓ air
- energy
- gravity

Mass and weight

Suppose you had two sealed boxes of matter. If both boxes were the same size, how could you tell which box contained more matter without opening the box? One way would be to *weigh* the boxes. If the first box weighed 100 pounds and the second box weighed only 50 pounds, you would know that the first box contained more matter. This is true because **weight** is *a measure of the pull of gravity on an object,* and gravity pulls harder on objects that contain more matter. For example, an elephant weighs more than a mouse because an elephant contains more matter than a mouse.

Although weight can help us find out how much matter an object contains, *the weight of an object changes from place to place.* This is true because gravity is stronger in some places than in others. For example, a 6th grader who weighs 100 pounds on the earth's surface would weigh 17 pounds on the moon, 38 pounds on Mars, 253 pounds on Jupiter, and 2800 pounds on the sun! The amount of matter in the person does not change, but the force of gravity upon the person (and therefore his weight) would change greatly.

Earth

moon

Mars

100 lb.

17 lb.

38 lb.

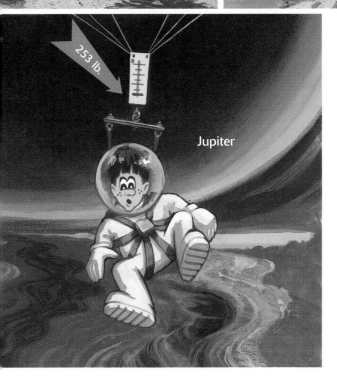

253 lb.

Jupiter

unit—about the mass of a large paper clip—a larger unit called the *kilogram* (1000 grams) is more common in everyday use. An object with a mass of 1 kilogram weighs about 2.2 pounds on the earth's surface. Thus, a person who weighs 110 pounds has a mass of 50 kilograms.

Concept Check

Check the correct answer.

1. Astronaut Neil Armstrong has
- ☐ more *mass* on the earth.
- ☐ more *mass* on the moon.
- ✓☐ the same *mass* wherever he is.

2. Astronaut Neil Armstrong has
- ✓☐ more *weight* on the earth.
- ☐ more *weight* on the moon.
- ☐ the same *weight* wherever he is.

3. Because gravity weakens as you move farther from the center of the earth, you would weigh slightly more
- ☐ at a beach.
- ✓☐ at the top of Mount Everest.

Because the strength of gravity varies from place to place, scientists use a different term to refer to the amount of matter in an object. The amount of matter that makes up an object is called the object's **mass.** Although the weight of a box changes from place to place, the mass of the box would remain the same.

Measuring mass. A metric unit called the **gram** is used to measure an object's mass. Because the gram is a very small

◼ Density

You know that some materials seem naturally heavier than others. A handful of lead shot is heavier than a handful of feathers, for example. But we cannot say that lead is always heavier than feathers, because it depends on how much we have of each material. There is an old riddle that asks, "Which is heavier, a pound of feathers or a pound of lead?" The answer is that they are equally heavy; a pound is a pound. The pound of lead merely takes up less space than the pound of feathers. But if you compared a truckload of feathers with a handful of lead, feathers would be heavier than lead.

In other words, it is not always correct to say that lead is heavy, because it depends on how much lead we are talking about. An ounce of lead is not heavy at all. Neither is it always true that feathers are light, because a truckload of feathers would be far too heavy for you to lift.

A box of lead weighs more than the same volume of feathers.

Density explained. What we really have in mind when we think of a material as light or heavy is not its weight, but its density. **Density** is *the amount of matter (mass) in one unit of volume (space).*

Imagine that we have two identical, empty boxes sitting side by side. Now suppose that we fill one of the boxes with lead and the other with feather fluff. If we were to weigh the boxes, we would find that the box of lead weighs much more than the box of feathers, even though the volume of lead and the volume of feathers are the same. The box of lead simply packs more matter (mass) into the same amount of space. Thus, we can say that lead is *denser* than feathers because lead contains more mass per unit of volume. The two boxes

Weight of 12-inch cubes of common substances

lead	iron	cork	water	carbon dioxide
700 lb.	493 lb.	15 lb.	62.4 lb.	0.112 lb.

demonstrate that *if two objects have the same volume but different densities, the object made of the denser substance weighs more.*

As another example, suppose we have two bricks of exactly the same size, one made out of iron and the other of clay. Since iron is denser than clay, the iron brick would be the heavier of the two. If we wanted the two bricks to weigh the same, we would need to make the clay brick bigger, increasing its volume until it could contain the same amount of matter found in the smaller iron brick. The two bricks show us that *two objects made of material with different densities can either be of the same volume and different weights, or of the same weight and different volumes.*

Measuring density. We can measure the density of an object by measuring both its mass and its volume. We can then divide the mass by the volume to find out how much mass is contained in each unit of volume.

For example, imagine that we want to find the density of a cube-shaped piece of concrete. We will first need to find the *mass* of the block of concrete. Using a balance or a scale, we determine that the block has a mass of 3000 grams (3 kilograms).

Next, we will need to find the *volume* of the piece of concrete. Since the gram is a metric unit, we will also use metric units to find the volume. Using a ruler, we find that the cube is 10 centimeters wide, 10 centimeters front to back, and 10 centimeters high. The volume of an object is equal to length × width × height (also written $V = l \times w \times h$). So the volume of the concrete is 10 cm × 10 cm × 10 cm, or 1000 cubic centimeters (1000 cm³).

Now, to find the density, all we have to do is divide the mass of the block (3000 grams) by the volume (1000 cubic centimeters). We find that the density of the concrete block is 3 grams per cubic centimeter, abbreviated 3 g/cm³. (One cubic centimeter is about the size of a sugar cube.)

Notice that if the amount of mass is measured in grams, and the cubic centimeter is used as the unit of volume, then density is measured in *grams per cubic centimeter.* One of the most familiar substances, water, has a density of exactly 1 gram per cubic centimeter.

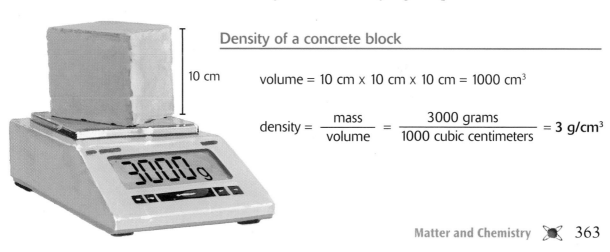

Density of a concrete block

volume = 10 cm x 10 cm x 10 cm = 1000 cm³

$$\text{density} = \frac{\text{mass}}{\text{volume}} = \frac{3000 \text{ grams}}{1000 \text{ cubic centimeters}} = 3 \text{ g/cm}^3$$

10 cm

Densities of other common materials are shown in Table 6.1. What do you suppose happens to those substances less dense than water when they are placed in water? What happens to those substances more dense than water?

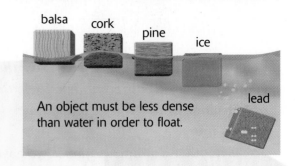

An object must be less dense than water in order to float.

Table 6.1 **Densities of various substances**	
Substance	**Density** (g/cm³)
hydrogen gas	0.00009
air	0.0013
balsa wood	0.13
cork	0.24
white pine wood	0.4–0.5
oak wood	0.6–0.9
gasoline	0.68
ice	0.92
water	**1.00**
seawater	1.03
sugar	1.59
clay	1.8–2.6
sandstone	2.1–2.4
salt	2.16
sand	2.32
glass	2.4–2.8
marble	2.6–2.8
granite	2.6–2.8
aluminum	2.7
limestone	2.7–2.8
cement	2.7–3.0
diamond	3.0–3.5
iron	7.9
copper	8.9
silver	10.5
lead	11.4
mercury	13.6
uranium	18.7
gold	19.3
platinum	21.4
osmium	22.5

lightest

heaviest

This diagram shows the actual volumes for 5 grams (about the mass of one unsharpened pencil) of each substance.

platinum

gold

lead

silver

granite

concrete

sugar

coal

milk

water

petroleum

pine

charcoal

air

Concept Check

Use Table 6.1 to answer the following questions.

1. Which of these objects could float in water?

☐ ice

☐ clay

☑ wood

☑ marble

2. Which of these trees has wood of the greatest density?

☑ white pine

☐ balsa

☐ oak

3. These rocks all have the same volume. Which weighs the most?

☐ sandstone

☑ granite

☐ marble

☑ limestone

4. These metal cubes all have the same weight. Number them in order from the least to the most dense.

☑ copper

☐ iron

☐ gold

☐ aluminum

Comprehension Check 6.1

Clues. Give the word or term that best fits each clue.

1. The study of what substances are made of, and how one substance can be changed into another

2. Anything that takes up space and has weight

3. The difference between mass and weight

4. The units in which mass is measured

5. The amount of matter (mass) in one unit of volume

Explain.

6. Which is more dense, oak wood or aluminum? (See Table 6.1.)

7. Which would weigh more, a brick made of iron or the same size brick made of lead?

8. When the head of an axe fell into the water, the prophet Elisha caused it to float (2 Kings 6:1–7). Why was this miraculous? Would it still have been a miracle if, instead of the axe head, the wooden handle had floated in the water?

6.2 Atoms: Building Blocks of Matter

Definition of atom

All matter is composed of tiny particles called **atoms.** For example, suppose you could somehow take a solid copper penny (pre-1982) and cut it into a million pieces; then you took the smallest piece and cut *it* into a million pieces; and so on. Eventually, you would reach a point at which the particles could not be made any smaller and still remain particles of copper. These smallest possible particles of copper would be the copper atoms.

How many atoms of copper would a solid copper penny contain? The answer may surprise you: nearly 30 billion trillion atoms, or 3 followed by 22 zeroes (30,000,000,000,000,000,000,000). If you could count a billion atoms per second, it would take you 930,000 years to count that many atoms! An ordinary half-ounce cookie contains even more atoms—just over one septillion (1 followed by 24 zeroes). You can see that the smallness of an atom defies the imagination.

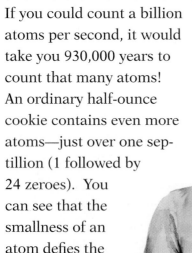

"I will now devour one septillion atoms!"

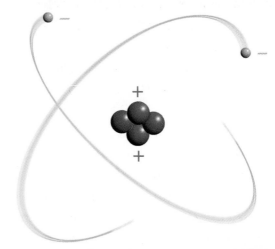

| electron (−) | proton (+) | neutron (no charge) |

Structure of an atom

Anatomy of an atom

Energetic electrons. Imagine for a moment that you enlarged an atom to the size of a person. What would you see? Actually, you would see almost nothing at all, because an atom is mostly empty space. At the center is a tiny, extremely dense core called the **nucleus,** and around the nucleus swarms from one to over a hundred tiny particles called **electrons.** But as you peered intently at the greatly oversized atom in front of you, all these particles would escape your notice, for the nucleus would be much smaller than the dot on an *i*, and the electrons would be still smaller. Moreover, the electrons would be moving at tremendous speed. A single electron circles the nucleus one hundred quadrillion (1 followed by 17 zeroes) times each second. But you should not think that an electron follows a regular orbit, such as the orbit of a planet about the sun. Rather, it darts here and there along a seemingly unpredictable path; its ever-changing course is suggested by the flight of a bee around a hive. Being nearly everywhere at once, the electrons zooming about a nucleus form a shield that prevents other atoms from moving into the same space. These fast-moving electrons are commonly described as an **electron cloud.**

The fuzzy outline of the electron cloud around an atom can be seen through extremely powerful microscopes. An instrument called the *scanning-tunneling microscope* is able to examine the texture of a surface so closely that it can detect the tiny bump due to each individual atom.

The central nucleus. The nucleus of an atom is a cluster of separate particles. These are of two kinds, **neutrons** and **protons.** Although in pictures we often see neutrons, protons, and electrons portrayed as little round balls and a nucleus portrayed as something like a bunch of grapes, the truth is that we do not know what any of these things look like. When we attempt to see them with light, the light rays spread apart and give us extremely fuzzy pictures. Trying to observe particles so small is like trying to feel the difference between a penny and a dime when you are wearing heavy gloves.

A normal atom has exactly the same number of protons and electrons. In smaller atoms the number of neutrons is about the same as the number of protons and electrons, but in larger atoms the number of neutrons is considerably larger. For example, one common atom has 14 protons, 14 electrons, and 14 neutrons; another has 82 protons, 82 electrons, and 125 neutrons.

Although the neutron and the proton are nearly equal in mass, both are about 1800 times more massive than an electron. More than 99.9% of the mass of an atom is concentrated in the nucleus. A nucleus is so dense that a pinhead of nuclear material would weigh ten million pounds.

scanning-tunneling microscope image of a silicon surface

Charges in an atom

Unlike the neutron, both the proton and electron bear an electric charge. This means simply that an electric force exists between any proton and any electron, or between any two electrons, or between any two protons. An electric charge may be either **positive** or **negative.** As you have probably learned before, *opposite charges attract, and like charges repel.* Therefore, since the proton is positive and the electron is negative, the force between them is one of attraction. This attractive force is what binds the electrons of an atom to the atom's nucleus. Between any two particles of the same charge, however, the force is one of repul-

like charges repel

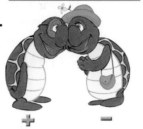

opposite charges attract

sion. The bump you feel when you run into a wall is due to the strong rejecting force between the electron clouds of your body's atoms and the electron clouds of the wall's atoms.

As we said earlier, a normal atom has an equal number of protons and electrons. Although the charge on a proton is the opposite of the charge on an electron, the two charges are of equal strength. Thus, in a normal atom, the total positive charge is in perfect balance with the total negative charge. The atom as a whole has no charge of either kind; in other words, the overall charge of the atom is zero. Anything lacking an electrical charge is said to be **neutral.**

Structure of some common atoms

There are many hundred different kinds of atoms. The simplest kind, having a single electron whirling about a single proton, is the main building block of the substance called *hydrogen.*

A typical *helium* atom contains two of each kind of particle. A cluster of two protons and two neutrons forms the nucleus, and around the nucleus fly two electrons.

hydrogen atom

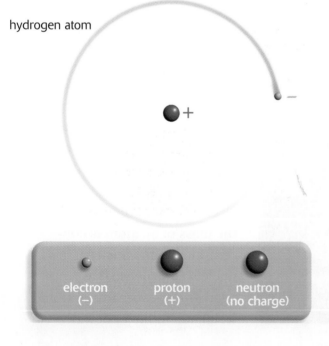

electron (−)   proton (+)   neutron (no charge)

helium atom

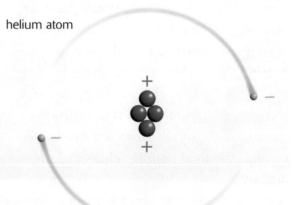

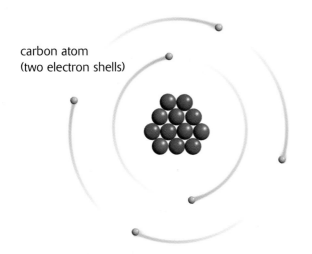

carbon atom
(two electron shells)

A typical atom of a substance called *sodium* provides an example of an atom with three electron shells. Of the eleven electrons, two are in the inner shell, eight are in the second shell, and one is in the third shell. Just as there are eleven electrons in orbit, so there are eleven protons in the nucleus. But in this case, the number of neutrons is not the same as the number of protons; there are twelve neutrons.

A slightly more complex atom is illustrated by a typical *carbon* atom. Six electrons move about a nucleus of six protons and six neutrons. Notice that the four additional electrons are in an orbit farther from the nucleus. Electrons in orbit at roughly the same distance from the nucleus are said to be in the same **shell.** Although the shell closest to the nucleus has a capacity of only two electrons, the second shell can hold as many as eight electrons. Thus, the first two shells are sufficient to accommodate all six electrons of a carbon atom. Much larger atoms require more shells, however. A third shell holds up to 18 electrons, and a fourth shell holds up to 32 electrons. The largest atoms require as many as seven electron shells.

The nucleus of a typical *oxygen* atom is crowded with four additional particles, bringing the number of protons and the number of neutrons to eight apiece. Around the nucleus are electrons in two shells, the inner shell containing two electrons and the outer shell containing six electrons. Eight electrons are needed to balance the total positive charge of the nucleus.

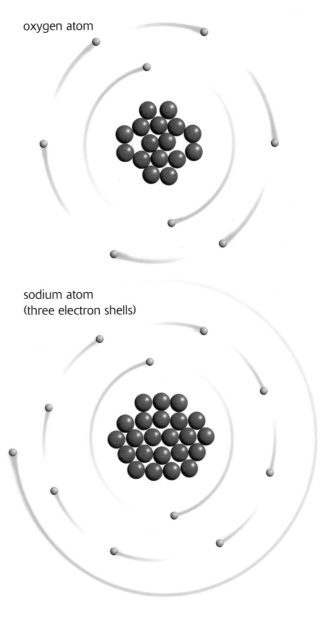

oxygen atom

sodium atom
(three electron shells)

Atomic numbers

A copper atom is distinctly different from a gold atom, a carbon atom, or a hydrogen atom. But how can we tell different types of atoms apart? What is it that makes one atom carbon and another copper?

Although all types of atoms have the same overall structure, *atoms of different elements contain different numbers of protons*. For example, a carbon atom always contains exactly six protons. If an atom contains five or seven protons, it is not carbon. *Any* atom that contains six protons is a carbon atom.

Likewise, copper atoms always contain 29 protons. If an atom contains 29 protons, it is a copper atom, but an atom with 28 protons or 30 protons cannot be copper.

Because the number of protons in an atom is a very important number, it has been given a special name: the **atomic number.** A carbon atom, containing 6 protons, would have an atomic number of 6. Copper has an atomic number of 29, and gold has an atomic number of 79. Because every element is composed of a unique type of atom, *every element has its own atomic number.*

✓ *Concept Check*

Complete the chart.

Kind of atom	Number of electrons	Number of protons	Number of neutrons
hydrogen	1	1	0
helium	2	2	2
carbon	6	6	6
oxygen	8	8	8
sodium	11	11	12

Comprehension Check 6.2

Clues. Give the word or term that best fits each clue.

1. The tiny particles that matter is composed of

2. The tiny, extremely dense core at the center of an atom

3. The tiny particles that swarm at tremendous speed around the nucleus of an atom

4. The two types of particles which make up the nucleus of an atom

5. Anything lacking in an electrical charge

6. The simplest kind of atom, with only a single electron whirling around a single proton

7. Name for the number of protons in an atom

Definition of element

Some substances are composed of only one type of atom. For example, a piece of pure copper is made of individual atoms of copper. Similarly, a piece of pure gold is made of gold atoms, and a piece of carbon is made of carbon atoms. However, not all substances are made of only one type of atom. For example, water is *not* made of "water atoms," but of hydrogen and oxygen atoms bonded tightly together.

Substances that are composed of only one type of atom are called **elements.** Copper, gold, and carbon are examples of elements. Substances that are composed of more than one type of atom bonded together are not elements, but are called **compounds** instead. Water is an example of a compound.

Atomic names and numbers

Scientists have identified well over a hundred different elements. The known elements range from little hydrogen, with only 1 proton in the nucleus, to big ununoctium [ō͞on′ō͞on·ŏk′tē·əm], with 118 protons in the nucleus! Since the atomic number of an element is equal to the number of protons, the atomic numbers of the known elements range from 1 to 118. Some well-known elements and their atomic numbers are shown in Table 6.2.

Elements and compounds

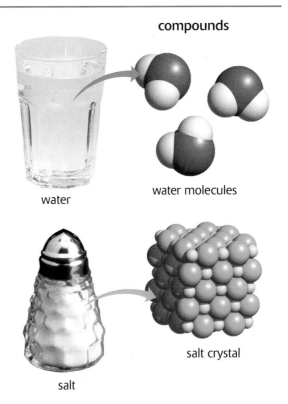

elements

copper

copper atoms

sulfur

sulfur molecule

compounds

water

water molecules

salt

salt crystal

Table 6.2 Selected elements and their symbols		
Atomic number	Element	Symbol
1	hydrogen	H
2	helium	He
3	lithium	Li
4	beryllium	Be
5	boron	B
6	carbon	C
7	nitrogen	N
8	oxygen	O
9	fluorine	F
10	neon	Ne
11	sodium	Na
12	magnesium	Mg
13	aluminum	Al
14	silicon	Si
15	phosphorus	P
16	sulfur	S
17	chlorine	Cl
18	argon	Ar
19	potassium	K
20	calcium	Ca
22	titanium	Ti
24	chromium	Cr
25	manganese	Mn
26	iron	Fe
28	nickel	Ni
29	copper	Cu
30	zinc	Zn
33	arsenic	As
36	krypton	Kr
43	technetium	Tc
47	silver	Ag
50	tin	Sn
53	iodine	I
61	promethium	Pm
76	osmium	Os
78	platinum	Pt
79	gold	Au
80	mercury	Hg
82	lead	Pb
92	uranium	U
94	plutonium	Pu
114	ununquadium	Uuq
118	ununoctium	Uuo

Notice that *each element has its own atomic number.* This is true because *each element is composed of a unique type of atom.* Remember that it is the atomic number (number of protons) that determines the type of atom.

Notice that each element has a symbol as well as a name. The symbol is in some cases the first letter of the name; thus, hydrogen is *H* and oxygen is *O*. In other cases, the symbol has been formed by joining another prominent letter to the first; thus, chlorine is *Cl* and calcium is *Ca*. In a few cases, the symbol is based not on the English name but on the Latin name of the element. For example, iron is represented *Fe* because the Latin name for iron is *ferrum.*

Most of the first 92 elements occur naturally. The only exceptions are technetium [tĕk·nē′shē·əm: atomic number 43] and promethium [prə·mē′thē·əm: atomic number 61]. These as well as all the elements beyond the first 92 are man-made elements. Except under rare circumstances, they do not occur naturally.

carbon

carbon (diamond)

oxygen

gold

silver

copper

sulfur

Naturally occurring elements

Atomic number	Element	Symbol
1	hydrogen	
2	helium	
6	carbon	
7	nitrogen	
8	oxygen	
11	sodium	
13	aluminum	
16	sulfur	
17	chlorine	
20	calcium	
26	iron	
30	zinc	
47	silver	
79	gold	
82	lead	
92	uranium	

The highest-numbered element that occurs naturally in significant quantities is *uranium,* with atomic number 92. The man-made elements with higher atomic numbers are called the *transuranium* [trăns′yoo·rā′nē·əm] *elements,* which means the elements *beyond* uranium. As of 2001, transuranium elements as high as number 118 had been produced by scientists. The most abundant of the transuranium elements is **plutonium** [ploo·tō′nē·əm], which has an atomic number of 94.

Today, whenever a new element is created, it is given a temporary name based on its atomic number. For example, the temporary name of element 118, ununoctium, means simply "one, one, eight." Eventually, the temporary name is replaced by a permanent name, often based on the name of a famous scientist, a state, or a country.

Generally, the higher the atomic number of an element, the denser the element. This is true because adding additional protons and electrons significantly increases the mass of an atom, but does not greatly increase the size of the atom's electron cloud. For this reason, the densest elements tend to have high atomic numbers. For example, the element gold (atomic number 79) is over seven times as dense as aluminum (atomic number 13) and more than twice as dense as iron (atomic number 26). There are exceptions to this general rule, however. Lead (atomic number 82) is slightly less dense than gold even though it has a higher atomic number. The densest element of all is **osmium** [ŏz′mē·əm: atomic number 76], a metal similar to platinum. A brick made of osmium would weigh about 56 pounds. In other words, two osmium bricks would about balance your weight on a seesaw.

plutonium

Table 6.3 shows that the chief elements both in our environment and in our bodies have low atomic numbers. At the head of both lists is oxygen, element 8. Elements beyond iron, element 26, are relatively rare, accounting for less than 0.2% of the atoms in the earth's crust. In the universe as a whole, about 92% of the atoms are hydrogen and 7% are helium. All the other elements combined make up only 1% of the total.

Table 6.3a
Elements that make up the earth's crust, oceans and atmosphere

Element	Percent by mass	Atomic number
oxygen	49.1	8
silicon	26.1	14
aluminum	7.5	13
iron	4.7	26
calcium	3.4	20
sodium	2.6	11
potassium	2.4	19
magnesium	1.9	12
hydrogen	0.88	1
titanium	0.58	22
chlorine	0.19	17
carbon	0.09	6
all others	0.56	

Table 6.3b
Elements your body is made of

Element	Percent by mass	Atomic number
oxygen	64.6	8
carbon	18.0	6
hydrogen	10.0	1
nitrogen	3.1	7
calcium	1.9	20
phosphorus	1.1	15
chlorine	0.40	17
potassium	0.36	19
sulfur	0.25	16
sodium	0.11	11
magnesium	0.03	12
iron	0.005	26
zinc	0.002	30

Table 6.3c
Elements in the universe

Element	Percent by mass	Atomic number
hydrogen	92	1
helium	7	2
all others	1	

EYEwitness reporter

Observing elements

Although most substances around us are made of compounds, a surprising number of everyday objects are made of mostly individual elements. Collect objects representing as many different elements as you can (see pages 208–211 and 378–386 for ideas). How many different elements can you come up with?

Comprehension Check 6.3

Clues. Give the word or term that best fits each clue.

1. A substance that is made of only one type of atom

2. The element with the lowest atomic number (See Table 6.2.)

3. The symbols for hydrogen, oxygen, and chlorine (See Table 6.2.)

4. The transuranium element that is the most abundant

5. The densest element of all

6. The most abundant element in the earth's crust; in your body; and in the universe as a whole (See Table 6.3.)

Explain.

7. Explain the difference between an element and a compound.

8. Can two atoms of the same element ever have different atomic numbers? Why or why not?

6.4 Groups of Elements

The periodic table of the elements

About the time of the American Civil War, a total of 65 elements had been isolated and named. Enough was known about them to show that a typical element resembles several other elements. The first attempt to group the elements into families was undertaken in the 1860s by the Russian chemist Dmitri Mendeleev [d'mē′trē mĭn·dĭl·yā′yĕf]. After gathering all available

Dmitri Mendeleev

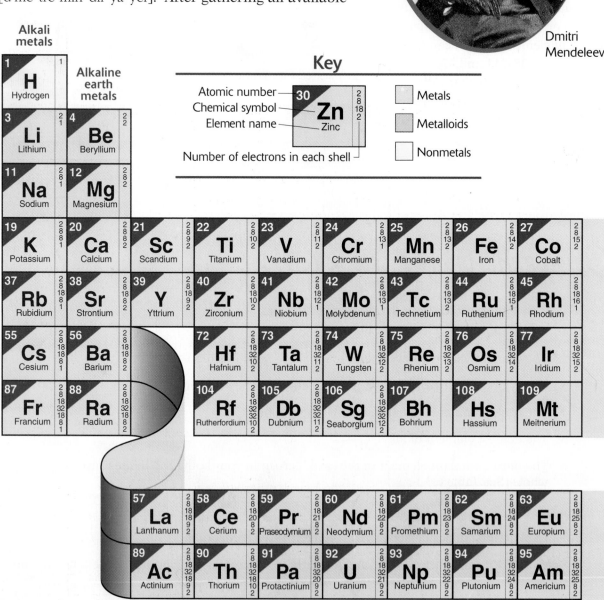

Key

Atomic number — 30
Chemical symbol — **Zn**
Element name — Zinc
Number of electrons in each shell

2
8
18
2

☐ Metals
▨ Metalloids
☐ Nonmetals

information about the elements known at the time and then making many attempts to arrange them, he at last constructed what we now call the **periodic table of the elements.**

In a modern version of Mendeleev's table, shown below, the elements are organized into rows and columns. The sequence from upper left to lower right sets them in order according to their atomic number. Each column contains a family of elements with similar characteristics.

The blocks of color in the periodic table indicate the *three main groups of elements.* All the elements in blue are **metals,** all those in yellow are **non-metals,** and all those in pink are considered **semimetals;** that is, they resemble metals in some respects and nonmetals in other respects.

Periodic table of the elements

Noble gases*

Halogens

Element	Atomic number	Symbol	Name	Electron shells
	2	He	Helium	2 (4.003)
	5	B	Boron	2, 3
	6	C	Carbon	2, 4
	7	N	Nitrogen	2, 5
	8	O	Oxygen	2, 6
	9	F	Fluorine	2, 7
	10	Ne	Neon	2, 8
	13	Al	Aluminum	2, 8, 3
	14	Si	Silicon	2, 8, 4
	15	P	Phosphorus	2, 8, 5
	16	S	Sulfur	2, 8, 6
	17	Cl	Chlorine	2, 8, 7
	18	Ar	Argon	2, 8, 8
	28	Ni	Nickel	2, 8, 16, 2
	29	Cu	Copper	2, 8, 18, 1
	30	Zn	Zinc	2, 8, 18, 2
	31	Ga	Gallium	2, 8, 18, 3
	32	Ge	Germanium	2, 8, 18, 4
	33	As	Arsenic	2, 8, 18, 5
	34	Se	Selenium	2, 8, 18, 6
	35	Br	Bromine	2, 8, 18, 7
	36	Kr	Krypton	2, 8, 18, 8
	46	Pd	Palladium	2, 8, 18, 0
	47	Ag	Silver	2, 8, 18, 1
	48	Cd	Cadmium	2, 8, 18, 2
	49	In	Indium	2, 8, 18, 3
	50	Sn	Tin	2, 8, 18, 4
	51	Sb	Antimony	2, 8, 18, 5
	52	Te	Tellurium	2, 8, 18, 6
	53	I	Iodine	2, 8, 18, 7
	54	Xe	Xenon	2, 8, 18, 8
	78	Pt	Platinum	2, 8, 18, 32, 17, 1
	79	Au	Gold	2, 8, 18, 32, 18, 1
	80	Hg	Mercury	2, 8, 18, 32, 18, 2
	81	Tl	Thallium	2, 8, 18, 32, 18, 3
	82	Pb	Lead	2, 8, 18, 32, 18, 4
	83	Bi	Bismuth	2, 8, 18, 32, 18, 5
	84	Po	Polonium	2, 8, 18, 32, 18, 6
	85	At	Astatine	2, 8, 18, 32, 18, 7
	86	Rn	Radon	2, 8, 18, 32, 18, 8
	110	Uun	Ununnilium	
	111	Uuu	Unununium	
	112	Uub	Ununbium	
	114	Uuq	Ununquadium	
	116	Uuh	Ununhexium	
	118	Uuo	Ununoctium	
	64	Gd	Gadolinium	2, 8, 18, 25, 9, 2
	65	Tb	Terbium	2, 8, 18, 27, 8, 2
	66	Dy	Dysprosium	2, 8, 18, 28, 8, 2
	67	Ho	Holmium	2, 8, 18, 29, 8, 2
	68	Er	Erbium	2, 8, 18, 30, 8, 2
	69	Tm	Thulium	2, 8, 18, 31, 8, 2
	70	Yb	Ytterbium	2, 8, 18, 32, 8, 2
	71	Lu	Lutetium	2, 8, 18, 32, 9, 2
	96	Cm	Curium	2, 8, 18, 32, 25, 9, 2
	97	Bk	Berkelium	2, 8, 18, 32, 26, 9, 2
	98	Cf	Californium	2, 8, 18, 32, 28, 8, 2
	99	Es	Einsteinium	2, 8, 18, 32, 29, 8, 2
	100	Fm	Fermium	2, 8, 18, 32, 30, 8, 2
	101	Md	Mendelevium	2, 8, 18, 32, 31, 8, 2
	102	No	Nobelium	2, 8, 18, 32, 32, 8, 2
	103	Lr	Lawrencium	2, 8, 18, 32, 32, 9, 2

Metals

Aside from reddish-brown copper and yellowish gold, all the metals have a lustrous silvery color. Moreover, nearly all are solids at room temperature. The sole exception is **mercury,** the silvery liquid that moves back and forth along the thin tube inside some thermometers. The metal gallium [găl′ē·əm: atomic number 31] will melt in your hand like chocolate; cesium [sē′zē·əm: number 55] would too except that it is too toxic and harmful to the skin to be handled. Electricity flows easily through most metals, which is why metals such as copper and aluminum are used for electrical wires. Metals also tend to be good conductors of heat.

In chapter 3, we studied several important metals, including **gold, platinum, silver, iron, copper,** and **aluminum.** However, several other metals are also important. Shiny **chromium,** or "chrome," is often applied to polished steel to protect it from rusting; the chrome layer also gives the steel a mirror-like surface. Steel coated with the metal **zinc** is called *galvanized steel* and is commonly made into such items as chainlink

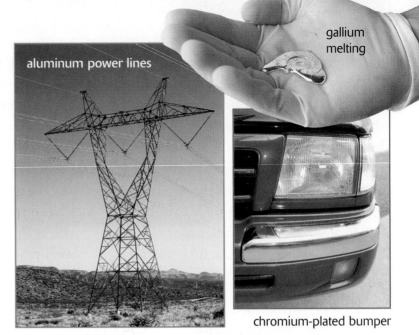

aluminum power lines

gallium melting

chromium-plated bumper

fences, trash cans, roofing nails, and car bodies. Zinc is also an ingredient in flashlight batteries. **Nickel,** a very hard metal, is an important ingredient in stainless steel and rechargeable batteries; it is also used as a lining for tanks holding corrosive chemicals. The five-cent U.S. coin called the "nickel" is made of an alloy (mixture) of 25% nickel and 75% copper.

Zinc

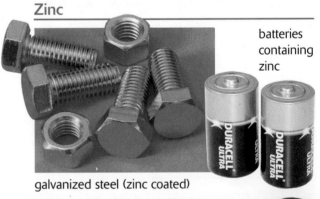

batteries containing zinc

galvanized steel (zinc coated)

Nickel

stainless steel (7–9% nickel)

nickel coins (25% nickel)

cell phone battery containing nickel

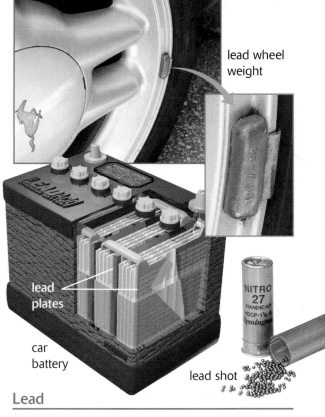

lead wheel weight

lead plates

car battery

lead shot

NITRO 27 HANDICAP HDCP-1⅛ Remington

Lead

The densest of the everyday metals is **lead.** The Latin word for lead, *plumbum,* is the source of the English word *plumbing,* so-called because until modern times most plumbing was made of lead. However, lead is no longer used for plumbing because even very small quantities of lead are harmful to humans and animals if eaten. Lead poisoning is especially harmful to the brain. Today, the main use of lead is in car and truck batteries, but it is also used to make wheel weights and firearms ammunition.

Nonmetals

The nonmetals include many solids and several gases. One nonmetal, **bromine** [brō'mēn], is liquid at ordinary room temperatures and pressures. The nonmetals show a variety of colors. Sulfur is yellow, carbon is black, phosphorus is sometimes red, bromine is reddish-brown, iodine is deep purple, and chlorine is greenish-yellow.

Gaseous nonmetals. Among the nonmetals is the very first element in the periodic table, **hydrogen.** As a colorless and odorless gas at room temperature, hydrogen is difficult to detect; a glass jar filled with hydrogen gas would appear absolutely empty. Very little of earth's abundant supply of hydrogen exists in pure form, because hydrogen combines readily with other elements. However, pure hydrogen can be obtained by splitting natural gas, petroleum, or water molecules. Hydrogen is very flammable; if a mixture of hydrogen and air is ignited, the hydrogen combines with the oxygen in the air to form water molecules (in the form of steam).

Hydrogen is most commonly used in chemical factories, but its most famous use may be in rocket engines such as those of the space shuttle. When hydrogen combines with oxygen in a rocket engine to

Colorful nonmetals

red phosphorus

sulfur

chlorine

iodine

bromine

hydrogen-burning main
engines of space shuttle

water (H_2O) and of most rocks and minerals. Over 50% of our bodies consists of oxygen because we are largely made of carbon-hydrogen-oxygen compounds in a watery fluid. Breathing is a process of taking in oxygen from the air and expelling carbon dioxide. The oxygen combines with food substances in reactions that produce energy useful to the body. Carbon dioxide is one byproduct of these reactions. Tanks of oxygen are used in welding torches, in deep-sea scuba diving, and in medical settings to make breathing easier.

oxygen cutting torch

produce steam, a large amount of heat is released. The super-hot steam shoots out of the rocket nozzle at tremendous speed, causing the rocket to move in the opposite direction.

Also grouped with the nonmetals are two other extremely important gases, *oxygen* and *nitrogen*. Together, they make up almost 99% of the earth's atmosphere. ***About 78% of the atmosphere is nitrogen, and about 21% is oxygen.***

Like hydrogen, **oxygen** is colorless and odorless. Oxygen is the most abundant element at the earth's surface because it is an ingredient not only of air, but also of

Table 6.4
Composition of Dry Air

Name of gas	Percent by volume	Percent by weight
nitrogen	78.09%	75.53%
oxygen	20.95%	23.16%
argon		
carbon dioxide		
neon	less than 1%	less than 1%
helium		
krypton		
hydrogen		
xenon		
ozone		

nitrogen

oxygen · other gases

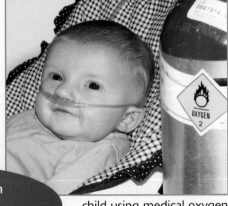

child using medical oxygen

Nitrogen is a colorless, odorless gas that is much less prone than oxygen to react with other elements. Nitrogen compounds are used in fertilizers, rocket fuels, and explosives. Nitrogen is also an ingredient in the compounds called **proteins** that much of our body tissues are made of.

Solid nonmetals and semimetals. Although several nonmetals are gases, most nonmetals and semimetals are solid at ordinary temperatures. Some of the most important of these are carbon, sulfur, and phosphorus (all nonmetals) and silicon (a semimetal).

In its elemental state, **carbon** has several different forms. One is graphite, a black, slippery solid used for lubrication and as an ingredient in strong, lightweight plastics called *graphite composites* [kəm·pŏs'ĭts]. The "lead" of your pencil is a mixture of graphite and clay. Another form of elemental carbon is diamond, the hardest of all minerals. Carbon is also a basic building block of the complex compounds found in your body and in all living organisms.

Compounds of both sulfur and phosphorus are also important in body chemistry. At room temperature, **sulfur** is an odorless, yellow solid, called *brimstone* in the Bible. Sulfur melts at 250°F and

powdered sulfur

liquid sulfur

⚠ **DANGER / POISON**

| SHIELD EYES EXPLOSIVE GASES CAN CAUSE BLINDNESS OR INJURY | NO · SPARKS · FLAMES · SMOKING | SULFURIC ACID CAN CAUSE BLINDNESS OR SEVERE BURNS |

skunk

sulfuric acid

Sulfur

remains liquid all the way to 446°F; hot liquid sulfur can cause severe burns and must be handled with great care. Sulfur is also flammable and burns easily, producing choking, poisonous vapors.

Many sulfur compounds have strong smells, such as those in skunk spray. Another notable sulfur compound, the gas *hydrogen sulfide* (H_2S), is responsible for the stench of rotten eggs. Most of the sulfur obtained from mining is used to make *sulfuric* [sŭl·fyŏŏr'ĭk] *acid,* a highly corrosive chemical used in car batteries and chemical manufacturing.

Carbon

diamonds

tennis racket made of graphite composite

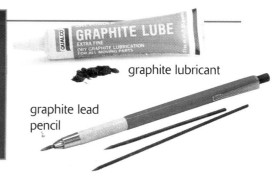

GRAPHITE LUBE
EXTRA FINE
DRY GRAPHITE LUBRICATION
FOR ALL MOVING PARTS

graphite lubricant

graphite lead pencil

Phosphorus is a waxlike solid with two forms: white phosphorus and red phosphorus. White phosphorus is so flammable that it spontaneously bursts into flames if it comes in contact with air; it must be stored underwater to prevent fires. Red phosphorus is more stable, but still ignites easily and burns with a brilliant flame. Compounds of phosphorus and oxygen known as *phosphates* are used as fertilizers and food preservatives.

Because the element **silicon** [sĭl′ĭ·kən] has characteristics of both metals and nonmetals, it is considered a *semi-metal*. Common sand, the mineral quartz, and glass are all made of a silicon-oxygen compound called *silicon dioxide*. Silicon in pure form is used to make computer chips, the tiny "brains" of computers and other electronic devices.

white phosphorus

red phosphorus

Families of elements

So far, we have discussed very general groups of elements, such as metals and nonmetals. However, elements can also be arranged into more specific groups or families. The periodic table of the elements is arranged in such a way that each column of the table contains a family of elements with similar characteristics. For example, the metals in the far left column are all soft, have low densities (three of them will float in water), and share a strong tendency to combine with other elements. Likewise, the elements in the far right column show little tendency to combine with other elements, and all but one are gases at room temperature.

Alkali metals. The metals in the first (far left) column of the periodic table are called the **alkali metals.** The alkali metals **sodium** and **potassium** are common in the rocks, soils, and oceans of the earth, although neither occurs

purified silicon

worker inspecting computer chips

Silicon

computer chip from personal computer

sodium vapor streetlights

sodium metal being cut with a knife

Sodium

lye soap

Alkaline earth metals. The second column of elements in the periodic table contains a group of metals called the *alkaline earth metals.* Like the alkali metals, the alkaline earth metals have a strong tendency to react with other substances. However, the alkaline earth metals are somewhat harder than the alkali metals and do not react quite as vigorously.

The most common alkaline earth metal is a metal called **calcium.** Although there are not many uses of the pure metal, calcium compounds are *very* important. For example, the bones of your body are made of a compound of calcium and phosphate. A compound known as *calcium carbonate* ($CaCO_3$) is the chief ingredient in seashells, limestone, and concrete. Another alkaline earth metal called **magnesium** is strong but lightweight and is used in parts for airplanes and some cars.

naturally in pure form. Pure sodium is used in many electric streetlights, which can be recognized by their yellow or orange hue. Besides sodium chloride (familiar table salt) the most important compound of sodium is probably **sodium hydroxide** [hī·drŏk′sīd′], also known as *lye* or *caustic soda;* the formula for this compound, useful in the production of many other chemicals, is NaOH. Like sulfuric acid, lye is extremely harmful to human flesh. The result of a little bit accidentally touching your skin would be a painful sore resembling a burn. Lye is used in chemical manufacturing and is an ingredient in many oven cleaners and drain cleaners. Lye reacts with animal fats or vegetable oils and turns them into soap; in pioneer days, most Americans used home-made lye soap to take baths and wash their clothes.

Alkaline earth metals

calcium metal

magnesium wheel

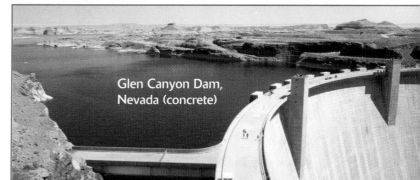

Glen Canyon Dam, Nevada (concrete)

Concept Check

List the first two families of elements on the periodic table of the elements.

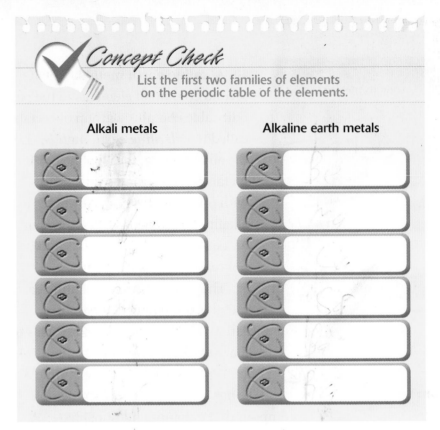

Alkali metals	Alkaline earth metals

Halogens. The seventh column of the periodic table contains the family of elements known as the **halogens** [hăl′ə·jənz]. These are all highly reactive, showing a special tendency to form compounds with alkali and alkaline earth metals. Can you name such a compound? The one that should come to your mind is **sodium chloride.** Only the first four halogens—fluorine [flŏŏr′ēn], chlorine, bromine, and iodine—occur naturally in significant quantities. Fluorine is most commonly obtained from minerals, but the other halogens are usually obtained from seawater. Fluorine and chlorine are gases at room temperature, bromine is a liquid, and iodine is a solid.

The halogen **fluorine** has a variety of uses. A form of fluorine known as *fluoride* strengthens tooth enamel and is added to drinking water and toothpaste to help prevent tooth decay, particularly in children. Compounds containing fluorine are used as coolants in refrigerators and air conditioners. The nonstick surface on some of your mother's pots and pans consists of Teflon®, a slippery plastic made from fluorine and carbon. Fluorine is also used in high-powered military *lasers,* devices that project intense beams of very pure light.

Fluorine

hydrogen fluoride military laser

fluoride toothpaste

Teflon®–coated pan

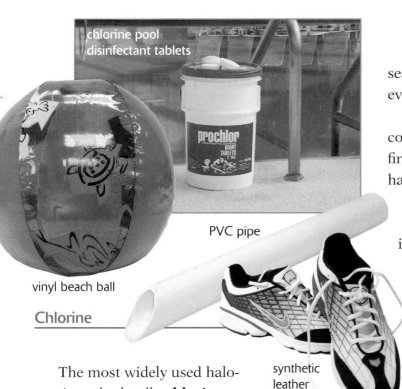

chlorine pool disinfectant tablets

vinyl beach ball

PVC pipe

Chlorine

synthetic leather (PVC)

The most widely used halogen is undoubtedly **chlorine.** *Bleaches* containing chlorine compounds (most commonly sodium hypochlorite, NaOCl) are often used to remove stains from light-colored clothing and are also excellent disinfectants (germ-killing agents). Small amounts of chlorine compounds are added to swimming pools and drinking water to prevent dangerous infections. A chlorine-containing plastic called *polyvinyl* [pŏl′ē·vī′nəl] *chloride* (PVC), or "vinyl" for short, is used to make everything from athletic shoes to plumbing pipes.

One of the chief uses of **bromine** is in the compound *silver bromide,* which provides the sensitive coating on most photographic film. Bromine, a liquid at room temperature, is difficult to store. If its container is not tightly

sealed, fumes escape and corrode everything in sight.

As you look down the halogen column in the periodic table, the first solid you see is **iodine.** Iodine has a strange property setting it apart from most other solids. When heated, it **sublimes;** that is, instead of melting, the crystals turn directly into a gas. Whereas the nearly black crystals have only a tinge of purple, the purple color of the gas is beautifully clear and rich. You may have noticed the word *iodized* on a box of table salt. This means that a small quantity of iodine has been added to prevent a deficiency of iodine in our diet. Such a deficiency produces an enlarged thyroid gland, a condition known as *goiter.* Iodine is also used in some medical antiseptics because it is very effective at killing germs.

Iodine

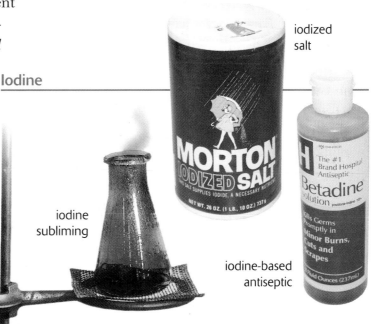

iodized salt

iodine subliming

iodine-based antiseptic

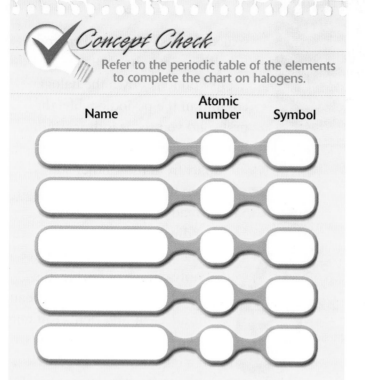

Concept Check

Refer to the periodic table of the elements to complete the chart on halogens.

Name	Atomic number	Symbol

it is commonly used as a filler in incandescent light bulbs. You have heard the word *neon* in connection with the colorful signs that are lit at night along busy city streets. The signs are constructed of tubes filled with **neon** gas. When an electric current is sent through the gas, the neon atoms omit light of a fiery red color. Other colors can be obtained by coating the inside of the tube or by mixing the neon gas with other chemicals. The noble gases helium, neon, krypton, and argon are also widely used in lasers.

Noble gases

All the naturally occurring elements in the last column of the periodic table are gases. They are called *noble gases* because they do not, except under very unusual circumstances, combine with anything else. That is why balloons today are generally inflated with **helium,** a noble gas, rather than hydrogen, the gas often used in the past. A hydrogen-filled balloon is easily set on fire, but a balloon filled with unreactive helium is perfectly safe.

The other noble gases include argon and neon. About 1% of the air you breathe is **argon** [är′gŏn]. Because argon is the most plentiful of the noble gases,

helium-filled balloons

Noble gases

neon sign

Comprehension Check 6.4

Clues. Give the word or term that best fits each clue.

1. The only metal that is liquid at room temperature

2. The most abundant nonmetal gases in the atmosphere

3. The element that comes in the forms of graphite and diamond

4. The semimetal that is used to make computer chips

Explain.

5. What term refers to the elements toward the left side of the periodic table that tend to have a lustrous silvery color and are good conductors of electricity and heat?

6. Give one use each of chromium, zinc, nickel, and lead.

7. Name two alkali metals, two alkaline earth metals, two halogens, and two noble gases.

8. Describe the unusual behavior of iodine when it is heated.

6.5 Molecules and Compounds

Molecules

What is a molecule? Most substances do not exist as individual, isolated atoms, but as groups of two or more atoms bound together. For example, the oxygen you breathe is not made of single oxygen atoms, but of tiny groups of two oxygen atoms bound tightly together. Each group of two oxygen atoms is called an oxygen *molecule*. A **molecule** is a tiny group of two or more atoms that are bonded tightly together.

Compounds

What is a compound? In section 6.3, an *element* was defined as a substance that consists of only one type of atom bonded together. All of the millions of different substances in the world around us are made from fewer than a hundred different elements. A few of these substances, such as copper, oxygen, and sulfur, consist of only one type of atom. However, most substances consist of *different types* of atoms that are bonded tightly together. Substances that are composed of more than one type of atom bonded together are called **compounds.**

Atoms and molecules

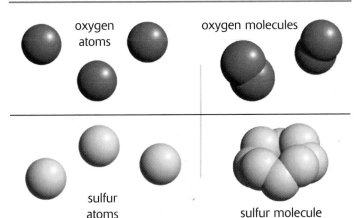

oxygen atoms

oxygen molecules

sulfur atoms

sulfur molecule

Elements and compounds

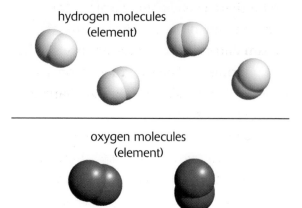

hydrogen molecules
(element)

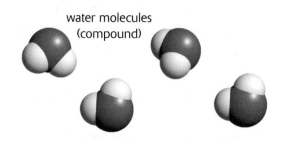

oxygen molecules
(element)

water molecules
(compound)

One of the most common compounds that we see around us is water. Water is not an element; there is no such thing as a "water atom." Instead, water is a *compound* of hydrogen and oxygen atoms that are bonded tightly together. Each tiny group of hydrogen and oxygen atoms in water is a water *molecule*. Each water molecule contains two hydrogen atoms and one oxygen atom.

If you were to take a drop of water and divide it into the smallest possible pieces, a water molecule would be the smallest piece you could have that would still be water. In order to divide the water molecule into still smaller particles, you would have to break up the water molecules into hydrogen and oxygen atoms. Then you would no longer have water, just the elements hydrogen and oxygen.

Formulas of compounds. More than 200 years ago, some pioneering *chemists*—scientists who study chemistry—invented a simple way to describe the composition of a molecule. They first wrote down the symbol for each element in the molecule. (For element symbols, see Table 6.2 on page 372.) Next to each symbol, they wrote the number of atoms of that element in the molecule. For example, water consists of hydrogen (H) and oxygen (O). Since there are two atoms of hydrogen and one atom of oxygen in each molecule, the formula for water is H_2O.

This system can be used for all molecules, from simple oxygen molecules (O_2) to more complex molecules like table sugar ($C_{12}H_{22}O_{11}$). Formulas of some well-known molecules are shown in Table 6.5.

Table 6.5 **Formulas of Some Common Molecules**	
Compound	**Formula**
water	H_2O
oxygen	O_2
carbon dioxide	CO_2
ammonia	NH_3
sulfuric acid	H_2SO_4
propane	C_3H_8
glucose	$C_6H_{12}O_6$
table sugar	$C_{12}H_{22}O_{11}$

water molecule

oxygen molecule

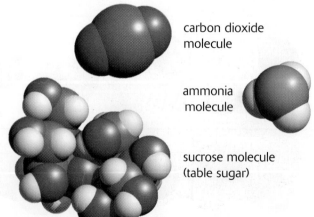

carbon dioxide molecule

ammonia molecule

sucrose molecule
(table sugar)

Nonmolecular compounds

All of the compounds we have studied so far have been composed of individual molecules; such compounds are called **molecular compounds** because they are made of molecules. However, *not all compounds are composed of individual molecules.* Instead, some substances are made of geometric structures containing many trillions of atoms all bonded together.

The most familiar example of a nonmolecular compound is probably ordinary table salt, or *sodium chloride* (NaCl). Because NaCl is the formula for sodium chloride, you might think that the basic fragment of this compound is a molecule containing a single sodium atom and a single chlorine atom. But no such molecule exists. Instead, the atoms of sodium and chlorine are fitted together in such a way as to build a beautifully geometric structure called a **crystal.** Everywhere within the crystal the arrangement of atoms is the same; each sodium atom is surrounded by six chlorine atoms, and each chlorine atom is surrounded by six sodium atoms.

The formula for sodium chloride is given as NaCl because throughout the crystal there is one chlorine atom for every sodium atom; in other words, the sodium and chlorine atoms are present in equal numbers. The way these atoms are arranged gives a simple angular shape to the crystal as a whole.

The most common type of nonmolecular compound consists of atoms or groups of atoms that have either gained or lost electrons, so that they are no longer neutral (section 6.2) but have an electrical charge. An atom that gains an electron becomes negatively charged, and an atom that loses an electron becomes positively charged. Because opposite charges attract, the charged atoms attract each other and become bonded together in a crystal.

Because charged atoms are called *ions* [ī′ŏnz], compounds composed of charged atoms or groups of atoms are called **ionic** [ī·ŏn′ĭk] **compounds.** Sodium chloride is an example of an ionic compound because it is composed of sodium and chlorine ions.

All ionic compounds form crystals of various shapes and colors. Several well-known ionic compounds are shown in Table 6.6. Note that many ionic compounds are composed of more than two elements, and some are quite complicated.

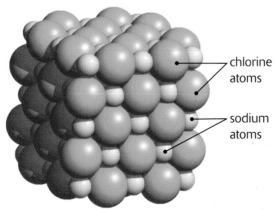

chlorine atoms

sodium atoms

sodium chloride crystal

Table 6.6 Formulas of Some Ionic Compounds	
Compound	**Formula**
sodium chloride (table salt)	NaCl
sodium hydroxide (lye)	NaOH
calcium carbonate (limestone)	$CaCO_3$
sodium bicarbonate (baking soda)	$NaHCO_3$
magnesium sulfate (Epsom salts)	$MgSO_4$ (mostly)
rust	Fe_2O_3 (mostly)
gypsum	$CaSO_4$ (mostly)
emerald (beryl)	$Be_3Al_2Si_6O_{18}$

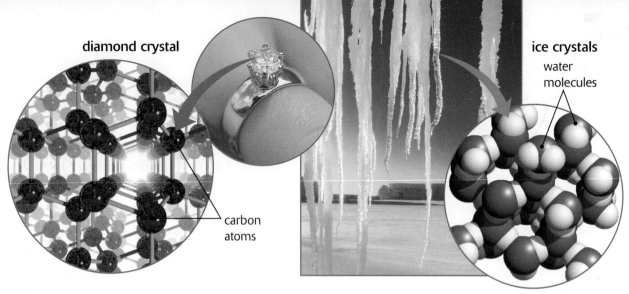

diamond crystal

carbon atoms

ice crystals
water molecules

Other kinds of crystals

Not all crystals have ions as building blocks. A **diamond** is a network of individual carbon atoms, each lacking an electric charge. The bond between any two neighboring carbon atoms is like the bonds formed in a molecule. Because the bonds between adjacent carbon atoms in a diamond are very strong, diamond is *the hardest of all known substances.* However, it is also quite brittle; it is much easier to break a diamond than to wear away or scratch one of its surfaces.

Another kind of crystal is illustrated by **ice,** which of course is frozen water (H_2O). The building blocks of ice are not single ions or atoms but whole molecules. The molecules are arranged in layers of interlocking hexagons.

Compounds vs. mixtures

It is important to understand that a compound such as water is not just a *mixture* of hydrogen and oxygen. If you simply mix a small amount of hydrogen gas and oxygen gas in a balloon, for example, you do not have a balloon full of

water; you just have a mixture of the two elements. *In order for a blend of two different substances to be called a compound, the different types of atoms have to become bonded together.*

Mixture or compound? One way to tell whether a substance is a compound or just a mixture of elements is by what it takes to separate them. For example, we know that air is composed mostly of the elements nitrogen and oxygen. Is air just a mixture of the two gases, or is it made of molecules of "nitrogen oxide"? We can tell by attempting to separate the gases. If the air is cooled to –300 °F, the oxygen turns into a liquid, but the nitrogen remains a

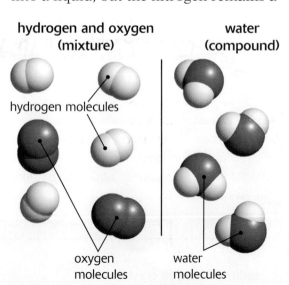

hydrogen and oxygen (mixture)

hydrogen molecules

oxygen molecules

water (compound)

water molecules

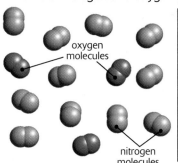

air
(mixture of nitrogen and oxygen)

oxygen
molecules

nitrogen
molecules

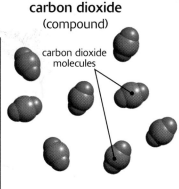

carbon dioxide
(compound)

carbon dioxide
molecules

gas. The fact that simply cooling air can separate it into nitrogen and oxygen tells us that air is only a *mixture* of nitrogen and oxygen; air is not made of nitrogen oxide molecules.

On the other hand, the gas carbon dioxide *cannot* be separated into carbon and oxygen by simple physical processes. Only chemical processes that can actually break molecules apart can separate carbon dioxide. This tells us that carbon dioxide is truly a compound.

Separating mixtures. *In order to separate a mixture, you must find a method that affects the substances in the mixture differently.* For example, sugar dissolves in water, but sand does not; therefore, a mixture of sugar and sand could be separated by adding water to dissolve the sugar, leaving the sand behind. However, you would have to use a different method to separate sugar and salt because both substances dissolve equally well in water.

A mixture of sugar and water can be easily separated because water evaporates, but sugar does not. Thus, heating the mixture to evaporate the water, leaving the sugar behind, is a useful way to separate the two. A mixture of water and salt can be separated the same way.

Many alcohols, such as rubbing alcohol, evaporate more easily than water. Therefore, heating a mixture of water and rubbing alcohol will cause the alcohol to evaporate, leaving the water behind.

EYE witness
reporter

Separating mixtures

To see how mixtures can be separated, you will need some *table salt,* some *white sand,* a *spoon, three disposable clear plastic cups, water* (room temperature or warmer), a *coffee filter, paper towels,* and a *magnifying glass* (optional).

Forming the mixture. First, measure a spoonful of salt into the first plastic cup and a spoonful of sand into the second cup. Examine the physical properties of each, listing as many properties as you can think of.

Now pour all of the salt from the first cup into the cup of sand and mix the two substances together with a spoon. Can you tell the sand and salt apart? Do you think the combined substances form a mixture or a compound? Actually, they are a mixture, since the sand and salt do not become chemically bonded together. If you look closely with a magnifying glass, you will notice that the individual grains of both substances have not changed.

Separating the mixture. In order to separate a mixture, you must use a method that affects the two substances differently. One difference between between salt and sand is that salt dissolves in water, whereas sand does not.

Set the cup of salt-sand mixture on a level surface and fill it ¾ full of water. Using the spoon, stir the sand and salt for at least a minute until half of it (the salt) seems to have disappeared.

Press the coffee filter slightly into the third cup so that it forms a little bowl resting in the mouth of the cup. Then slowly pour the salt-sand-water mixture into the filter, taking care not to spill any water. (You may need to hold on to the edge of the coffee filter or

tape it in place to keep it from falling into the cup.)

When you are finished, you should have a pile of moist sand trapped in the filter and a cup of salt water beneath it. If you wish, you can rinse the sand with more water (over a sink or another cup) to remove any last traces of salt. Finally, set the filter containing the sand on a folded paper towel to dry overnight. By this process, you have separated the mixture and recovered the pure sand. Can you think of a way to separate the salt from the water in the cup?

Chemical reactions

If you have ever mixed vinegar and baking soda, you undoubtedly discovered that these two substances do not form a simple mixture. Instead, they form a foaming, bubbling mass that gives off a sharp odor and leaves behind a gummy residue. Furthermore, once the vinegar and baking soda are combined, they cannot be separated; they somehow become permanently changed by being mixed together.

baking soda + vinegar → carbon dioxide + sodium acetate

$$NaHCO_3 + HC_2H_3O_2 \longrightarrow CO_2 + NaC_2H_3O_2$$

What happens to the vinegar and baking soda when they are mixed is an example of a **chemical reaction**—*a process in which atoms of elements or compounds are rearranged to form new substances.* When vinegar and baking soda come into contact, they *react* to form new substances—carbon dioxide gas (CO_2) and a residue called sodium acetate ($NaC_2H_3O_2$).

Still more dramatic is the transformation that occurs when sodium reacts with chlorine. The product is the compound known to us as common table salt but known to chemists by its scientific name, ***sodium chloride.*** The difference between this compound and its elements could hardly be greater. Both sodium and chlorine are poisonous, but sodium chloride is flavorful and nontoxic—indeed, essential to the human diet. Sodium chloride is neither a metal like sodium nor a gas like chlorine. Whereas sodium is gray and chlorine is greenish yellow, sodium chloride is white. Finally, rather than being explosively reactive like sodium or chlorine, sodium chloride is extremely stable. (The number *2* in front of *Na* and *NaCl* show us that there are two atoms of sodium and two units of sodium chloride involved.)

One of the most common types of chemical reactions is **combustion,** or burning. Combustion occurs *whenever a substance reacts rapidly with oxygen.* Examples of combustion include wood

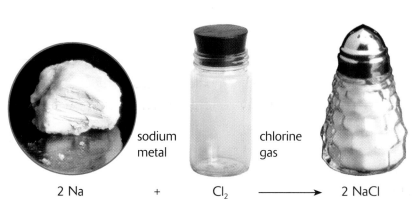

sodium metal + chlorine gas → sodium chloride (table salt)

$$2\ Na + Cl_2 \longrightarrow 2\ NaCl$$

combustion reactions
in jet engines

burning in a fireplace; the burning of fuel in a car engine, jet, or rocket; and the burning of coal in a power plant.

Perhaps the most important chemical reactions of all are those that power your own body. Your body uses chemical reactions to break down foods to produce energy. Every cell in your body, whether in your brain, your heart, or your muscles, is powered by chemical reactions.

EYE witness reporter

Chemical reactions

Whenever atoms of elements or compounds are rearranged to form new substances, a chemical reaction is said to have occurred. To observe a chemical reaction, you will need *an empty 20-oz. plastic soda bottle, a large balloon (uninflated), vinegar, baking soda, a transparent bowl, a tablespoon, a small measuring cup, a shallow baking pan,* and *a kitchen funnel.*

First, insert the funnel into the mouth of the balloon and pour one tablespoon of baking soda into the empty balloon. Remove the balloon from the funnel and set it aside for now. Second, pour approximately ¼ cup of vinegar into the empty soda bottle so that the bottom of the bottle is covered.

Pick up the balloon by its mouth and shake it gently to settle the baking soda. Now, stretch the mouth of the balloon over the end of the bottle, keeping the balloon bent so that no baking soda falls into the vinegar yet.

When you are ready to watch the reaction, pick up the end of the balloon so that the baking soda falls down into the vinegar, and stand back. What happens? Can you identify the gas that fills the balloon? Where did it come from?

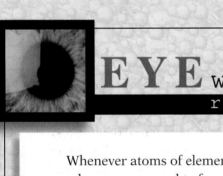

Science Speaks

Robert Boyle: Pioneer of Modern Chemistry

What a wonderful, orderly world we live in! Whether we look up at the vastness of the universe or down at the intricate design of the atom, we see marvels that demonstrate the power and wisdom of God. Science is a search for the laws that govern our world and the universe, and most of the world's greatest scientists have believed that the laws of nature were established by God at Creation. One pioneer scientist whose belief in God led to the discovery of important truths about atoms, molecules, and elements was Robert Boyle.

Robert Boyle was born in a castle in Ireland in 1627, the fourteenth of fifteen children. Robert's wealthy father, the Earl of Cork, was a devout Christian who was careful to give God the glory for his good fortune. After eight years of schooling at home with a tutor, Robert entered Eton College at the age of nine. When he was twelve or thirteen, he traveled to Europe for further studies. While he was in Switzerland, Robert accepted Christ as his Savior. Robert's studies gave him a strong desire to learn more about God's creation and how it worked. Not surprisingly, Robert eventually decided that God was calling him to be a scientist.

Robert had to overcome many obstacles as he studied science. Chemistry in the 1600s was still dominated by the "science" of alchemy [ăl′kə·mē], which was a combination of superstition,

wizardry, and primitive scientific methods. Some alchemists sought to accomplish remarkable feats in order to gain great fame and fortune. For example, many alchemists tried to change lead into gold. In this scientific wilderness Boyle overcame his discouragement and became a scientific pathfinder. He observed and experimented. He denounced superstition and laid the foundations of chemistry, the science of matter. He was the first to use such terms as *element* and *compound*. Boyle's pioneering efforts in the study of matter contributed greatly to the development of modern chemistry as we know it.

Boyle's great mind refused to be limited to chemistry alone, however. He did valuable work in optics (the study of light and vision), acoustics [ə·kōō′stĭks: the study of sound], and many other fields of physical science.

Robert Boyle

His most famous discovery, which explains what happens to the volume of a gas when its pressure changes, is today called *Boyle's law*. He is most admired, however, for replacing the mystical practices of alchemy with objective experimentation and observation.

Throughout his life, Robert Boyle diligently studied the Bible and tried to apply its teachings to his life and scientific studies. He firmly believed that the goals of science were to glorify God the Creator and to benefit mankind. He wrote an entire book (called *The Christian Virtuoso*) to show how faith in God goes hand in hand with the study of nature. He supported missionary work, including the ministry of John Eliot to the American Indians, and he supervised several translations of the Bible. In whatever he attempted, he did all to the glory of Christ. Robert Boyle died in 1691 at the age of 64. His was a life dedicated to turning men from the darkness of sin and superstition to the light of God's Word. Boyle's life and work can be summed up by a statement from one of his books: "When . . . I study the book of nature, I find myself oftentimes reduced to exclaim with the Psalmist, 'How manifold are Thy works, O Lord! in wisdom hast Thou made them all!' "

Comprehension Check 6.5

Clues. Give the word or term that best fits each clue.

1. A tiny group of two or more atoms that are bonded tightly together

2. A substance composed of more than one type of atom bonded together

3. The formula for water; the formula for carbon dioxide (See Table 6.5.)

4. The hardest of all known substances

5. The difference between a mixture and a compound

6. A process in which atoms of elements or compounds are rearranged to form new substances

7. The type of chemical reaction that occurs whenever a substance reacts rapidly with oxygen

Explain.

8. Why is sodium chloride not considered a molecular compound? What type of compound is it?

Chapter Checkup

I. Define these terms.

chemistry
matter
weight
mass
density
atom
nucleus
electrons

neutrons
protons
neutral
electron cloud
shell
atomic number
element
compound

periodic table of
the elements
metals
nonmetals
halogens
sublime
noble gases
molecule

molecular compound
crystal
ionic compound
mixture
chemical reaction
combustion

II. Know what is special about each of these substances.

plutonium
osmium
mercury
bromine
oxygen and nitrogen
iodine
diamond

III. Know these metals.

chromium
zinc
nickel
lead

IV. Know these nonmetals.

hydrogen
two forms of carbon
sulfur
phosphorus
silicon

V. Know these alkali metals and alkaline earth metals.

sodium
potassium
calcium
magnesium

VI. Know these halogens.

fluorine
chlorine
bromine
iodine

VII. Know these noble gases.

helium
argon
neon

Glossary

Pronunciation Key

Symbol • Example		Symbol • Example	
ā	āte	ô	côrd, taught, saw
â	dâre	ŏ	nŏt
ă	făt	oi	boil
ä	fäther	o͞o	bro͞od
ə	ago (ə·gō′)	o͝o	bo͝ok
ch	chin	ou	out
ē	ēven	sh	shark
ĕ	ĕgg	th	thin
*ẽ (ər)	pondẽr	t̶h̶	t̶h̶ere
g	good	*ṱû (cho͞o)	virṱûe
ī	īce	ū	ūnit
ĭ	ĭt	û	ûrn
j	jog	ŭ	ŭp
ks	perplex (ks = x)	zh	azure (zh = z)
kw	quart (kw = qu)	'	little (lĭt′'l;
ng	song		shows that the
ō	ōver		vowel is not
			sounded)

*Note: For simplicity, the alternate symbols are used for ẽr and ṱû.

Abbreviation Key

adj. adjective *n.* noun *v.* verb *pl.* plural *sing.* singular

absolute magnitude *n.* the actual brightness of a star; how much light a star produces

acorn *n.* the fruit of an oak tree

active volcano *n.* a volcano that has erupted recently or is considered likely to erupt in the near future

adult *n.* the final stage of an insect's life

aftershock *n.* a smaller earthquake or tremor that can occur after a major earthquake

air sacs *n.*
(1) small berrylike parts of large algae that help the fronds to float
(2) a structure in insects which is similar to lungs

Aldebaran [ăl·dĕb′ər·ən] *n.* a large orange star that represents the eye in the constellation Taurus

alga [ăl′gə] *n.* one of the smallest green plants; *pl.* algae

algin [ăl′jĭn] *n.* a substance obtained from seaweed that is used to thicken many foods

Algol [ăl′gŏl′] *n.* a bright, variable star in the constellation Perseus

alkali metals *n.* the metals in the first (far left) column of the periodic table, such as sodium and potassium

alkaline earth metals *n.* the metals in the second column of the periodic table, such as calcium and magnesium

aluminum *n.* a lightweight, silver-colored metal that is an important substitute for steel and copper; the most widespread metal in the earth's crust

American elm *n.* the most popular type of elm tree

American lobster *n.* a type of lobster prized for its enormous pincers and meaty tail; also called Maine lobster

amoeba [ə·mē′bə] *n.* a common protozoan which has a shape that changes continually as it moves

Andromeda [ăn·drŏm′ĭ·də] *n.* a constellation in the Northern Hemisphere that seems to depict the figure of a lady bound with a chain

Andromeda galaxy *n.* a slightly larger galaxy than the Milky Way that is located in the Local Group; the most distant object that can be seen with the naked eye

annual [ăn·yŏŏ′əl] *n.* a type of plant that lives for only one year

annual growth ring *n.* an inner band of light spring wood and an outer band of dark summer wood that make up one year's growth

ant *n.* a wingless social insect in the order Hymenoptera

antenna [ăn·tĕn′ə] *n.* a long, movable structure on the head of an invertebrate, used to feel, taste, smell, or hear; *pl.* antennae [ăn·tĕn′ē]

anthracite *n.* a hard, shiny, black coal that is the most expensive to mine

antivenin [ăn′tē·vĕn′ĭn] *n.* a medicine that deactivates venom

aphid *n.* a tiny insect in the order Homoptera

Apollo 11 *n.* the first space mission to actually land on the moon

apparent magnitude *n.* the apparent brightness of a star as seen from Earth

arachnid [ə·răk′nĭd] *n.* an arthropod with two distinct body regions, eight legs, simple eyes, no wings, and a book lung; examples include spiders, scorpions, ticks, and mites

argon [är′gŏn] *n.* the most plentiful of the noble gases; commonly used as a filler in incandescent light bulbs

Armstrong, Neil *n.* (1930–) the first person to set foot on the moon

arthropod [är′thrə·pŏd′] *n.* an invertebrate that has an external skeleton, jointed appendages, and a segmented body

asteroid [ăs′tə·roid] *n.* a small, rocky object that orbits the sun

asteroid belt *n.* a region between the orbits of Mars and Jupiter where most asteroids are located

astrology *n.* a false belief, or superstition, which claims to tell people's futures by studying the influence of the sun, planets, and stars on people's lives

astronaut *n.* a person who journeys into space

astronomer *n.* a scientist who studies outer space

astronomical unit *n.* the distance between the earth and the sun; equal to 93 million miles

astronomy *n.* the study of the stars, planets, and all other heavenly bodies

atmosphere *n.* a blanket of air that makes the earth hospitable for living things

atom *n.* a tiny particle from which all substances are composed; the smallest particle of an element

atomic number *n.* the number of protons in an atom

aurora [ô·rôr′ə] *n.* a breathtaking display of light that occurs when solar wind particles collide with molecules of air in the earth's atmosphere

aurora borealis [bôr′ē·ăl′ĭs] *n.* an aurora that appears in the Northern Hemisphere; also called "northern lights"

axis of rotation *n.* an imaginary line around which the earth rotates that stretches from pole to pole through the interior of the earth

bald cypress *n.* a tree in the redwood family that grows in swamps, shallow lakes, and lagoons of the South

ballooning *n.* the method by which young spiders sail through the air on silk strands that carry them from their place of birth to new homes

balsam fir [bôl′səm] *n.* one of the best-known fir trees; produces a fragrant liquid called Canada balsam

bamboo *n.* a woody grass that grows primarily in Southeast Asia and can reach over 100 feet high and 1 foot wide

banyan tree [băn′yən] *n.* a type of tree that sends thick roots down from its branches to the ground

baobab tree [bā′ō·băb] *n.* a type of tree known for its huge trunk, which stores water to last throughout the dry season

barnacle *n.* a small crustacean that cements itself to an object and builds a hard shell around itself

barred spiral *n.* a spiral galaxy in which the spiral arms are attached to a straight "bar" that runs through the center of the galaxy

basalt [bə·sôlt′] *n.* an extrusive igneous rock formed from thin, runny lava that often solidifies in vast mounds or sheets

bee *n.* a social, flying insect in the order Hymenoptera that has two pairs of filmy, membranelike wings and lives in a colony

beetle *n.* an insect in the order Coleoptera that has hard forewings that fit over its body like a shell and form a straight line down its back

Betelgeuse [bēt′'l·jōōz] *n.* a bright supergiant star in the constellation Orion; represents Orion's right shoulder

biennial [bī·ĕn′ē·əl] *n.* a type of plant that lives for two years

Big Dipper *n.* a familiar saucepan-shaped grouping of stars in the constellation Ursa Major

binary star *n.* a group of two stars that circle around each other just as the moon circles around the earth; a double star

bituminous coal *n.* the most common type of coal, also called soft coal, that is widely used by industry and used to produce electricity in power plants

bivalve [bī′vălv] *n.* a mollusk that has two matching, fan-shaped shells joined by hinges, such as mussels, oysters, and scallops

black spruce *n.* one of the most common varieties of spruce in North America

black widow *n.* a spider that is poisonous to humans and is recognizable by the "hourglass" on its abdomen

bladderwort *n.* an insectivorous (insect-eating) plant that uses special water-containing leaves to trap insects

blade *n.*
(1) the long, narrow part of a grass leaf that sticks out from the stem
(2) a leaflike part of large algae

blue crab *n.* a crab in the eastern United States that is a popular seafood dish

blue spruce *n.* a type of spruce tree that has frosty blue needles

book lung *n.* an organ in a spider in which several thin sheets of tissue filled with blood vessels are stacked like pages in a book

botanist *n.* a scientist who studies the plant kingdom

Boyle, Robert *n.* (1627–1691) a pioneer of modern chemistry responsible for discovering Boyle's law (explains what happens to the volume of a gas when its pressure changes)

bracts *n.* colorful leaves used to attract insects to the flower that may take the place of petals, as in a poinsettia

brass *n.* a metal made from copper and zinc

Braun, Wernher von [broun] *n.* (1912–1977) a scientist who helped the United States become the world leader in space exploration; generally considered to be the most knowledgeable astronautical engineer in the world until his death

breccia [brĕch′ē·ə] *n.* a type of sedimentary rock that consists of sharp-edged pebbles embedded in hardened sand or clay

brine shrimp *n.* one of the smallest types of shrimp, with unusual "gill-feet"

bristlecone pine *n.* a type of tree that is perhaps the oldest living thing on earth

broadleaf tree *n.* a tree with broad, flat leaves which are usually flower-bearing and seed-producing

bromine *n.* brown halogen that is liquid at ordinary room temperatures and pressures; used as an ingredient in photographic film

bronze *n.* a metal made from copper and tin

brown recluse *n.* a spider that is poisonous to humans and is recognizable by its dark violin-shaped mark on top of its body and its six eyes grouped in three pairs

bud *n.*
(1) a developing flower
(2) a small knobby structure at the tip of a tree stem that produces new growth

bulb *n.* an underground part of a plant, made of layers of thick, fleshy leaves that surround a very short stem, that serves to insulate and nourish the plant during the winter

butterfly *n.* a flying insect in the order Lepidoptera that has thousands of microscopic scales on each wing

calcium *n.* a silver-gray element that is the most common alkaline earth metal; an ingredient in limestone, cement, teeth, and bones

calcium carbonate *n.* a calcium compound that is the chief ingredient in seashells, limestone, and concrete

caldera [käl·dā′rä] *n.* a huge, bowl-shaped depression formed when an empty magma chamber collapses after a volcanic eruption

California redwood *n.* the tallest living tree in the world

cambium layer *n.* the part of the tree where growth takes place

candlenut tree *n.* a type of tree whose unusual nuts contain an oil that burns very well; also called *kukui*

Canis Major [kā′nĭs] *n.* a constellation in the Northern Hemisphere that is located near Orion; the Big Dog

carapace [kăr′ə·pās] *n.* a single sturdy shell that protects crabs and certain other crustaceans

carbon *n.* a nonmetal that is a basic building block of the complex compounds found in your body and in all living organisms

carnivore *n.* a flesh eater

carrageenan [kăr′ə·gē′nən] *n.* a substance obtained from seaweed that is used to thicken many foods

Cassiopeia [kăs′ē·ə·pē′ə] *n.* a constellation in the Northern Hemisphere named after a mythical queen of Ethiopia; has the shape of a huge *M* or *W*

castings *n.* soil that has passed through an earthworm's body

Castor [kăs′tər] *n.* one of the brightest stars in the constellation Gemini

cave *n.* any hollow space in the earth's crust that has formed naturally and is large enough for a person to enter

cave pearls *n.* cave formations that occur when layers of calcium carbonate build up around a grain of sand in a shallow pool

cave rafts *n.* cave formations that occur when evaporating water leaves behind a thin, floating disk of calcium carbonate in an underground pool

cavern *n.* a very large cave

cedar *n.* a tree in the cypress family that is known for its aromatic wood

cedar of Lebanon *n.* a tree in the pine family that Solomon used to build the Temple

cell *n.* the smallest living unit in any living organism, made up of the cell membrane, cytoplasm, and nucleus

cell membrane *n.* a thin, flexible covering that encloses a cell and protects it

cellulose [sĕl′yə·lōs′] *n.* a tough, fibrous material made from glucose that is used to make the cell walls of plant cells

cell wall *n.* a strong structure made of cellulose that surrounds and protects a plant cell

Centaurus [sĕn·tôr′əs] *n.* a large constellation in the Southern Hemisphere that resembles a centaur, a mythical creature with the body of a horse and the chest, arms, and head of a man

centipede *n.* an arthropod with a flattened body and one pair of legs in each segment except the last two, which have no legs at all; name means "one-hundred footed"

cephalopod [sĕf′ə·lə·pŏd′] *n.* a type of mollusk in which the foot and head are combined into a single headlike structure

cephalothorax [sĕf′ə·lə·thôr′ăks] *n.* a body region of a spider or crustacean that is like a head and thorax combined

Cepheus [sē′fē·əs] *n.* a five-sided constellation in the Northern Hemisphere named after Cassiopeia's husband; looks like a house with a sharply pointed roof

cereal grass *n.* a type of grass that is harvested for the nutrients in its seeds, or grains

chalk *n.* an organic sedimentary rock formed from the cemented skeletons of microscopic sea animals, formerly used in the classroom to write on chalkboards

chemical reaction *n.* a process in which atoms of elements or compounds are rearranged to form new substances

chemical sediment *n.* a type of sediment formed when minerals in a rock are dissolved by water and carried elsewhere, where they may later crystallize or settle out of the solution

chemical weathering *n.* a type of weathering that occurs when natural acids slowly eat into a rock and break it apart

chemistry *n.* the study of what substances are made of and how one substance can be changed into another

chigger *n.* the immature form of the red harvest mite

chitin [kīt′′n] *n.* a tough material that helps make up an arthropod's external skeleton

chlorine *n.* a gaseous nonmetal that is the most widely used halogen

chlorophyll [klôr′ə·fĭl] *n.* the pigment, or coloring, that makes plants green and helps carry out photosynthesis

chloroplast [klôr′ə·plăst] *n.* a tiny package of chlorophyll within a plant cell

chromium *n.* a metal that is often applied to polished steel to protect it from rusting and give the steel a mirrorlike surface; commonly known as chrome

chromosome [krō′mə·sōm] *n.* a threadlike structure in a cell's nucleus that contains the instructions for running the cell and making needed parts

chromosphere [krō′mə·sfîr] *n.* the part of the sun's atmosphere closest to the sun's surface; "sphere of color"

cicada [sĭ·kā′də] *n.* a large insect in the order Homoptera, known for the loud, shrill sound the male makes

cilia [sĭl′ē·ə] *n.* the tiny, hairlike structures that cover a paramecium and allow it to swim

cinder-cone volcano *n.* a type of volcano that is formed when eruptions composed mostly of tephra build up a cone-shaped mountain

class *n.* a group smaller than a phylum but larger than an order, used in the classification of plants and animals

classification *n.* the process of arranging animals or other things into groups according to their similarities

cleaner shrimp *n.* a species of shrimp that cleans parasites from fish

coal *n.* a useful fuel, commonly found in sedimentary rock, that comes from decayed plants and is used for heating, industrial purposes, and generating electricity

coal tar *n.* a tarlike substance that is made from coal and used to make plastics, detergents, and other products

cockroach *n.* a common insect in the order Orthoptera

coconut *n.* the large, hard fruit of the coconut palm

Coleoptera [kō′lē·ŏp′tər·ə] *n.* an order of insects that include beetles, June bugs, and fireflies; means "sheath wings"

column *n.* a cave formation that occurs when a stalagmite grows tall enough to reach the ceiling of a cave or joins with a stalactite hanging from the ceiling

coma [kō′mə] *n.* a cloud of gas and dust around a comet's nucleus

combustion *n.* a chemical reaction in which a substance reacts rapidly with oxygen

comet *n.* an asteroid-sized object that develops a huge, bright tail when it comes near the sun; means "long-haired star"

complete metamorphosis *n.* a type of metamorphosis in which an insect goes through the stages of egg, larva, pupa, and adult

composite family *n.* the largest family of flowering plants, having flowers made of a combination of many smaller flowers; includes daisies, goldenrods, thistles, and dandelions

composite volcano *n.* a type of volcano that is formed when alternating layers of fluid lava and tephra build up a steep, symmetrical mountain

compound *n.* a substance that is composed of more than one type of atom bonded together

compound eyes *n.* a pair of large, faceted eyes in most insects that enable them to see in many directions at once

conch [kŏngk] *n.* a one-shelled mollusk that lives in salt water and has a ridged, or bumpy, shell

conglomerate rock *n.* a type of sedimentary rock that consists of rounded pebbles embedded in hardened sand or clay

conifer *n.* a cone-bearing tree

constellation *n.* the stars outlining an imaginary picture in the sky

Copernicus, Nicolaus [kō·pûr′nə·kəs, nĭk′ō·lā′əs] *n.* (1473–1543) a Polish astronomer who believed in a sun-centered universe

copper *n.* the reddish-orange metal that covers a penny and is a good conductor of electricity

coral polyp [pŏl′ĭp] *n.* a tiny relative of the sea anemone that builds limestone colonies called coral

coral reef *n.* a ridge of coral rock that lies at or near the surface of the water

core *n.*
(1) the innermost region of the earth
(2) the central, hottest region of the sun

corona *n.* a haze of very hot gases that extends hundreds of thousands of miles from the surface of the sun; the hottest region of the sun's atmosphere

cotyledon [kŏt′əl·ēd′ən] *n.* one or two structures within the seed that contain stored food for the growing plant

cowrie *n.* a one-shelled mollusk (univalve) that lives in salt water and has a glossy shell

crab *n.* a crustacean that has a broad, flat body and two large pincers

crater *n.*
(1) a depression at the top of a volcano
(2) a depression formed by the impact of an asteroid, comet, or meteoroid

crayfish *n.* a small freshwater lobster that feeds on small animals in lakes, ponds, streams, or drainage creeks; also called crawfish or crawdad

crescent phase *n.* the stage of the visible moon when it waxes from the new moon to the first-quarter moon

crest *n.* the high point of a wave

cricket *n.* a common insect in the order Orthoptera

crude oil *n.* petroleum in its natural form

crust *n.* the outermost layer of the earth

crustaceans [krŭ·stā′shənz] *n.* a class of arthropods with hard, crusty shells; examples include shrimp, lobsters, and crabs

crystal *n.* a geometric arrangement of atoms

cuticle *n.* the waxy covering that coats the skin of a leaf and prevents water from escaping

cuttlefish *n.* a cephalopod that has ten tentacles with suction cups and an internal shell that helps support and protect its "head"

Cygnus [sĭg′nəs] *n.* a constellation in the Northern Hemisphere located on the other side of the Big Dipper in the Milky Way; the Swan

cytoplasm [sī′tə·plăz′əm] *n.* the jellylike fluid that fills the volume of a cell

damselfly *n.* an insect in the order Odonata that has a long, slender body, large eyes, and two pairs of equal-sized transparent wings

day *n.* the period of light that the sun shines on the earth as it rotates on its axis

deciduous tree [dĭ·sĭj′ o͞o·əs] *n.* a tree that loses its leaves in the fall

dehydration *n.* the loss of moisture

dendrologist [děn·drŏl′ə·jĭst] *n.* a scientist who studies trees

Deneb [děn′ĕb] *n.* a white supergiant star that is the brightest star in the constellation Cygnus

density *n.* the amount of matter (mass) in one unit of volume (space)

diamond *n.* a hard, crystalline form of carbon that is the hardest of all known minerals

diamond pipe *n.* a deep, tubelike formation that appears to be the clogged vent of an extinct volcano and contains diamonds

diatomite *n.* a sedimentary rock formed when the glassy shells of dead diatoms collect on the ocean floor

diatoms [dī′ə·tŏmz′] *n.* one-celled algae that live in damp soil, ponds, lakes, and oceans; known for their intricate, glassy shells

dicot *n.* a type of flowering plant characterized by seeds with two cotyledons, broad and flat leaves, veins that branch, taproots, and flower petals in multiples of four or five

dinoflagellate [dī′nō·flăj′ə·lĭt] *n.* a one-celled alga that resembles both animals and plants

Diptera [dĭp′tər·ə] *n.* an order of insects that includes flies, gnats, and mosquitoes; means "two wings"

disk flowers *n.* in a composite flower, the individual flowers that make up the disk

dormant *adj.*
(1) describing a seed that is inactive
(2) describing a volcano which erupted many years ago and is now inactive, but which may erupt again

Draco [drā′kō] *n.* a constellation in the Northern Hemisphere that has a long tail curving around the Little Dipper; the Dragon

dragonfly *n.* an insect in the order Odonata that has a long, slender body, huge eyes, and two pairs of equal-sized transparent wings

drapery *n.* a thin, wavy sheet of hanging rock that occurs when water runs down a ceiling or wall of a cave at an angle

Dutch elm disease *n.* a fatal disease of elm trees that is caused by a fungus and is most often spread by beetles that live within the trees' bark

Earth-centered universe *n.* the erroneous view that all heavenly bodies—stars, planets, sun, and moon—revolve around a stationary earth

earthquake *n.* any trembling or shaking of the earth's crust

earthworm *n.* a burrowing invertebrate that eats soil, enriching the soil as it burrows

Eastern white pine *n.* an important American pine with needles in bundles of five

Edwards, Jonathan *n.* (1703–1758) America's greatest preacher in colonial times who often used nature illustrations in his sermons

egg cell *n.* a cell stored inside an ovule of a flower that when fertilized becomes the embryo of a new plant

electric field *n.* a region in which certain objects may be attracted or repelled by an electric force, as in "static electricity"

electromagnet *n.* a magnet that becomes magnetized only when it is hooked to a battery or some other source of electric current

electromagnetic spectrum *n.* an arrangement of electromagnetic waves according to frequency and wavelength

electromagnetic wave *n.* a wave consisting of an electric field and a magnetic field vibrating at right angles to each other

electron *n.* one of the tiny particles that circle around the nucleus of an atom

electron cloud *n.* the cloudlike shield around an atom's nucleus formed by the atom's fast-moving electrons; prevents other atoms from moving into the same space

element *n.* a substance that is composed of only one type of atom

ellipse *n.* a symmetrically shaped oval

elliptical galaxy [ĭ·lĭp′tĭ·kəl] *n.* a type of galaxy, often shaped like an egg or football that is not as structured as a spiral galaxy and does not contain as much free gas or dust

embryo [ĕm′brē·ō] *n.* a miniature, undeveloped plant located within a seed

emerald *n.* a green precious stone that is a form of the mineral beryl

Encke's comet [ĕng′kəz] *n.* the comet with the shortest recorded period—three years and four months

entomologist *n.* a scientist who studies insects

epicenter *n.* the place at ground level that is directly above the focus of an earthquake and often receives the most damage

epiphyte [ĕp′ə·fīt′] *n.* a plant that grows in the tops of trees and never touches the ground, such as the vanilla plant and Spanish moss

evergreen *n.* a tree that keeps its leaves year around

Explorer 1 *n.* the first satellite launched by the United States, in January 1958

exoskeleton *n.* an external skeleton; the strong, lightweight skeleton made primarily of protein and chitin that provides an arthropod with protection, strength, and support

extinct volcano *n.* a volcano that has not erupted in recorded history or is unlikely to ever erupt again

extrusive igneous rock *n.* igneous rock formed at the earth's surface, usually as a result of magma forced out of a volcano

fault *n.* the break that appears at the boundary between two moving masses of rock

feather star *n.* a frilly relative of the sea star and sea urchin

fertilization *n.* the process in which a sperm cell from a pollen grain unites with an egg cell of a flower, causing a seed to develop

fiddler crab *n.* a type of crab with one huge pincer or claw and a second pincer that is much smaller

filament *n.* a long string of cells laid end to end, formed by some algae

first law of motion *n.* an object in motion will continue moving in the same direction and at the same speed unless an outside force acts upon it

first law of planetary motion *n.* every planet orbits the sun in an ellipse, with the sun as one of the foci of the ellipse and an empty point in space as the other

first-quarter moon *n.* the phase of the visible moon when it is half light and half dark

fishing spider *n.* a type of large spider that can easily move across the surface of the water to catch insects and small frogs

flagella [flə·jĕl′ə] *n.* a small, movable hairlike structure that certain invertebrates use to swim or to move water through their bodies

flowstone *n.* a cave formation that occurs when water flows over broad areas of a wall or floor of a cave and deposits a sheet of minerals

fluorine [flo͞or′ēn] *n.* a gaseous nonmetal and halogen with many important uses

fly *n.* any of several insects in the order Diptera that have only two wings, short antennae, and wings that are held slightly out to the side when at rest

focus *n.*
(1) the point underground where an earthquake begins
(2) either of two special points inside an ellipse; *pl.* foci [fō′sī]

fold *n.* a rock formation formed when rock bends without cracking

foliated rock *n.* metamorphic rock made up of layers like the leaves (pages) of a book

food vacuole [văk′yo͞o·ōl′] *n.* a tiny storage container in a protozoan where food is digested and absorbed into the cytoplasm

fossil *n.* any trace left in rock by a plant or animal

fossil fuel *n.* a fuel derived from the remains of once-living things, such as coal

fractions *n.* different groups of hydrocarbons separated by a process called fractional distillation

fracture *n.* a rock formation formed when rock cracks but does not move in any way

frequency *n.* the term for how fast a wave oscillates

friction *n.* the force that resists motion

frond *n.*
(1) the leaves of a palm tree
(2) the leaves of a fern, which grow upward from the upper side of the stem

fruiting body *n.* a mushroom's large spore-forming structure, made of the stalk, cap, and gills

full moon *n.* the phase of the moon when we see the entire sunlit side

fumarole [fyo͞o′mə·rōl] *n.* a hole or crack in the ground that serves as an escape vent for underground gases

fungus [fŭng′gəs] *n.* a type of plant that does not contain chlorophyll and cannot make its own food; *pl.* fungi

funnel weaver *n.* a spider that shapes its web like a funnel with the broad opening facing upward and the narrow opening pointing toward the ground

Gagarin, Yuri [gə·gär′yĭn, yo͞or′yĭ] *n.* (1934–1968) the first person to travel in space

galaxy *n.* a star system containing from millions to billions of stars

Galileo [găl′ə·lā′ō] *n.* (1564–1642) the first astronomer to make extensive use of a telescope to study the heavens

Ganymede [găn′ĭ·mēd] *n.* a moon of Jupiter that is the largest moon in the solar system

garden spider *n.* a common, brightly colored spider that spins an orb web

gastropod [găs′trə·pŏd′] *n.* a mollusk with a muscular foot that it uses to slide forward; means "stomach-foot"

Gemini [jĕm′ə·nī] *n.*
(1) a constellation in the Northern Hemisphere that resembles twin brothers holding hands
(2) a series of manned U.S. space flights in the 1960s

gemstones *n.* small deposits of igneous and metamorphic crystals in rock

General Sherman Tree *n.* a giant sequoia tree in California that is the biggest tree in the world

genus *n.* in classification, a group smaller than a family but larger than a species; *pl.* genera [jĕn′ər·ə]

geologist *n.* a scientist who studies the earth

geology *n.* the study of the earth and its structure

geostationary orbit *n.* an orbit in which a satellite follows the direction of the earth's rotation in such a way that it stays in the same location in the sky

geotropism [jē·ŏt′rə·pĭz′əm] *n.* the growth of a plant in response to gravity

ghost crab *n.* a sand-colored, burrowing crab of Atlantic and Caribbean beaches

giant centipede *n.* a South American centipede that can grow over ten inches long

giant sequoia *n.* the largest tree in the world

gibbous phase [gĭb′əs] *n.* the term for the visible moon when it seems to bulge as it waxes from first quarter to full

girdling *n.* a procedure in which a ring of bark is removed from a tree's trunk, killing the tree

gland *n.* in spiders, an organ that produces silk

Glenn, John *n.* (1921–) the first American to orbit the earth

glucose *n.* a type of sugar that plants need to live

gnat *n.* a small, biting insect in the order Diptera

Goddard, Robert H. *n.* (1882–1945) an American scientist who built and launched the first liquid-fueled rocket; called the Father of Modern Rocketry

gold *n.* a valuable precious metal that is known for its yellowish color

Goliath birdeater *n.* the largest tarantula in the world

grain *n.* the seed in cereal grasses that is harvested for its nutrients, as in wheat, rice, and corn

gram *n.* a metric unit used to measure an object's mass

granite *n.* a strong, light-colored rock that contains mineral crystals such as quartz, feldspar, and mica; the most common igneous rock

granule *n.* a "bubble" of rising gas that rises to the surface of the sun and gives the sun's face a speckled or granulated look

grass family *n.* the most important family of food-producing plants; includes wheat, rice, and corn

grasshopper *n.* a common insect in the order Orthoptera

gravity *n.* the force of attraction that exists between any two objects

Great Red Spot *n.* a gigantic rotating storm on Jupiter twice as wide as the earth

Great Square *n.* a group of stars in the constellations Andromeda and Pegasus [pĕg′ə·səs]

greenhouse effect *n.* the ability of the atmosphere to retain heat around the earth

guard cell *n.* a pair of cells that surround the stoma on a leaf

gypsum [jĭp′səm] *n.* a type of sedimentary rock formed by chemical sediments that is used in construction materials such as plaster of Paris and plasterboard

halite *n.* rock salt; a type of sedimentary rock formed by chemical sediments that is used in making chemicals, tanning leather, salting roads, and flavoring food

Halley's comet *n.* a famous comet named for Edmund Halley, with a period of about 76 years

halogens [hăl′ə·jənz] *n.* elements in the seventh column of the periodic table, such as fluorine and chlorine, that show a special tendency to form compounds with alkali and alkaline earth metals

hardwood tree *n.* another name for a broadleaf tree

harvestman *n.* an arachnid with eight legs and only one body section; often called daddy longlegs

Hawaiian eruption *n.* type of eruption in which a volcano produces a large amount of fluid lava that surges from the volcano's vent like water from a fountain

helium *n.* a noble gas that replaced hydrogen as the gas with which to fill balloons because it is unreactive

Hemiptera [hĭ·mĭp′tər·ə] *n.* an order of insects that includes bedbugs, stinkbugs, and water striders; means "half wings"

herbivore *n.* a plant eater

hermit crab *n.* a crablike animal that lives in discarded mollusk shells

Herschel, William *n.* (1738–1822) the astronomer who discovered Uranus

high tide *n.* the highest point on shore that the ocean reaches

Hipparchus [hĭp·pär′kəs] *n.* a Greek astronomer and mathematician who developed a system of classifying stars by their brightness

holdfast *n.* a rootlike part of large algae that anchors the plant to the ocean floor

Homoptera [hō·mŏp′tər·ə] *n.* an order of insects that includes aphids, tree hoppers, and cicadas; means "same wings"

house spider *n.* a common spider that often weaves webs in the corners of a house and destroys tiny household pests

Hubble space telescope *n.* a reflecting telescope with an 8-foot-wide main mirror launched into orbit around the earth in 1990

hybrid [hī′brĭd] *n.* a new variety of a plant resulting from cross-fertilizing related plants

hydra [hī′drə] *n.* a tiny freshwater invertebrate with tentacles around its mouth

hydrocarbon *n.* a chemical substance made primarily of hydrogen and carbon

hydrogen *n.* the very first element in the periodic table; a colorless and odorless gas at room temperature

hydrotropism [hī·drŏt′rə·pĭz′əm] *n.* the growth of a plant in response to water

Hymenoptera [hī′mə·nŏp′tər·ə] *n.* an order of insects that includes bees, ants, and wasps; means "membrane wings"

hyphae [hī′fē] *n.* the tiny, white, hairlike structures in which bread mold is first seen

ice *n.* frozen water (H_2O)

igneous rock *n.* a rock that forms when molten rock solidifies either above or below ground

incomplete metamorphosis *n.* a process in which an insect goes through the stages of egg, nymph, and adult

inner planets *n.* the planets closest to the sun and made mainly of rocks and metals; Mercury, Venus, Earth, and Mars

insect *n.* a large class of arthropods that have three distinct body regions (head, thorax, and abdomen), three pairs of jointed legs, and one or more pairs of wings

insectivorous [ĭn′sĕk·tĭv′ər·əs] *adj.* insect eating

International Space Station *n.* a space station that sixteen nations worked together to build

intrusive igneous rock *n.* igneous rock formed when magma remains in pockets below the surface and slowly cools and hardens while still underground

invertebrate *n.* an animal without a backbone

iodine *n.* a nonmetal and halogen that is a purple solid at room temperature

ionic compound [ī·ŏn′ĭk] *n.* a compound composed of charged atoms or groups of atoms

iron *n.* a practical metal that is strong and abundantly available; the most commonly used metal

irregular galaxy *n.* a galaxy composed of stars clumped together in no definite shape, as in the Large Magellanic Cloud and the Small Magellanic Cloud

ivy *n.* a climbing plant that has special roots used for clinging

Japanese spider crab *n.* a giant crab that may weigh up to forty pounds and have legs nearly five feet long

jellyfish *n.* a bowl-shaped ocean invertebrate that has long tentacles that contain stinging cells

jet propulsion *n.* a type of movement in which a mollusk sucks water into a chamber of its body and then rapidly forces the water out

jumping spider *n.* a spider that uses extraordinarily keen eyesight to skillfully hunt and pounce on insects

juniper *n.* a tree in the cypress family that has unusual fleshy coats on its seed cones

Jupiter *n.* the fifth planet from the sun and the largest planet in our solar system

kelp *n.* the largest type of alga

Kepler, Johannes [kĕp′lər, yō·hän′əs] *n.* (1571–1630) a German astronomer who discovered that planets travel in elliptical orbits; formulated three laws of planetary motion

king crab *n.* an Alaskan crab that is a popular seafood dish

kingdom *n.* in classification, the largest group into which all living things can be organized

krill *n.* a crustacean that is small and shrimplike and feeds on plankton

Kuiper belt [kōō′pĕr] *n.* a belt of small, icy objects resembling comet nuclei that orbit farther from the sun than the planet Neptune

lac insect [lăk] *n.* a tiny insect in the order Homoptera that is the source of shellac

lapilli [lə·pĭl′ī] *n.* fragments of tephra that are smaller than bombs and blocks but larger than volcanic ash; means "little stones"

larch *n.* a type of deciduous conifer tree

larva *n.*
(1) a wormlike eating and growing stage of insects that undergo complete metamorphosis
(2) a young jellyfish that fastens to an object in the water and then grows to resemble a coral polyp

lava *n.* the name for molten rock after it reaches the earth's surface

lava cave *n.* a cave that forms when molten lava flows out from beneath a hardened surface of lava and leaves behind an underground chamber

law of universal gravitation *n.* the strength of the gravitational force between two objects depends on their masses (the amount of matter they contain) and the distance between them

lead *n.* the densest of everyday metals; used in car and truck batteries and to make wheel weights and firearms ammunition

leaf hopper *n.* a brightly colored insect in the order Homoptera

leech *n.* a parasitic worm that fastens to the skin of its host and feeds on the host's blood

legume *n.* the name for members of the pea family; its fruits grow in the shape of a pod

Leo *n.* a constellation in the Northern Hemisphere seen close to the eastern horizon on winter nights; the Lion

Lepidoptera [lĕp′ĭ·dŏp′tər·ə] *n.* an order of insects that is made up of butterflies and moths; means "scale wings"

lichen [lī′kən] *n.* a plant that consists of both fungi and algae

light year *n.* the distance light travels in one year; a unit for measuring distances in space equal to about 5.9 trillion miles

lignite coal *n.* the type of coal of the poorest quality; also called brown coal

lily family *n.* the family of plants whose flowers have petals in multiples of three, as in tulips, Easter lilies, and yuccas

limestone *n.* the most common type of organic sedimentary rock, made from calcium carbonate

Linnaeus, Carl [lĭ·nē′əs] *n.* (1707–1778) Swedish botanist who developed a system of classification for plants and animals; called the Father of Taxonomy

live oak *n.* a type of oak tree which is not deciduous

Livingstone, David *n.* (1813–1873) the missionary-explorer who spent thirty years opening the interior of Africa to Christianity, commerce, and civilization

lobe *n.* a rounded projection, such as the divisions of a leaf

lobster *n.* a crustacean that has a thick, muscular tail sticking out behind its narrow body

Local Group *n.* a cluster of about 40 galaxies including the Milky Way

locust *n.* a grasshopperlike insect in the order Orthoptera

low tide *n.* the lowest point on shore that the ocean reaches

lunar eclipse *n.* an event that occurs when the moon passes through the earth's shadow, causing the moon to appear darkened; can occur when the moon is full

lunar month *n.* the period of time it takes for the moon to revolve around the earth; 29 days, 12 hours, and 44 minutes

Luther, Martin *n.* (1483–1546) the great German reformer who encouraged a new interest in the study of science

magma *n.* melted rock

magma chamber *n.* a large reservoir a few miles beneath the earth's surface that contains magma

magnesium *n.* an alkaline earth metal that is strong but lightweight and is used in parts for airplanes and some cars

magnetic field *n.* the area surrounding a magnet in which the force of magnetism affects other objects

magnetism *n.* the force that pulls magnets apart or pushes them together

magnetosphere [măg·nē′tō·sfĭr] *n.* the region of space affected by the earth's magnetic field

magnitude *n.*
(1) the strength of an earthquake
(2) the brightness of a star

mange *n.* a skin infection of animals caused by mites

mantle *n.*
(1) in mollusks, the tissue that produces the shell
(2) the middle layer of the earth

marble *n.* an unfoliated metamorphic rock that was once limestone but was hardened by extreme heat and pressure within the earth

maria [mä′rē·ə] *n.* dark patches on the moon's surface once thought to be seas but now known to be rolling plains

Mars *n.* the fourth planet from the sun; called the red planet

mass *n.* the amount of matter that makes up an object

matter *n.* anything that takes up space and has mass and weight

Maxwell, James Clerk *n.* (1831–1879) the Scottish scientist who discovered electromagnetic waves and that light is a type of electromagnetic wave

mechanical sediment *n.* a type of sediment formed when rock is physically broken down and carried away by the "mechanisms" of nature; may later be pressed together to form sedimentary rock

medium *n.* the term for whatever carries a wave; *pl.* media

medusa [mĭ·do͞o′sə] *n.* the free-floating, umbrella-shaped stage of a jellyfish

mercury *n.* the only metal that is liquid at room temperature

Mercury *n.*
(1) the closest planet to the sun; the speediest planet
(2) a series of manned U.S. space flights during the early 1960s

metals *n.* a large group of elements that are typically shiny, with a silvery color, and are good conductors of electricity

metamorphic rock *n.* a rock produced by metamorphism of an igneous or sedimentary rock

metamorphism *n.* the change of a rock into a new type of rock by heat or pressure

metamorphosis *n.* the change in form that occurs during the life of an insect; can be complete or incomplete

meteor *n.* a meteoroid that enters earth's atmosphere

meteorite *n.* a meteor that has landed on the earth's surface

meteoroid [mē′tē·ə·roid′] *n.* a piece of space debris that orbits the sun and is smaller than the smallest asteroid

meteor shower *n.* a brief period during which the earth passes through a cluster of meteoroids, causing more meteors than usual to be seen

mid-oceanic ridge *n.* an underwater mountain range in the ocean where plates of the earth's crust are spreading away from each other

midrib *n.* a large vein that runs up the middle of a leaf

mildew *n.* a fungus that often grows on wet clothes, shower stalls, and plants

Milk Dipper *n.* a figure formed by the brightest stars in the constellation Sagittarius that extends into the Milky Way

Milky Way *n.* the barred spiral galaxy in which we live

millipede *n.* an arthropod with a rounded body and two pairs of legs in each segment; means "one-thousand footed"

minerals *n.* the individual substances that make up rocks

mite *n.* the smallest arachnids

Moho [mō′hō] *n.* the boundary between the earth's crust and mantle

molecular compound *n.* a compound composed of individual molecules

molecule *n.* a tiny group of two or more atoms that are bonded tightly together

mollusk *n.* a soft-bodied invertebrate such as clams, oysters, and squids

molt *n.* a process in which an insect sheds its external skeleton

monocot *n.* a type of flowering plant characterized by seeds with one cotyledon, leaves with parallel veins, fibrous roots, and flower petals in multiples of three

moon *n.*
(1) any natural heavenly body that orbits a planet
(2) the large natural satellite that orbits the earth

moon milk *n.* a soft paste of calcium carbonate that may form in a cave if the air is very humid

mosquito *n.* a biting insect in the order Diptera

moss *n.* a group of small green plants that have no true leaves, stems, or roots

moth *n.* a nocturnal insect in the order Lepidoptera that has a thick body and feathery antennae

mushroom *n.* a fungus with a fruiting body

mycelium [mī·sē′lē·əm] *n.* a network of cells strung together in a fungus; the main part of a fungus

nautilus *n.* a cephalopod with a beautifully designed external shell that protects its body

neap tide *n.* a weaker ocean tide that occurs during a first-quarter moon and a third-quarter moon, when the gravitational forces of the sun and moon work at right angles against each other

near-Earth asteroids *n.* a very important group of asteroids, located in the inner solar system, that are not part of the main asteroid belt; most of these asteroids cross paths with the earth

nebula *n.* a large cloud of gas and dust in space; *pl.* nebulae [nĕb′yə·lē]

nectar *n.* a sweet liquid stored in the bottom of a flower that helps attract insects to the flower

negative *n.* the type of electric charge carried by an electron

neon *n.* an element and noble gas that is commonly used in "neon signs"

Neptune *n.* the eighth planet from the sun

neutral *n.* anything lacking an electrical charge

neutron *n.* a particle that helps make up the nucleus of an atom

new moon *n.* the beginning of the lunar month when the sunlit side of the moon is turned away from Earth and completely hidden from view

Newton, Sir Isaac *n.* (1642–1727) the scientist who discovered the law of universal gravitation and that sunlight is a combination of many colors, developed the reflecting telescope, and discovered the three laws of motion

nickel *n.* a very hard metal that is an important ingredient in stainless steel and rechargeable batteries; also used as a lining for tanks holding corrosive chemicals

night *n.* the period of darkness that occurs as the earth rotates on its axis

nitrogen *n.* a colorless, odorless gas that is much less prone than oxygen to react with other elements; nitrogen compounds are used in fertilizers, rocket fuels, and explosives

noble gases *n.* the elements in the last column of the periodic table, such as helium and argon; they do not combine with anything else except under unusual circumstances

nocturnal *adj.* describing an animal that is active at night

nonmetals *n.* the elements in the periodic table that are not classified as metals or semimetals

Northern Cross *n.* the five brightest stars in the constellation Cygnus

nova [nō′və] *n.* an occurrence when a star suddenly flares up to many times its original brightness

nucleus [noo′klē·əs] *n.*
(1) the part of a cell that is often located in the center and directs the work of the cell
(2) a frozen chunk of rock, dust, and ice about the size of a small asteroid that is the heart of a comet
(3) a tiny, extremely dense core of an atom

nudibranch [noo′də·brăngk] *n.* a brightly colored gastropod that is one of the most beautiful sea creatures; also called sea slug

nymph [nĭmf] *n.* an immature insect that resembles a miniature adult

obsidian [ŏb·sĭd′ē·ən] *n.* a shiny, black igneous rock that resembles glass

octopus *n.* a cephalopod that has eight long tentacles and eyes that are much like the eyes of vertebrates

Odonata [ō′dō·nā′tə] *n.* an order of insects that is made up of dragonflies and damselflies; means "toothed"

ogre-faced spider *n.* a spider that uses its silk to make a tiny net to catch insects

optical double *n.* a pair of stars that appear very close together from our perspective on the earth, but which are actually far apart

orbit *v.* to revolve around

orb web *n.* a spider's web that has a wheel-shaped design

order *n.* in classification, a group smaller than a class but larger than a family into which plants and animals are divided

ore *n.* a rock containing a metal together with impurities

organelle *n.* a tiny organ in a cell

organic sediment *n.* sediments that consist of dead plants, shells, or animal skeletons

Orion [ō·rī′ən] *n.* the brightest of all constellations, located in the Northern Hemisphere; resembles a hunter holding a shield and a club with a sword at his side

Orthoptera [ôr·thŏp′tər·ə] *n.* an order of insects that includes crickets, grasshoppers, locusts, and roaches; means "straight wings"

oscillation *n.* a back and forth motion that repeatedly follows the same path

osmium [ŏz′mē·əm] *n.* a metal that is the densest element

outer planets *n.* the term for Jupiter, Saturn, Uranus, Neptune, and Pluto; except for Pluto, are much larger than the inner planets and are composed mainly of liquids and gases

ovary [ō′və·rē] *n.* the structure at the base of the pistil that holds one or more undeveloped seeds in a flower

overburden *n.* layers of rock and soil that lie on top of a coal bed and must be stripped away to expose the coal

ovule [ō′vyo͞ol] *n.* the undeveloped seeds in a flower

oxygen *n.* a colorless and odorless gas that animals and people require in order to live

ozone layer [ō′zōn] *n.* a region of the atmosphere, located between 10 and 30 miles above the surface of the earth, which filters out most of the sun's ultraviolet radiation

paper birch *n.* the most common type of birch tree in North America

paramecium [păr′ə·mē′shē·əm] *n.* a common protozoan that is covered with cilia and looks like a shoe or slipper under a microscope

parasite *n.* an organism (plant or animal) that gets its nourishment by attaching itself to another organism and continuously taking in that organism's body fluids

pea crab *n.* the smallest crab; hides its quarter-inch body in the shell of a live clam or oyster

pea family *n.* the large high-protein plant group whose fruits grow in the shape of a pod, or legume, as in clover, green beans, and peanuts

peat moss *n.* a type of moss that when mixed with soil keeps household and garden plants from drying out

Pegasus [pĕg′ə·səs] *n.* a constellation in the Northern Hemisphere that is named for a flying horse in Greek mythology

penicillin *n.* an antibiotic drug made from one kind of mold

perennial [pə·rĕn′ē·əl] *n.* a type of plant that does not die after one season of growth but lives for many years

period *n.* the amount of time it takes a comet to complete an orbit

periodic table of the elements *n.* a chart constructed by Dmitri Mendeleev [d′mē′trē mĭn·dĭl·yä′yĕf] to arrange the elements in such a way as to group similar elements together

Perseus [pûr′sē·əs] *n.* a constellation in the Northern Hemisphere seen during the winter that is named for a mythical hero who rescued Andromeda

petal *n.* the most noticeable, brightly colored part of a flower that helps to attract bees or other creatures

petroleum *n.* a fossil fuel that may have been formed from the remains of once-living creatures; means "rock oil"

phosphorus *n.* a nonmetal element that is a waxlike solid with two forms, white phosphorus and red phosphorus; compounds of phosphorus and oxygen known as phosphates are used as fertilizers and food preservatives

photosphere [fō′tə·sfîr] *n.* the sun's visible surface; "sphere of light"

photosynthesis [fō′tō·sĭn′thĭ·sĭs] *n.* a complex chemical process by which green plants use the energy of sunlight to change water and carbon dioxide into glucose for food

phototropism [fō·tŏt′rə·pĭz′əm] *n.* a plant's growth in response to light

phylum *n.* in classification, a group smaller than a kingdom but larger than a class into which plants and animals are divided; *pl.* phyla [fī′lə]

physical weathering *n.* a type of weathering that occurs when rock is broken down by water, ice, or windblown sand

pill bug *n.* a type of wood louse that rolls itself into a hard little ball whenever it senses danger and can expel an offensive odor; also called a roly-poly

pinyon pine [pĭn′yən] *n.* a type of conifer tree that produces tasty edible nuts and grows in the hot, dry climate of the Southwestern states

pistil *n.* a long tube in the middle of a flower that makes seeds

pistol shrimp *n.* a type of shrimp that has one large pincer that it uses as a type of stun gun

pitcher plant *n.* an insectivorous (insect-eating) plant that uses bright colors, a pleasant aroma, and slippery leaves to trap insects

planet *n.* any of the nine large heavenly bodies that orbit the sun

plankton *n.* colonies of microscopic plants and animals

plate *n.* large sections of the earth's crust that "float" on the soft rock of the upper mantle and slowly move about

platform spider *n.* a spider that blankets a small section of ground with a sheet web

platinum [plăt′ĭ·nəm] *n.* a precious metal that is more expensive than gold because of its rarity and many uses

Pleiades [plē′ə·dēz′] *n.* a star cluster located in the constellation Taurus

Plinian eruption *n.* an eruption that occurs when a volcano expels hot clouds of gas and dust high into the atmosphere, forming ash clouds that may travel completely around the world; usually the volcano has lain dormant for a long period of time

Pluto *n.* the ninth planet from the sun; the outermost planet in the solar system and the smallest planet

plutonium [plo͞o·tō′nē·əm] *n.* the most abundant of the transuranium elements

polar orbit *n.* an orbit in which a satellite travels perpendicular to the equator, passing over the polar regions as it circles the earth

Polaris [pə·lăr′ĭs] *n.* a star in the constellation Ursa Minor that is the North Star, or Pole Star

poles *n.* the places of a magnet where the magnetic field is most concentrated

pollen *n.* the dustlike yellow grains produced by the stamen of a flower

pollen cone *n.* a type of cone produced by a conifer tree that contains large amounts of pollen

pollen tube *n.* during pollination, a tube formed by a special cell down which two sperm cells travel from a pollen grain to the egg cell inside the ovule

pollination *n.* the transfer of pollen from the stamen of a flower to the pistil

pollinator *n.* the name for anything that pollinates flowers, such as bees and the wind

Pollux [pŏl′əks] *n.* one of the brightest stars in the constellation Gemini; one of Gemini's heads

polyp *n.* a stage in the life of a jellyfish, coral polyp, or hydra in which the animal has a nonswimming, cylinder-shaped body with its mouth and tentacles facing up

ponderosa pine [pŏn′də·rō′sə] *n.* one of the largest varieties of pine trees in the American West

Portuguese man-of-war *n.* a colony of several jellyfishlike creatures living and working together

positive *n.* the type of electric charge that a proton carries

prawn *n.* a type of shrimp that can grow to ten inches long

precious metal *n.* a metal known for its durability, rarity, and beauty

precious stones *n.* the rarest, most durable and beautiful gems

protein *n.* complex molecules found in living things that are necessary for life

proton *n.* a positively charged particle that helps make up the nucleus of an atom

protozoan [prō′tə·zō′ən] *n.* a miniature invertebrate made up of one cell, such as an amoeba or paramecium

Proxima Centauri *n.* the closest star to the earth besides the sun; located in the constellation Centaurus and part of the Alpha Centauri system

pseudopod [sōō′də·pŏd′] *n.* a projection in an amoeba that pushes it from place to place; means "false feet"

Ptolemy, Claudius [tŏl′ə·mē] *n.* an ancient Greek astronomer who believed in an earth-centered universe

pulsar [pŭl′sâr] *n.* a star that produces rapid bursts of radio waves

pumice [pŭm′ĭs] *n.* a lightweight extrusive igneous rock made from gas-filled lava

pupa *n.* the resting stage of an insect undergoing complete metamorphosis

pussy willow *n.* a type of willow tree that grows no larger than shrub size

quaking aspen *n.* a type of poplar tree that gets its name from the tendency of its leaves to tremble in the slightest breeze

radio telescope *n.* an instrument that collects radio waves from space and allows us to study the heavens using portions of the electromagnetic spectrum that are invisible to the human eye

ray *n.* an arm of a sea star

Ray, John *n.* (1627–1705) a Puritan botanist and naturalist who helped devise the system of classification of plants and animals that we use today

ray flower *n.* a petal-like part of a composite flower

red spinel [spĭ·něl′] *n.* a semiprecious stone commonly confused with ruby

redwood tree *n.* the tallest tree in the world

reflecting telescope *n.* a type of telescope that uses mirrors to produce an image

reflection *n.* the turning back or turning aside of any wave when it hits an obstacle

refracting telescope *n.* a type of telescope that uses lenses to gather light and form an image

refraction *n.* the bending of any wave's direction at the boundary between two wave media

regeneration *n.* the replacement of lost body parts

Regulus [rĕg′yə·ləs] *n.* the brightest star in the constellation Leo that marks one of the lion's front paws

revolution *n.* a single orbit around the sun or another heavenly body

rhizoids [rī′zoidz] *n.* a fern's roots that grow downward from the underside of the stem

rhizome [rī′zōm′] *n.* a thick storage stem that produces new plants and grows just below the ground

Richter scale [rĭk′tər] *n.* the most famous scale used to measure earthquake strength; invented by Charles Richter

Rigel [rī′jəl] *n.* one of the brightest stars in the constellation Orion; represents Orion's left foot

Ring of Fire *n.* the volcanic belt that encircles the edge of the Pacific Ocean

rock *n.* the hard material that composes the earth's crust

root cap *n.* a layer of thick protective cells covering the end of a growing root

root hair *n.* a tiny projection near the end of a root that finds water and dissolved minerals in the soil

root system *n.* the part of a plant that is below the ground

rose family *n.* a family of plants with blossoms with five petals or multiples of five; includes roses, strawberries, and apples

rotation *n.* the spinning of the earth or other object

roundworm *n.* a parasitic worm that can live in the lymph nodes, intestines, and muscles of a host and take its nourishment from the host's blood or partially digested food

ruby *n.* a transparent red precious stone that is a variety of the mineral corundum

runner *n.* a stem that grows along the surface of the ground; stolon

Sagittarius [săj′ĭ·târ′ē·əs] *n.* a constellation in the Southern Hemisphere that looks like an archer

sand dollar *n.* a type of sea urchin that has very small spines and lives off the coasts of North America

sandstone *n.* a rough, crumbly rock which consists of particles of quartz sand that have been fused together into rock; sometimes used to make glass

sap *n.* a watery substance in a tree that contains the sugar sucrose

sapphire *n.* a transparent precious stone that is a variety of the mineral corundum; may be blue, yellow, orange, or purple

saprophyte [săp′rə·fīt′] *n.* a fungus or other creature that feeds on dead matter

satellite *n.* any object that orbits a larger object

Saturn *n.* the sixth planet from the sun, known for its glorious rings

scabies *n.* a skin infection, caused by mites, which affects humans

scale insect *n.* a tiny insect in the order Homoptera

scaly leaves *n.* a flat layer of very small leaves that covers a branchlet and stays green all year

scientific name *n.* the name of a plant or animal derived from the genus name and the species name

scorpion *n.* a dangerous arachnid characterized by a long tail with a poisonous, needlelike point on the end; a scorpion bears live young and breathes entirely through book lungs

Scorpius [skôr′pē·əs] *n.* a constellation in the Southern Hemisphere that looks like a scorpion

sea anemone [ə·něm′ə·nē] *n.* a flowerlike ocean-dwelling invertebrate animal that has many stinging tentacles

sea cave *n.* a cave that forms when the ocean beats upon a weak area of a cliff and erodes a hole into the rock

sea cucumber *n.* a long, bumpy relative of the sea star and sea urchin

sea lily *n.* a flowerlike relative of the sea star and sea urchin

sea star *n.* a spiny-skinned, ocean-dwelling invertebrate that has two rows of tiny tube feet and at least five rays; also called a starfish

sea urchin *n.* a relative of the sea star that uses its long spines to protect itself and to turn itself over

second law of planetary motion *n.* as a planet moves closer to the sun, it travels faster; and as it moves farther away, it slows down

sediment *n.* a thick layer of sand and mineral fragments

sedimentary rock *n.* a rock that is formed from sediments that have been pressed together into solid rock

seed coat *n.* the part of a seed that covers and protects the embryo

seed cone *n.* a type of cone produced by the conifer tree that contains the ovules to be pollinated

seismic belts *n.* the regions of the earth where most earthquakes occur; located along plate boundaries

seismologist *n.* a scientist who studies earthquakes

seismology *n.* the study of earthquakes

semimetals *n.* the elements of the periodic table that have characteristics of both metals and nonmetals

semiprecious stones *n.* gems that are not as rare or as durable as precious stones

sepals [sē′pəlz] *n.* green, leaflike structures attached to the base of a flower; serve to protect the flower bud as it develops

setae *n.*
(1) sensitive hairs responsible for a spider's sense of touch
(2) the eight movable bristles on each segment of an earthworm that allow the worm to hold on to the soil

shale *n.* a type of rock formed from mud or clay that consists of much smaller particles than sand and is often found in layers of sandstone or limestone; used to make bricks

sheath *n.* the part of a grass leaf that is closely wrapped around the stem

sheet web *n.* a spider's web that is a flat maze of silk

shell *n.*
(1) a beautiful, hard covering of a mollusk
(2) a group of electrons in an atom that orbit at roughly the same distance from the nucleus

Shepard, Alan *n.* (1923–1998) the first American in space

shield volcano *n.* a type of volcano that forms when large amounts of fluid, runny lava gradually build up a dome-shaped mountain

shoot system *n.* the part of a plant that is visible above ground

shrimp *n.* a common crustacean that resembles a miniature lobster and can grow to two inches long

Sickle *n.* the bright stars that outline the constellation Leo's head

silicon [sĭl′ĭ·kən] *n.* a gray semimetal that in pure form is used to make computer chips and is an ingredient in common sand, the mineral quartz, and glass

silver *n.* a precious metal that is primarily mined for industrial and technical applications

simple eye *n.* a type of eye in insects and other arthropods that has only one lens; used in insects to detect light and shadow, but used in some spiders to see very clearly

Sirius [sĭr′ĭ·əs] *n.* the brightest star in the night sky, located in the constellation Canis Major

slate *n.* a foliated metamorphic rock derived from shale that is weather resistant and waterproof

slime mold *n.* a fungus that grows on tree trunks and decaying logs; sends out sticky threads that become spore-producing structures

slug *n.* a close relative of the snail that does not have a protective shell

snail *n.* a common garden gastropod that eats young plants

social insects *n.* insects such as bees, ants, or wasps that live together in colonies

soda straws *n.* cave formations that consist of thin, hollow tubes that hang from the ceiling of a cave

sodium chloride *n.* chemical name for ordinary table salt; formula is NaCl

sodium hydroxide [hī·drŏk′sīd′] *n.* an important compound of sodium also known as lye or caustic soda; formula is NaOH

soil *n.* small particles of rock and decomposed plant and animal matter that provide a place for plants to grow

solar eclipse *n.* an event that occurs when the earth's moon passes between the sun and the earth, temporarily blocking the sun's rays from a portion of the earth

solar flares *n.* tremendous bursts of energy on the sun caused by sudden changes in the sun's magnetic field

solar prominence *n.* a huge loop or streamer of cooler gas that erupts thousands of miles from the sun's chromosphere

solar system *n.* the sun and all the heavenly bodies that orbit it

solar wind *n.* a stream of potentially harmful particles that flows constantly from the surface of the sun, formed by particles of gas escaping into space at high speed

solar year *n.* the length of the earth's revolution around the sun, equal to 365¼ days

solution cave *n.* a cave formed by the dissolving of underground rocks by water

Southern Cross *n.* a group of four very bright stars that is the most familiar sight in the sky of the Southern Hemisphere; has an upright bar that points nearly due south

space probe *n.* an unmanned spacecraft that is launched specifically to explore the unknown

space shuttle *n.* an American spacecraft, first launched in 1981, that was the first spacecraft designed to be reused

space station *n.* a structure in space in which people can live and work for weeks or months at a time

Spanish moss *n.* a plant that has no roots and covers many old trees in the South; a type of epiphyte

special leaf *n.* a leaf that has a special design for a special task, such as a tendril or a spine

species [spē′shēz] *n.* the smallest group into which all living things can be organized

spectroscope *n.* a special device that can split light into a spectrum for analysis

speed of light *n.* the speed at which electromagnetic waves travel, equal to roughly 186,000 miles per second

speleology [spē′lē·ŏl′ə·jē] *n.* the scientific study of caves

sperm cell *n.* a cell located in a pollen grain that is needed for a seed to develop

spicules *n.* faint "spikes" of hydrogen gas that commonly rise from the sun's chromosphere to a height of several thousand miles

spine *n.* a special leaf that contains no chlorophyll and protects the water-storing stem of the cactus plant

spinneret *n.* the special tubelike structure in a spider that excretes liquid silk when pressure is applied

spiny lobster *n.* a lobster without pincers that uses its antennae for self-defense; also called rock lobster

spiracle [spīr′ə·kəl] *n.* a tiny opening in an insect's abdomen through which air enters the body

spiral galaxy *n.* a galaxy that looks like a giant pinwheel spinning through the void of space; has a central nucleus that resembles a flattened ball, to which are attached long, curved arms, and contains large amounts of gas and dust

spitting spider *n.* a spider that spits out a pair of strong, sticky threads to catch insects

sponge *n.* a stonelike or bushlike animal on the ocean floor that circulates water through the pores of its body in order to collect microscopic food particles

spore *n.* a single cell produced instead of a seed by ferns and some other plants

spore·case *n.* a tiny structure where spores develop

spring tide *n.* an especially high or low ocean tide that occurs during a new moon or a full moon, when the sun and moon are in line with the earth and their gravitational forces are working together

Sputnik 1 [spoōt′nĭk] *n.* a Russian satellite, launched in 1957, that was the first artificial object to orbit the earth

squid *n.* a cephalopod that has ten tentacles with suction cups and an internal shell that helps support and protect its "head"

stalactite *n.* an icicle-shaped rock formation that grows from the ceiling of a cave

stalagmite *n.* a steep mound or spike of calcium carbonate on the floor of a cave

stamens [stā′mənz] *n.* the structures arranged in a ring around the pistil of a flower that make and hold pollen

starch *n.* a substance made from sugar and used as a form of food storage by plants

steel *n.* an alloy of iron and carbon that makes up most iron products

stem *n.* the part of the plant that carries water and minerals to the leaves and food to the roots; sometimes also used to refer to the stalk that connects a leaf to a branch

stem tip *n.* the upper part of a plant stem where growth occurs

stigma *n.* a flat tip on the pistil of a flower that receives pollen

stinging cells *n.* cells in a jellyfish's tentacles that shoot a stinging poison into anything they touch

stolon [stō′lŏn] *n.* a stem that grows along the surface of the ground; a runner

stoma *n.* "little mouth"; a tiny hole or pore in a leaf; *pl.* stomata [stō′mə·tə]

Strombolian eruption *n.* a usually mild, frequent eruption of a volcano

sub-bituminous coal *n.* the second most common type of coal; softer and more crumbly than bituminous coal and widely used for generating electricity

sublime *v.* to turn directly from a solid into a gas

sucrose [soō′krōs] *n.* a kind of sugar into which a tree's stored food is converted in the spring; table sugar

sugar cane *n.* a woody grass that is filled with sweet-tasting pulp and is very juicy when crushed; a primary source of table sugar

sugaring *n.* the process of producing maple syrup and sugar from maple trees

sugar maple *n.* a type of tree that is found primarily in Canada and the northern forests of the United States that is the source of maple syrup

sulfur *n.* nonmetal element that is an odorless, yellow solid at room temperature; called brimstone in the Bible

sulfuric acid [sŭl·fyŏŏr′ĭk] *n.* a highly corrosive chemical used in car batteries and chemical manufacturing

sun *n.* the star that lies at the center of our solar system

sun-centered system *n.* the view that all planets orbit the sun

sundew *n.* an insectivorous (insect-eating) plant that uses sticky "dew drops" to trap insects

sunspot *n.* a patch of gas on the sun's surface that is cooler than the rest of the sun and therefore not as bright

supernova *n.* the violent explosion of a star

surface mining *n.* a method of mining a deposit of coal or minerals by removing the overlying rock; used only for deposits near the earth's surface

swimmeret *n.* a leglike limb that helps lobsters and other crustaceans when they are swimming and walking

tail *n.* a trail of dust particles and gases that stream away from the nucleus and coma of a comet

tamarack *n.* the most common type of larch tree in North America

tapeworm *n.* a parasitic worm that grows inside the intestines of a host and robs it of important nutrients

taproot *n.* a single main root of a plant that penetrates deeply into the ground

tarantulas *n.* the group of spiders that includes the largest spiders in the world

Taurus *n.* a constellation in the Northern Hemisphere that resembles a bull

taxonomy [tăk·sŏn′ə·mē] *n.* the science of classification

telescope *n.* a device to make distant objects appear clearer, brighter, or closer

tendril *n.* a special leaf by which a vine grasps a support

tephra [tĕf′rə] *n.* fragments of volcanic rock that form when thick magma explodes into pieces as it leaves the volcano; includes volcanic ash, lapilli, volcanic bombs, and volcanic blocks

Tereshkova, Valentina [tĕr′əsh·kô′və, vəl′yĭn·tēn′ə] *n.* (1937–) the first woman to fly in space

thigmotropism [thĭg·mŏt′rə·pĭz′əm] *n.* the growth of a plant in response to touch

third law of planetary motion *n.* shows the relationship between a planet's distance from the sun and the time it takes the planet to complete one orbit

third-quarter moon *n.* the stage of the visible moon when it is half dark and half light again

thorn *n.* a protective stem much like a leaf spine

tick *n.* an arachnid that feeds on the blood of living creatures

Titan [tī′tən] *n.* Saturn's largest moon; has its own atmosphere

tracheae [trā′kē·ē′] *n.* an insect's breathing tubes through which air travels

transuranium elements [trăns′yŏŏ′rə·nē·əm] *n.* the man-made elements with higher atomic numbers than uranium; the elements beyond uranium in the periodic table

trapdoor spider *n.* a spider that digs a hole in the ground, lines the hole with silk, builds a silk trap door over the hole, and lies in wait for passing insects

tree fern *n.* a type of fern tree that looks more like a palm tree than a fern; its stem grows upward like the trunk of a tree

tree hopper *n.* a brightly colored insect in the order Homoptera

tremor *n.* a weak earthquake

troglobite [trä′glō·bīt] *n.* an animal that lives only in caves and cannot survive above ground; means "cave dweller"

troglophile [trä′glō·fīl] *n.* an animal that can live its entire life either in a cave or above ground and can go from one place to the other; means "cave lover"

trogloxene [trä′glō·zēn] *n.* an animal that visits caves regularly but must return to the surface to find food; means "cave guest"

tropism [trō′pĭz′əm] *n.* the growth of a plant in response to a condition in its environment, such as gravity, water, light, or touch

trough *n.* the low point of a wave

true bug *n.* an insect in the order Hemiptera that has wings that cross over to form an *X* or a *V* at the base of the abdomen; known for the way it sucks sap from plants and body fluids from animals with its piercing-sucking mouth parts

tsunami [tsŏŏ-nä′mē] *n.* a monstrous wave that can occur after an earthquake or undersea landslide

tube feet *n.* the feet of sea stars and sea urchins that act like suction cups and help the sea star keep a firm grip on its prey

turf grass *n.* a type of grass which beautifies the land and protects it from erosion; used to cover lawns, athletic fields, golf courses, and playgrounds

underground mining *n.* a method of mining underground coal or mineral deposits by digging a tunnel down to the deposit

unfoliated rock *n.* metamorphic rock that does not have a layered appearance and cannot be split into thin layers like slate and other foliated rocks

univalve *n.* a one-shelled mollusk

Uranus *n.* the seventh planet from the sun, noted for being turned on its side

Ursa Major [ûr′sə] *n.* an easily recognizable constellation in the Northern Hemisphere that contains the Big Dipper; also called the Great Bear

Ursa Minor *n.* the constellation in the Northern Hemisphere containing Polaris; also called the Little Bear or Little Dipper

vacuum *n.* an area containing no air or any other matter

vanilla plant *n.* a plant that has green open-air roots that carry out photosynthesis; a type of epiphyte

vein *n.* in plants, a pipe that transports liquids and reinforces the structure of a leaf

vent *n.* an opening caused by trapped gases that blast their way through the earth's surface

Venus *n.* the second planet from the sun and hottest planet in our solar system; the brightest object in the night sky except for the moon; called the morning star and evening star

Venus flytrap *n.* an insectivorous (insect-eating) plant that uses hinged leaves to trap insects

vertebrate *n.* an animal with a backbone

vine *n.* a plant that climbs upward as it grows by clinging to tall objects such as walls or trees with its tendrils

visible spectrum *n.* the color sequence red, orange, yellow, green, blue, and violet, visible when white light is passed through a prism

vitamin *n.* a chemical that plants, animals, and people need in small amounts for nourishment

volcanic ash *n.* the smallest fragments of tephra; resembles dust or fine sand

volcanic block *n.* a type of large volcanic tephra

volcanic bomb *n.* a type of large volcanic tephra

volcano *n.* a vent that allows molten rock and hot gases to escape from within the earth

wane *v.* to shrink, as the moon seems to as it goes through its phases

wasp *n.* a common, stinging social insect in the order Hymenoptera

water spider *n.* a type of spider that lives its entire life underwater

wave *n.* a movement of energy from one place to another

wavelength *n.* the length of one complete wave or cycle of oscillation, measured from crest to crest or trough to trough

wax *v.* to grow larger, as the moon seems to as it goes through its phases

weathering *n.* a chemical or physical process that causes rocks to gradually break or crumble into smaller pieces

weeping willow *n.* a type of willow tree that has drooping leaves, giving it an almost mournful appearance

weight *n.* a measure of the pull of gravity on an object

white oak *n.* a type of oak tree whose edible acorns were used as food by American Indians and pioneers

white spruce *n.* one of the most common varieties of spruce in North America, characterized by the skunklike odor its needles give off when crushed or broken

wood louse *n.* a crustacean that lives on land in moist places under leaves and stones and has seven pairs of legs

year *n.* the period in which the earth revolves around the sun; 365¼ days

yeast *n.* a single-celled fungus that converts sugar into alcohol and carbon dioxide

zinc *n.* a metal used to galvanize steel; commonly made into such items as chainlink fences, trash cans, roofing nails, and car bodies; an ingredient in flashlight batteries

Index

Page numbers for illustrations are printed in *italic type*.

mussel 144
mycelium 84

N

nautilus 146, *146*
navigational satellite 333, *333*
Navstar *333*
neap tide 286, *286*
near-Earth asteroids 289, *289*
nebulae 244, *244, 252, 267, 298, 308, 374*
nectar 24
needlelike leaves 10, *10*, 67
needles 10, *10*, 67
negative charge 368
neon 386, *386*
Neptune
    discovery of, 277
    position in solar system, 277, 337, *337*
    moons of, 278, 352, *352*
    description of, 351–352, *351*
    gravity on, 352
neutral 368
neutron 367
New Madrid earthquake 180
new moon 284, *284*
Newton, Sir Isaac
    and gravity, 274, *274*
    and Creation, 275
    and light, 299, *299*
    and telescope, 306
    and laws of motion, 317
    life of, 318–319, *319*
nickel 211, 378, *378*
nitrogen 35, 380, 381
noble gases 377, 386, *386*
nonmetals 376–377, 377, 379–382, *379–382*
Northern Cross 249, *249*
nova 266
nucleus
    of cell, 159, *159*
    of galaxy, 242
    of comet, 290, *290*
    of atom, 366–367, *366*
nudibranch 144, *144*
nutmeg 50, *50*
nymph 100, *100*

O

oak 50, 60–61, *60*
oats 39, 40

objective lens 305–306, *306*
obsidian 194, *194*
octopus 146, *146*
Odonata 103
ogre-faced spider 116, *116*
oil (*see* petroleum)
olive tree 47, *47*
Olympus Mons 343, *343*
onion
    structure of, 8, *8*
optical double 266, *266*
orange 27
orb web 112–113, *113*
orbit
    defined, 270
    elliptical, 271–274, *273*
    of comet, 290–291, *291*
    of satellite, 317–318, *318*, 332, 333, *333*
    geostationary, 332, *333*
    polar, 333, *333*
orbiter (*see* space shuttle)
order *94*, 95, 100, *101*
ore 208
organelle 159, *159*
organic sediments 200
Orion 246, 250–251, *250*
Orthoptera 102
oscillation 300
osmium 364, 373
ostrich 78
outer core *168*, 170, *170*
outer planets 278, 337, *337*, 344–353
ovary 23, *23*, 26–27, *27*
overburden 216, *216*
ovule 23, *23*
oxygen
    atom, 369, *369*
    importance of, 374, *374*, 380
    uses of, 380, *380*
    molecule, 387, *387*
    and combustion, 393–394, *394*
oyster 144
ozone layer 281, *281*

P

palm tree 75, *75*
paper 50
paper birch 61, *61*
paramecium *157, 158*, 161, *161, 163*
parasite 84
Paricutín 181–182, *181*, 187, *187*, 189

Pathfinder 335, *336, 342*
pea crab 128, *128*
pea family 34–35, *34*
peach 35
pear 35
peat moss 81
Pegasus 248, *248*
penicillin 85, 89
perennial 46
period 291
periodic table of the elements 376–377, *376–377*
permafrost 343
Perseus 248, *248*
petal 22, *22*
petroleum 217–219, *217–219*
Phobos 343
Phoebe 347
phosphates 382
phosphorus 382, *382*
photosphere 257, *257*
photosynthesis 4–5, *5*
phototropism 20, *20*
phyla *94*, 95
    (*see also* phylum)
phylum *94*, 95, 100, *101*
physical weathering 171, *171*
pill bug 132, *132*, 135
pincer *126, 127*
pine
    uses of, 50
    examples of, *47, 47, 65, 68, 68*
    (*see also* pine family)
pine family 68–70, *68–70*
pinyon pine 68, *68*
pistil 23, *23*
pistol shrimp 131, *131*
pitcher plant 9, *9*
planet
    known by ancient astronomers, 268
    Earth as, 270
    laws of motion of, 272–274
    defined, 276
    around other stars, 278
    of solar system, 337–353
    sizes of, *337*, 344
    (*see also individual planets*)
plankton 127
plants 3–89
    importance of, 3
    insectivorous, 8–9, *8, 9*
plaster of Paris 199, *199*

scallop 144, *144*

scaly leaves 10, *10*, 67

scanning-tunneling microscope 367, *367*

scientific name 95, *95*, 100

scorpion 122–123, *123*

Scorpius 252, *252*

Scotch pine 71, *71*

sea anemone 150, *150*

sea cave 221, *221*

sea cucumber 149, *149*

sea lily 148

sea slug (*see* nudibranch)

sea star 147–148, *147*, *148*

sea urchin 148, *148*

seaweed 82–83, *82*, *83*

sedimentary rock 193, 197–200, *197–200*

sediments 168, 197, 198–200

seed 27–29, *27–29* (*see also* grain)

seed coat 29, *29*

seed cone 66, *66*

seismic belt 180, *180*

seismologist 177

seismology 177 (*see also* earthquake)

semimetal 377, *377*, 382, *382*

semiprecious stone 207, *207*

sepal 22, *22*

sequoia (*see* giant sequoia)

setae of spider, 109, *109* of earthworm, 140, *140*

shale 198, *198*

sheath 39, *39*

sheet web 115, *115*

shell of mollusk, 142 of atom, 369, *369*

shelly limestone 200, *200*

Shepard, Alan 321, *321*

shield volcano 186–187, *187*

shoot system 13, *13*

shooting star (*see* meteor)

shrimp 130–131, *130*, *131*

Sickle 249, *249*

silicon 382, *382*

silk 110–111

silver 209, *209*, 372

silver bromide 385

simple eyes 99, *99*, 109, *109*

Sirius 250, 251, 262, 265, *265*

Sirius B 265, *265*

Skylab 237, 326, *326*

slate 202, *202*

slime mold 86–87, *86*

slug 143, *143*

Small Magellanic Cloud 241, *241*

snail 142–143, *142*, *145*

soap 383, *383*

social insect 104

soda straws 222, *222*

sodium 369, *369*, 382–383, *383* 393, *393*

sodium chloride 384, 385, 389, *389*, 393, *393* (*see also* salt)

sodium hydroxide 383, *383*

soft coal 215

soil 171, *171*

solar eclipse 258

solar flare 260, *260*

solar prominence 257, 259, *259*

solar system defined, 276 location in Milky Way, *242*, 243, 280 description of, 276–278, *276–277* around other stars, 278 small bodies of, 287–295 planets of, 276–278, 337–353 (*see also individual planets*)

solar wind 229, *229*, 260, 290

solar year 279 (*see also* year)

solution cave 221

Sombrero galaxy 242

Southern Cross 252, *252*

space characteristics of, 236–238, *236* traveling to, 314

space probe 335–336, *335*, *336* early space probes, 320

space shuttle *281*, 328–330, *328*, *329* engines of, 379–380, *380*

space station 325–327, *326*, *327* astronauts and, *237*, *238*, 327

spacecraft Vostok, 321, *321* Mercury, 321, *321* Voskhod, 322 Gemini, 322, *322* Apollo, 322–324, *322–324* space shuttle, 328–329, *328*, *329* future, 329–330, *330*

Spanish moss 16, *16*

special leaf 7–9, *7–9*

species 94, 95, 100, *101*

spectra 309, *309*

spectroscope 309, *309*

spectrum visible, 299 electromagnetic, 302, *302* spectroscopy, 309, *309*

speed of light 302

speleology 220

sperm cell 23

spicules 259, *259*

spider 109–121 classification of, 109

spider crab 128, *128*

spinel 207, *207*

spines 7, *7*

spinnerets 111

spiny lobster 130, *130*

spiracles 99, *99*

spiral galaxy 241, 242–243, *242*, *243*

spitting spider 117, *117*

sponge 149, *149*

spore case 79, *79*

spores 79

spring constellations 246

spring tide 286, *286*

spruce 69, *69*

Sputnik 1 320, *320*

Sputnik 2 320–321, *320*

spy satellite 334, *334*

squash bug 105, *105*

squid 146, *146*

stag beetle 103, *103*

stainless steel 210, *210*, 378, *378*

stalactite 222, *223*

stalagmite 223, *223*

stamen 23, *23*

star sizes of, 250, 265, *265*, 309 brightest, 251 nearest, 252 distances to, 261–262 magnitude, 262–263, *263* temperature, 264, *264*, 282 classification of, 264–265, *264* twinkling of, 307 smallest, *265*, 311 (*see also* constellations; sun)

starch 16

starfish 147–148, *147*, *148*

steel 210, *210*

stem 17–19 of leaf, 6 special, 18–19, *19*

Scripture Index

Credits

Credits are listed in order from left to right, top to bottom on a page. Abbreviations are used for major sources: AA or ES–Animals Animals/Earth Scenes; CRF–CorbisRoyalty-Free; PR–Photo Researchers Inc.; WEF–William E. Ferguson. Location on some pages is noted by abbreviations: t-top, c-center, b-bottom, r-right, l-left.

Spot photos used in special features, charts, and diagrams throughout are taken from royalty-free photo CDs by Corbis, Corel, and Stockbyte and are not separately credited. Credits to the publisher (ABB) are given only as needed to show locations of other images on a page.

Photos of planets and Earth, pages 276-277, 289, 291, 292, 337: Venus-NSSDC, Earth-CRF, Mars-JPL/Malin Space Science Systems/NASA, Jupiter-JPL-U. of Arizona/NASA, Saturn-USGS, Uranus-K Seidelman/U. S. Naval Observatory/NASA, Neptune-NASA, Pluto-NASA/JPL/Caltech.

Illustrations of constellations are from *The Stars: A New Way to See Them*, by H. A. Rey. Copyright ©1952, 1962, 1967, 1970, 1975, 1976 by H. A. Rey. Adapted and reprinted by permission of Houghton Mifflin Company. All rights reserved.

Cover–NASA (space station), all others CRF; inside cover–CRF; i–CRF; iii–CRF, Simon D. Pollard/PR, Matthew Shipp-SPL/PR; iv–CRF, NASA, Digital Vision; 2–CRF; 3–CRF; 4–CRF; 7–Stephen Parker/PR, Eastcott-Momatiuk/ES; 8–ABB, Zig Leszczynski/ES; 9–WEF, G. I. Bernard/ES, David M. Schleser-Nature's Images/PR, CRF, WEF; 16–George Bernard/ES, Mindy Klarman/PR, ABB; 22–CRF; 23–Corel (tl); 24–WEF; 28–E. R. Degginger/ES, Eastcott-Momatiuk/AA; 29–E. R. Degginger/ES (bl); 30–The Granger Collection; 32–CRF; 34–Corel, John Gerlach/ES, Richard Shiell/ES; 35–Marcia Griffen/ES, Corel, Corel; 36–Corel; 37–Stephen Ingram/ES, Stephenie S. Ferguson/WEF, Fletcher & Baylis/PR; 40–CRF, WEF, Bill Beatty/ES; 41–Ryan Baldwin/ES, Joyce Photographics/PR; 45–CRF; 47–Renee Lynn/PR, Phyllis Greenberg/ES, Jerome Wyckoff/ES; 48–Patti Murray/ES, Philip Perry/PR; 50–Hans Reinhard-Okapia/PR, Nils Reinhard-Okapia/PR, Dani-Jeske/ES; 55–CRF; 56–CRF; 57–CRF; 58–Richard Kolar/ES, Peter Miller/PR; 59–Gordon E. Smith/PR; 60–Eastcott-Momatiuk/PR; 61–WEF; 62–Geoff Bryant/PR; 65–WEF, WEF; 73–Breck P. Kent; 75–CRF; 76–WEF; 79–Biophoto Associates/PR; 80–Stephenie S. Ferguson/WEF, Peter Lilja/ES; 81–WEF; 82–Andrew J. Martinez/PR, Scott Camazine/PR; 83–Randy Morse/AA; 84–Breck P. Kent; 85–Richard Shiell/ES; 86–Charlie Ott/PR, Marcia Griffen/ES, Marcia Griffen/ES, Richard E. Ferguson/WEF; 90–CRF; 92–Paddy Ryan/AA; 93–Simon D. Pollard/PR; 109–David Dennis/AA, Larry West/PR; 110–C. W. Schwartz/AA, C. W. Schwartz/AA (inset), Rod Planck/PR; 111–Nuridsany et Perennou/PR; 112–Donald Specker/AA; 113–J. A. L. Cooke-OSF/AA (all); 115–Peter Miller/PR;116–Biophoto Associates/PR, Charles W. Mann/PR, OSF/AA; 117–Patti Murray/AA, Simon D. Pollard/PR; 118–Rod Planck/PR, Gary Meszaros/PR, OSF/AA; 120–E. R. Degginger/AA, S. Camazine-K. Visscher/PR; 121–John Mitchell/PR, Simon D. Pollard/PR, ABB; 122–Scott Camazine/PR; 123–James H. Robinson/AA, Stephen Dalton/AA; 124–Bill Beatty/AA; 127–Mike Johnson/Marine Natural History Photography, E. R. Degginger/PR; 128–Tom McHugh/PR, E. R. Degginger/PR (inset), Eastcott-Momatiuk/PR, WEF; 129–Tom McHugh-Steinhart Aquarium/PR, Andrew J. Martinez/PR; 130–Andrew G. Wood/PR, Bruce Watkins/AA, Tom McHugh-Steinhart Aquarium/PR; 131–Anthony Mercieca/PR, Zig Leszczynski/AA, E. R. Degginger/PR; 132–James A. Robinson/AA, Breck P. Kent/AA; 134–Tom McHugh/PR; 137–Jeanne White/PR; 138–WEF, Andrew J. Martinez/AA; 139–E. R. Degginger/AA; 140–OSF/AA; 142–John Watney/PR, Eastcott-Momatiuk/AA; 143–Joyce & Frank Burek/AA, G. I. Bernard-OSF/AA, Donald Specker/AA; 144–James Watt/AA, Andrew J. Martinez/PR; 145–Michael Lustbader/PR; 146–G. I. Bernard-OSF/AA, Tom McHugh-Steinhart Aquarium/PR, Tom McHugh/PR, Carl

Roessler/AA; 147–Herb Segars/AA; 148–Fred Winner-Jacana/PR, WEF, Steve Earley/AA, David Hall/PR; 149–Fred McConnaughey/PR, Joyce & Frank Burek/AA; 150–R. Jackman-OSF/AA, Mary Beth Angelo/PR, Stockbyte; 152–F. Stuart Westmoreland/PR, Mike Johnson/Marine Natural History Photography; 153–W. Gregory Brown/ES; 154–Corel (shells); 157–Dr. Dennis Kunkel/Phototake (paramecium); 162–reproduced by permission fo Pfizer Inc., all rights reserved; 163–E. R. Degginger/ES; 164–Simon D. Pollard/PR; 166–CRF; 167–Matthew Shipp-SPL/PR; 168–Mountain High Maps ©1993 Digital Wisdom Inc.; 170–Mountain High Maps ©1993 Digital Wisdom Inc.; 171–E. R. Degginger/ES, WEF, CRF, Corel; 173–©MAPS IN MINUTES™2000; 175– Mountain High Maps ©1993 Digital Wisdom Inc., Bettmann/Corbis; 176–U. S. Geological Survey Library (both); 177–Ken M. Johns/PR; 178–U. S. Geological Survey/G. K. Gilbert; 179–Sherwin Crasto/AP; 180–©MAPS IN MINUTES™2000; 181–Corbis; 183–©MAPS IN MINUTES™2000; 184–WEF; 185–Krafft-Explorer/PR, Francois Gohier/PR, WEF, ABB; 187–WEF, Krafft-Explorer/PR; 188–Stephen & Donna O'Meara/PR, George Ranalli/PR, CRF, CRF; 189–Bernhard Edmaier-SPL/PR, CRF, CRF; 190–Robin Holcomb/WEF, Soames Summerhays/PR; 191–Roger Ressmeyer/Corbis, API-Explorer/PR; 192–David Weintraub/PR; 193–CRF (t); 194–WEF (bl), Joyce Photographics/PR (br); 195–Richard Cummins/Corbis (t), WEF (br); 197–Michael Giannechini/PR; 198–WEF (bl); 199–WEF, WEF, ABB, Charles D. Winters/PR (halite), Solvay Chemicals; 200–Breck P. Kent/ES, Kaj R. Svensson-SPL/PR, Biophoto Associates/PR, Corel; 202–WEF (br); 203–The Granger Collection; 205–Crown Copyright-Historic Royal Palaces (both); 206–Charles D. Winters/PR; 207–©1982 Gemological Institute of America-reprinted by permission, Crown Copyright-Historic Royal Palaces, Richard T. Nowitz/PR, Breck P. Kent/ES, Breck P. Kent/ES, Charles D. Winters/PR; 208–Tom McHugh/PR (tr); 209–CRF (br); 210–Lowell Georgia/PR (t), GM Electro-Motive (cr); 211–Corel (car), U. S. Mint (coin), Emmet Bright/PR (bl); 214–CRF; 215–Breck P. Kent/ES, Andrew J. Martinez/PR, Andrew J. Martinez/PR, Mark A. Schneider/PR; 216–WEF, CRF; 217–Astrid & Hans Freider Michler-SPL/PR; 218–Shell Group, Stena Bulk AB/Conny Wickberg, Shell Group; 220–Dave Bunnell/Good Earth Graphics; 221–Dave Bunnell/Good Earth Graphics, Corel; 222-T. Middleton-OSF/AA; 223–Bruce Roberts/PR; 224–Dave Bunnell/Good Earth Graphics (all); 225–John J. Bamgma/PR, Tom McHugh-Steinhart Aquarium/PR, Charles E. Mohr/PR; 227- Charles D. Winters/PR; 228–Mountain High Maps ©1993 Digital Wisdom Inc.; 229–Corel; 230–B. & C. Alexander/PR; 232–Matthew Shipp-SPL/PR; 234–David Nunuk-SPL/PR; 235–CRF; 236–NASA-JPL-Caltech; 237–NASA/Photri; 238–NASA; 240–Jerry Schad/PR, Space Telescope Science Institute/NASA; 241–Tony & Daphne Hallas/Astrophoto; 242–Hubble Heritage Team (AURA/STScI)/NASA, European Southern Observatory; 243–European Southern Observatory (all); 244–Hubble Heritage Team(STScI)/NASA, NSSDC-A. Caulet ESA/NASA, Tony & Daphne Hallas-SPL/PR, NSSDC-A. Caulet ESA/NASA; 245–Pekka Parviainen-SPL/PR; 246–©MAPS IN MINUTES™2000; 250–Tony & Daphne Hallas-SPL/PR; 251–Royal Observatory Edinburgh-AAO-SPL/PR; 252–Jerry Lodriguss/PR; 256–CRF; 258–SOHO-MDI(ESA & NASA), SOHO (ESA & NASA), CRF (inset); 259–SOHO (ESA & NASA) both; 260–TRACE/NASA, Dr. Fred Espenak-SPL/PR; 263–©MAPS IN MINUTES™2000 (globe); 265–CRF; 266–©MAPS IN MINUTES™2000 (globe), AAO (bl, br); 267–European Southern Observatory; 270–Paul Almasy/Corbis; 273–Bettmann/Corbis; 279–CRF; 280–Mountain High Maps ©1993 Digital Wisdom Inc.; 283–John Sanford-SPL/PR; 284–Mountain High Maps ©1993 Digital Wisdom Inc. (earth); 285–Jerry Schad/PR, CRF, Mountain High Maps ©1993 Digital Wisdom Inc. (2); 286–Michael P. Gadomski/PR, Michael P. Gadomski/PR, Mountain High Maps ©1993 Digital Wisdom Inc.; 288–JHUAPL/NASA, JPL/NASA; 290–Dr. Horst Uwe Keller/Max-Planck-Institute fur Aeronomie, Tony & Daphne Hallas/Astrophoto; 291–Peter McGregor-NSSDC/NASA (tc), Hubble Space Telescope Imaging Jupiter Team/NASA (tr);